Three Ways Wharf, Uxbridge

A Lateglacial and Early Holocene hunter-gatherer site in the Colne valley

MOLA Monograph Series

For more information about these titles and other MOLA publications
visit the publications page at www.museumoflondonarchaeology.org.uk

Three Ways Wharf, Uxbridge

A Lateglacial and Early Holocene hunter-gatherer site in the Colne valley

John S C Lewis with James Rackham

MOLA MONOGRAPH 51

MUSEUM OF LONDON ARCHAEOLOGY

Published by Museum of London Archaeology

Copyright © Museum of London 2011

A CIP catalogue record for this book is available from the British Library

Production and series design by Tracy Wellman
Typesetting and design by Sue Cawood
Reprographics by Andy Chopping
Copy editing by Simon Burnell
Series editing by Sue Hirst/Susan M Wright

Printed by the Lavenham Press

*Front cover: Early Mesolithic flint refitting group 10 from scatter C west; this
blade sequence shows faceted butts (top left), and bruised blade (lame mâchurée)
FFN 8189 (right)*

CONTRIBUTORS

Principal authors	John S C Lewis with James Rackham
Animal bone	James Rackham with Alan Pipe
Bone taphonomy and cut marks	Peter Andrews, Barbara Ghaleb
Molluscs	Martin Bates
Plant remains	John Giorgi
Palynology	Patricia E J Wiltshire
Lithics	Roger Grace
Micromorphology	Richard Macphail
Sedimentology	Simon Collcutt
Scientific dating	Alex Bayliss
CAD and spatial data analysis	John S C Lewis, James Rackham
Graphics	Helen Jones, Carlos Lemos, †Kikar Singh
Photography	Andy Chopping, Maggie Cox
Project manager	David Bowsher, Richard Malt
Editor	Sue Hirst

CONTENTS

FIGURES

TABLES

SUMMARY

Uxbridge, Middlesex, is situated at the north-west periphery of Greater London and adjacent to the River Colne, a major tributary of the Thames. Three Ways Wharf occupies a low-lying site in the Colne floodplain on the north-west edge of the modern town (NGR 505225 184560). Excavations between 1986 and 1990 revealed a total of five *in situ* lithic and faunal scatters.

Scatter A consisted of a Lateglacial 'long blade' lithic industry associated with horse and reindeer faunal remains. Two radiocarbon dates on the horse remains suggest a human presence *c* 10,000 BP. A third, more recently obtained radiocarbon determination confirmed the earlier dates.

Scatters B and D were small and difficult to date, but scatter D should probably also be dated to the Lateglacial.

Scatter C was composed of two chronologically distinct occupations, C east and C west. Scatter C east was associated with a 'long blade' lithic industry and horse and reindeer faunal remains. No radiocarbon date could be obtained from the skeletal material, but this phase probably falls within the period from 10,300 BP to *c* 9600 BP and is thus at least broadly contemporary with scatter A.

Scatter C west consisted of a dense concentration of Early Mesolithic lithic material and a faunal assemblage dominated by red deer. This was confirmed by three radiocarbon dates suggesting human activity in the early Postglacial at 9200 BP. The analysis of the faunal assemblage suggested a late winter or spring season of occupation, with a concentration on extracting grease and marrow from stored red deer long bones.

The main thrust of the Three Ways Wharf project has been to date and characterise human activity and subsistence strategies at the Glacial/Postglacial transition, a period poorly understood in Britain. This has been achieved through analysis of the lithic technology and typology, the faunal remains, and the spatial patterning of the artefacts and skeletal fragments. In the course of the analysis many further avenues of unforeseen research have presented themselves, while others have proved unproductive. Consideration has been given to the possible implications for changing social structure in this period of prehistory.

ACKNOWLEDGEMENTS

With any project that has taken decades to reach publication, a large number of people will have participated at one time or another. The authors would like to thank Trafalgar Brookmount PLC for generously funding (in the pre-PPG16 era) the trial and main excavations in 1986 and 1988. We would also like to thank English Heritage for partly funding the main excavation in 1988, as well as all the subsequent post-excavation analysis. This publication was funded by English Heritage and is the product of a joint venture between English Heritage and Museum of London Archaeology (MOLA; prior to 2009 known as MoLAS, the Museum of London Archaeology Service) to publish backlog sites identified in the London post-excavation review (Hinton and Thomas 1997). The post-excavation and publication phases of this work were monitored by Brian Kerr and Barney Sloane for English Heritage and by Gordon Malcolm and David Bowsher for MOLA.

John Lewis would like to thank Nick Barton, Chris Bergman, Andrew David and Roger Jacobi for their support and advice at various points during the course of the project. He also wishes to express his thanks to Michael Reynier for generously permitting the use of data from his unpublished PhD thesis. James Rackham would like to thank Peter Rowley-Conwy for making available information about his material from Barry's Island (a peat 'island' site in a farmer's field not far from Star Carr) in advance of publication, and Tim Schadla-Hall for his comments on the Seamer Carr, Lake Flixton material.

John Lewis also wishes to thank the members of the West London Archaeological Field Group who helped with the excavations, particularly the late Barbara Eastop and Tony Lewis, and also Keith Sudell and David Smith. Don and Geri Corti undertook the painstaking marking of the flints. Eric Harris was an enthusiastic excavator as well as expertly maintaining the site plumbing, pumps, shelters and performing any other maintenance task that was required, in addition to being a good friend. John Lewis would also like to thank the staff of the West London section of the former Department of Greater London Archaeology (DGLA) of the Museum of London for all their contributions, particularly the late Margaret Wooldridge who was an ever-present source of help and support and, again, a very good friend. John Mills did much to facilitate the initial exploratory work on the site, as well as undertaking invaluable historical research on the Tudor gatehouse and medieval occupation. John Lewis would like to express particular thanks to Jon Cotton not only for giving him the opportunity to direct the excavation, but also for allowing him the chance to analyse and publish the site, as well as providing incalculable advice and support over the years. Peter Hinton and Carrie Cowan provided much-appreciated support during the long process of applying for the initial post-excavation funding.

John Lewis would especially like to thank the site excavation and sieving team, which consisted of (among others) Mark Burley, Andy Boucher, Heather Fear, Guy Hollman, Debbie Mattocks, Nick Truckle, Fiona Walker, Doug Walsh and Antonia Watkins. Martin Bates was in charge of the on-site environmental and sieving programme, which continued under his supervision at Fulmer quarry. The facilities at Fulmer were kindly made available by Tim Penfold of Drinkwater Sabey Ltd. Sharon Gerber-Parfitt assisted with the sieving and the flint and bone sorting from the residues, and also entered all the flint identification data on the site database during post-excavation analysis. Alan Pipe made the initial primary records for the animal bone and produced a catalogue.

John Lewis would also like to thank all the specialist contributors to this report, in particular Pat Wiltshire for her continuing friendship and, finally, all those not mentioned by name who have supported his desire to achieve the publication of this report.

PREFACE

John S C Lewis

It has taken at least 20 years to publish the excavations at Three Ways Wharf and, in order to understand the content of the monograph, it is useful to summarise the history of the project over those two decades.

The main excavations finished at the end of August 1988, although some further work was undertaken in 1990 during the construction of the building which now occupies the site.

The post-excavation and publication programme can be broken up into a number of phases. The period from 1988 to the end of 1992 was characterised by the production of numerous research designs and grant applications to English Heritage to fund the assessment and post-excavation programme. A valuable phase of assessment was funded in 1990 and informed the subsequent research designs. Subsequently the original research design was rewritten to follow the guidelines in the first edition of the *Management of archaeological projects* (English Heritage 1989). A year later, the project design was once more rewritten in accordance with the second edition, MAP2 (English Heritage 1991). Finally, the project became included in the substantial package of funding to address the post-excavation backlog of the Museum of London's former Department of Greater London Archaeology (DGLA).

A brief interim note on the site was published in 1991 (Lewis 1991). The main phase of analysis and writing started late in 1992. There was a break of about a year around 1994 while the microwear and other specialist analyses were being carried out. James Rackham undertook the analysis of the faunal data on the then Museum of London Archaeology Service (MoLAS) environmental department computer system and, when he left the Museum, on his own systems. Lithic analysis was undertaken in the offices of MoLAS. The thousands of flint artefacts were laid out in the drawers of map chests. Although efficient in terms of space utilisation, this did mean that none of the assemblages was ever visible in its entirety at any one time, which inevitably affected the already very constrained refitting programme. However, the use of a database and CAD system to analyse the assemblages was, in those pre-GIS times, a real advance and proved essential. Modern GIS packages would now make the process far simpler.

The draft text was begun in 1995 and completed by the end of July 1996, when John Lewis left MoLAS. Some references to research and new sites published since 1996 have been worked into the main body of the text. However, this short preface seeks to address some of the main issues that have emerged during the last ten years without having to substantially alter the main text.

Several articles and books have been published since 1995

(Barton 1997; 1998; 2005; Barton and Dumont 2000) which are relevant to British 'long blade' studies. Within the context of Greater London, a review of the Upper Palaeolithic and Mesolithic was published (Lewis 2000), but is now in need of revision.

A number of pieces of research were about to be published as the draft text was being written in 1995–6, but were not available for consultation. For example, Fagnart and Plisson (1997) suggested that the characteristic bruising on some of the long blades (the *lames mâchurées*) was the product of their use to modify the soft-stone hammers used in core reduction. Later, Froom (2005, 34–8) developed the theory that the bruising was a product of the use of large flakes and blades as 'hammers' to partially facet and adjust the core platform edges in Lateglacial assemblages. In contrast, the accepted theory of the time was that the heavy bruising on blades and flakes was caused by chopping bone and in particular antler (Barton 1986). The data from scatter C east at Three Ways Wharf show that *lames mâchurées* were detached early in the reduction sequence and were associated with the densest parts of the lithic scatters, factors which would support the 'bruised blades as hammers' theory. However, the longest and most robust pieces will usually be detached early in the reduction sequence and, by definition, most material will be in the densest parts of the scatter, otherwise there would be no dense parts of a scatter! This author sees no reason why these theories should be mutually exclusive.

Also regarding soft-stone hammers, a paper was published exploring the characteristics of their use for core reduction (Pelegrin 2000). As this only appeared after the analysis of the Three Ways Wharf assemblage, soft-stone hammer mode was not recorded in the database, only hard and soft hammer use (Ohnuma and Bergman 1982).

While the Three Ways Wharf text was being completed in 1996, Baales (1996) published a consideration of Ahrensburgian seasonal use of the landscape, and in particular the part that reindeer migrations played in shaping patterns of human activity. In essence this work suggested that the main summer grazing areas of reindeer were the central German uplands (*Mittelgebirge*) and the uplands of central England. During the spring and autumn the reindeer migrated to the wintering grounds of the north European plains and the (now submerged) North Sea basin. This is broadly in accordance with the views presented in the Three Ways Wharf text, but it would have been useful to have had access to Baales's publication.

Since 1996, new 'long blade' sites have been excavated in Britain and some, together with older sites, have been published. Examples include the site at Launde, Leicestershire (Cooper 2006), and the sites in the Kennet valley (Froom 2005). The Launde site is particularly important, since although it produced no faunal material and had been damaged, the assemblage did contain microliths with very distinctive concave truncations which are very similar to those from Three Ways Wharf scatters A and C east, and from Ahrensburgian sites on the Continent. These similarities are mentioned in the main text of this report, and discussed in far more detail elsewhere (Cooper 2006). Other sites, such as Underdown Lane in Kent

(Gardiner et al in prep) are awaiting slots in journal publication schedules, and at the time of writing the final publication of Seamer Carr in North Yorkshire (Conneller and Schadla-Hall 2003; Lane and Schadla-Hall in prep) is imminent. Analysis and reporting of the 'long blade' assemblage from Church Lammas, Staines, Surrey, was completed by this author by 2000, but remains unpublished.

Fieldwork continues to recover 'long blade' material: for example, Wessex Archaeology have recorded artefacts on a number of projects in the Kennet and Colne valleys as well as north Kent in the last 12 years. However, at the time of writing it would appear that only the two Colne valley sites of Three Ways Wharf and Church Lammas, Staines, have produced faunal material, and only Three Ways Wharf has yielded radiocarbon dates. It is essential that 'long blade' sites with associated fauna are located, excavated and published if we are to move studies of this period on to a new level.

Across the North Sea, Ahrensburgian radiocarbon dates have been reviewed for the Netherlands (Deeben et al 2000), and more sites have been excavated in the last 12 years in Germany, the Low Countries and northern France. These include Oudehaske and Gramsbergen in the Netherlands (Johansen and Stapert 1997–8) and the Buhot site at Calleville (Eure) in France (Biard and Hinguant 2004). In France, volumes containing contributions examining the final Palaeolithic have appeared (eg Fagnart and Thévenin 1997).

The volume of research into the final Palaeolithic has increased significantly since the Three Ways Wharf site was excavated in 1988 and the analysis completed in 1995–6. There is now even more of a sense that 'long blades' and the Ahrensburgian form part of a much larger north-west European phenomenon than when an international conference on the Lateglacial was held in Oxford in September 1989. That conference gave rise to the publication of a volume (Barton et al 1991) which shaped British research into this period for many years. It might well be time to hold another conference and to review progress over the past 20 years.

Turning to the Mesolithic, there have been many excavations over the past 12 years of lithic scatters in southern Britain, most unfortunately lacking preserved faunal material. One exception is the site of Faraday Road, Newbury, in the Kennet valley in Berkshire (Ellis et al 2003). This site was an extension of the Greenham Dairy Farm site partially excavated in 1963. The recent excavations recovered a flint assemblage containing a limited repertoire of tools, a faunal assemblage dominated by wild boar, and radiocarbon dates spanning the period *c* 9000 BP to 8000 BP. Although slightly later than the occupation at Three Ways Wharf scatter C west, the Faraday Road site is important in that it appears to represent a specialised autumnal site where wild boar carcasses underwent initial processing before the meat was carried elsewhere. It thus provides an interesting contrast to Three Ways Wharf scatter C west: the main prey is wild boar not red deer; the season is autumn not late winter/early spring; and the activity is more closely associated with the kill in the *chaîne opératoire* of meat procurement than at Three Ways Wharf, where processing of cached long bones was one of the main occupations. Faraday Road and Three Ways Wharf thus provide insights into human subsistence strategies at different times of the year, using different animal resources at different locations in the landscape.

Just such a picture will also emerge when the Seamer Carr material is fully published (Conneller and Schadla-Hall 2003; Lane and Schadla-Hall in prep), since this project has explored very large areas of the Vale of Pickering in Yorkshire.

Closer to Three Ways Wharf, an Early Mesolithic flint assemblage was recovered from the former Jewsons Yard site on Harefield Road, Uxbridge (Barclay et al 1995). Although the lithic material had been disturbed it was broadly comparable with scatter C west. Perhaps of most interest is the site's location, *c* 300m to the east of Three Ways Wharf and situated on the higher ground providing a good vantage point overlooking the Colne valley; it thus would have formed another activity location within a complex system of landscape utilisation.

Further evidence of the intensity of Mesolithic occupation of the Colne valley has come from excavations at the former Sanderson factory, a few hundred metres to the north-east of Three Ways Wharf (Halsey 2006). They recovered several Early Mesolithic flint scatters and faunal material adjacent to hearth areas. Analysis is at an early stage, but the faunal material includess red deer, boar and beaver. Radiocarbon dates centre on 9200 BP. This would make the site contemporary with scatter C west at Three Ways Wharf, and comparisons of the lithic and faunal assemblages essential.

Currently, Wessex Archaeology are undertaking a programme of evaluation and excavation on a site on the Colne valley floodplain at New Denham, *c* 1km to the west of Three Ways Wharf. Several Early Mesolithic flint scatters have been identified, as well as a low density of 'long blade' material.

When these recent excavations and continuing fieldwork and analysis are considered within the framework of the sites reported by Lacaille (1961; 1963; 1966), Three Ways wharf can be seen to be part of an extremely complex early Lateglacial and Early Mesolithic landscape on a par with that of the Kennet valley and perhaps the Vale of Pickering. The major challenge of the future will be to analyse the data from individual sites so that a narrative of landscape habitation can be written.

1

Introduction

The town of Uxbridge (London Borough of Hillingdon), Middlesex, lies on the north-west periphery of modern Greater London. Commencing in 1983, the Department of Greater London Archaeology (DGLA) of the Museum of London, a predecessor of Museum of London Archaeology (MOLA), undertook a programme of excavations in Uxbridge with the aim of studying the pre-12th-century origins and subsequent development of the medieval market town (Mills 1984). As part of this programme, trial excavations were carried out at Three Ways Wharf, a large site adjacent to the River Colne. Formerly, the main London to Oxford road had run along Uxbridge High Street, out of the town and through the Three Ways Wharf site. In addition, the remains of a twin-towered gatehouse associated with a Tudor mansion were known from documentary research to have been located on the site. Corresponding medieval and Tudor remains were duly encountered there, and the archaeological record of these periods is stored in the archives of the Museum of London.

The history of the fieldwork is given below (1.3), but here it may be noted that it was during the investigation of the medieval and post-medieval archaeology of Three Ways Wharf that the remains of *in situ* flint and faunal scatters were found by chance. In retrospect this should not have been surprising. A D Lacaille published a series of papers in the early to mid 1960s (Lacaille 1961; 1963; 1966) which reported on numerous finds, made by himself and others, of Mesolithic flintwork from gravel workings in the Colne and middle Thames valleys. Although none of this material had been retrieved by careful excavation, some stratigraphic detail was available. For instance, Lacaille makes it clear that the Mesolithic flintwork was usually found on the surface of the basal gravels of the floodplain, and was often contained in the base of, or sealed by, peat deposits which could be attributed to the Boreal phase (pollen zone VI) of the postglacial Holocene sequence. In particular, the sites at Willowbank and Sandstone in Buckinghamshire followed this pattern and were discussed by Lacaille in some detail. Both were located close to Three Ways Wharf, in similar stratigraphic and topographical positions.

In the light of this knowledge, the finds from the trial excavations at Three Ways Wharf were originally thought to date to the Early Mesolithic. However, an initial examination by Andrew David of the Ancient Monuments Laboratory, English Heritage, led to the suggestion that the material might in fact be of Lateglacial date and have affinities with the (at the time) little-known 'long blade' industry of north-west Europe. At the suggestion of Andrew David, Nick Barton also examined the flintwork and agreed that, on the basis of a small sample, the preliminary findings did suggest a 'long blade' connection. This was apparently confirmed by identification of some of the faunal remains as being horse and reindeer, both open environment species which had become extinct by the early Postglacial.

Subsequent major excavations clarified the nature of the Lateglacial activity (scatter A), which was further refined by two radiocarbon dates on the horse remains, suggesting a human presence *c* 10,000 BP. Excavation also revealed three further scatters of lithic and faunal material. Two of these (scatters B and D) were small and difficult to date, but the third (scatter C) consisted of many thousands of flint artefacts and skeletal fragments in two main clusters, C west and C east. Initial conclusions were that C west dated to the Early Mesolithic, as suggested by the lithic typology and the faunal remains which were predominantly of red deer. This was confirmed by three radiocarbon dates suggesting human activity in the early Postglacial at 9200 BP. It was expected that scatter C east would prove to be contemporary with this phase; however, preliminary examination of the microliths from scatter C led Roger Jacobi to suggest that C east represented an earlier phase, possibly broadly contemporary with scatter A. Subsequent faunal and lithic analysis has shown that there is indeed an earlier phase of activity represented by C east and associated with cut-marked reindeer bones. Unfortunately, it proved impossible to obtain a radiocarbon date from this skeletal material, and so this phase of activity lacks an absolute physical date. However, it is likely to be contained within the period from 10,300 BP to *c* 9600 BP, and thus broadly if not exactly contemporary with scatter A.

1.1   A summary interpretation of the site

The following is an interpretation based on our view of the evidence presented in this volume. Other interpretations are of course possible, depending on the point of view of the reader.

Scatter A: Lateglacial/Early Holocene (Loch Lomond Stadial/early Pre-Boreal, *c* 10,300 BP– *c* 9700 BP)

At some time during the Lateglacial/Early Holocene, a small group of four to six humans occupied part of a low ridge running from the valley side of the River Colne out into the floodplain. The occupation was probably brief and seems to have been concerned with the processing of at least one and a maximum of two reindeer, although a horse may also have been processed. The carcasses seem to have undergone initial butchery, probably at the original kill site, before arriving at Three Ways Wharf. Once at the site, the selected meat-bearing carcass elements were completely processed. The location of the kill site is unknown, though it probably would have been nearby at a fording point on the Colne. Local flint nodules from the Colne were collected and reduced to produce debitage and a tool kit which was typologically restricted. However, a range of tasks including fish processing and wood and antler working were also undertaken. These tasks, along with carcass processing, seem to have been carried out around a possible hearth, and low meat-bearing bones disposed of around the periphery of the site. No evidence survived for exploitation of vegetable matter. After two to four days the site was abandoned and the group moved on.

Scatter C east: Lateglacial/Early Holocene (Loch Lomond Stadial/early Pre-Boreal, *c* 10,300 BP– *c* 9700 BP)

A second area of the low ridge at Three Ways Wharf was similarly occupied by a group of four to six humans. Whether this was contemporary with scatter A is unproven, although several strands of evidence suggest that it may have been slightly later. As with scatter A, the occupation of scatter C east involved the processing of at least three reindeer which had already undergone some initial butchery at the kill site. The main meat-bearing bones appear to have been processed and discarded adjacent to a hearth, while other skeletal elements were discarded on the site periphery. Local river flint nodules were reduced to produce a wider range of retouched tools than in scatter A, and these were mainly utilised and discarded adjacent to the hearth. Other tasks such as bone, wood, hide and antler working were also carried out, but these can perhaps be seen in the context of maintenance of hunting/survival equipment carried by a mobile group, rather than being connected with a 'base camp'. There is some evidence for a curation technology, in that some microliths may have been brought to the site from elsewhere, while it is possible that some were manufactured on site and then removed. Similarly, the nature of the antler working suggests the reduction of larger beams into smaller segments for removal elsewhere. Two of the reindeer carcasses were completely processed at the site, while part of the third may have been removed to provide food while the group shifted location. No evidence for the exploitation of vegetable matter survived. Many of these activities occurred on the southern side of the hearth, suggesting either a prevailing wind from the south or the presence of a shelter to the north. Following a period of two to three weeks, the group abandoned the site and moved on.

Scatter C west: Early Holocene (early Boreal, 9200 BP)

Following an interval of at least 500 radiocarbon years, the low ridge at Three Ways Wharf was again occupied, possibly in late spring. In this instance the occupation was more substantial, and may have involved up to 20 humans. Unlike the earlier phases, the main concern of this occupation was the extraction of marrow, fat and grease from at least 15 red deer and two roe deer. These were supplemented by other species, particularly birds (such as swan) and possibly beaver. The deer carcasses appear to have undergone extensive butchery elsewhere, to the extent that it is possible that most of the meat had already been stripped from the limb bones prior to these elements reaching the site. The fat extraction process appears to have been carried out adjacent to the hearth and the majority of material discarded in a 'midden'. The faunal elements, therefore, represent the very last stage in a complex process of animal carcass processing, apparently involving a number of locations. Flint nodules from the River Colne were selected for production of tools, although possibly from a different source to that exploited in the earlier phases. Tool production and fat extraction were located around a central hearth, while bone and some lithic material were discarded away from the central area. A wide range of tasks were carried out in addition to the animal processing, and unlike the earlier phases of occupation these tasks – such as adzing wood – could be seen as associated with a less temporary occupation. Use-wear analysis suggests that they are indicative of a more permanent 'base camp' (Chapter 6.4) and the faunal analysis suggests a relatively long potential period of occupation (Chapter 6.3). There is evidence of a curation technology among the tools, since some axes and microliths appear to have been brought (?hafted) to the site, while others were manufactured there and then removed. However, notably absent were bone tools such as mattocks or barbed points, or any evidence of their production. Faunal analysis suggests that the suitable raw materials were not brought to the site and hence manufacture of these implements was not carried out. This is not surprising given the apparently specialised marrow/fat extraction nature of the faunal assemblage. This level of specialisation around the hearth argues for other parts of the 'settlement' or site being beyond the excavated area. Certainly the butchery of 17 deer carcasses and any other animals could be expected to leave considerable quantities of debris and, if the animals were killed while still carrying their antlers and their skins were kept, then this site must surely include other areas where antler, phalanges and other parts of the skeleton were discarded. If the presence of shelters on site is discounted, then one is left with the interpretation of scatter C west as being an activity area concerned primarily with the very last stages of carcass processing. This was carried out adjacent to the hearth, and it is possible to envisage members of the group or other groups congregating around the hearth as a sociable location to carry out other maintenance tasks such as bone, antler and wood working. Thus scatter C west need not be seen as a 'base camp', but rather a (perhaps specialised) activity area within a much wider landscape of kill, butchery, antler-working and dwelling sites.

Post-occupation

Following the final phase of occupation at Three Ways Wharf, the rising water table led to the formation of an organic mud representing a sedge swamp, which covered the entire site and lasted from *c* 9000 BP to 7500 BP. Human occupation of the valley continued, however, and the microscopic charcoal present in the humic clays may be indicative of widespread (?anthropogenic) forest burning at this period.

1.2 Three Ways Wharf: site location, geology and topography

Site location

Uxbridge, Middlesex, is situated at the north-west periphery of Greater London and adjacent to the River Colne, a major tributary of the Thames (Fig 1). Three Ways Wharf occupies a low-lying site in the Colne floodplain on the north-west edge of the modern town (Fig 3, a). Present ground surface on the site is at *c* 33m OD. However, excavation revealed the Lateglacial/

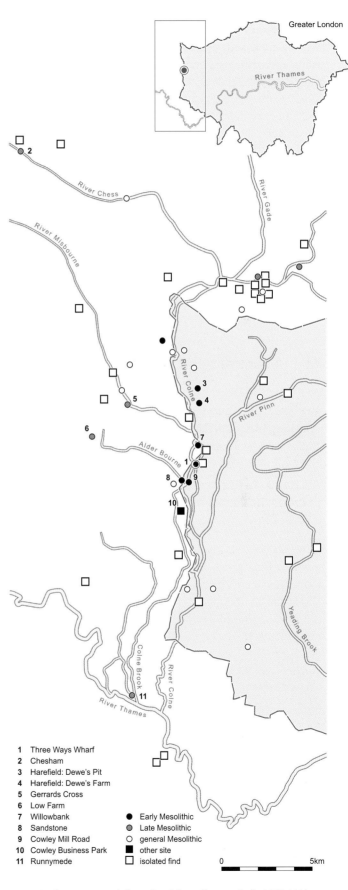

1	Three Ways Wharf
2	Chesham
3	Harefield: Dewe's Pit
4	Harefield: Dewe's Farm
5	Gerrards Cross
6	Low Farm
7	Willowbank
8	Sandstone
9	Cowley Mill Road
10	Cowley Business Park
11	Runnymede

● Early Mesolithic
● Late Mesolithic
○ general Mesolithic
■ other site
□ isolated find

0   5km

Fig 1 Site location map including other Colne valley sites (scale 1:200,000)

early Postglacial land surface at *c* 31.4m OD, the overburden mainly being the result of medieval and post-medieval activity and Holocene alluvial sediments.

The site is located at NGR 505225 184560, *c* 75m east of the present course of the river and *c* 120m from the break of slope, where the eastern valley side rises from the floodplain to an altitude of *c* 60m OD. To the west, the Colne floodplain stretches as a flat expanse for *c* 2.5km before the western side of the valley slowly rises up. Three Ways Wharf is situated between the confluences of two of the Colne's tributaries, the Alder Bourne and the Misbourne.

The site is thus located at the eastern edge of the Colne floodplain and overlooked by the high ground of the valley side immediately to the east. To the west the flat floodplain is visible for a considerable distance, particularly from the high ground overlooking the site (Fig 2). The location of Three Ways Wharf therefore offers a number of advantages. It is in a sheltered position on the floodplain, close to water. The high ground to the east would have provided good views of the floodplain and the opportunity to monitor the movements of prey animals from some distance, at least during more open vegetational conditions. The site was also ideally placed to exploit the differing vegetational resources of the floodplain to the west and the claylands to the east, while the close proximity of two tributary valleys provided easy routes into the chalk uplands of the Chilterns.

Geology of the lower Colne valley

The lower Colne valley is aligned north–south (Fig 1), but bends sharply eastwards at Rickmansworth. North of Denham, the Colne valley cuts through the Upper Chalk. In the Chess and upper reaches of the Misbourne, both tributaries of the Colne, the Middle Chalk is exposed (BGS sheet 255). South of Denham the valley cuts through Pleistocene Thames terrace sediments which rest on Lower Tertiary deposits of London Clay (Gibbard 1985, 82).

Throughout the length of the Colne valley a continuous spread of gravel and sand underlies the postglacial floodplain

Fig 2 View of Three Ways Wharf looking west from the top of an adjacent office building; the height of view is roughly equal to the highest point of the adjacent valley side

deposits, and this has been termed the Colney Street Gravel member (Gibbard 1985, 82). Organic-rich channel sediments within the Colney Street Gravel have been observed at several localities (ibid). These have produced dates ranging from 14,320±210 BP to 11,230±120 BP. Together with associated fossils indicative of cold climate, the radiocarbon dates demonstrate that the Colney Street Gravel accumulated during the Late Devensian substage (ibid, 81).

The lithology of the Colney Street Gravel comprises 92–93.5% total flint, predominantly angular but with consistent amounts of rounded type. Vein quartz and quartzite content is variable, being 3.5–7.5% for the former and 0.25–2% for the latter. Greensand chert is virtually absent from Colne gravel except where adjacent to outcrops of Thames gravel terrace deposits (Gibbard 1985, 83).

Regionally, the Colne valley separates the chalklands of the Chilterns in the west from two main geological bodies in the east. North of Uxbridge and stretching eastwards across north London, the geology is dominated by Tertiary London Clay. South of Uxbridge and following the Thames valley are the Pleistocene Thames river gravel terraces capped by the fine-grained Langley Silt Complex (Gibbard et al 1987). Thus Uxbridge is situated near the boundary of three main geological zones, each of which has played a part in the shaping of the topography of the region.

Topography of the Uxbridge locality

The effect of the solid geology on the topography of the Colne valley is subtle but perceptible. Generally the eastern side of the valley is steeper throughout the lower Colne. North of Denham, where the river cuts through chalk, this asymmetric pattern is present, with both valley sides steeper and the floodplain narrower. Thus the chalk bedrock above Denham has had the effect of constricting the River Colne to a narrower, steeper-sided valley.

South of Denham, where the Colne cuts through softer Pleistocene and Tertiary deposits, the valley sides become less steep, although the east–west asymmetry is maintained but more markedly until just south of Uxbridge. The width of the Colne floodplain alluvial deposits at Uxbridge is also greater (c 2.5km). South of Uxbridge, the valley broadens out even more and the steepness of both sides becomes barely perceptible until the Colne and the Thames merge at Staines. Hence the modern town of Uxbridge is situated on one of the last vestiges of high ground on the eastern side of the Colne valley, formed by Pleistocene gravel deposits. This high ground is further defined c 1km to the east by the River Pinn, whose valley bisects the London Clay and runs parallel to the Colne which it joins c 4km to the south of Uxbridge. The three main western tributaries of the lower Colne, namely the Chess, the Misbourne and the Alder Bourne, all cut through the chalk of the Chilterns. The Chess joins the Colne c 12km and the Misbourne 1.5km upstream from Uxbridge, while the modern confluence of the Alder Bourne is c 1.3km to the south of Uxbridge.

1.3 Aims and results of the fieldwork and post-excavation analysis

Fieldwork history and aims

The fieldwork can be broken down into three main phases:
1) the evaluation (1986–7);
2) the main excavation (1987–8);
3) subsequent site watching and further evaluation (1989–90).
The aims of the evaluation were necessarily different from that of the main and subsequent fieldwork and were concentrated on the archaeology of medieval and post-medieval Uxbridge. Thus it was entirely fortuitous that excavation of the basal sediments located in situ flint and faunal material thought to date from the Lateglacial/Early Holocene.

In order to meet the aims of the initial evaluation, three trenches were excavated (Fig 3, b). Trenches A and B were to the north of the canal dock and parallel to the course of the medieval High Street, and trench C was to the south, on the site of the 16th-century gatehouse (site code UX86 VIII).

Apart from modern disturbances, only medieval ditches were recorded in trenches A and B.

Trench C was machine-excavated to the top of the surviving walls of the eastern hexagonal tower of the 16th-century gatehouse. This structure was recorded, and the sequence of deposits beneath its foundations excavated by hand. While excavating a section of medieval ditch it was noted that the fill contained a comparatively large quantity of struck flints, in good condition. This suggested that the ditch had been cut through a layer containing prehistoric flintwork (Fig 4). It became apparent with the removal of the black organic layer (SU50) that the grey alluvial layer beneath contained the struck flint. At first, the flints were simply bagged by context; later the positions of the flints were planned but they were not assigned unique numbers, and so could not be matched with their coordinates. Nevertheless, the number of artefacts treated in this way was relatively small since it was quickly realised that each flint had to be fully three-dimensionally recorded and uniquely catalogued. In the latter stages of the evaluation, an area corresponding to half the internal area of the gatehouse was excavated in 5cm spits and all the spoil retained for sieving.

Construction of a proposed double-basemented building threatened to destroy the archaeologically important deposits. In the light of the results of the trial evaluation, it was clear that a much larger area needed to be examined, and that a systematic but flexible excavation, recording and sieving strategy had to be employed.

In December 1987, an area measuring c 34 x 24m was reduced to a depth of c 1.8m (ie to just above the black clay deposit SU50). Three test trenches were also cut to assess the nature of the deposits north of the backfilled canal dock. Manual excavation then commenced, initially in the area of the flint and faunal scatter (A) detected during the trial work. To map the topography of the sediments and to detect further flint scatters, the site was sampled using 1.0m² test pits located at 4.0m intervals. This resulted in the discovery of scatters B and C.

This main phase of excavation was funded by the developers Trafalgar-Brookmount until the end of May 1988, whereupon English Heritage funding allowed the excavation to continue until the end of August 1988 (site code UX88 VIII).

In 1989, a short visit was made to the site to record the stratigraphy exposed in the test pits excavated by the structural engineers on behalf of the clients (site code UX89 VIII). The location of these pits is shown in Fig 3, b.

In 1990 the site was acquired by new owners who redesigned the proposed building and altered its location within the site. Accordingly, a further evaluation was undertaken by Andy Boucher (site code UX90 VIII). This work involved the examination of five large trenches in the northern area of the site, within the new footprint of the proposed building. A number of 1.0m² pits were excavated within these trenches using the same recording system as that employed during the main excavation. A number of test pits were also examined outside the trenched areas. Observations were also made of a section located in the western part of the main 1988 excavation area. This section cut through the basal Colney Street Gravels and was excavated by the contractors as part of the construction of the new development, and could only be rapidly recorded and sampled.

The importance of the *in situ* material meant that the aims of the main and subsequent fieldwork phases were radically different from that of the evaluation. The overriding emphasis was placed on the early prehistoric material, with later features being excavated and recorded only where they disturbed the lithic and faunal scatters. Nonetheless, the remains of the Tudor gatehouse of the 'Place House' mansion were recorded, as were a number of possible later prehistoric and medieval features. These fall outside the scope of the present report.

The aims of the main and subsequent phases of fieldwork were relatively straightforward and can be summarised as follows.

1) To locate, fully excavate and record *in situ* scatters of lithic and faunal material dating to the Lateglacial/Early Holocene, prior to their destruction by redevelopment.

2) To date, using radiocarbon and other physical methods, the faunal material from the various phases of occupation and thereby date the associated lithic assemblages.

3) To record the sediments containing the archaeological material in such a way that the palaeotopography could be three-dimensionally modelled. This would allow the evolution and development of the palaeo-landscape to be studied, as well as placing the lithic and faunal material in its microtopographical setting.

4) To employ a multi-disciplinary approach to the analysis of the range of palaeoenvironmental evidence preserved on site. This would allow the reconstruction not only of the environment prior to, during and following the human occupation of the site, but also permit the interpretation of the regime of deposition of the sediments and their effect on site formation processes.

5) The product of all these questions was to be used to consider

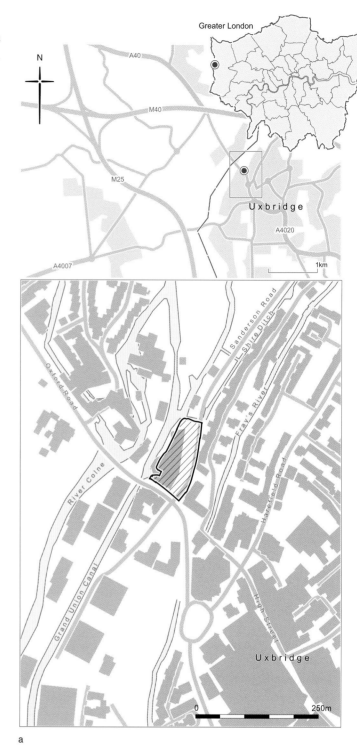

Fig 3 a – Map showing the location of the site within Uxbridge (scale 1:7500); b – plan of trenches within the site (scale 1:1000)

the character of the site in relation to hypotheses concerning other sites, particularly Star Carr, North Yorkshire (Legge and Rowley-Conwy 1988).

Excavation recording methodology

Recording was based on a 1.0m grid, with each square subdivided into four quarters ('quads' of 0.25m²), A, B, C and D, effectively giving a 0.5m grid. Sediment was removed in 20–50mm spits,

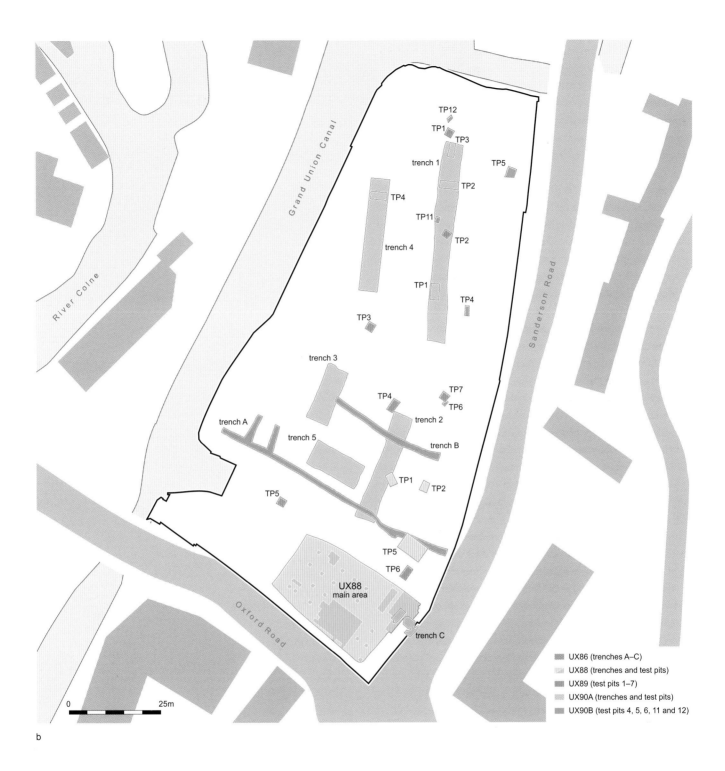

b

with the spot heights of each spit being recorded at the corners of the square and at the centre. No attempt was made to keep spits of uniform height and depth between squares (Fig 5). This policy was adopted for two reasons:

1) the state of preservation of the bone and the threat of vandalism precluded the exposure of large areas, thus making it difficult to coordinate spit heights between squares;

2) harmonising spit heights would have slowed down the excavation considerably.

This approach did not prove to have any major drawbacks during post-excavation analysis.

The level and location of stratigraphic units exposed in test pits and trenches across the entire site were recorded during each phase of fieldwork. These data were combined with those from the main excavated area to build detailed reconstructions of the palaeotopography of each stratigraphic unit (SU) (Chapter 2.2).

All flints >10mm and bone fragments >50mm long were

Fig 4 Section showing medieval ditch and stratigraphy (2.0m scale)

Fig 5 View showing excavation of Mesolithic flint and bone scatter in progress

three-dimensionally recorded. Finds under these sizes were assigned to their respective quadrant and spit. In addition, identifiable faunal remains such as teeth which were <50mm long were also three-dimensionally recorded.

Initially the orientation as well as the angle of dip of the long and short axis of all three-dimensionally recorded lithic and faunal material was recorded. However, during the excavation of scatter C it was decided in consultation with English Heritage to abandon the recording of these data and instead take vertical photographs of each quad and spit prior to lifting of the lithic and faunal material in order to speed up excavation.

Sieving methodology

The excavated sediment (in excess of 30 tonnes) was sieved on site or as part of the post-excavation sieving programme. This had two objectives, namely the recovery of microdebitage and of microfauna. The latter involved sieving the sediment from selected squares at a mesh size of 0.85mm. For microdebitage, all artefact-bearing sediment from the flint scatters was sieved at mesh sizes of 3mm and 1.5mm (Fig 6). It was hoped that debitage of >3mm would provide an understanding of the taphonomy of the site, while residue of >1.5mm would be selectively sampled to boost the microdebitage and microfaunal data. However, practicalities dictated that only 3mm samples were sorted for microdebitage, with 1.5mm samples remaining unsorted. Environmental samples sieved at 0.85mm were resieved at 3mm and the microdebitage collected from this residue to ensure standardised sample parameters. Given the long delay between the initial excavation of the site and the final processing of the samples, a certain degree of sample degradation and loss was inevitable.

A large number of samples remained unprocessed at the end of the excavation. Eventually, these remaining 186 samples were wet-sieved on a 3mm mesh sieve under garden sprinklers in a manner very similar to that carried out on site (above). This material was not floated.

In addition to these samples, 14 samples were wet-sieved and floated for the recovery of carbonised and waterlogged plant remains. These were processed in a Siraf tank over a 1mm residue mesh and floated into a 0.5mm flot sieve. John Giorgi determined that the preserved organic material from the samples, composed largely of 'monocotylendous' root material, did not justify study and rather than being contemporary with the archaeological horizon had penetrated from deposits above. A study was, however, made of the identifiable material from these and the carbonised remains from the sorted samples. This concluded that the presence of modern contaminants precluded further analysis (below, 1.4).

Summary of results of the fieldwork

Stratigraphic sequence

The evaluation phase established that the *in situ* lithic and faunal material was located within the upper portion of fine-grained alluvial sediments which overlay basal gravels dating to the Late Devensian. These basal deposits were assigned to numbered stratigraphic units (SU) 20–60 (Fig 7). Each scatter of lithic and faunal material was contained in the grey fine-grained argillaceous sediment SU40 and with decreasing density in the underlying orange argillaceous sediment SU30. Thus the artefactual material was distributed over a vertical depth of *c* 15–20cm. The artefact-bearing fine-grained sediments were sealed by a black humic clay (SU50) which in turn was overlain in places by a thin calcareous tufa deposit (SU60).

The thickness of these deposits varied across the site, and will be dealt with in detail in Chapter 2. Stratified above this sequence was up to *c* 1.6m of later prehistoric and historic period deposits. Several features dating to these later periods had unfortunately cut through the underlying artefact-bearing sediments and disturbed the lithic and faunal scatters in some places (Fig 19).

Fig 6 View of sieving taking place on site

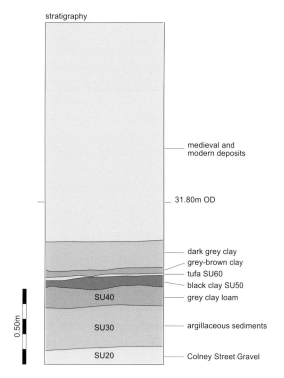

stratigraphy

medieval and
modern deposits

31.80m OD

dark grey clay
grey-brown clay
tufa SU60
black clay SU50
grey clay loam

SU40

argillaceous sediments

SU30

Colney Street Gravel

SU20

0.50m

*Fig 7 Section through the stratigraphic
sequence (scale 1:25) and close-up view of
the site stratigraphy (0.5m scale)*

Spatial patterning and structure of the lithic and faunal scatters

Four main lithic and faunal scatters were located: A, B and C to the south of the site, and D located further north (Fig 8). Of the four scatters, it can be seen that C had by far the densest concentrations of lithic and faunal material, followed by A. Scatters B and D were far more ephemeral.

Preliminary refitting suggested that the lithic material in all four scatters had undergone minimal horizontal dispersal, thus preserving anthropogenically produced spatial patterning.

Scatter A consisted of relatively low densities of three-dimensionally recorded lithic and faunal material (Fig 9) which can be divided into two spatially distinct sub-assemblages (SAS) 10 and 11. This is even more apparent when the flintwork distribution is contoured by numbers per 0.25m² (Fig 10), which shows that the frequency of burnt flintwork and bone in scatter A was very low compared to that in scatter C (below, 3.3, for detailed discussion). Furthermore, scatter A had been relatively more severely disturbed by later features, making the differentiation of hearth areas very difficult. However, it is possible to suggest that the area immediately to the north of the medieval ditch may have been the site of a fire, since six of the burnt pieces of flint were found here. In addition, four more pieces recovered during the initial phase of fieldwork and not coordinated were located in this area. Fig 10 shows this *possible* hearth location.

The lithic material in scatter C (Fig 11) was much more extensive in comparison with scatter A, and could be divided into two main scatters, C west and C east. Scatter C west could in turn be divided into five sub-assemblages (SAS 1, 2, 6, 7 and 8), while C east could be divided into four (SAS 3, 4, 5 and 9).

Contouring the flint densities by 0.25m² shows this patterning more clearly (Fig 12). It should be noted that the presence of later intrusive features has had the effect of distorting the spatial distributions slightly: for instance, it is likely that SAS 2 and 6 were originally the same sub-scatter, and similarly with SAS 1 and 7.

The densest concentration of faunal material (Fig 13) occurred to the south-east of and between the two densest concentrations of lithic material in C west (SAS 1 and 2) (Fig 14). This pattern is particularly apparent if the weight of bone per 0.25m² is contoured (Fig 15). Study of the fragmentation and composition of the faunal material in this area (Chapters 4 and 6) suggests that this particular deposit represents a 'midden' or disposal area of long bones which had been processed for marrow and grease extraction.

The final major element in the spatial patterning of scatter C is the distribution of burnt lithic and faunal material, which falls into two main concentrations, one in C west and the other in C east (Fig 16). The concentration of the burnt flint is more apparent when it is contoured at intervals of three flints per 0.25m². This acts to filter out the general 'background noise' of burnt flint. Fig 16 shows that the distribution of burnt faunal material also coincides with the burnt lithic concentrations. The two concentrations were, therefore, interpreted as hearths or areas of burning. Fig 17 shows that the main concentrations of lithic and faunal material are concentrated around the two hearths. Thus, the lithic and faunal material in both C west and C east is interpreted as being the product of hearthside activity. Detailed lithic and faunal analysis in Chapters 3 and 4 strongly suggests that the two hearth-centred scatters, C west and C east, were not contemporary, with the former dating to *c* 9100 BP and the latter to sometime between 10,300 BP and 9700 BP.

Fig 8 *Plan showing the location of lithic and faunal scatters (scale 1:200)*

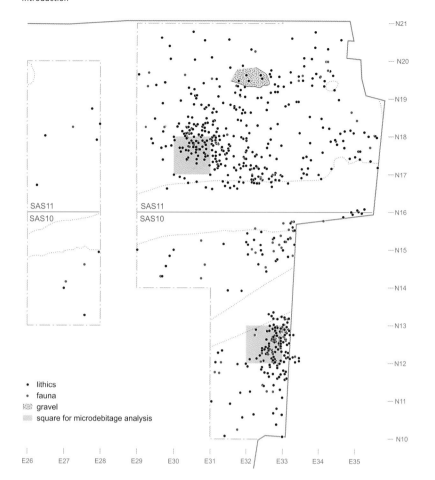

Fig 9 Scatter A, 3D-recorded flintwork and faunal material subdivided into two sub-assemblages (scale 1:100)

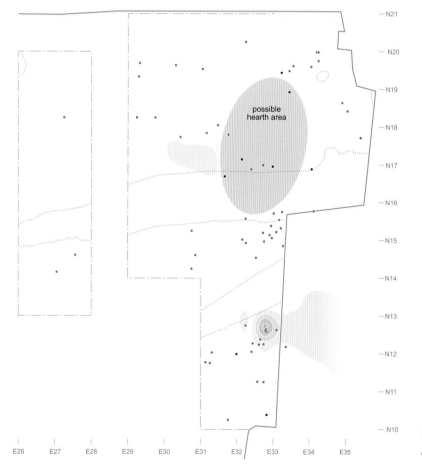

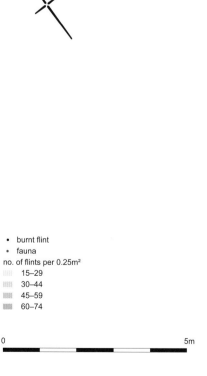

Fig 10 Scatter A, flintwork contoured by 0.25m²; burnt flint and all faunal material shown as 3D points (scale 1:100)

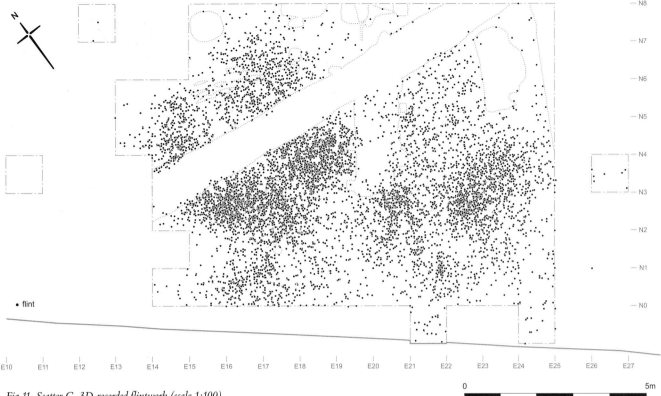

Fig 11 Scatter C, 3D-recorded flintwork (scale 1:100)

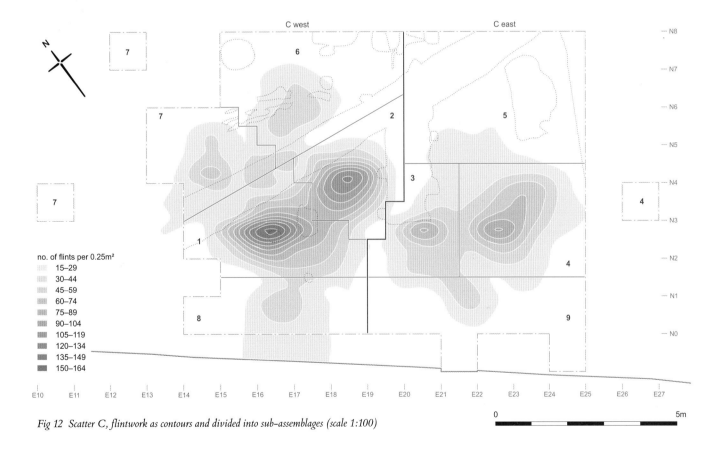

no. of flints per 0.25m²
15–29
30–44
45–59
60–74
75–89
90–104
105–119
120–134
135–149
150–164

Fig 12 Scatter C, flintwork as contours and divided into sub-assemblages (scale 1:100)

Features and structures

The majority of features excavated at Three Ways Wharf consisted of later prehistoric (or more frequently) medieval and post-medieval ditches and pits. A number of features cutting SU40 were initially interpreted as stakeholes; however, excavation revealed that they had penetrated from above SU50 and were probably root holes. In scatter C west, features interpreted as root disturbance from above SU50 were apparent. Very few features could be tentatively identified as being

Fig 13 View of top of SU40 through
densest area of faunal material along grid
E18 (0.5m scale)

contemporary with the Lateglacial/Early Holocene occupations. This may be due to two factors. Firstly, human activity simply may not have entailed the excavation of substantial pits and postholes. Secondly, the post-depositional changes which SU40 has undergone may have led to the blurring of any features that might have existed (Chapter 2).

A single possible feature [431] could be contemporary with the lithic scatters. This was located in squares E17N01 and E17N02 in scatter C west (Fig 19) and consisted of a small subrectangular pit 0.86m long by 0.44m wide and 0.25m deep. The pit appeared to be sealed by SU50 and the bottom of the feature rested on the underlying gravel (SU20). The fill, [483], was virtually indistinguishable from the surrounding sediment of SU40.

The validity of this pit as an archaeological feature remains unproven. Unlike all the later intrusive features it does not disturb the *in situ* flintwork, and it is located between the two densest concentrations of lithic material in C west and adjacent to the hearth area. In Chapters 3 and 6 it is suggested that if contemporary with the lithic scatters, the pit [431] could be associated with the heating or boiling of water as part of the process of marrow extraction. However, no significant quantity of charcoal was recovered from the pit. Moreover, if the pit were contemporary it might be expected to have caused some alteration to the distribution of the lithic material. Instead, the flintwork seems undisturbed by the feature in any way. It is possible to interpret feature [431] as a natural phenomenon caused

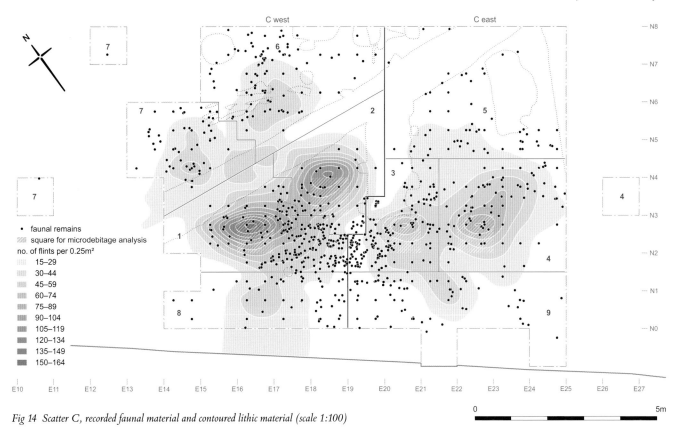

Fig 14 Scatter C, recorded faunal material and contoured lithic material (scale 1:100)

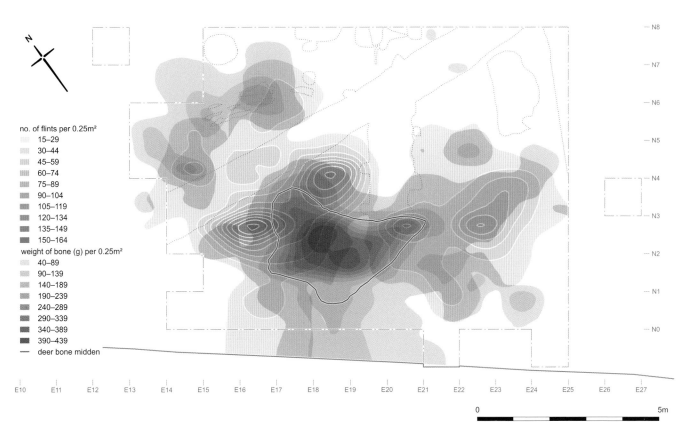

Fig 15 Scatter C, contoured lithic material and contoured weight of faunal material in g per 0.25m² (scale 1:100)

either by differential iron staining, giving the impression of a feature, or by natural vegetation or animal action. It would, therefore, be prudent to regard feature [431] as being of uncertain origin.

A concentration of pebbles and cobbles also occurred in scatter C east in square E21N01. This scatter was spatially

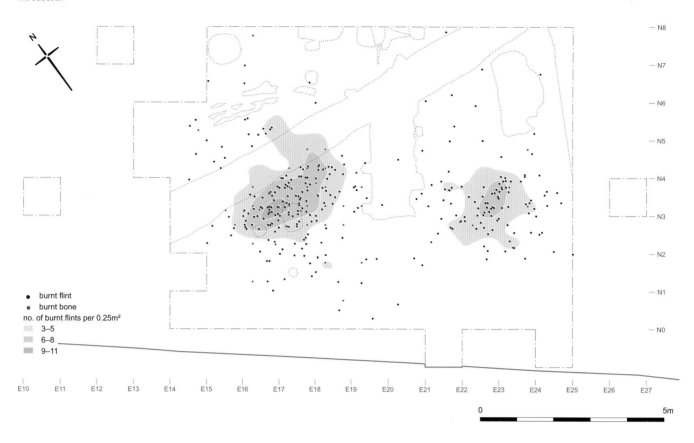

Fig 16 Scatter C, 3D-recorded burnt flint and bone, and burnt flint contours showing hearth areas (scale 1:100)

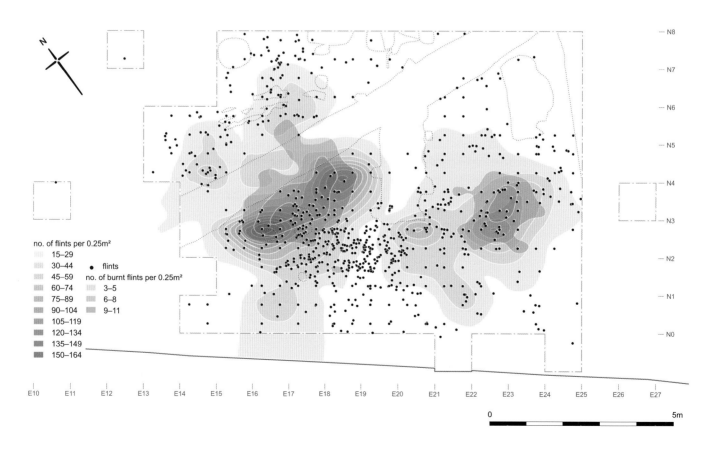

Fig 17 Scatter C, contoured distribution of flintwork and hearths together with all 3D-recorded faunal material (scale 1:100)

concentrated (Fig 65) and included a partially worked cobble. In this instance it is possible to interpret the flint cobbles as perhaps representing a dump of raw material or possibly associated with bone processing.

The only other feature of possible anthropogenic origin was a spread (1.0m long by 0.6m wide and 0.05m thick) of medium to coarse flint gravel clasts [256] within SU40 and directly above SU30 in the northern area of scatter A (Fig 9). The clasts varied in size from cobbles to small pebbles under 10mm in diameter, with *c* 40% of the clasts being in the cobble size range. None of the cobbles were struck, and while this feature could be interpreted as an area of hardstanding, it is equally possible that the pebbles were deposited by natural fluvial processes which may perhaps have included rafting on vegetation.

Dating

The very low or non-existent collagen levels preserved in the faunal material made radiocarbon dating extremely difficult. Even using the Oxford AMS accelerator, the only red and roe deer remains which could be dated were some of the teeth. None of the reindeer material was datable, and only a molar and samples from within a mandible provided dates on the horse material. Five radiocarbon dates were obtained in all (Table 1), by identifying groups of teeth from specific individuals and pooling the collagen extracted from those teeth to produce a single date. However, even the dates which did not fail were only of single-run precision since there was not enough CO_2 for a second ampoule to be counted.

In 2008, FB 83387 was redated (OxA-18702) by Jacobi and Higham using the ultrafiltration method (Higham et al 2006). The new date was in close agreement with the original date obtained in 1987. In addition, a single thermoluminescence date was obtained from a piece of burnt flint (OX89 TL772F1, with a date of 8000±800 BP). However, even with a single standard deviation error of 10%, the thermoluminescence date would appear to be too young when compared with the radiocarbon dates (Table 1).

The distribution of the dated material is shown in Fig 18 and Fig 19. It is apparent that no material was radiocarbon-dated from scatter C east, and neither was any reindeer material dated from scatter A. This proved a major problem, since the horse material in scatter A need not necessarily be associated with human activity (Chapters 3, 4 and 6) while, conversely, the reindeer in scatter C east definitely was associated with human activity (Chapter 4.6) but was undatable.

The probability distributions have been calculated by Mary Ruddy using OxCal v4.0 (Bronk Ramsey 1994; 2001) and calibrated using the IntCal04 curve (Reimer et al 2004). Each scatter is enclosed as a phase (Fig 20; Fig 222) and date ranges for each radiocarbon determination are presented in Table 1. Due to the use of the rigorous ultrafiltration method (which removes modern age contaminants and proves particularly useful when dating bones greater than 2–3 half-lives of ^{14}C such as these: Higham et al 2006) the scatter A date of 10,026–9334 cal BC (OxA-18702) is considered more reliable than previous scatter A results.

The determinations from within scatter A were not statistically significantly different, neither were those from within scatter C, although the measurements from scatter A and scatter C are statistically significantly different from each other (Ward and Wilson 1978). The fact that three individual animals of two different species produced dates statistically indistinguishable suggests that scatter C west was a single 'event,' but this cannot be demonstrated with enough precision.

In conclusion, the following points may be made.
1) Scatter A is not definitely associated with the horse fauna and hence its dating is not secure. However, if the horse material was the product of human activity, then that activity dates from the end of the 11th to the middle of the 10th millennium BC.
2) The reindeer fauna in scatter C east was cut-marked and thus definitely the product of human activity. Unfortunately, however, none of this material was datable.
3) The red and roe deer fauna in scatter C west was definitely the product of human activity and *may* have been the product of a single short phase of activity in the middle of the 9th millennium BC.

Table 1 Successfully dated faunal material from Three Ways Wharf

Scatter	FB no.	Species	Lab no.	Radiocarbon age (BP)	Unmodelled calibrated date range 99.7% probability (cal BC)	Modelled calibrated date range 99.7% probability (cal BC)
A	83387	horse	OxA-18702	10060±45	10026–9334	10024–9367
A	83390	horse	OxA-1778	10270±100	10717–9445	10448–9380
A	83387	horse	OxA-1902	10010±120	10290–9157	10141–9238
C west	84084	red deer	OxA-5557	9280±110	9140–8227	8803–8252
C west	90377	roe deer	OxA-5558	9265±80	8801–8271	8752–8287
C west	84107	red deer	OxA-5559	9200±75	8715–8241	8701–8272

Note: the probability distributions are calculated using OxCal v4.0 (Bronk Ramsey 1994; 2001) and calibrated using the IntCal04 curve (Reimer et al 2004)

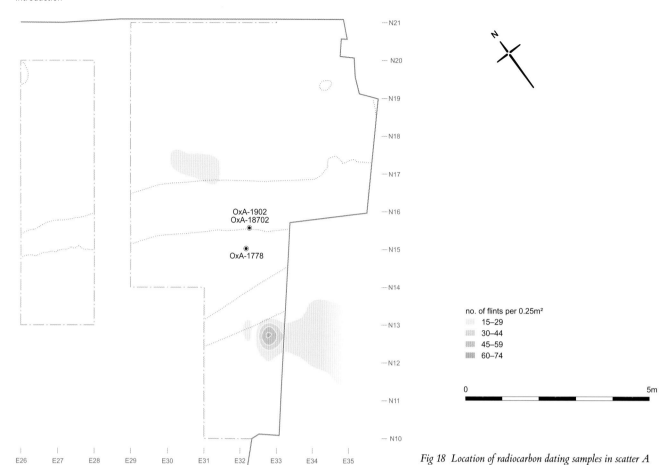

Fig 18 Location of radiocarbon dating samples in scatter A (scale 1:100)

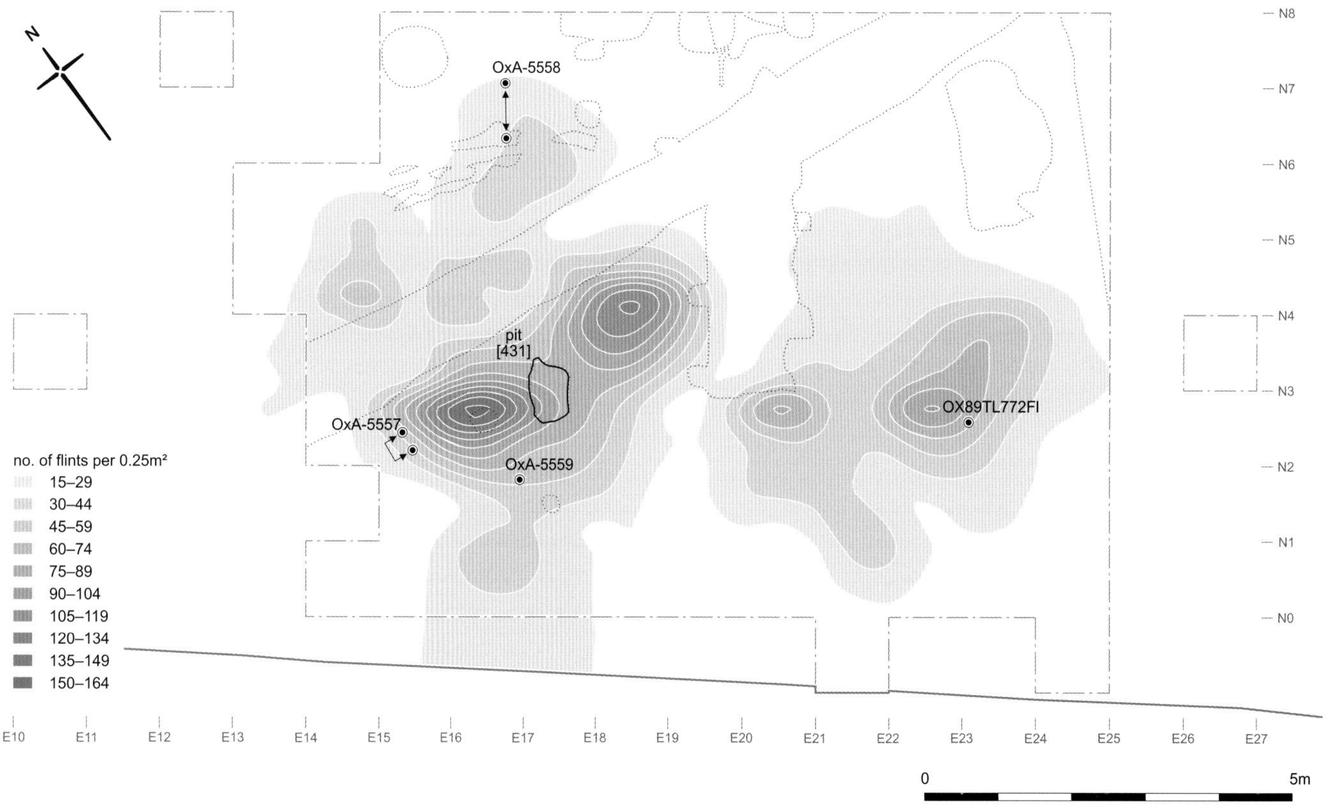

Fig 19 Location of radiocarbon (and thermoluminescence) dating samples in scatter C (scale 1:100)

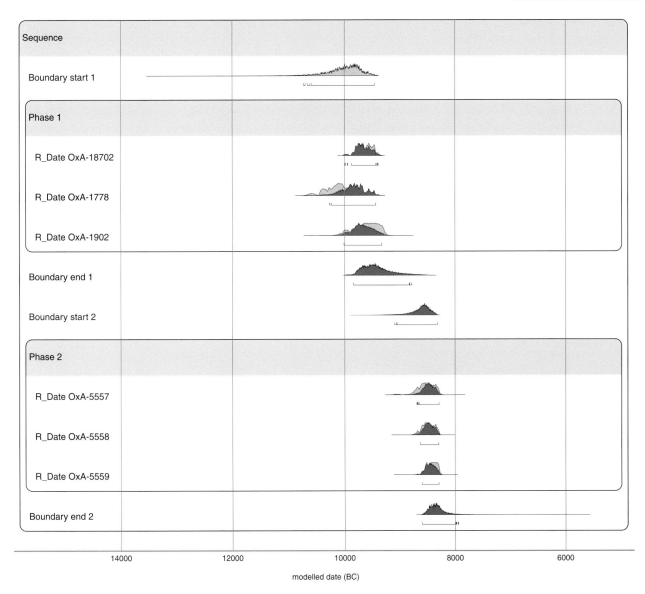

Fig 20 Probability distributions for all radiocarbon dates from Three Ways Wharf

1.4   Post-excavation aims and methodologies

Post-excavation aims and research design

Academic objectives

The main phase of fieldwork was planned as a multi-disciplinary project employing as many different analytical techniques as possible, thus allowing a range of academic objectives to be addressed.

1) *Typological analysis* of Lateglacial and Early Flandrian lithic assemblages, to aid understanding of the evolution of lithic technology in this transitional period.

2) *Physical dating* of the *in situ* flint assemblages by radiocarbon assay of the associated fauna, to place the scatters within a tight chronological framework.

3) *Analysis of the environmental changes throughout the period of*

occupation. Determination of the processes of deposition of the sedimentary sequence, reconstruction of the local environment during phases of occupation, and dating and characterising the organic layer immediately post-dating the occupation were all priorities. Most importantly, the species composition of the assemblages might help determine the periods of occupation at the site, and variations in the distribution of particular species (both vertical and horizontal), such as the red deer and reindeer, might permit the separation of superimposed archaeological horizons. The lithic and faunal scatters were to be placed against the background of the sedimentary and environmental history of the site. These studies would have implications for the archaeological potential of alluvial deposits in other tributary valleys of the Thames.

4) *Study of the palaeotopography of the site.* The exact topographical situation of the site was to be studied, since this would have a bearing on why the site saw several phases of occupation over a considerable length of time. The identification of a

'favoured location' for hunter-gatherer activity could have implications for predicting the likely existence of other sites.

5) *Assessing the degree of post-depositional disturbance and taphonomic processes affecting the site.* Establishing the integrity of the phasing of the lithic and faunal scatters was essential.

6) *Determination of the character, span and season of human activity.* Recent work at Boxgrove, West Sussex (Roberts 1986), has shown that relatively small-scale occupation can generate large quantities of flint material. Information on the character and span of the Late Palaeolithic and Mesolithic occupation would therefore best be tackled from the faunal evidence. It was important for the faunal analysis to identify how many individual prey animals were present on the site, which bones were likely to derive from 'each' individual, and which parts of 'each' individual were present. The distribution and fragmentation of the bone elements would be compared with the recent work on Star Carr (Legge and Rowley-Conwy 1988) and assessed within the model of hunting and base camps proposed by those authors. The results could lead to a reassessment of these most recent conclusions for the Star Carr assemblage and an interpretation of the Three Ways Wharf group.

7) *The study of functional behaviour* within Lateglacial/Early Flandrian hunter-gatherer groups by reconstructing the patterns of production, use and discard of lithic tools. Flint refitting would play an important part in this analysis. Study of the faunal material would allow butchery practices to be ascertained. Lithic and faunal studies might be directly linked by the three-dimensional data to determine which artefacts are spatially correlated with associated animal bone.

The framework for these strategies has been current for many years and is made explicit in Binford's approach, where in his introduction to *Nunamiut ethnoarchaeology* (Binford 1978b, 12) he offers the following two hypotheses.

1) 'We could display patterns of assemblage variability against scales of resource utility as a basis for evaluating the degree to which the patterning reflected consistent strategies relative to the use of the animals. Patterning in faunal frequencies might then be reasonably viewed as resulting from variable strategies in the use of food sources.'

2) 'If we could elucidate the models of dynamics standing behind faunal variability we might then use such understanding as a reference dimension for evaluating variability in stone tools.'

At the time of the excavation of Three Ways Wharf these formulae were an accepted element within the framework of prehistoric studies, although no excavations of Late Palaeolithic and Mesolithic open sites had been conducted in Britain to which they could be applied, apart from work by Schadla-Hall at Seamer Carr (Schadla-Hall 1987; 1989) and the excavations by Mellars of the Mesolithic shell middens on Oronsay (Mellars 1987). The first significant application in Britain of Binford's model for faunal patterns reflecting human behaviour and strategy was the work of Legge and Rowley-Conwy (1988) on the re-analysis of the Mesolithic faunal collections from Star Carr, but since they were working with a collection excavated

over 30 years earlier they had none of the spatial data to work with, or the recovery control introduced on more recent excavations. The association of flint and significant numbers of animal bones at Three Ways Wharf makes this a particularly important site and the hypotheses quoted above were very much to the fore when designing the excavation strategy. For instance, the spatial distribution of the faunal remains might reflect the human behaviour and activities associated with the butchery, processing, consumption and disposal of the animal carcasses and their parts. The association of identifiable flint tools with any particular patterns of faunal distribution, and/or their wear patterns, might allow a positive correlation between tool and function.

The area of study which in retrospect was given the least attention, but deserved much more, was the detailed fragmentation of the faunal material. This is considered below and was an aspect of the post-excavation research design, but a more detailed descriptive field record made by an archaeozoologist during the excavation would perhaps have opened up a more informed taphonomic study of the varying impact of human and natural processes on the fracture and breakage of the faunal assemblage.

The following sections detail the methodologies employed to analyse the material recovered from the excavations in pursuit of the aims articulated in the research design.

Techniques of environmental analysis

The fine gravels and overlying fine-grained sediments were sampled where appropriate for the various environmental analytical techniques. Fig 21 shows the main environmental sampling locations within the area of the main excavation, and the type of sample taken. The sampling strategy aimed to achieve a good spatial distribution of samples for the various environmental specialists across as wide an area of the site as possible.

Sedimentary examination

The examination of the gross sedimentology was conducted by Simon Collcutt during a field visit while excavation was in progress. The sediments were examined at a number of exposures across the site and noted, although no samples were taken for laboratory analysis.

Soil micromorphology

Richard Macphail

Three undisturbed soil samples were taken from a 50cm monolith located in scatter A (Fig 21) through layers 4, 3 and 2 (black humic clay). Layers 3 and 2 were similarly sampled in scatter C by two kubiena boxes (Fig 21). Layers 1 and 2 from the centre of the site were also sampled to investigate the tufa and the base of the overlying later prehistoric level. A further 50cm long monolith taken from the exact location of the area which yielded pollen could not be studied because of problems with impregnation, despite two attempts being made to embed the sample.

Complementary samples for the bulk analysis of grain size, loss on ignition, calcium carbonate and organic carbon (Avery and Bascomb 1974) were also taken (Table 2). Undisturbed samples were air-dried, impregnated with polyester resin (Murphy 1986), made into thin sections (Guilloré 1985), described according to Bullock et al (1985) and interpreted using the guidelines of Courty et al (1989); full details can be found in the archive report (Macphail 1990). Soil microfabrics are usually interpreted on a hierarchical basis. At Three Ways Wharf, the earliest features of alluvial sedimentation and pedogenesis,

relating to the Upper Palaeolithic and Early Mesolithic archaeology, needed to be differentiated from later features resulting from post-depositional biological activity such as the in-mixing of tufa material. There was also patchy sewage sludge inwash and associated vivianite neoformation from later soil contamination.

Palynology

Patricia E J Wiltshire

During the excavation period, a total of six sediment profiles from the site, including areas close to scatters A and C, were

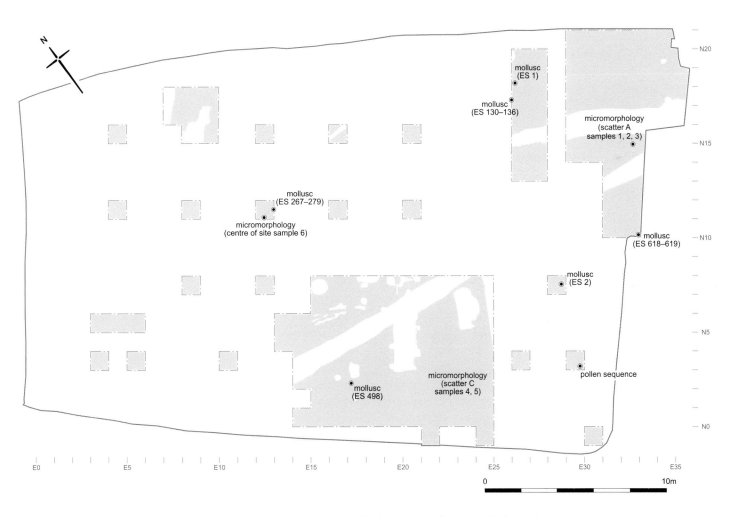

Fig 21 Plan showing the location and type of environmental samples collected within the main areas of excavation (scale 1:200)

Table 2 Soil analytical data from Three Ways Wharf

Area	Sample no.	Layer no.	Depth (cm)	Thin section	Organic carbon (%)	Calcium carbonate (%)	Loss on ignition (%)	Clay (%)	FZ (%)	MZ (%)	CZ (%)	Silt (%)	VFS (%)	FS (%)	MS (%)	CS (%)	VCS (%)	Sand (%)	Texture
Scatter A	{1}	2/3	97–104	A	1.50	0.70	9.6	22	29	14	12	55	7	9	5	<1	<1	23	clay loam
	{2}	3/4	107–114	B	1.70	0.77	7.2	27	11	11	19	41	24	4	1	2	1	32	clay loam
	{3}	4	117–124	C	8.20	0.70	11.5	25	10	10	19	39	28	4	1	2	1	36	clay loam
Scatter C	{4}	2	17–24	D	1.60	0.08	15.7	47	11	6	10	27	17	4	2	1	2	26	clay
	{5}	3	25–33	E	0.43	0.12	7.9	27	11	12	17	40	20	7	3	1	2	33	clay loam

assessed (Fig 21). A monolith of 10 x 10 x 50cm was obtained from each profile, wrapped in polythene, and stored at 3°C. Preliminary assessment showed that only one of the monoliths (from immediately adjacent to scatter C) was polleniferous and only the black humic clay (SU50) contained sufficient palynomorphs to make a study feasible; even here, they were exceedingly sparse and generally in a poor state of preservation. Pollen analysis was also carried out on black organic clay obtained from a site situated on the Colne floodplain, 1.4km south of Three Ways Wharf at Cowley Mill Road, Uxbridge (Fig 1). Here, excavations revealed small *in situ* Early Mesolithic flint scatters (I Stewart, pers comm) sealed beneath a black clay similar to that found at Three Ways Wharf and the nearby site of Sandstone, Buckinghamshire.

In all sections studied at Three Ways Wharf, the sediments underlying and overlying the black clay layer (SU40 and SU60) contained only the occasional grain of Poaceae (grasses) or undifferentiated monolete spores of Pteropsida (ferns). Microscopic charcoal fragments were abundant in all the layers, but were particularly dense within the black layer. Because the upper and lower clay horizons were barren of pollen, ten contiguous samples of 10mm thickness were prepared from the black polleniferous layer, with samples {1} and {10} being transitional between the black layer and the adjacent clays. Each 10mm sample consisted of a lateral spit of 20g of sediment.

The organic, clay matrix was removed using standard treatments for soils (Dimbleby 1985, 155) and the sample suspended in 1.0ml of glycerol jelly after staining with safranine. Slides were examined with phase-contrast microscopy at x400 and x1000 magnification where necessary. Counts of palynomorphs ranged between 638 and 2931, with an average of *c* 730. Because of the very large concentration of charcoal, it proved impossible to count the fragments by standard techniques (Clark 1982, 527–31). Palynomorph nomenclature follows that of Moore et al (1991), Bennett et al (1994) and Stace (1991).

Data are expressed as percentage of total pollen (TP), excluding spores. Spores were expressed as a percentage of TP and spores. The diagram of selected pollen and spore taxa (Fig 23) was produced using TILIA and TILIA★GRAPH programs (Grimm 1991). The diagram was zoned subjectively and divided into TWW(1) and TWW(2). Minor taxa not shown in Fig 23 are listed in Table 5.

Molluscan analysis

Martin Bates

The molluscs were sampled by the author at the site during excavation. All stratigraphic units were sampled at a number of locations in order to obtain a clear idea of the three-dimensional variation in mollusc assemblage composition. The units sampled, the sample numbers and sample locations are given in Table 3. Molluscan sample locations are shown in Fig 21. Sample volumes were dependent on the relative abundance of

Table 3 Stratigraphic units sampled for molluscs, their locations, sample numbers and contexts

Stratigraphic unit	Location by site grid square						Context no. related to sample nos
	E26 N18	E28 N0	E25 N17	E13 N11	E17 N02	E33 N10	
Upper clays				{267} {268} {269}}	{498}	{615} {616}	[314]: {267}; {268} [404]: {269}; {498} [432]: {615}; {616}
Tufa	{1}	{2}					-
Black unit			{130}	{270}		{617} {618}	[433]: {130}; {617}; {618} [342]: {270}
Archaeological unit			{131} {132}	{271} {272} {273}		{619} {620} {621}	[348]: {271}; {272}; {273} [333]: {131}; {132}; {619}; {620}; {621}
Lower clay-silts			{133} {134} {135} {136}	{274} {275} {276} {279}		{622} {623} {624} {625}	[345]: {274}; {275}; {276}; {279} [334]: {133}; {134}; {135}; {136} [407]: {622}; {623}; {624}; {625}

Key: {no.} = ES no.; [no.] = context no.

molluscs and the nature of the sedimentary units. It was unusual to find well-preserved molluscan assemblages at Three Ways Wharf, and sample sizes (Table 4) were therefore larger than usual for malacological study. Sampling intervals depended on the thickness of the stratigraphic units. Considerable lateral variation in sediment thickness was observed at the site, and hence the more deeply stratified sequences towards the south-east corner of the site produced a greater number of samples per stratigraphic unit. The presence of the author at the site throughout the excavation allowed numerous areas to be examined for molluscan material.

Samples were air-dried and weighed prior to immersion in water to facilitate disaggregation of the sediment. In the case of partial disaggregation the procedure was repeated until a slurry was produced. In a limited number of cases the samples were prepared with hydrogen peroxide (33% diluted H_2O_2) and warm water and left for 12 hours. After disaggregation the slurry was sieved through a 500µm sieve. The residue was air-dried and sorted under a binocular microscope.

Total shell counts are given in Table 4. Totals and percentages calculated exclude the counts for *Bithynia* opercula. To simplify the presentation and discussion of these results, the freshwater species have been grouped according to Sparks's classification (Sparks 1961) and group frequencies are presented as a percentage of total freshwater shells and shown as closed histograms (Fig 22). The terrestrial molluscs have been classified into three main ecological categories as follows (Preece and Robinson 1982).

Table 4 Mollusc data from Three Ways Wharf

Species	ES 1	ES 2	ES 130	ES 131	ES 132	ES 133	ES 134	ES 135	ES 136
Valvata cristata Müll		108	18	7	5	1		2	2
Valvata piscinalis (Müll)	92	237	27	15	17	6	4	8	5
Bithynia tentaculata (Linn)	64	4	2	2					
Bithynia opercula	250	56	4	11	3	4	2	2	1
Carychium tridentatum (Risso)	1								
Carychium sp									
Lymnaea truncatula (Müll)	17	18							
Lymnaea palustris (Müll)	5								
Lymnaea stagnalis (Linn)									
Lymnaea peregra (Müll)	1								
Planorbis planorbis (Linn)	6								
Planorbis sp									
Anisus leucostoma Millet	7	1							
Bathyomphalus contortus (Linn)	20	23	1	1		2	1		
Gyraulus albus Müll	3	15		1	3				
Armiger crista (Linn)	6	2							
Ancylus fluviatilis Müll	9	17							
Acroloxus lacustris (Linn)	1	4							
Succinea/Oxyloma sp	91		1	1					
Cochlicopa lubrica (Müll)	1			1		1			
Cochlicopa sp	5		1	2	1	1	1		
Vertigo antivertigo (Drap)		1							
Vertigo pygmaea (Drap)				3					
Vertigo moulinsiana (Dupuy)									
Vertigo substriata (Jeffreys)				1					
Pupilla muscorum (Linn)	4	2	2						
Vallonia costata (Müll)	3	1		7			1		
Vallonia pulchella (Müll)	34		1						
Vallonia excentrica (Sterki)	2								
Vallonia pulchella/excentrica	47		1	14					
Acanthinula aculeata (Müll)	6	1	1	3					
Punctum pygmaeum (Drap)	1								
Discus rotundatus (Müll)	6	1		1					
Nesoivitrea hammonis (Ström)	5			5				1	
Aegopinella nitidula (Drap)	4			1		1			2
Oxychilus sp	3		1						
Limax/Deroceras	5	6	4	13	9	5	9	7	
Euconulus fulvus (Müll) agg									
Cecilioides acicula (Müll)		2	8	12	18	18	12	6	3
Clausilia bidentata (Ström)	1								
Clausiliidae	2	2		2					
Trichia hispida (Linn)	35	4	3	26	2	4	6	2	1
Arianta arbustorum (Linn)	*	*		*	*			*	
Cepaea sp *nemoralis*	*	*	*	*	*		*		
Cepaea/Arianta	2	1		3		2			
Spherium sp		*							
Pisidium amnicum (Müll)	7	1		1					
Pisidium casertanum (Poli)	1	28				1			
Pisidium milium Held	4	*			3	2			
Pisidium nitidum Jenyns	7	4			1		2		
Pisidium pulchellum	2	1							
Pisidium mortessierianum Paladihle	19	12		2					
Sample weight (kg)	2.2	2.2	4.4	13.3	12.5	9.7	9.7	11.4	9.7
Total no. of shells (excluding *Bithynia* opercula)	529	496	71	124	59	44	36	26	13
Shells per kg of sediment	240	225	16	9	5	5	4	2	1

Species	ES 498	ES 615	ES 616	ES 617	ES 618	ES 619	ES 620	ES 621	ES 622	ES 623	ES 625
Valvata cristata Müll	3		6		363	134	2		1		1
Valvata piscinalis (Müll)	6		1		86	6	1			1	
Bithynia tentaculata (Linn)	2				51	5					
Bithynia opercula	31	4	47	73	104	13	2	1		1	1
Carychium tridentatum (Risso)											
Carychium sp	3		1		1						
Lymnaea truncatula (Müll)	2		3		4	1					

23

Table 4 (cont)

Species	ES 498	ES 615	ES 616	ES 617	ES 618	ES 619	ES 620	ES 621	ES 622	ES 623	ES 625
Lymnaea palustris (Müll)											
Lymnaea stagnalis (Linn)					2						
Lymnaea peregra (Müll)											
Planorbis planorbis (Linn)	3				3						
Planorbis sp			I			I					
Anisus leucostoma Millet	I										
Bathyomphalus contortus (Linn)					7	2	I				
Gyraulus albus Müll					20						
Armiger crista (Linn)					8	I					
Ancylus fluviatilis Müll					19	4					
Acroloxus lacustris (Linn)					3						
Succinea/Oxyloma sp	15		2		35						
Cochlicopa lubrica (Müll)					3						
Cochlicopa sp	5		2		4	I					
Vertigo antivertigo (Drap)				I	I						
Vertigo pygmaea (Drap)	2				2						
Vertigo moulinsiana (Dupuy)					I						
Vertigo substriata (Jeffreys)											
Pupilla muscorum (Linn)	4		I		6	I					
Vallonia costata (Müll)					17					I	
Vallonia pulchella (Müll)	4				6						
Vallonia excentrica (Sterki)	4		3		10						
Vallonia pulchella/excentrica	42		9		95	2					
Acanthinula aculeata (Müll)	5		I		5						
Punctum pygmaeum (Drap)	I										
Discus rotundatus (Müll)	I				4	*					
Nesovitrea hammonis (Ström)	5				14	I	I				
Aegopinella nitidula (Drap)						I					
Oxychilus sp	I				2						
Limax/Deroceros	26	4	6		10	6	4			2	
Euconulus fulvus (Müll) agg					2	I					
Cecilioides acicula (Müll)					I						
Clausilia bidentata (Ström)											
Clausiliidae					2						
Trichia hispida (Linn)	38		8		4	2					
Arianta arbustorum (Linn)	*		*			*	*				
Cepaea sp *nemoralis*	*				I	*	*				
Cepaea/Arianta	9				8	I					
Spherium sp											
Pisidium amnicum (Müll)					2						
Pisidium cassertanum (Poli)					25	2					
Pisidium milium Held					4			I			
Pisidium nitidum Jenyns					14	2		I			
Pisidium pulchellum					8						
Pisidium mortessierianum Paladihle					8	2					
Sample weight (kg)	7.0	2.0	2.5	2.0	2.0	1.0	1.5	1.5	1.5	2.0	1.3
Total no. of shells (excluding *Bithynia* opercula)	182	4	44	I	861	176	11		I	4	I
Shells per kg of sediment	26	2	18	0.5	430	176	7		I	2	I

Species	ES 267	ES 268	ES 269	ES 270	ES 271	ES 272	ES 273	ES 274	ES 275	ES 276	ES 509	ES 510
Valvata cristata Müll		I									3	
Valvata piscinalis (Müll)		3										
Bithynia tentaculata (Linn)		I										
Bithynia opercula	81	107	16	26	16	7	7	I	4	4	2	
Carychium tridentatum (Risso)												
Carychium sp												
Lymnaea truncatula (Müll)												I
Lymnaea palustris (Müll)												
Lymnaea stagnalis (Linn)												
Lymnaea peregra (Müll)												
Planorbis planorbis (Linn)												
Planorbis sp												
Anisus leucostoma Millet												
Bathyomphalus contortus (Linn)												

Table 4 (cont)

Species	ES 267	ES 268	ES 269	ES 270	ES 271	ES 272	ES 273	ES 274	ES 275	ES 276	ES 509	ES 510
Gyraulus albus Müll												
Armiger crista (Linn)														
Ancylus fluviatilis Müll												
Acroloxus lacustris (Linn)												
Succinea/Oxyloma sp		3										
Cochlicopa lubrica (Müll)												
Cochlicopa sp												
Vertigo antivertigo (Drap)											3	
Vertigo pygmaea (Drap)												
Vertigo moulinsiana (Dupuy)											5	
Vertigo substriata (Jeffreys)												
Pupilla muscorum (Linn)												
Vallonia costata (Müll)											5	
Vallonia pulchella (Müll)												
Vallonia excentrica (Sterki)											3	
Vallonia pulchella/excentrica												
Acanthinula aculeata (Müll)												
Punctum pygmaeum (Drap)												
Discus rotundatus (Müll)												
Nesoivitrea hammonis (Ström)											*	
Aegopinella nitidula (Drap)											4	2
Oxychilus sp												
Limax/Deroceros	2	18								2		
Euconulus fulvus (Müll) agg												
Cecilioides acicula (Müll)		2									8	
Clausilia bidentata (Ström)												
Clausiliidae												
Trichia hispida (Linn)											18	15
Arianta arbustorum (Linn)		*										*
Cepaea sp *nemoralis*		*										
Cepaea/Arianta												2
Spherium sp												
Pisidium amnicum (Müll)												
Pisidium cassertanum (Poli)												
Pisidium milium Held												
Pisidium nitidum Jenyns												
Pisidium pulchellum												
Pisidium mortessierianum Paladihle												
Sample weight (kg)	7.0	4.5	2.0	5.5	4.0	3.5	4.0	6.5	5.0	3.5	6.1	3.6
Total no. of shells (excluding *Bithynia* opercula)	2	31								2	53	26
Shells per kg of sediment		7									9	7

Note: In the Limax/Deroceros row, single specimens (|) are present in ES 270, ES 271, ES 273, ES 274, and ES 509. In the Total no. of shells row, single specimens (|) occur in ES 270, ES 271, ES 273, and ES 274.

Key: * = present but not quantifiable

1) Swamp species: *Succinea/Oxyloma*, *Vertigo antivertigo*, *V moulinsiana*.

2) Terrestrial 'A': *Cochlicopa*, *Punctum*, *Nesovitrea*, *Limax/Deroceros*, *Euconulus*, *Cepaea/Arianta*.

3) Terrestrial 'B': *Acanthinula*, *Aegopinella*, Clausiliidae.

It may be noted here that alternative schemes of classification of mollusc assemblages could have been used (eg that proposed by Evans et al 1992). Frequencies of terrestrial molluscs have been calculated as a percentage of total freshwater molluscs and are represented by open histograms (Fig 22).

Identification of specimens was based on complete shells and/or diagnostic fragments. Totals were based on apical fragments, with bivalve totals being halved. Differential destruction and corrosion of the shell surface caused identification difficulties. Post-depositional decalcification had occurred throughout the site (below), resulting in the total destruction of the shell material from certain areas. Elsewhere, only the more robust elements, such as *Bithynia* opercula and slug plates (*Deroceros/Limax*) survived. Where molluscs were preserved decalcification had frequently removed shell surface sculpture and colouration, rendering the identification of smaller shells and fragments difficult.

Mollusc frequencies in sample column ES 130–6 are, with the exception of ES 130 and 131, too small to allow standard percentage histograms to be drawn. It was therefore decided to combine the results from the numerically significant samples taken across the site. This has allowed broad inferences to be made regarding the ecological conditions prevalent during deposition of the sediment matrix, the sequence of events at the site, and the taphonomic processes involved in the production

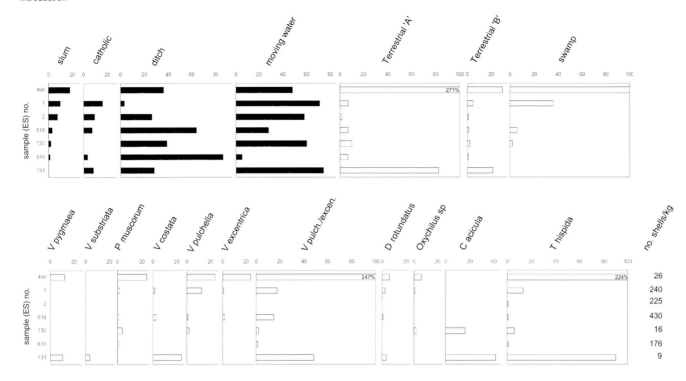

Fig 22 Numbers of terrestrial and aquatic mollusc shells per kilogram of sediment from selected samples; key: closed bars – aquatic molluscs; open bars – terrestrial molluscs

of the assemblage; where more than one sample is available from a single stratigraphic unit an indication of lateral variability may be gained. This methodology is not standard malacological practice and it should not be assumed that changes across stratigraphic boundaries are necessarily synchronous across space. The results are presented in stratigraphic order (Fig 22), but it should be remembered that the lateral relationship within and between units may be more complex than the stratigraphic sequence would suggest (above). It may be unwise to assume contemporaneity of sedimentary layers across the site and hence the contemporaneity of the molluscan assemblages, even within discrete units, must be treated with caution.

Other environmental techniques

Samples were taken for both ostracods and diatoms. Unfortunately, the results proved negative due to poor preservation.

Contamination and differential preservation

Palynology

Patricia E J Wiltshire

The results from Three Ways Wharf are shown in the pollen diagram (Fig 23) and table of minor taxa (Table 5). It should be noted that these data were first prepared for publication in the early 1990s (Lewis et al 1992). The patterns observed in the pollen curves strongly suggest that the black humic clay has stratigraphic integrity and it is assumed, therefore, that the

pollen record reveals vegetation change in the environs of the site.

When the pollen spectra are examined, it is obvious that species richness was low, with only 22 taxa being recorded in the black clay layer. Differential preservation is, therefore, an important factor to be kept in mind during interpretation of the data (Havinga 1964; 1967; 1971; Faegri 1971; Elsik 1971; Correia 1971). Much of the observational and experimental evidence for differential susceptibility to decay of pollen and spores is contradictory, so that only generalisations can be made. Broadly, the breakdown and disappearance of palynomorphs appears to be related to the oxidation susceptibility and the sporopollenin content of the exine, as well as the redox potential and pH of accreting sediments. The area from which the polleniferous sediment was obtained must, therefore, have offered a different physico-chemical environment from that of the other areas of the site which were studied. It probably remained waterlogged and anaerobic throughout the period during which the black humic clay was deposited, whereas elsewhere the site may have experienced drier, more aerobic conditions, at least periodically.

Nevertheless, the pollen of vulnerable taxa was present alongside that of very resistant taxa (Chapter 2.2, 'Black humic clay (SU50)'). It is assumed, therefore, that real vegetational changes are reflected in the pollen diagram rather than simply the effects of differential preservation.

The presence of macroscopic contamination of the artefact-bearing layers (SU40 and SU30) by medieval fish bones and brick dust is noted below. This contamination appears to have had little effect on the stratigraphic patterning of the pollen diagram. One possible explanation of this is that the underlying strata were contaminated with coarser-sized material moving

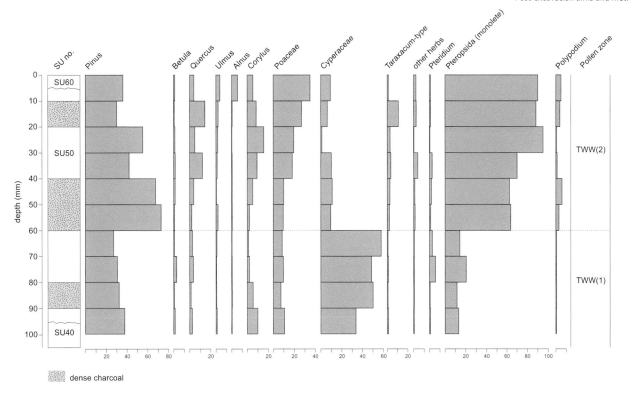

Fig 23 Diagram of selected pollen and spore taxa; pollen expressed as % total pollen (TP) excluding spores; spores expressed as % total pollen plus spores

Table 5 Pollen minor taxa from Three Ways Wharf; pollen expressed as % total pollen (TP) excluding spores; spores expressed as % total pollen plus spores

Pollen zone	Sample no.	Depth (mm)	*Salix*	Rosaceae	Apiacaeae	Caryophyllaceae	Aster-type	*Centaurea nigra*-type	*Rumex* indeterminate	*Plantago lanceolata*	Ranunculus-type	*Sphagnum*
	{1}	0–10						1.9				
	{2}	10–20								2.0		
TWW(2)	{3}	20–30										
	{4}	30–40			0.5				1.6	1.0	0.5	
	{5}	40–50							0.8			
	{6}	50–60						0.9				
	{7}	60–70		0.2		0.2	0.2					
TWW(1)	{8}	70–80			0.2							
	{9}	80–90	0.2		0.3	0.3						0.3
	{10}	90–100	0.4		0.4							

Note: Depth is from top of sequence

downwards through root holes. Microscopic pollen grains, on the other hand, may have been too small to have been disturbed by this scale of contamination, and remained locked within the fine-grained clay matrix.

Molluscs

Martin Bates

Mollusc frequencies for the samples examined are typically low. Column samples ES 130–6 exhibit the most consistent frequencies of shells, while the other column samples, ES 267–79 and ES 615–25, exhibit very low frequencies of preserved mollusca (Table 4). Individual samples within these columns do, however, contain greater frequencies of shells, for instance ES 618 and 619. It is, therefore, obvious that great lateral variation in mollusc frequencies exists at the site. Samples ES 130–6 contain mollusc numbers that allow graphical representation of the results. Fig 24 illustrates the plot for total number of shells per kilogram of sediment and includes total shell frequencies (shkg), total freshwater shells (wkg) and total terrestrial shells (lkg). All curves illustrate a rapid decrease in abundance of shells with increasing depth. Shell totals, never high, decline from *c* 15/kg in the black, humic horizon (ES 130) to fewer than 2/kg in the basal unit (ES 136).

Plots of the *Bithynia* opercula/slug plate frequency as a percentage of the total sample (including *Bithynia* opercula and slug plate totals) and the absolute frequencies of *Bithynia*

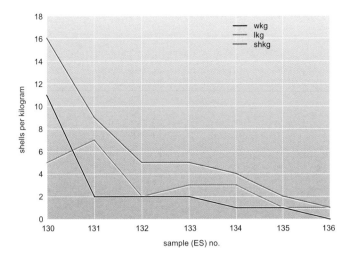

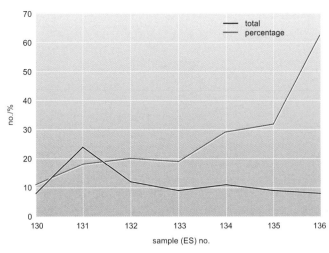

Fig 24 *Absolute frequencies of mollusc shells per kilogram of sediment from grid square E25N17; key: wkg – aquatic molluscs per kg; lkg – terrestrial molluscs per kg; shkg – total numbers of molluscs per kg*

Fig 25 *Frequencies of* Bithynia *opercula and slug plates from grid square E25N17*

opercula and slug plates (Fig 25) show that absolute frequencies are consistent through the profile, but that the percentage increases with depth. This illustrates an inverse relationship between shell preservation and depth. Both *Bithynia* opercula and slug plates are relatively more resistant than normal mollusc shells and thus may, in certain circumstances, be used as an index of differential destruction of the mollusc assemblage. Therefore, it is suggested that there is evidence within this column for differential destruction of the mollusc assemblage with depth. The period at which the destruction commenced is at present unknown.

Differential destruction of the mollusc assemblages is suggested to account for at least part of the lateral variability in the presence and absence of molluscs in the sedimentary sequence at Three Ways Wharf. It is likely that differential destruction of the mollusc assemblage may have affected all the samples, and not only those for which few, if any, shells remain. All sample frequencies and conclusions drawn from them should, therefore, be treated with caution.

Contamination of other categories of organic material retrieved by sieving and differential preservation

The initial processing stages and sorting of the residues of the environmental samples revealed a number of finds that were quite clearly intrusive in the deposits. Those items that could be categorically identified as intrusive included small fragments of glass, brick and coal. All these fragments, which occurred in many samples, including the lowest sampled layers on the site, were all very small and rarely more than 3–4mm in diameter. This was initially viewed with some surprise, since the stratigraphy at the site is quite clear (Fig 7) and shows little visual evidence of disturbance. The stratigraphy of the lower layers has remained sufficiently intact to indicate that these were not seriously disturbed by soil formation processes, and these intrusive elements must have made their way into the deposits

from the upper layers of the stratigraphy on the site in the medieval or post-medieval period.

The only plausible explanation for the presence of this material is that it moved down through root voids and worm holes passing vertically through the deposits from the upper levels. This would also explain the small size of the intrusive fragments identified. While modern glass and small fragments of brick and coal are readily identified as intrusive, other elements of the finds are more problematic. This is particularly true of botanical and zoological material surviving in the deposits, and analysis of some of these elements also suggests intrusion of much later material into the early prehistoric horizons.

BOTANICAL MATERIAL

Both waterlogged and charred plant remains were extracted from soil samples taken from the Lateglacial and Early Holocene archaeological horizons. A study of these indicates that most of the material must derive from later deposits at the site. The presence of carbonised cereal grains, including bread wheat (*Triticum aestivum*) and six-row hulled barley (*Hordeum sativum*), in the samples is clearly out of context in an Early Holocene archaeological horizon, and the survival of a grape (*Vitis vinifera*) pip in a waterlogged condition in context [348], SU40, throws into question the status of other surviving waterlogged seeds found in these contexts. Much of the waterlogged plant material in these lower layers was unidentifiable root or stem material and it appears likely that most of this constitutes the surviving roots, through waterlogging, of plants that were growing on the surface of the alluvial deposits in the medieval period or later.

SMALL VERTEBRATES

A number of small vertebrates were recovered from many of the sieved residues. These included fragments of the bones and teeth of small mammals, a few bird bones and the bones of fishes. Several hundred identifiable fragments of bones were recovered from some 400 of the sorted samples. These included, among the terrestrial vertebrates, bones and teeth of rat, mice, vole, mole and amphibian. All these fragments were small and of similar size to the carbonised cereal grains or pieces of glass and brick also found in the samples. The presence of rat, a species not introduced to Britain before the Roman period (Rackham 1979), makes it clear that much if not all of this material may be intrusive, and little reliance can be placed on the occurrence of any individual species.

No species were identified that could be confidently assigned to the various archaeological occupations on the basis of their ecology, including species that might have been associated with the Lateglacial occupation of the site. Disconcertingly, a large number of bones of marine fish species were extracted from the samples, as well as freshwater species. The majority of those recovered from a selection of 400 samples were herring, although eel bones were in fact the most numerous of the fishes. The occurrence of so many marine species including

fragments of cod, whiting and estuarine species must cast into doubt the contemporaneity of these bones with the deposits in which they lay. The distribution of the fish bones has been analysed. In Fig 26 the eel and herring bones have been plotted in terms of their frequency at depths below the top of SU40. This figure also includes the total number of processed samples from each level. The distribution shows that the frequency of both eel and herring bones is positively correlated with sample frequency. Unfortunately, few samples were collected from the deposits overlying the archaeological horizon and it has not, therefore, been possible to test whether fish bones continued to occur with similar frequency in the deposits overlying SU40. The remaining fish species (ie excluding eel and herring) were plotted in a similar manner after being amalgamated into freshwater, estuarine and marine groups (Fig 27). Again the marine species distribution shows a positive correlation with sample numbers, but the freshwater species demonstrate much less of a tendency to fall with sample numbers, and bones of cyprinids and other freshwater species occurred at frequencies

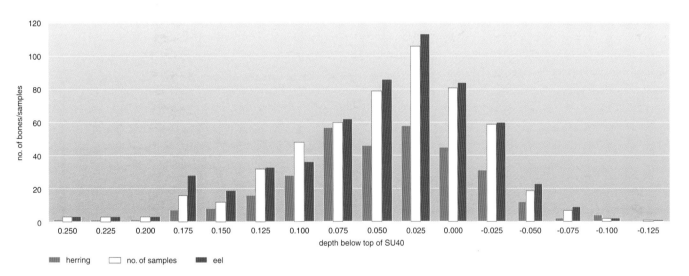

Fig 26 Vertical distribution of eel and herring bones in SU40

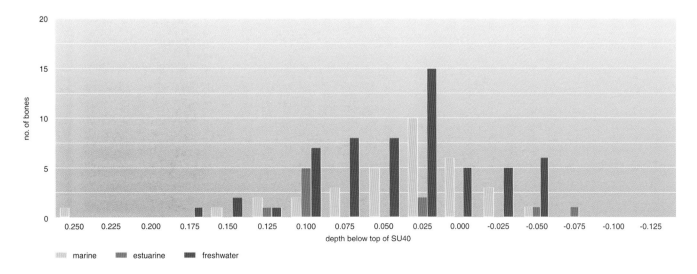

Fig 27 Vertical distribution of fish bones (excluding eel and herring) in SU40

greater than expected at depths immediately below and above those with the greatest number of samples. Fish remains were distributed throughout the excavated area where samples were sieved, with frequencies of both freshwater and marine fish being as high in scatter A as in scatter C.

It may be that an element of the freshwater assemblage is contemporary with the deposits but this cannot be substantiated. It is unfortunate that none of the fish bones can be positively associated with the prehistoric occupation, but these data serve to caution against the use of small material from soil samples even where the stratigraphic evidence would suggest that deposits were well sealed.

LARGER VERTEBRATES

The discussions above have been concerned largely with finds that rarely exceeded 3–5mm in diameter and which can plausibly be seen as contaminants through moving down through the soil. It therefore becomes necessary to consider whether any of those bones that we might attribute to the archaeological deposits could also be contaminants. The analyses below show that the bones of reindeer, red deer and roe deer are sufficiently frequent and concentrated within a defined distribution to preclude their occurrence as intrusive elements in the deposits. Furthermore, the size of many, if not most, of these fragments is too large to have allowed their movement through the soil without a much more severe disruption of the stratigraphy. This factor can also be used to exclude the bones of swan and beaver, and the teeth and bones of horse, as candidates for intrusion, and consequently these are regarded as being contemporary with the other Lateglacial/Early Holocene fauna.

However, fragments of pig, pine marten, rabbit, hare, cat, fox, wolf or canid, duck and swallow are possible candidates for intrusion. These fauna were assessed on the basis of their preservation, surface condition, size and spatial distribution. Of these the fox is almost certainly contemporary, with the wolf/canid and marten possibly also. None of the other species can be confidently assigned to these faunas. A detailed discussion of the selection criteria and reasoning underpinning this assessment is included in the site archive.

The foregoing discussions indicate a high level of contamination of the early archaeological horizons by small bones and fragments, and by cereal grains. This jeopardises the context for many of the smaller elements of the flora and fauna, including charcoal, and raises many questions for future and past assemblages that may come under scrutiny. Housley's comment on the characteristically young age obtained from many charcoal samples (Housley 1991) may reflect this movement of material through the soil. The Thatcham rabbits are an excellent illustration of this problem: despite being found sealed within an algal marl, 9in (23cm) below the top of this deposit and apparently well stratified, they have yielded a post-medieval radiocarbon date (Yalden 1991).

In conclusion, contamination of the Lateglacial/Early Holocene occupation strata (SU50–30) was largely confined to macroscopic fragments 3–4mm in size which had travelled down root holes and worm burrows. Microscopic material such

as pollen grains appears unaffected by this movement, as does the overwhelming proportion of the larger elements of the flint and faunal assemblages. Therefore, while the evidence of the small vertebrate assemblages must be discounted and the mollusc evidence treated with caution, contamination of the main lithic and faunal assemblages is minimal.

1.5 Organisation of this report

Structure of the report

The report first of all presents the sedimentary and stratigraphic sequence, integrated with the findings of the environmental analysis and interpretations. Chapter 3 contains a description of the lithic assemblages including refitting, technological trends, comparisons between the lithic scatters and spatial patterning. Chapter 4 describes the faunal assemblages, species identifications and the ecology of the identified species. Chapter 5 considers the site formation processes, including preservation of faunal material, recognition of different phases of occupation, and the degree of vertical and horizontal dispersal of lithic material. Chapter 6 is principally concerned with spatial and functional analysis of the lithic and faunal assemblages, and the interpretation of the social structures of the prehistoric inhabitants. Chapter 7 concludes by examining the Three Ways Wharf assemblages in their national and European contexts.

The archive

The excavation records, research archive, digital archive and finds from the site have been deposited with the London Archaeological Archive and Research Centre (LAARC), referenced by the site code (UX88; also UX86 and UX89). The archive may be consulted by prior arrangement with the archive manager at the LAARC, Mortimer Wheeler House, 46 Eagle Wharf Road, London N1 7ED.

1.6 Textual and graphical conventions

Textual conventions

The flints and bones were numbered in two series in the databases and in this publication as FFN + no. (final flint no.) and FB + no. (final bone no.). Environmental samples are distinguished in the text by ES + no. The abreviation SAS is used to refer to a sub-assemblage.

For purposes of analysis and in this publication contexts were grouped into 'stratigraphic units' (SU) and assigned numbers (20–70) (Chapter 2.2).

Graphical conventions

The graphical conventions used in this report are shown on Fig 28. All plans are oriented with site north to the top, except Fig 3 which is in OS grid orientation.

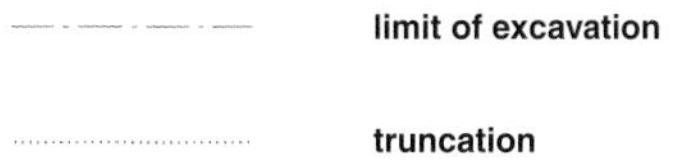

— · — · — · — **limit of excavation**

················· **truncation**

Fig 28 Graphical conventions used in this report

2

Site sequence
and development

2.1 Introduction

The sequence of gravels and fine-grained sediments were assigned context numbers while under excavation. During post-excavation analysis the contexts were grouped into 'stratigraphic units' (SU) and assigned numbers (20–70). This was based on context descriptions including colour and texture which were observed in the field and supported by soil analytical data produced by the soil micromorphological analysis (Table 2). However, it is accepted that the lack of a detailed sedimentological analysis means that the homogeneity of the stratigraphic units cannot be supported by detailed quantified data. In particular, it is difficult to demonstrate that the stratigraphic units are not time-transgressive across the site. Nonetheless, soil micromorphology suggests (below, 2.2) that variations in the sequence between different areas of the site are due to differential post-depositional changes.

Six main stratigraphic units were recognised (Fig 7; Fig 29). These will be described below in ascending order. Incorporated within the description are the results of the sedimentological examination and the soil micromorphological, palynological and malacological studies to produce an integrated stratigraphic narrative and interpretation. Computer-generated interpolations of the palaeotopography of the various stratigraphic units were produced from hundreds of spot heights recorded during fieldwork, and these are included below (Fig 30; Fig 31). In the case of the wire-net surfaces, a vertical exaggeration of 25 was used to draw out subtle topographical changes in an essentially flat landscape.

2.2 The site sequence, including palaeoenvironmental evidence and palaeotopography

Basal gravels (SU20)

The basal deposits consisted of undisturbed, very sandy fine to medium gravels which were very well bedded and of fluvial origin. These deposits have been correlated with the Colney Street Gravels and ascribed to the Late Devensian (Gibbard 1985, 81–2). No pollen or molluscan remains survived within the matrix of this unit.

The morphology of the gravel body was complex, consisting of an irregular body forming a low bank swinging across the site from west to east to the north of trench D (Fig 30). Some imbricated structures were present, indicating very local flow directions. Larger-scale directional structures (such as cross-bedding) were not observed, and palaeocurrent direction could not be inferred.

Fig 30 shows that the low 'gravel bank' ran in an east–west direction from the valley side to a higher gravel plateau to the west. The gravel dipped relatively steeply away to the south-

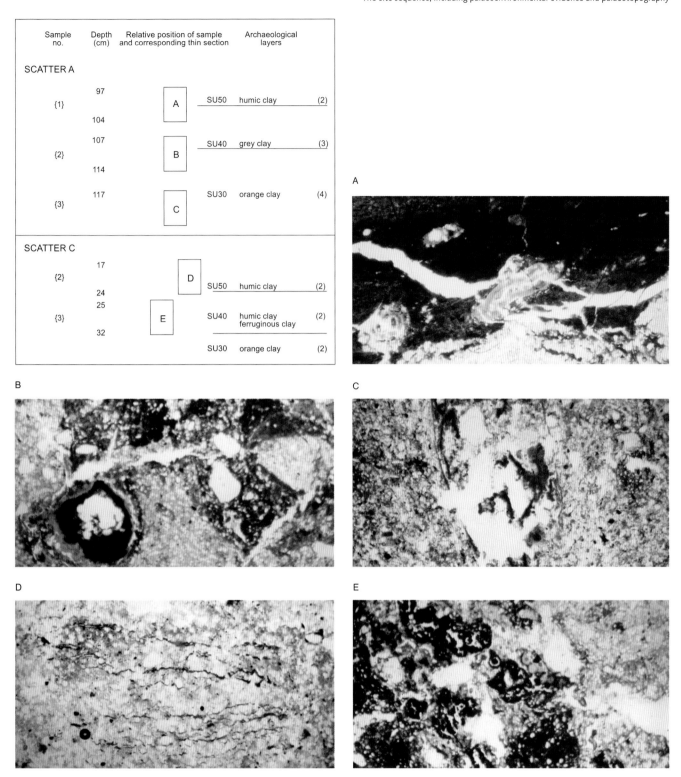

Sample no.	Depth (cm)	Relative position of sample and corresponding thin section	Archaeological layers		
SCATTER A					
{1}	97 104	A	SU50	humic clay	(2)
{2}	107 114	B	SU40	grey clay	(3)
{3}	117	C	SU30	orange clay	(4)
SCATTER C					
{2}	17 24	D	SU50	humic clay	(2)
{3}	25 32	E	SU40	humic clay ferruginous clay	(2)
			SU30	orange clay	(2)

A

B

C

D

E

Fig 29 Stratigraphic units and soil micromorphology samples with photomicrographs of thin sections A–E: A – banding in humic clay relating to variations in concentration of included fine charred organic matter; bright yellow infills probably relate to post-depositional contamination process which produces amorphous organic/phosphorus/iron features (plane polarised light (PPL), frame L 5.56mm); B – illustrates biological mixing of humic layer 2 material (? also mixed with calcitic soil from layer 1) into the more mineral layer 3; also vivianite-like material can be seen associated with the orange and very dark brown ferruginous module, indicative of cess input (PPL, frame L 5.56mm); C – root replaced pseudomorphically by calcium carbonate (a possible relict feature of late lastglacial decalcification) in layer 4, a homogenised and partially decalcified subsoil (PPL, frame L 5.56mm); D – uppermost part of layer 3: iron and clay depleted, structureless silty topsoil of the Early Mesolithic profile with very thin organic matter laminae, now replaced by iron; these laminae are interpreted as wetting-front phenomena caused by flooding of the site with highly organic clays, like 'fibre' formation in the structureless Ea horizons of podzols (PPL, frame L 3.35mm); E – near surface soil roots (black features), probably contemporary with the Mesolithic occupation, have been replaced pseudomorphically by iron and manganese as a result of gleying probably brought about by a rise in water table associated with the flooding of the site; ferruginised clay infills of the coarse biological porosity probably also relate to flood inundation amd alluvial sedimentation, but possibly could also have resulted from earlier surface soil disturbance (trampling) by Early Mesolithic people occupying the site (PPL, frame L 5.56mm)

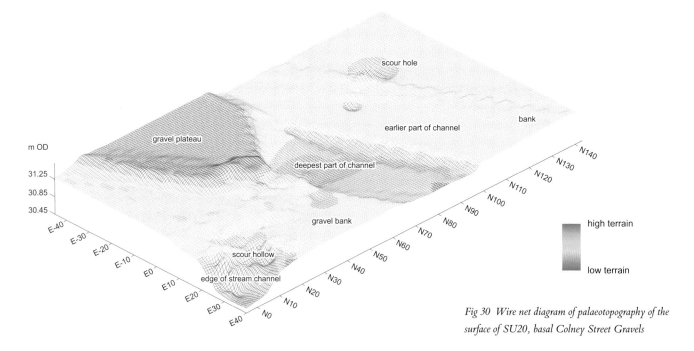

m OD

31.25
30.85
30.45

high terrain

low terrain

Fig 30 Wire net diagram of palaeotopography of the surface of SU20, basal Colney Street Gravels

west corner of the site, via a small 'scour hollow'. The marked drop-off in height of the basal gravels in the south-west corner of the site could be interpreted as the edge of a stream channel.

To the north of the 'gravel bank' the gravel dipped down to form a 'channel', the northern 'bank' of which is quite clear.

Beyond this palaeochannel 'bank' the gravel was locally much deeper, and overlain by a sequence of brown clays containing lenses of organic material. Fig 30 shows this to be very localised and it is interpreted as a 'scour hole' in the underlying gravel. However, this interpretation is based on a single exposure and the true extent of this feature remains uncertain.

It is noticeable that the general trend of all the features seen in Fig 30 is east–west. This is at odds with the axis of the river valley and present river system which is north–south (Fig 1). However, the area of the floodplain examined during the project was relatively small; a larger study area would allow a better understanding of the palaeotopography of the sedimentary units.

In general the morphology of the gravel unit SU20 was constructional and not erosive; that is, the gravel was laid down as a low feature and the later fine-grained sediments were draped conformably around and upon it, probably with no great hiatus in sedimentation.

Fine-grained argillaceous sediments (SU30 and SU40)

Overlying the basal gravels and often infiltrating into their originally openwork top was a sequence of upwardly fining mineral sediment, usually with a dominant mode in the clay and fine to medium silt grades. The thickness of this deposit varied with the height and topography of the underlying gravel. The sequence was subdivided into two stratigraphic units, SU30 and SU40. The evidence of the soil micromorphological study,

soil analytical data (Table 2) and the field sedimentary examinations suggested that SU40 and SU30 are facies of a single sedimentary unit. This unit contained the *in situ* lithic and faunal material; predominantly concentrated in the upper part of SU40, the frequency of this material diminished with depth (Chapter 5).

The lower of the two facies (SU30) was redder than the upper and clearly contained more iron compounds. Secondary carbonate concretions were also quite common. At some exposures (with no interpretable spatial patterning) SU30 seemed very slightly coarser than other clay/silt facies, there being a small coarse silt and even fine sand component. The upper facies (SU40) was a greyish silty clay with rare isolated fine gravel clasts. There was little relief in the vicinity to generate substantial wash deposits and a dominant wind-blown dust component is unlikely. Therefore, deposition of much of the fine sediment could be attributed to gentle overbank flooding, which implies that stream level kept pace with sedimentation throughout the period.

Towards the south-east corner of trench D, tongues of fine to medium sand interdigitated with the clay/silt facies SU30. These sandy subunits were thicker and coarser nearer the base of the sequence, where they also possibly encroached a little further north-westwards on to the flank of the low gravel rise. Such sediments represent the limit of more active water; that is, they marked the fluctuating edge of the contemporary stream *sensu stricto*. The geometry of the sand subunits suggested that the active stream was migrating south-eastwards with progradation of finer sediment in the sheltered zone thus abandoned.

By the time the site was occupied, the active stream margin already lay outside the site area. This can be seen in Fig 31 which shows the topography of the upper surface of SU40. The dip of sediments to the south-east, caused by deposition of sediment by the migrating stream, is clearly evident (1). It can

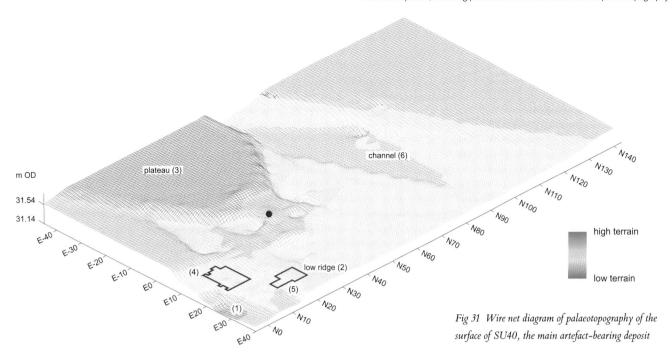

Fig 31 Wire net diagram of palaeotopography of the surface of SU40, the main artefact-bearing deposit

be seen that although the gravel body SU20 was now cloaked with fine-grained sediment (SU30 and SU40), it still determined the microtopography of the site. Thus the low east–west aligned ridge (2) was now more prominent, as was the plateau to the west (3). It is noticeable that both scatters A and C (4) were located on the side and not the top of the low ridge, presumably in order to be closer to the active stream. This more sheltered location (31.20–31.40m OD) probably played a part in the excellent preservation of the material in these scatters. In contrast, scatters B and D were located on higher ground (c 31.55m OD) around the margins of the ridge and plateau (5). As well as a much lower density of lithic material (eg ten pieces in scatter D), the artefacts were also more dispersed in these scatters. This may be partly explained by the more exposed topographic position, perhaps subjecting these scatters to more disturbance.

To the north of the ridge (2), SU30 and SU40 had filled in the channel (6). This was confirmed by the sequence observed in test pit 7 (UX89 TP4, Fig 3), which consisted of a series of clays and gravels which dipped away to the south, into the deepest part of the channel (Fig 30).

The basic sequence varied across the site; for example, the eastern half of scatter C exhibited signs of iron compound deposition within the upper grey clay (SU40), a phenomenon not observed in scatter A. Soil micromorphology was employed to study the differences between the two areas, as well as those between the different stratigraphic units. No pollen was preserved within SU30 or SU40, although mollusc shells did survive in low frequencies.

Scatter A

The upward fining sequence of alluvium over the gravels comprised some 300mm of moderately calcareous, coarsely mottled, yellowish-brown (Munsell 1992, 10YR5/6) clay loam

(Fig 29, samples {2} and {3}), containing chalk clasts and mollusc fragments (SU30), with some 160mm of finely mottled light yellowish-brown (ibid, 2.5Y6/4), mainly non-calcareous clay loam sediment above (SU40) (cf Table 2, sample {5}, scatter C).

At scatter A, SU30 (Fig 29, A) contained evidence of both calcium carbonate depletion (weathered chalk fragments, fine fabric depleted of calcium carbonate) and flushing by calcium carbonate-enriched water (micritic pseudomorphic impregnation of roots). These features, which are typical of Late Devensian sediments, could relate to the rapid decalcification of sediments under cool and high water flow conditions (Catt 1979). At scatter A the sediment seems to have been homogenised by biological activity and no microfabrics related to sedimentary structures or cryogenic processes remained. Thus, possibly during the Late Devensian, the site was probably damp, but vegetated and the soil biologically active. The upper part of the soil (SU40) (Fig 29, B) retained only poor microfabric evidence of later microstructure, which is quite comparable to the soil fabrics extant during activity at scatter C. In any case, biological activity (over an as yet unknown length of time) is assumed to have continued up to and until increased site wetness caused a valley 'swamp' to form (SU50, below) during the Early Mesolithic. Molluscan evidence (Fig 32) confirmed that SU40 (ES 131) contained a greater abundance of terrestrial shells than the overlying sediments represented by SU50 (ES 619) (77% and 9% respectively). Terrestrial molluscs dominated the assemblage in sample ES 131, in particular the terrestrial 'A' group (Fig 22) of wide ecological tolerance. Associated with this are high frequencies of species adapted to open ground grassland environments, for example the Vallonids and *Trichia hispida*. Small percentages of terrestrial 'B' group and *Discus rotundatus* (Fig 22) suggest that shaded conditions indicative of tree cover were present within the catchment area of the assemblage. However, the proximity of this ecological zone to the site was difficult to determine. The

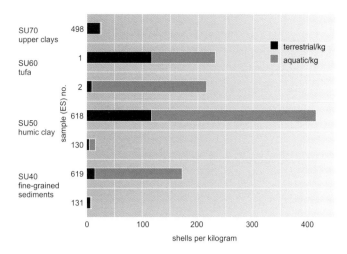

Fig 32 Numbers of terrestrial and aquatic mollusc shells per kilogram of sediment from selected samples (samples arranged by stratigraphic unit)

freshwater molluscs from ES 131 were dominated by ditch and moving water groups (Fig 22), as in general were other samples from SU30/40.

Scatter C

The basic sequence was similar to that in scatter A (Table 2). The increased frequency of iron compounds was noted within the area of scatter C, and particularly in its eastern half. Here SU40 was assigned to the upper 'grey clay', and the lower 'ferruginous clay' was labelled SU30. In SU40 in scatter C, evidence of pedological activity, in an otherwise iron and clay depleted microfabric, was differentially preserved. This preservation resulted from strong iron and manganese impregnation of features caused by later hydromorphism (Bouma et al 1990). The impregnation preserved a soil (Table 2; Fig 29, C; Fig 7) with a fine subangular and channel microstructure that was perforated by medium to coarse roots and well worked by earthworms. This biological activity was present throughout the depth of SU40 and suggests a lower water table at this typical alluvial gley soil (Avery 1980) during the Early Flandrian. This must have had an impact on the present distribution of bone and artefacts. For instance, the surfaces of the red deer bones in scatter C showed little evidence of root etching, while the contrary is true for the reindeer bones in this scatter. Even though close to the stream, this site can be considered to have been fully terrestrial at this time and may well have had a cover of vegetation that could root successfully in shallow ripened sediments (Bal 1982). The soil itself in SU40 contains rare fine charcoal that might be contamination from the overlying charcoal-rich SU50, but could alternatively have been of Early Mesolithic origin or earlier. In addition, some of the clay coatings and infill affecting the biological porosity may possibly relate to surface soil disturbance brought about by the trampling of humans and/or animals on the site (Courty et al 1989, 124–5, fig 17d). In contrast, pale dusty clay inwash into the soil is more likely to relate to increased wetness on the site, which may be linked to a

rise in water table subsequent to the human occupation. This would account for the strong iron and manganese impregnation of soil features caused by hydromorphism (above), and the presence of iron concretions on many of the lithic and faunal material in the 'ferruginous clay'. Thus the rise in water table must have post-dated the human occupation. It is unclear why a rising water table should have mobilised iron and manganese compounds predominantly in the eastern half of scatter C, although factors such as sediment grain size, porosity, underlying gravel structure and the unpredictability of water table movements may have contributed to this phenomenon. The formation of the 'ferruginous clay' in the eastern part of scatter C may have led to the boundary of SU30 and SU40 becoming indistinct in this part of the site.

The rise in water table led to gleying and caused mottling; relict roots were pseudomorphically replaced with iron and manganese. Similar features relating to a rising water table can be cited from Swanscombe, Kent (Kemp 1985). Soil fabrics in general across the Three Ways Wharf site became depleted of iron and lost their structure (Table 2; Fig 29, D). The uppermost 6cm were most strongly affected by hydromorphic iron and clay depletion, and loss of structure on slaking (Bouma et al 1990). The deflocculated or dispersed soil caused clay and fine silt to be washed down the profile, and this material probably forms the pale dusty coatings that affect the relict biological structure lower down. Similar effects (slaking, loss of structure, formation of pseudo-layering) on soils caused by increased wetness have been recorded in Neolithic palaeosols in Essex (the River Blackwater estuary: Macphail 1994) and also from soils which had been occupied in the Lower Palaeolithic at Boxgrove, West Sussex (Goldberg and Macphail 1990). Because of these post-depositional transformations, SU40 (the Mesolithic soil) is now leached and grey in the upper part of the horizon and ferruginous in the lower part. In addition, the uppermost 1–2cm of SU40 contained iron-replaced laminae of organic matter (Fig 29, D) that are considered to relate not to *in situ* sedimentary features but to wetting-front phenomena, that is, when organic-rich swamp water infiltrated into the structureless topsoil. Again, similar features are recorded in Essex (Macphail 1994). All these effects (slaking and loss of structure, and formation of pseudo-layering) and rooting activity of plants can make it very difficult to identify junctions between buried soils and overlying alluvium.

In summary, SU30 and SU40 represented two facies of a Lateglacial/early Postglacial fluvially deposited clay loam which was damp but vegetated and biologically active. This substrate was occupied at a date contemporary with the lithics and horse and reindeer fauna in scatter A (*c* 10,000 BP), and possibly contemporary with the corresponding material in scatter C east.

By the early Postglacial, SU40 had developed into an earthworm-worked and well-structured alluvial gley soil. Terrestrial molluscan evidence suggests a local open ground environment, typified by damp open grassland. Within the catchment area for the molluscan assemblage, closed conditions – perhaps indicative of woodland cover – were present, although the proximity of this ecological zone is difficult to determine.

A further phase of occupation (scatter C west, *c* 9200 BP) took place on this land surface. Bioturbation led to the greater vertical displacement of the lithic and faunal material in scatter A relative to scatter C (Chapter 5). Biological activity was curtailed relatively soon after the occupation at 9200 BP (scatter C) due to increasing site wetness caused by a rise in water table. This formed a prelude to the deposition of the black humic clay, SU50.

Black humic clay (SU50)

Martin Bates and Patricia E J Wiltshire

A sub-sequence of weakly banded, moderately organic (1.6% organic carbon) clays (SU50) (Table 2, sample {4}) overlay SU40 throughout the site. The boundary between SU50 and SU40 was often sharp but not obviously erosive. Although some rootlet penetration down from the base of SU50 could be seen macroscopically, this did not appear to be a true rootlet bed. The organic matter was finely divided and lacking in fibrous structure, the mineral content was still high (clay 47%), and there was no apparent post-depositional destruction of organics. The deposition of the black clay (SU50) filled in the lower-lying areas, completely cloaking the lithic scatters. Both pollen and molluscs were preserved in SU50, though at very low concentrations.

Plots of the percentage of terrestrial and freshwater shells (Fig 32) show that the occupation horizon (SU40) in grid square E25N17 (ES 131) was much drier, with a greater abundance of terrestrial shells, than it was in E33N10 (ES 619) (77% and 9% respectively). Within the overlying black humic horizon (SU50) the percentage of freshwater mollusc species in the two squares was similar (ES 130, 32% and ES 618, 28%). Information from column samples through square E25N17 (ES 130–6) shows a relative increase in the frequencies of freshwater shells in the black humic horizon (SU50) (Fig 33, ES 130; Table 4), which is perhaps indicative of more widespread flooding. However,

there was an absence of true fast-flowing species such as *Theodoxus fluviatilis*, although moving water types present include *Bithynia tentaculata*, *Pisidium nitidum*, *P milium* and *Armiger crista*. Other species such as *Lymnaea truncatula* and *Anisus leucostoma* suggest more localised areas of marshy ground or muddy pools possibly prone to periodic drying out. It is likely that the assemblage is derived from a number of sources that may result from local vegetation factors and patterns of flooding and fluvial sedimentation. The abundance of *Valvata cristata* in E33N10 (ES 618–19) may be related to the occurrence in this area of reedy vegetation. The presence of a contemporary stream towards the southern corner of the site may have produced the flooding. The black humic horizon (SU50) contained a more homogeneous assemblage similar in character to the assemblages below (from SU40) and perhaps indicative of more widespread flooding. The molluscan evidence suggests that wetter conditions continued during the deposition of the overlying tufa (SU60, samples {1} and {2}; Fig 22; Fig 32).

At scatter A, SU50 contained laminated microscopic charred material (Fig 29, E; Table 2, sample {1}). In the area of scatter C, SU50 (Fig 29, D; Table 2, sample {4}) was essentially a weakly banded, moderately organic clay, with 47% clay and 1.6% organic carbon. It contained much microscopic charcoal as well as charred monocotyledonous epidermis and amorphous organic debris. Indeed, at both scatters A and C, SU50 contained so much fine charred organic matter that some laminae were almost opaque. In the palynology section, the prepared samples showed that although charcoal was exceedingly abundant throughout the layer, it appeared to be concentrated in three particularly dense bands at 10–20mm, 40–60mm and 80–90mm (Fig 23). However, the sampling method obscured its true distribution, with the charcoal laminae (revealed by the soil micromorphology) inevitably being bulked together in each pollen sample. The size of fragments found in all contexts ranged from <100µm^2 to >5000µm^2, so that both microcharcoal and macrocharcoal (*sensu* MacDonald et al 1991, 57–9) were present. Along with the finds of charred epidermis, the relatively large size of the fragments provides additional support for the contention that at least some of the burning occurred *in situ*. However, it must be said that the great majority of fragments fell into the microcharcoal size classes, and this may be due to the fact that pollen preparation methods would inevitably break up fragile particles.

In spite of the obvious influence of differential preservation, the pollen of supposedly vulnerable taxa, such as *Ulmus* (elm) and *Quercus* (oak), were present in most samples of SU50. Furthermore, these increased in frequency in the upper part of the sequence together with undifferentiated monolete fern spores, *Polypodium* (polypody fern) and *Pinus* (pine), which are generally considered to be resistant to decomposition and are often over-represented where preservation is poor. There is little doubt that differential preservation has resulted in a reduced and biased pollen record at Three Ways Wharf. However, survival of more vulnerable pollen taxa suggests that there were microsites within the sediments which offered conditions conducive to preservation, and so real vegetation

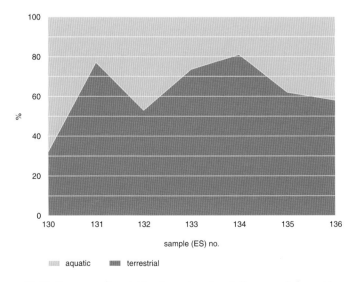

Fig 33 Percentage of terrestrial and aquatic mollusc shells per sample from grid square E25N17

changes are being reflected.

Pollen zone TWW(1) included the transition between the underlying clay (SU40) and the black humic layer (SU50) (Fig 23). Pine reached values of 30–40% of the sum in this zone, which indicates that the tree was abundant around the site. Modern pollen studies have shown that values of pine pollen can drop from 80% to 4% within 100m of the edge of a pine plantation (P Wiltshire, pers obs). It is, therefore, reasonable to assume that pine trees were growing close to the sample site, possibly on the sloping ground rising away to the north. Deciduous woody taxa such as oak, elm, *Betula* (birch) and *Corylus* (hazel) were also growing in the catchment, with ferns, possibly *Dryopteris carthusiana* (narrow buckler fern) or *Thelypteris palustris* (marsh fern), locally abundant. In view of its very poor pollen dispersal, the presence of *Salix* (willow) in the two lowermost samples suggests that willow bushes were growing very close by. The area around the sampling site seems to have been dominated by Cyperaceae (sedges) and Poaceae (grasses), and other herbaceous taxa (Table 5) attest to the openness of the immediate locality.

A band of very dense charcoal was found at 80–90mm, and this appears to coincide with a marked rise in sedges and a decline in other taxa (Fig 23). Woody taxa seem to have declined progressively throughout this zone in favour of sedges and *Pteridium* (bracken), and it might be reasonable to suggest that these changes were related to burning. The micromorphological evidence and the nature of the pollen spectra suggest a wet, relatively open environment at the sampling site.

The boundary between zones TWW(1) and TWW(2) was drawn at 60mm (Fig 23). This coincides with a very dense band of charcoal extending up to 40mm and also with large changes in the pollen/spore values. Pine and ferns (including polypody fern but excluding bracken) increased very markedly and there was a dramatic reduction in sedge pollen. Elm, hazel, grasses and other herbaceous taxa exhibited slight increases, while oak and bracken declined; but it is difficult to assess the degree of significance of these small changes in the spectra.

It is interesting that the character of the herbaceous flora seems to change in zone TWW(2). Grasses increased progressively and herbs associated with grass-dominated communities and/or disturbed soils were recorded, such as Fenestrate Asteraceae (dandelion-like plants), *Plantago lanceolata* (ribwort plantain), *Centaurea nigra*-type (eg knapweed) and *Rumex* (docks). The whole of zone TWW(2) is characterised by continued low levels of sedges and high levels of fern spores. While there was an erratic but sustained decline in pine above the charcoal band at 40–60mm, most other taxa showed increased values. Another dense charcoal band occurred at 10–20mm but was not accompanied by very marked changes in the pollen and spore record. *Alnus* (alder) was found only in the uppermost samples at 0–5mm.

The massive increase in pine pollen and fern spores, and dramatic drop in sedge pollen, at the boundary of zones TWW(1) and TWW(2) might be explained in several ways. Firstly, the sudden changes might be more apparent than real, and could be artefacts of crude sampling. The temporal resolution was very poor because of the need to take relatively large amounts of sediment to obtain enough palynomorphs for counting, and information has almost certainly been lost. Secondly, it is possible that there was a loss of information at the zone boundary because of a hiatus in sedimentation. This could occur if dry conditions had become established locally, and it might mean that the observed differences between the two zones reflect real vegetation change. If there had been a significant drop in water table, the reduction or loss of plants favouring wet soils such as sedges, willow and *Sphagnum* moss may be explained. These taxa were found only in zone TWW(1). Other pollen taxa such as Apiaceae, Caryophyllaceae, *Aster*-type and Rosaceae all include plant species which are characteristic of waterlogged soils, and it is conceivable that their absence from TWW(2) might also be related to changes in water table and the establishment of drier conditions. Certainly, sediment accumulation could have virtually ceased under dry conditions and, if dryness were significant, it would be reasonable to suppose that pine woodland, with an understory of ferns, was able to spread over the sampling site. It might be argued that such high levels of pine and ferns could have been a function of differential decomposition, but it is equally feasible that they represent an increase in these plants. Palynological assessment has recently been carried out on sediments of similar age at a site in the lower Colne valley at Staines, Surrey (Wiltshire 1996). A pollen diagram has been produced which shows increases in fern spores which are correlated with layers of parenchymatous tissue, conducting elements and bands of spores. These could possibly have been derived from ferns, although further work is necessary to confirm this suggestion.

Another possible reason for the marked changes between TWW(1) and TWW(2) is that prior burning and removal of woodland on the adjacent slopes could have resulted in soil instability; reworked soil, laden with older pine pollen and fern spores, might then have been washed into the site. However, it is difficult to sustain this argument when the high levels of pine and ferns continue throughout zone TWW(2), where more gradual vegetation changes are also being recorded. To be represented throughout the zone through the agency of inwash, the process would have to have been continuous throughout TWW(2).

The erratic but sustained decline of pine, and increase of ferns, grasses and other open habitat indicators in the upper part of zone TWW(1) suggest an opening-up of the regional pine woodland canopy (Fig 23). The increased frequency of trees such as oak and elm, and the appearance of alder at the top of TWW(2), also indicate that the Holocene succession and establishment of mixed deciduous woodland was being recorded in the pollen diagram. The very high concentrations of charcoal throughout the sequence suggest that fire might have played a role in local vegetation changes.

The palynological results from Three Ways Wharf record a changing environment around the site which could reflect fluctuations in water table as well as the impact of fire in the region. Whether the fires were natural or man-made, small and localised, or more regional in scale, is difficult to ascertain from such limited data. However, palynological results from Enfield Lock in the Lea valley, where sediments of greater depth were analysed (Chambers and Mighall 1991), have aided interpretation of the events at Three Ways Wharf. Detailed comparison of the two pollen diagrams has already appeared (Lewis et al 1992) and will only be mentioned here. At Enfield Lock, the sediments were 50cm deep as opposed to the 10cm (and elsewhere on the site, 4cm) of black humic silt at Three Ways Wharf, and the results from Uxbridge can be readily understood as a crude and telescoped version of those from Enfield Lock (ibid).

Because of the possibility of contamination (Chapter 1.4) radiocarbon dating of SU50 was not attempted, and the chronology of this black clay must rely on pollen evidence alone. At Three Ways Wharf, in spite of the consistently low values for birch and relatively low levels for hazel, the pollen spectra point to a Boreal landscape during the period represented by SU50. In zone TWW(1), the dominance of pine and low values of deciduous trees imply the early Boreal, possibly zone V/VIa (*sensu* Godwin 1940), while in zone TWW(2) the increasing values for oak, elm and hazel, and the later appearance of alder, suggest the later Boreal, zones VIb and VIc. The absence of *Tilia* (lime) might confirm that the sediments date from the Boreal since pre-6500 BP records for this thermophilous tree are rare (Godwin 1975; Scaife 1982). The appearance of alder in the uppermost level also points to the late Boreal (Devoy 1979, 139; Chambers and Mighall 1991, 14–15). The pollen assemblages from Cowley Mill Road and the nearby site of Sandstone, Iver (Lacaille 1963), further indicate that the black deposit from these sites is of Boreal age.

In summary, during the early to mid Boreal, humic clays and muds (SU50) accumulated under waterlogged conditions in an open, sedge-dominated habitat. Pine woodland dominated the region's drier soils, but birch, oak and hazel (see zone TWW(1)) were also present in the catchment. The accumulating organic sediments contained varying amounts of very abundant microscopic charred organic matter (derived from frequent and/or intense burning). The presence of charred epidermal cells in pollen preparations indicated that the surface vegetation had been burned as well as that further away. In the later Boreal (zone TWW(2)) there might have been a drier phase in the site's history when sedimentation was much diminished. Subsequently, pine woodland seems to have spread at the expense of open habitat plants, but it declined as the succession of temperate, deciduous woodland proceeded. The site has a record of repeated burning throughout the period represented by SU50, and the nature and origin of these fires is of considerable interest. Certainly, evidence is accumulating to show that fires were very frequent, widespread, or intense in the Mesolithic period (Wiltshire and Edwards 1993; P Wiltshire, pers obs) and it is possible that fire had some impact on the local woodland succession at Three Ways Wharf. If Mesolithic people were indeed responsible for these fires, it means that the area continued to be exploited long after the period of occupation represented by the flint scatters.

Reworked tufa (SU60)

Lenses of tufaceous material (SU60) occurred discontinuously across the site at the upper boundary of SU50. The internal structure of these calcareous pellets showed them to be true tufa and not merely weathered chalk fragments. Recent research on cool freshwater tufa deposits has shown that a wide variety of different forms of tufa may be found in the Holocene stratigraphic record (Pedley 1990) in southern and central Britain. These freshwater carbonate deposits often vary in type across space (ie they form facies relationships) and can be diagnostic of the environments of deposition. In southern England tufa deposition appears to have taken place between the Lateglacial and *c* 7500 BP (Goudie et al 1993).

However, most of the material in SU60 consisted of quite well rounded particles 'floating' in clay/silt; at best some lenses had particles with more irregular 'spiky' surfaces but no continuous framework. It was originally thought that, although the material originated from algal growth in waters charged with calcium carbonate, it was redeposited material and not *in situ* tufa.

The fragility of this material as well as the similar fragility of the associated molluscan debris suggested that the tufa had not moved far, possibly from the break of slope some tens of metres to the west. However, this interpretation has since been revised. Tufa pellets, strictly known as cyanolith 'oncoidal' tufa (Ordóñez and Garcia del Cura 1983), are rounded to oblate pellets consisting of an internal nucleus (sometimes a shell or sediment particle) around which successive layers of carbonate have been concreted. Oncoliths vary from pea-sized to golf-ball-sized and from rounded to highly oblate, with well rounded varieties forming in fast-flowing water. Oncoidal tufa is commonly found in braided fluviatile (often shallow) river systems where beds (graded and cross-bedded in places) of oncoids may occur with finer micritic tufa and stromatolithic tufa growths. Normal sedimentary dynamics relating particle size to water velocities and other factors do not apply when tufa oncoid size/shape and water velocities are considered. Thus the tufa in SU60 may have formed *in situ*. However, the soil containing the tufa had been so strongly reworked, both biologically and by down-wash from a possible trample horizon in the clays above (SU70), that its origin remains enigmatic. Nonetheless, there is no reason to suggest that the tufa particles (or the mollusca) were not broadly contemporary with their stratigraphic position.

The molluscan evidence (Fig 32) points to subtle changes in microtopography. For example, comparison between the percentages of mollusc types in the samples from SU60 showed that ES 1 was relatively drier (at *c* 31.45m OD), with a greater number of terrestrial shells (51%) than ES 2 (4% at *c* 31.35m OD). Sample ES 618 at 31.32m OD was also dominated by aquatic shells (*c* 70%).

Upper clays (SU70)

The upper sequence of clays was not subjected to detailed palaeoenvironmental study. However, terrestrial molluscs dominate the assemblages in sample ES 498 (Fig 22), particularly those of terrestrial 'A' group of wide ecological tolerance. Associated with this are high frequencies of species adapted to open ground grassland environments, such as the Vallonids and *Trichia hispida*. The presence of *Vallonia excentrica*, a shade-intolerant species, confirms an open ground aspect to the fauna. Small percentages of terrestrial 'B' and *Discus rotundatus* are also present, suggesting that shaded conditions did exist within the catchment area of the assemblage. Thus SU70 (of probably later prehistoric date) shows a clear trend away from fluvially dominated assemblages towards a predominantly terrestrial assemblage. This is characterised by a near total absence of shade-loving species, with the exception of *D rotundatus*. It appears that by this time the fluvial input had disappeared and grassland conditions prevailed.

2.3   Summary and conclusions

The sequence at Three Ways Wharf represents a naturally occurring fluviatile sequence whose initial deposition commenced in the Lateglacial. Between at least 10,270 BP and 8080 BP (10,480–8030 cal BP) a soil developed on top of the stable land surface represented by SU40. This landscape saw several phases of human activity associated with subsistence strategies based initially on reindeer and, latterly, on red and roe deer exploitation. Detailed soil micromorphological trends at

Three Ways Wharf can be paralleled at other floodplain sites of this period, such as Gatehampton Farm, Oxfordshire, in the Thames valley (Collcutt and Macphail 1995, 12) and Church Lammas, Staines, Surrey, near the mouth of the Colne (Macphail in prep). Both sites show evidence of Lateglacial/ Early Holocene pedogenesis. In particular, at Church Lammas a lithic assemblage and reindeer fauna comparable to those at Three Ways Wharf scatters A and C east were situated in a deposit which showed evidence of being a vegetated and biologically active soil. The Church Lammas soil also appears to have become increasingly wet and prone to flooding.

Following the latest human occupation the site shows signs of increasing wetness and a rising water table, leading eventually to the formation of the sedge swamp represented by SU50 during the Boreal period. Organic deposits of similar date have been recorded elsewhere on the Colne and other tributaries of the Thames (for discussion see Lewis et al 1992). The landscape of this period consisted of regional pine woodland with frequent and/or intense burning in the area. In the late Boreal pine woodland declined as the succession of temperate deciduous woodland proceeded. Once again high levels of burning were present in the upper levels of SU50. The significance of the burning episodes has been discussed in detail elsewhere (ibid), but it could be interpreted as representing repeated human modification of the vegetation cover of the Colne valley.

The formation of tufa (SU60) over SU50 points to a return to clearer, calcium-rich water conditions, prior to the development of a dry terrestrial soil (SU70).

3

Lithic material

3.1 Introduction

This chapter seeks to identify and analyse each chronologically distinct assemblage. Scatter A is dealt with separately, since it was spatially and probably chronologically distinct from the bulk of material in scatter C. The small assemblages in scatters B and D are also described separately since they too were spatially distinct. The very small quantity of material from the numerous test pits is dealt with as one assemblage.

The spatial distribution of material in scatter C, together with other factors which are covered in previous or subsequent chapters, suggested that there was a chronological or functional difference in the nature of occupation within scatter C. Put simply, the occupation arranged around the western hearth (assemblage C west, composed of sub-assemblages (SAS) 1, 2, 6, 7 and 8) could be seen to correspond with the radiocarbon dates centring on 9200 BP. The activity around the eastern hearth (assemblage C east, composed of SAS 3, 4, 5 and 9) was more problematic, since it might represent a difference in functional activity between the two hearth areas, or an earlier phase of occupation altogether. The latter interpretation is based on faunal differences and subtle changes in lithic technology between C west and C east. Given the differences between C west and C east, a report which dealt with the lithics as a single assemblage would give a false picture of two potentially chronologically distinct assemblages. However, there are also problems associated with treating scatter C as two separate assemblages. Firstly, in theory each of the sub-assemblages could represent a single distinct phase of activity, perhaps representing repeated seasonal occupation. However, this is unlikely given the spatial arrangement and patterning around both hearths. Secondly, SAS 3, although incorporated within C east, is located between the two hearth areas and could be related to either. This sub-assemblage has, however, produced the clearest technological evidence of an early phase of occupation, and it is conceivable that the cold fauna present in scatter C was associated with SAS 3. Thus the eastern hearth and SAS 4 and 5 could be later and contemporary with the main occupation around the western hearth. Thirdly, refitting shows (below, 3.6) that the products of knapping are not confined within the spatial boundaries of respective sub-assemblages. For instance, while the majority of the components of refitting group 10 are located within SAS 3, a significant number (especially tools) are found in SAS 2, 4, 5, 6, 8 and 9. The anthropogenic and non-anthropogenic factors affecting horizontal dispersal of lithic material discussed in Chapters 5 and 6 have inevitably led to some mixing of the assemblages. Therefore a report which divided scatter C into two assemblages would suffer from not necessarily assigning all the material to the relevant phase of occupation. The problem inherent in treating scatter C as a single undifferentiated assemblage would be duplicated in this approach.

In order to address these problems the lithic report has treated scatter C as a single assemblage, but within each artefact class the differences in technology, typology and distribution between C west and C east are discussed on the assumption that most of the material within the sub-assemblages and hearth areas can be attributed to the phase of activity which produced these concentrations. Table 6 and Table 7 show the numbers and percentage composition of the assemblages in scatters A, B, C (subdivided into C west and C east) and D. Similar data for the sub-assemblages within each scatter can be found below, where there are also data summarising the typological, technological and functional differences between the assemblages in scatters A, C west and C east.

Methodology

Each piece of struck flint was examined and classified according to the type system developed by A David, English Heritage, for the analysis of the Lateglacial/Early Mesolithic assemblage from Seamer Carr in the Vale of Pickering, North Yorkshire. This system was adapted by the author for use at Three Ways Wharf. The format of the report is based on that produced by Barton and Bergman for the Hengistbury Head, Dorset, assemblages (Barton 1992), and the terms and definitions employed in that report have been used here.

Artefacts were classified by their type (eg burin on truncation, dihedral burin) with each type forming part of a group of similar types (eg burins).

The maximum length, breadth and thickness (excluding the bulb) of each complete piece of debitage and each retouched tool was measured. In addition, selected pieces and types such as cores and partially worked nodules were weighed.

Qualitative attributes recorded included the type of raw material, colour, inclusions, degree of patination, percentage coverage of cortex, completeness and butt type. An attempt was also made to determine the hammer mode using the characteristics described by Ohnuma and Bergman (1982). These characteristics allowed the differentiation of soft- and hard-hammer percussors, but not that of soft-stone percussors. Work on determining soft-stone percussion techniques (Fagnart and Plisson 1997; Pelegrin 2000) was only published after this text was produced in 1995, and the Three Ways Wharf assemblages have not been re-analysed in the light of that work.

The analysis was limited to lithic artefacts which were securely stratified within and beneath the black organic clay (SU50). Artefacts from above this layer, and which were recovered from the numerous later intrusive features, were excluded from the analysis.

Lithic material retrieved by sieving

Retouched pieces were extracted from each sorted sample and given a unique catalogue number. Arbitrary X, Y and Z coordinates were also assigned based on the square, quad and spit of the sorted sample. Particularly large (c >30mm) items of debitage were also treated in this way. However, due to time constraints, the quantity of debitage >10mm–<30mm was

Table 6 Composition of lithic assemblages in scatters A–D and test pits

Artefact groups	A	B	C west	C east	Total C	D	Test pits	Grand total
				Scatters				
I Microliths	9	0	48	31	79	0	0	88
2 Scrapers & truncated blades	1	0	96	35	131	0	0	132
3 Notched pieces	0	0	10	7	17	0	0	17
4 Burins	0	0	6	15	21	0	0	21
5 Axes	0	0	4	0	4	0	0	4
6 Multi tools & awls	0	0	2	5	7	0	0	7
7 Retouched pieces	9	1	73	48	121	0	0	131
Total tools	19	1	239	141	380	0	0	400
8 Utilised pieces	4	0	21	18	39	0	0	43
Lames mâchurées	1	0	0	8	8	0	0	9
Total utilised pieces	5	0	21	26	47	0	0	52
13 Microburins	0	0	18	2	20	0	0	20
14 Burin spalls	0	0	13	13	26	0	0	26
17 Axe debitage	1	0	89	17	106	0	0	107
Total tool debitage	1	0	122	32	154	0	0	155
9 Flakes & fragments	352	3	2126	1434	3560	1	2	3918
10 Blades & fragments	244	14	1935	1164	3099	4	1	3362
11 Core preparation pieces	42	3	201	161	362	2	0	409
12 Cores & fragments	12	1	62	42	104	2	0	119
15 Unworked >100g & partially worked nodules	6	0	21	38	59	1	0	66
Total 3D-recorded debitage	656	21	4345	2839	7184	10	3	7874
Total 3D-recorded flints	681	22	4605	3006	7611	10	3	8327
Sieved debitage	251	0	4820	2828	7648	0	0	7899
Total debitage (sieved & 3D-recorded)	907	21	9165	5667	14832	10	3	15773
Total flints	932	22	9544	5866	15410	10	3	16377
Hammer stones	0	0	2	7	9	0	0	9
Grand total (incl hammer stones)	932	22	9546	5873	15419	10	3	16386

Table 7 Percentage composition of lithic assemblages in scatters A–D and test pits

| | Scatters % | | | | | | | |
Artefact groups	A	B	C west	C east	Total C	D	Test pits (%)	Grand total (%)
I Microliths I	-	I	I	I	-	-	I	
2 Scrapers & truncated blades	<I	-	I	I	I	-	-	I
3 Notched pieces	-	-	<I	<I	<I	-	-	<I
4 Burins	-	-	<I	<I	<I	-	-	<I
5 Axes	-	-	<I	-	<I	-	-	<I
6 Multi tools & awls	-	-	<I	<I	<I	-	-	<I
7 Retouched pieces	I	5	I	I	I	-	-	I
Total tools	2	5	3	2	2	-	-	2
8 Utilised pieces	<I	-	<I	<I	<I	-	-	<I
Lames mâchurées	<I	-	-	<I	<I	-	-	<I
Total utilised pieces	I	-	<I	<I	<I	-	-	<I
I3 Microburins	-	-	<I	<I	<I	-	-	<I
I4 Burin spalls	-	-	<I	<I	<I	-	-	<I
I7 Axe debitage	<I	-	I	<I	I	-	-	I
Total tool debitage	<I	-	I	I	I	-	-	I
9 Flakes & fragments	38	I4	22	24	23	I0	67	24
I0 Blades & fragments	26	64	20	20	20	40	33	21
II Core preparation pieces	5	I4	2	3	2	20	-	2
I2 Cores & fragments	I	5	I	I	I	20	-	I
I5 Unworked >I00g & partially worked nodules	I	-	<I	I	<I	I0	-	<I
Total 3D-recorded debitage	70	95	46	48	47	100	100	48
Total 3D-recorded flints	73	100	48	51	49	100	100	51
Sieved debitage	27	-	50	48	50	-	-	48
Total debitage (sieved & 3D-recorded)	97	95	96	96	96	100	100	96
Total flints	100	100	100	100	100	100	100	100
Hammer stones	-	-	<I	<I	<I	-	-	<I
Grand total (incl hammer stones)	100	100	100	100	100	100	100	100

recorded from each sample but not analysed further. Unretouched microdebitage and spalls <10mm in size are not included in the main lithic analysis, but are dealt with in Chapter 6.4. All data are stored in dBASE IV files and form part of the site archive (Chapter 1.5).

3.2 Raw material

Almost all the artefacts from scatters A, B, C and D were of flint, with the exception of quartzite hammer stones and a possible anvil stone.

The raw material consisted almost entirely of water-worn, well rounded and weathered flint and chert cobbles. The numerous inclusions (below), together with a tendency for hinge and columnar breakage, make the quality of the raw material relatively poor, certainly when compared with flint freshly derived from a chalk outcrop. These features point to the raw material being river-transported flint nodules, derived from the Colney Street Gravels which would have been exposed along the banks of the River Colne. Identical flint nodules can still be collected from this gravel deposit today. The majority of the raw material may have been collected from locations in very close proximity to the site. The assemblage also contains pieces of struck flint which are grey-black in colour and have a chalky white cortex. These are almost certainly derived from chalk outcrops, the nearest of which occurs at Harefield, *c* 7km to the north. The presence of this material within the Colney Street Gravels is to be expected; thus their immediate source is probably the same as the river gravel nodules which form the bulk of the raw material. Similarly, the small quantity of chert encountered on site could also be derived from the Colney Street Gravels, as chert has been shown to be a component of this lithostratigraphical member (Gibbard 1985, 82). The 'chalk-derived' flint and the chert were mainly located in scatter C west.

Colour

The colour of the flint was very variable, with numerous variations and combinations of shades of brown, yellow and grey. Some artefacts (eg a broken axe and refitting fragments in scatter C west) had a distinctive mottled yellow-brown colour. Other distinctive colours were yellow-orange (as represented by several axe thinning flakes and a rough-out in scatter C west) and a blue-grey colour, the latter partly caused by patination. Refitting has shown that colour can vary extensively within a nodule and should, therefore, be treated with caution. During analysis, the colour of the flintwork was assigned to one of nine colour categories, although due to the variations noted above, these were fairly arbitrary. Fig 34 shows the composition of the total assemblages by colour. In this case burnt flint has been omitted.

Lithic material

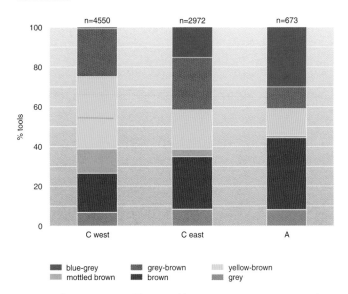

Fig 34 Colour composition of flint assemblages in scatters C west, C east and A

It is clear that there are major differences in the colour of the raw material utilised in the three areas. Subjectively the colour composition of scatter C east is closer to that of scatter A than C west. The spatial distributions of flintwork by colour show no particular patterning of grey, brown, grey-brown and yellow-brown flints, as they are represented over most of scatter C. Mottled brown and yellow flintwork is confined mainly to the western flint concentrations, with only minor amounts in the

eastern area. Grey-black flints are also mainly found in the west, and in particular in the concentration in SAS 2. In contrast to these, Fig 35 shows that the distinctive blue-grey flintwork is found mainly in the eastern area of scatter C and in scatter A. As stated above, the blue-grey colour is partly a product of raw material type and partly of patination, so this distribution may have resulted from localised groundwater and soil conditions as well as differences in raw material and chronology.

Patination

During analysis the degree of patination of each flint was recorded in 25% increments, and the results are shown in Fig 36.

The plot shows that scatters A and C east are almost identical, but totally different from C west. It has already been noted that patination played a part in producing the blue-grey colour prevalent in scatters C east and A, so the increased patination in these areas might partly explain the higher incidence of that colour there (Fig 35). Moreover, refitting has shown that entirely unpatinated pieces refit to patinated artefacts (eg burin spalls to burins). Therefore, the degree of patination is not solely a chronologically dependent phenomenon but is affected by variables such as groundwater conditions, soil mineral composition and flint type. Differences within SU40 between the areas of scatter C west and C east have been noted in Chapter 2.2, and these could have contributed to variations in patination between these areas. It is nonetheless suggested that

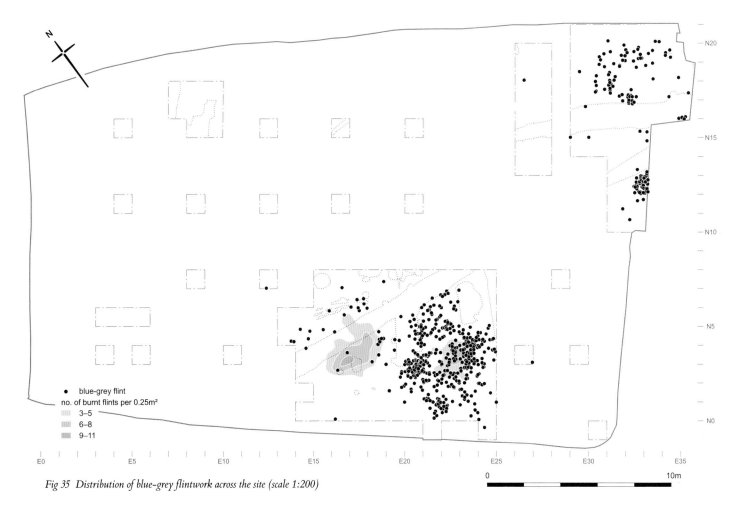

Fig 35 Distribution of blue-grey flintwork across the site (scale 1:200)

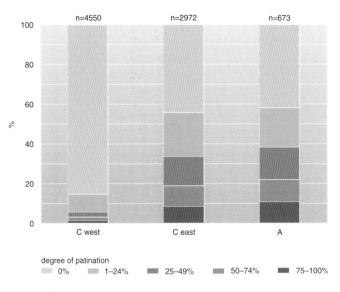

degree of patination
0%   1–24%   25–49%   50–74%   75–100%

Fig 36   Flint patination in scatters C west, C east and A

chronological differences, in particular length of exposure to the atmosphere following knapping, have also affected the degree of patination of the assemblages as a whole.

Inclusions

Chert and fossil inclusions were very numerous in scatters A and C, in fact so numerous that they were not recorded. Occasionally, 'cortex'-filled voids were present, as were rectangular voids. In one nodule (refitting group 10, scatter C east), a translucent quartz vein ran through the nodule. Crystalline quartz inclusions were present on several yellow flakes (particularly in scatter C west), as were purple manganese crystals.

Conclusions

The raw material which was used to produce scatters C west, C east and A consisted overwhelmingly of flint and occasional chert nodules derived from the Colney Street Gravels, probably from within close proximity to the site. Variations in the colour of the lithics suggest that the immediate source and/or the selection of raw material in scatter C west may have differed from scatters C east and A. Variations in the degree of patination between these three areas also suggest (while acknowledging the role of other factors) that there may be a chronological difference between scatter C west and scatters C east and A.

3.3   The lithic artefacts in scatters B and D and the test pits

The remainder of this chapter deals with the analysis of the lithic scatters. The smaller assemblages from the test pits and scatters B and D are briefly discussed below, before moving on to the more substantial scatters A and C.

Test pits

Very little material stratified from below SU50 was recovered from the numerous test pits excavated over the several phases of investigations at Three Ways Wharf (Table 6). Those which did produce material usually indicated the presence of the larger scatters or could be associated with them by proximity. Thus, in general, the scarcity of lithic material from test pits is indicative of the tight spatial distribution and concentration of lithics into discrete scatters.

Scatter B

Scatter B was located (like scatters A and C) on the southern slope of the low ridge projecting from the valley side (Fig 8). However, unlike A and C, scatter B was situated near the highest part of the ridge (Fig 31).

The area of scatter B had undergone extensive disturbance by two medieval ditches, the fills of which contained flintwork which was probably derived from scatter B. This material has not been included in the following discussion, leaving 22 securely stratified pieces forming scatter B. The only retouched tool present was a small retouched flake. The debitage consisted of three flakes, 14 blades, three core preparation pieces and an opposed platform core.

Due to the small size of the assemblage, no detailed analysis has been attempted. However, a few comments can be offered.

1) The raw material consisted of river gravel flint of predominantly grey-brown colour and was unpatinated.
2) Of the seven blade butts which could be recorded, six were plain and a further example was plain with platform edge abrasion.
3) Only one piece (a blade fragment) was burnt.
4) Scatter B was the product of *in situ* flint knapping as can be demonstrated by refitting group 55. This consists of the opposed platform core FFN 312 and blade FFN 539. The core was an opposed platform prismatic blade core. The posterior of the core had transverse flake scars probably produced during decortication, and there were traces of cresting along the edge of the anterior flaking face. Both platforms were plain and one had its edges abraded. The raw material is very similar to that used in core FFN 6470 in scatter C east. Thus, in terms of morphology and raw material, core FFN 312 is very similar to a number of cores in the east of scatter C. The core was probably abandoned due to size and the occurrence of hinge terminations halfway down the flaking face.

The lack of patination and absence of faceted blade butts suggests that scatter B could date to the Early Mesolithic, but there are not enough artefacts to establish this with any certainty.

Scatter D

In contrast to scatters A–C, scatter D was located on the northern side of the ridge projecting from the valley side (Fig 8; Fig 31). Scatter D consisted of ten pieces over an area of *c* 40m², and was thus of low density and very diffuse. It comprised one flake, four blades or blade fragments (two fragments conjoined following recent breakage), one core tablet, one uni-directionally crested blade, two refitting cores and a very large partially worked nodule.

As with scatter B, the low numbers of artefacts in scatter D preclude detailed analysis, but the following points are pertinent.

1) The raw material was river gravel flint of predominantly blue-grey colour and most pieces were patinated.

2) Of the four identifiable butts in the assemblage, three were plain and one was faceted.

3) Only one piece was burnt.

4) Scatter D was, like the other scatters at Three Ways Wharf, the product of *in situ* knapping. This is illustrated by refitting group 43 and the large partially worked nodule FFN 21009. The latter was a large (172mm long) river rolled nodule weighing 1310g. It had clearly been modified with a view to decortication and/or the production of a frontal crest, both of which represent the initial stages of core preparation. The piece was probably abandoned as unsuitable due to the numerous hinge terminations produced during flaking. Refitting group 43 (Fig 37) was originally a large opposed platform prismatic fully opposed platform blade core, with one plain and one faceted platform (Fig 37, b). The flaking faces produced by the two platforms were rotated through 90° from one another. Following a number of removals from both platforms, the core was rejuvenated by breaking the piece in half. FFN 21008, the fragment with the faceted platform, was abandoned and saw no further reduction, and the shape of the flaking face of this fragment was probably the cause of the rejuvenation event. The other fragment, FFN 21004, underwent further extensive reduction and became an opposed platform prismatic blade core in its own right. Both

platforms of 21004 were plain.

5) In terms of raw material, colour, patination, faceting of butts and platforms, and core morphology there are great similarities between the cores in refitting group 43 and elements of scatters A and C east.

6) Although refitting group 43 demonstrates the process of *in situ* knapping, the associated debitage is very sparse and, where present, diffuse. This could be accounted for by the topographical position of scatter D, on a relatively elevated and exposed portion of the ridge extending from the valley side. This may have meant less protection from post-depositional non-anthropogenic taphonomic processes, which led to only a few of the larger pieces remaining *in situ*.

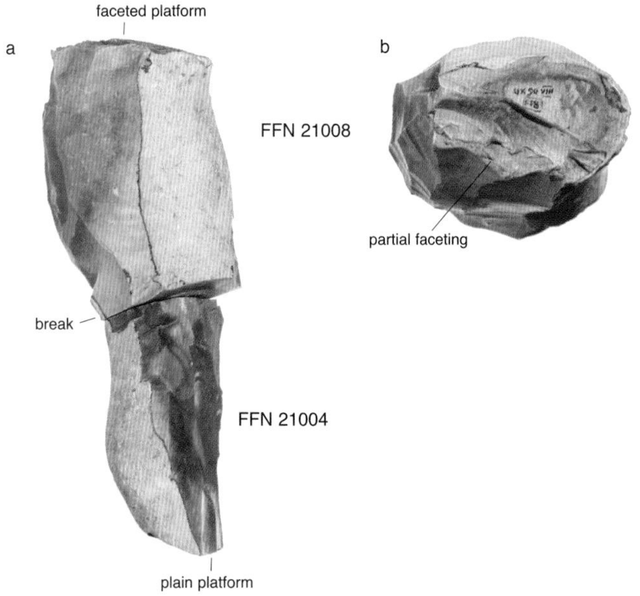

The patination and the presence of faceting on a blade and core platforms suggest that scatter D could date to the Lateglacial, but there are not enough artefacts to establish this with any certainty.

3.4 The lithic artefacts in Lateglacial scatter A

Scatter A consisted of 681 securely stratified, individually catalogued artefacts together with a further 251 items of debitage >10mm recovered from sieving (Table 6). The density distribution (Fig 9) suggests that the scatter continued eastwards under the road which formed the site boundary. The retouched tool assemblage forms a very low proportion of the total assemblage (Table 7). The range of retouched tools is very restricted, and there is no tool debitage such as microburins or burin spalls. Only 11 pieces of flint were burnt, all being blade or flake fragments except for two small struck pebble fragments.

Debitage

Debitage composed by far the largest proportion of the total assemblage. Some 660 pieces were individually catalogued, while a further 255 pieces were recovered from sieving (Table 6; Table 7) but not individually catalogued.

Flakes

Flakes comprised 37.8% of the total assemblage, of which 188 (53.4%) were complete and 164 (46.6%) were broken (Table 8; Fig 38). The flakes have been classified by the amount of cortex covering their dorsal surface.

QUANTITATIVE ATTRIBUTES

In general the flakes were broad, wide and thick (Table 9), with some (eg refitting group 22) obviously the product of decortication of nodules prior to blade production. The division between flakes and blades is somewhat arbitrary, as combining the scatter plots of length to breadth ratios for both classes of artefact would show a gradual gradation from one to

Fig 37 Scatter D refitting group 43: a – large opposed platform core, broken in two (FFN 21008 and 21004); b – partially faceted platform of core FFN 21008, the abandoned portion of refitting group 43 (scale 1:2)

Table 8 Condition and composition of flake assemblage (n=352) in scatter A

	No. (burnt)	% (burnt)
Complete flakes		
Primary flakes (75–100% cortex)	21 (0)	6.0 (0.0)
Secondary flakes (1–74% cortex)	72 (0)	20.5 (0.0)
Tertiary flakes (0% cortex)	94 (1)	26.7 (0.3)
Unclassified debitage	1 (0)	0.3 (0.0)
Total complete	188 (1)	53.4 (0.3)
Broken flakes		
Proximal fragments	55 (2)	15.6 (0.6)
Mesial fragments	30 (3)	8.5 (0.8)
Distal fragments	76 (2)	21.6 (0.6)
Unclassified fragments	3 (0)	0.9 (0.0)
Total broken	164 (7)	46.6 (2.0)
Total complete & broken	352 (8)	100.0 (2.3)

Table 9 Quantitative data for complete flakes (n=185) in scatter A

	Range	Average	Standard deviation
Length (mm)	84–9	29.4	16.9
Width (mm)	69–7	24.6	12.5
Thickness (mm)	24–1	5.5	4.5

the other. The mean thickness of flakes of 5.5mm ± 4.5mm compares well with that of blades at 5.1mm ± 4mm.

QUALITATIVE ATTRIBUTES

Fig 39 shows that the predominant butt type is plain, with preparation in the form of platform edge abrasion increasing as core reduction proceeds. A similar pattern is clear with hammer type. Fig 40 shows that soft-hammer technique is predominant among the complete flakes and increases as core reduction proceeds.

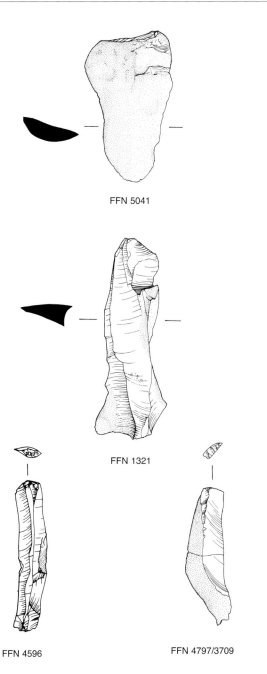

FFN 5041

FFN 1321

FFN 4596

FFN 4797/3709

Fig 38 Flake (FFN 5041) and blades (FFN 1321, 4596 and 4797/3709) from scatter A (scale 1:2)

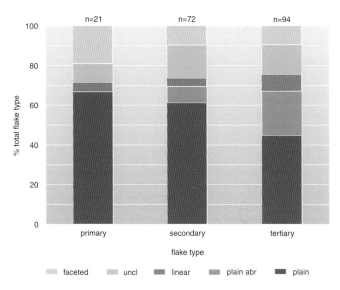

Fig 39 Butt morphology of flakes in scatter A

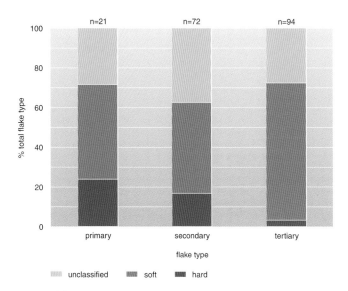

Fig 40 Flake hammer mode in scatter A

47

The interlinked patterns of increasing butt preparation and soft hammer usage are exactly what would be expected as finer flakes were produced as core reduction proceeded. This pattern is continued in the production of blades, where soft-hammer technique and prepared butts dominate (Table 12).

DISTRIBUTION

Together with blades, flakes form the main constituent of the lithic concentrations in scatter A. There was no apparent spatial patterning of flake types and they are not differentiated in Fig 41.

Blades

The 244 blades comprise 26.2% of the total assemblage (Table 6; Table 7). Table 10 shows a high breakage rate (75%) for this class of artefact. This high breakage rate can be explained by:

1) relatively poor raw material, leading to increased breakage during manufacture;
2) the longer, laminar form of blades, making them more susceptible to breakage by post-depositional processes.

QUANTITATIVE ATTRIBUTES

The lengths of most of the blades cluster in the range 25–65mm, and Table 11 demonstrates that there is no real distinction between blades and bladelets.

Table 10 Condition of blade assemblage (n=244) in scatter A

	No.	%
Complete	62	25.4
Proximal fragments	80	32.8
Mesial fragments	34	13.9
Distal fragments	68	27.9
Unclassified	0	0.0
Total broken	182	74.6
Total complete & broken	244	

Table 11 Quantitative data for complete blades in scatter A

	Range	Average	Standard deviation
Length (mm)	109–12	45.7	20.7
Width (mm)	41–3	15.7	7.7
Thickness (mm)	23–1	5.1	4.0

QUALITATIVE ATTRIBUTES

Thirty-six of the complete blades have no cortex on their dorsal surface, which is to be expected as generally blade production followed initial core preparation, which often involved decortication of the original nodule.

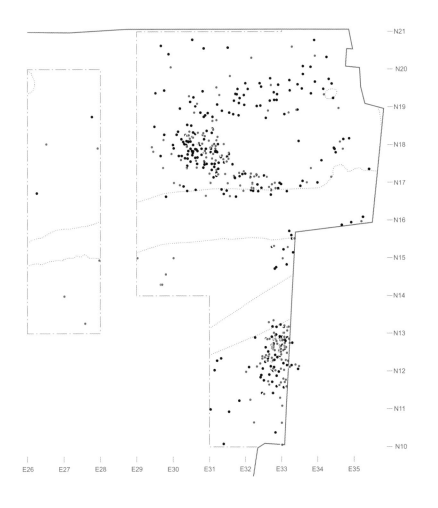

Fig 41 Distribution of flakes and blades in scatter A (scale 1:100)

Butt types are mainly plain, plain butts with platform abrasion (eg Fig 38, FFN 4596) forming the largest group. Faceted butts constituted a significant component of the assemblage (eg Fig 38, FFN 4797/3709). Platform preparation in the form of abrasion and faceting formed an important part of the blade production process (Fig 42).

Soft hammer types were the preferred flaking tools used for blade production, with 79% of the measured assemblage being manufactured in this way (Table 12).

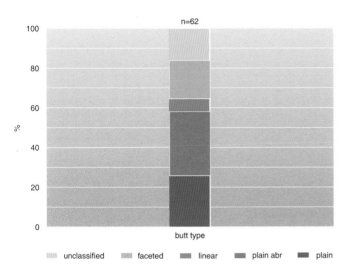

Fig 42 Butt morphology of complete blades in scatter A

Table 12 Blade hammer mode in scatter A

Hammer mode	No.	%
Hard	1	1.6
Soft	49	79.0
Unclassified	12	19.4
Total	62	

DISTRIBUTION

Together with flakes, blades form the major part of the main lithic concentrations in scatter A (Fig 41).

Core preparation pieces

The 42 core preparation pieces comprise 4.5% of the total assemblage (Table 6; Table 7).

CRESTED PIECES

Seventeen crested pieces were present in the assemblage, of which seven were complete (Table 13). None of these pieces were burnt. In addition, the one *lame mâchurée* (bruised blade) present in the assemblage was also a crested piece (Fig 43; and see below).

All of the seven complete crested pieces are of blade proportions, which is unsurprising since cresting is usually

Table 13 Quantitative data for crested pieces in scatter A

	Range	Average	Standard deviation
Length (mm)	107–51	79	20
Width (mm)	40–25	25	6
Thickness (mm)	13–8	12	2

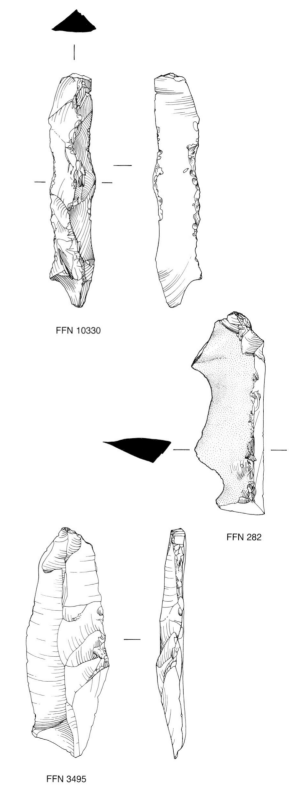

FFN 10330

FFN 282

FFN 3495

Fig 43 Core preparation pieces: bi-crested blade and lame mâchurée *FFN 10330; uni-crested blades FFN 282 and 3495 (scale 1:2)*

employed to prepare cores for the production of blades or to rejuvenate the flaking face of a blade core. Five of the seven complete pieces were bi-directionally crested (Fig 43), while seven of the ten broken pieces were uni-directionally crested (Fig 43). The cresting on the *lame mâchurée* was also bi-directional.

CORE TABLETS AND REJUVENATION FLAKES

A total of nine core tablets (*sensu* Barton 1992, 264) were recorded, of which eight were complete and none were burnt. In addition, 15 other miscellaneous core preparation flakes were recorded, of which nine were unbroken and none were burnt. The large blade FFN 3495 is an example of the miscellaneous category (Fig 43). This piece retains traces of faceting and platform abrasion at its proximal end and extending around the lateral edge, and it is possible that FFN 3495 was intended to rejuvenate the flaking face of the core. Other examples

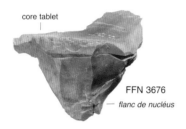

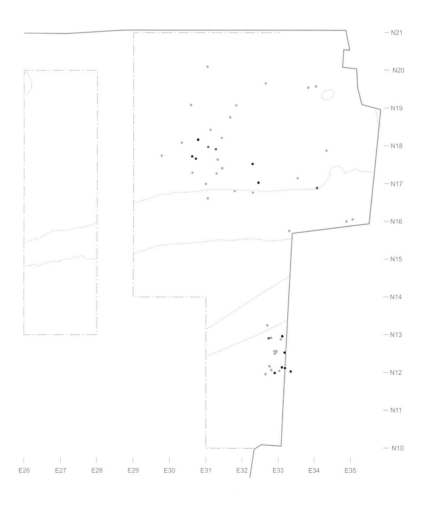

Fig 44 Refitting group 17: flanc de nucléus *and core tablet (scale 1:2)*

consisted of flakes which had not removed the entire striking platform of the core, and it is probable that many of these were the by-product of platform faceting. A single *flanc de nucléus* (FFN 3676, part of refitting group 17; Fig 44) (ibid, 267) was also present in the assemblage.

DISTRIBUTION

Fig 45 shows the distribution of cores and core preparation pieces in scatter A.

Cores

Scatter A contained seven complete cores and five core fragments. Of the complete cores, five were blade or bladelet cores, while two were flake cores.

MORPHOLOGY

All the blade cores were opposed platform types, and predominantly prismatic in shape (Table 14). Almost all were fully bi-polar (ie with more than two removals from the flaking face of each platform). One of the flake cores (FFN 104) may originally have been a blade core but reduction led to flakes being the final product of this piece.

QUALITATIVE ATTRIBUTES

All the blade cores display evidence of pre-forming and platform preparation prior to and during blade production.

Fig 45 Distribution of cores and core preparation pieces, and partially worked nodules, in scatter A (scale 1:100)

Table 14 Complete blade and flake morphology in scatter A

Type	Prismatic	Pyramidal	Globular	Irregular	Total
Blade cores					
I-platform	0	0	0	0	0
2-platform (opposed)	3	0	I	I	5
Total	3	0	I	I	5
Flake cores					
I-platform	0	0	0	I	I
2-platform (offset)	0	0	I	0	I
Total	0	0	I	I	2

The backs of four of the five blade cores were flaked, probably during the initial decortication of the nodule. Striking platforms were prepared and rejuvenated by faceting and core tablet removal, which corresponds to the butt data for flakes and blades. Faceting occurred on two cores (Fig 46, FNN 5048; Fig 47, FNN 10174) and one core fragment. In each case the faceting was slight and confined to the front of the platform, a technique described as partial faceting (Barton 1992, 106). The scars produced by faceting terminated in hinge fractures. Prior to partial faceting, the platform of FFN 10174 (refitting group 21) was subjected to two large overlapping flake removals (Fig 47).

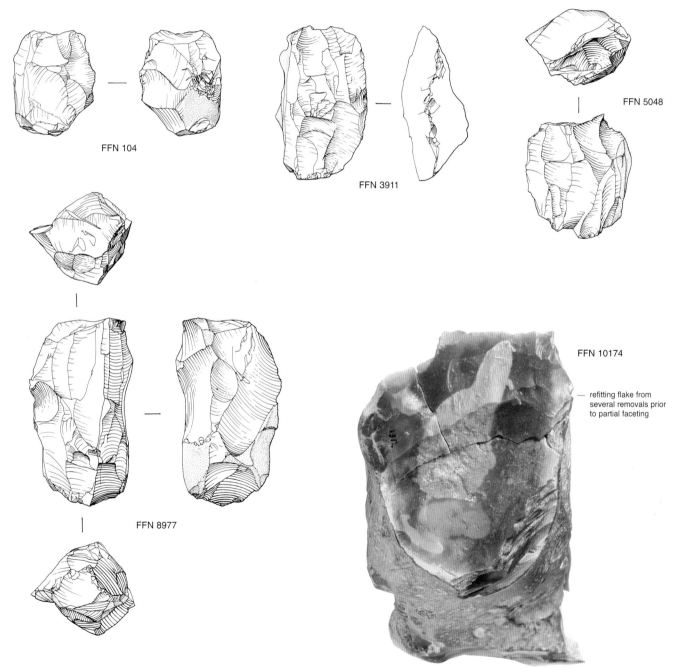

FFN 104

FFN 3911

FFN 5048

FFN 8977

FFN 10174

— refitting flake from several removals prior to partial faceting

Fig 46 Cores FNN 104, 3911, 5048 and 8977 (scale 1:2)

Fig 47 Refitting group 21: large opposed platform core (FFN 10174) with faceted platform (scale 1:1)

Core preparation in the form of platform edge abrasion (which serves to strengthen the platform (Barton 1992, 106)) was present on five cores (eg Fig 46, FNN 8977, 5048, 3911; Fig 47, FNN 10174) and one core fragment.

The remains of cresting were present on two cores. On FFN 3911 (Fig 46) the cresting (uni-directional) was confined to one of the lateral edges of the flaking face.

QUANTITATIVE ATTRIBUTES

The cores are thus relatively large (Table 15), particularly two examples, FFN 10174 (Fig 47) and 8977. The variation in the dimensions can be explained by the shape, quality and amount of reduction of the original raw material. All the cores retain some part of their original grey to chalky white cortical exterior.

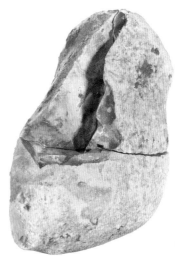

Fig 48 Refitting group 45: shattered partially worked nodule (scale 1:2)

Table 15 Quantitative data for blade cores in scatter A

	Range	Average	Standard deviation
Length (mm)	112–55	82.2	21.7
Width (mm)	58–31	50.2	10.2
Thickness (mm)	57–32	40.6	8.8
Weight (g)	390–75	199	111

DISTRIBUTION

Fig 45 shows, unsurprisingly, that the distribution of cores corresponds to the areas of highest debitage density.

Partially worked and unworked nodules

A total of ten partially worked and unworked pebbles/nodules were recovered from scatter A. The majority of the unworked pieces were pebbles, with only one approaching the size required for artefact production. However, since this piece had a natural perforation in it, an artefact seems unlikely, and all except the burnt fragments may be natural occurrences. Of the partially worked nodules, only one was heavier than 100g. This was FFN 3277, part of refitting group 45, the other elements of which were located in the eastern area of scatter C. Refitting has demonstrated that this nodule was deliberately broken, either to test its quality or to produce smaller fragments for knapping (Fig 48).

Two other partially worked pieces weighed 85–90g and formed part of refitting group 18. This was a large flint cobble derived from river gravels and which, like refitting group 45, had been deliberately smashed (below, 3.6).

DISTRIBUTION

Fig 45 shows the distribution of partially worked nodules.

The retouched tool assemblage

The retouched tool assemblage was composed of 19 pieces (2% of the total assemblage), of which nine were microliths or fragments of microliths and one was a scraper. The remainder of the assemblage was composed of retouched fragments of flakes and blades which did not fall within any formal tool type (Table 6; Table 7).

Microliths

There were nine microliths or microlith fragments in the assemblage (1% of the total assemblage), of which four were complete (Table 16). Two of the remaining five fragments were conjoined (refitting group 12), giving a total of eight microliths within the excavated assemblage. None were burnt, and none retained cortex on their dorsal surfaces. At least four of the microliths were detached from opposed platform cores.

Four of the microliths belonged to Clark's non-geometric 'A' type obliquely backed points (Clark 1933). All were retouched on the left side (with point uppermost) and in all cases this had been carried out from the ventral surface.

Two microliths (Fig 49, FFN 3957, 3479) were bi-truncated examples (Clark's 'C' type) each with oblique proximal truncation on the left side and additional distal truncation on the right side. The proximal truncation of FFN 3479 was carried out from both the dorsal and ventral surfaces, perhaps indicating anvil technique. The remaining truncations of both pieces were all from the ventral surface.

Probably related to this class were two broken microliths (FFN 4454/8943 (Fig 49), FFN 10281) which were distally

Table 16 Microlith typology (n=9) in scatter A

Microlith type	No.
A1a	3
?A1a	1
C1a	2
Distally retouched fragments	2
Refitting fragment	1
Total	9

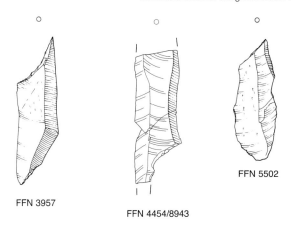

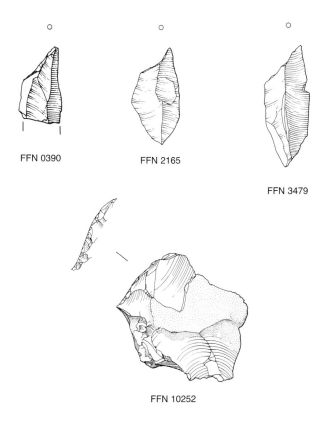

Fig 49 Microliths and scraper refitting group 12: FNN 4454/8943, 3479, 3957, 2165, 5502, 0390 and 10252 (scale 1:1)

truncated from the ventral surface on the right side. Due to breakage of the proximal end the classification of these pieces could not be further refined.

Since only four microliths were complete, full quantitative data is not presented, but the range of their main dimensions was as follows: length 37–26mm; width 13–11mm; and thickness 3–2mm.

The proximal angle of oblique truncation for the five examples which could be measured varied from 41° to 55°. The distal truncation angles of the two quantifiable examples (both 'C' types) were 40° and 45°. These angles would indicate a low degree of 'pointedness' for the assemblage.

However, the degree of 'pointedness' is also influenced by the shape of the truncation. For instance, of the four 'A' type microliths, two had concave truncations while the other two were straight. Of the two 'C' type microliths, one (FFN 3957, Fig 49) had a very concave proximal truncation, while the proximal truncation was slightly concave on FFN 3479 (Fig 49). On both examples the distal truncation was straight. It is apparent that, with a very oblique truncation, the greater the concavity of the truncation the more 'pointed' the piece becomes. The combination of truncation angle, type and position makes the small number of microliths in scatter A very distinctive, and identical to those in the eastern part of scatter C (below, 3.5).

Scrapers

Only one piece could be classified as a scraper (FFN 10252, Fig 49). It consisted of a large flake generated during initial core

decortication (refitting group 24, Fig 111). One of the distal margins has had a minimal amount of abrupt dorsal retouch. Although the piece could be classed as a flake end scraper, it is a crude, rather *ad hoc* example.

Miscellaneous retouched pieces

This category was composed of nine small flake or blade fragments. Most pieces have localised retouch on lateral or distal margins, and do not appear to be fragments of formal tool types. Rather, they seem to be opportunistically modified and used.

Utilised debitage

A number of pieces within the assemblage show signs of edge damage or discontinuous retouch. In the majority of cases it is clear that this has been caused either by post-depositional factors such as movement or by the process of excavation (eg FFN 4596). However, five pieces could be categorised as *a posteriori* tools (*sensu* Bordes 1970b). These may be defined as artefacts with no deliberate modification, but which show signs of utilisation. The five pieces were composed of one blade, one blade fragment, two flakes and a crested blade. All except the crested blade showed signs of localised minor edge damage along their lateral margins.

The crested blade (Fig 43, FFN 10330) showed the clearest evidence of damage caused by utilisation. The piece was 123mm long, 26mm wide and 13mm thick. It was bi-directionally crested and triangular in section. The proximal end was missing, and the break may possibly have been slightly modified to remove a sharp burr. The distal end showed some signs of retouch, although this may have been produced spontaneously. The damage was confined to the lateral edges of the mid-section of the blade, and was predominantly on the ventral surface. The damage consisted of stepped, invasive scars on the ventral surface and crushing of the lateral margins. 'Bruised' blades such as this have been described as *lames mâchurées* (Bordes 1967, 30), and experimental work (Barton 1986) suggests that this characteristic damage can be produced by heavy chopping of antler or bone. However, others have suggested that the blades were used to hone sandstone hammers (Fagnart and Plisson 1997) or to partially facet core platforms and prepare core fronts (Froom 2005). However, the assemblage from Launde, Leicestershire, has only three bruised pieces (none of them blades or flakes), yet a high proportion of the blades had faceted butts. One would expect there to be more 'hammers' and 'sharpeners' if these theories were correct. Such 'bruised' pieces are highly diagnostic of the 'long blade' industries of southern Britain and north-west Europe which date to *c* 10,000 BP (Barton 1991).

Distribution of retouched and utilised tools

The distribution of retouched tools and utilised pieces is shown in Fig 50.

Tool debitage

Only one item of possible tool debitage was recovered, FFN 264. This consisted of a broken flake with evidence of bi-directional removals from the dorsal surface. Although this could be interpreted as an axe thinning flake, it is equally likely to have been the product of core preparation. This is particularly true given the amount of flaking carried out to the back of the opposed platform cores present in the assemblage.

Discussion

It must be remembered that the excavated area of scatter A probably lay on the periphery of the major activity area, and the sample analysed is, therefore, probably biased. Nevertheless, some trends are clear.

Table 6, Table 7 and Fig 51 clearly illustrate the very low proportion of tools and utilised pieces to debitage in the scatter A assemblage as a whole. Within the retouched tool assemblage,

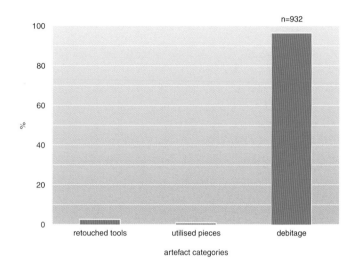

Fig 51 Assemblage composition in scatter A

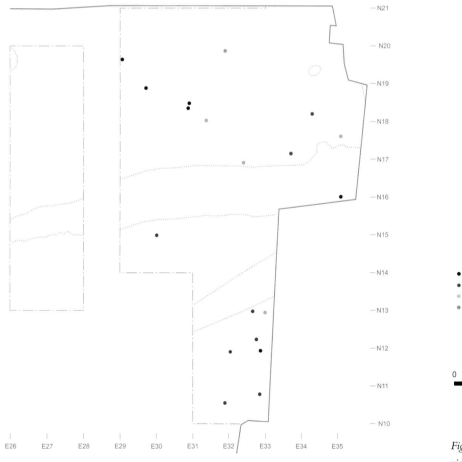

Fig 50 Distribution of all retouched and utilised pieces in scatter A (scale 1:100)

miscellaneous retouched flakes and fragments form the largest category, followed by microliths and a single scraper. The very low numbers and restricted range of formal tool types is noteworthy. The debitage assemblage is clearly orientated towards blade and flake production, as these types dominate.

3.5 The lithic artefacts in scatter C (including C west and C east)

Table 6 shows that scatter C was by far the largest lithic assemblage at Three Ways Wharf, consisting of over 15,000 pieces. The spatial distribution of these artefacts can be subdivided into nine sub-assemblages (SAS 1–9), which in turn can be grouped into two scatters, C west and C east (Fig 12). The following deals with the scatter C assemblage as a whole, but notes contrasts between C west and C east where pertinent or possible.

Debitage

Flakes and unclassified debitage

A total of 3508 flakes were present in the assemblage, together with 52 unclassified pieces of debitage. In total they form 23.1% of the entire scatter C assemblage (Table 7).

Flakes have been divided into three categories using the same criteria as those adopted for scatter A. These divisions (primary, secondary and tertiary) are derived from observations of core preparation strategies as reconstructed by refitting (below, 3.6). When analysing the composition of the flake assemblage, only complete flakes have been considered, since only complete examples can provide reliable quantitative and qualitative data. The details of the condition and composition of the flake assemblage are shown in Table 17.

The lower breakage rate of flakes (49%) compared with blades (63%) may be explained by the relatively more robust shape and dimensions of flakes. As with the blades, burning played a very minor role in breakage, with the major factors likely to be quality of the raw material, trampling and post-depositional processes.

Since the quantitative data from C west and C east showed little variation, these data are presented in Table 18 for scatter C as a whole.

QUALITATIVE ATTRIBUTES

The percentage composition of each butt type within each of the three flake categories is set out in Table 19 and represented graphically in Fig 52. The flake assemblage (particularly in C west) will inevitably contain axe thinning flakes which could not definitely be classed as such. These flakes will have inadvertently boosted the proportions of flakes with faceted butts.

Fig 52 shows a tendency towards increased platform preparation (in the form of abrasion and faceting) as core reduction progresses. This is particularly true of C east, where faceting is especially prevalent. A comparison with Fig 39 shows the similarity between scatters A and C east. This pattern of increasing platform preparation as the core is reduced accords

Table 17 Condition and composition of flake assemblage (n=3560) in scatter C

	No. (burnt)	% (burnt)
Complete flakes		
Primary flakes (75–100% cortex)	79 (0)	2.2 (0.0)
Secondary flakes (1–74% cortex)	690 (5)	19.4 (0.1)
Tertiary flakes (0% cortex)	1024 (10)	28.8 (0.3)
Unclassified debitage	20 (0)	0.6 (0.0)
Total complete	1813 (15)	51.0 (0.4)
Broken flakes		
Proximal fragments	569 (37)	16.0 (1.0)
Mesial fragments	284 (35)	8.0 (1.0)
Distal fragments	765 (49)	21.5 (1.4)
Unclassified fragments	129 (20)	3.5 (0.5)
Total broken	1747 (141)	49.0 (3.9)
Total complete & broken	3560 (156)	100.0 (4.3)

Table 18 Quantitative data for complete flakes (n=1792) in scatter C

	Range	Average	Standard deviation
Length (mm)	105–2	30.50	12.89
Width (mm)	112–8	26.85	13.06
Thickness (mm)	49–1	4.99	3.86

Table 19 Flake butt morphology (n=1792) in scatters C west and C east

Flake type & assemblage	Butt type					Total
	Plain	Plain abraded	Linear	Faceted	Unclassified	
Primary C west	28	4	3	0	2	37
Secondary C west	246	69	20	17	36	388
Tertiary C west	311	163	41	59	66	640
Total C west	585	236	64	76	104	1065
Primary C east	33	3	0	1	5	42
Secondary C east	159	35	18	50	40	302
Tertiary C east	156	67	34	86	41	384
Total C east	348	105	52	137	86	728

with the increasingly greater degree of precision and skill required to maximise the productivity of the core as reduction progresses.

Fig 53 shows the data for hammer type by flake type in scatters C west and C east. In contrast with C west, hard hammer usage in scatter C east remains fairly constant, but at a relatively lower frequency than in C west. Soft hammer usage is correspondingly greater in scatter C east. Scatter C east

compares most closely with scatter A (Fig 40), with the marked decrease in hard hammer use during core reduction in A also being present in C east.

DISTRIBUTION

The distribution of flakes and blades is shown in Fig 54, and no differences are apparent between them. Neither could any differential spatial patterning be observed in the distribution of

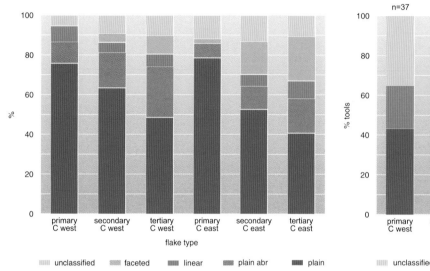

Fig 52 Flake butt morphology in scatters C west and C east

Fig 53 Flake hammer mode in scatters C west and C east

Fig 54 Distribution of flakes and blades across the whole site (scale 1:200)

The lithic artefacts in scatter C (including C west and C east)

Fig 55 Distribution of complete blades with faceted butts across the whole site (scale 1:200)

primary, secondary and tertiary flakes, and they are displayed undifferentiated.

Flakes with plain and plain/abraded butts were likewise found in all the major debitage concentrations. Flakes with faceted butts were also present in each of the major concentrations, although there was a tendency for them to occur more often in the eastern area of scatter C. However, this tendency was not as marked as in the distribution of blades with faceted butts (Fig 55).

Blades

Blades and bladelets numbered 3099 or 20% of the total assemblage (Table 6; Table 7). Six of the complete blades were burnt in contrast to 101 of the broken examples, suggesting that burning had contributed in a minor way to the degree of breakage. However, it is more likely that factors such as quality of raw material and trampling underfoot played the major part in producing such a high breakage rate of 63.1% (Table 20).

Of the complete examples, only 309 had a width of less than 12mm and could thus be classed as bladelets. Many more small bladelets and fragments were recognised in the sieved residues, but time and funding precluded their detailed recording, and they are classed as general debitage. Scatter plots of length to breadth ratios showed that there was no clear division between blades and bladelets. Table 21 shows the differences in lengths of blades in scatter C subdivided into C

west and C east. These data suggest that there was a tendency for blades in C east to be longer than those in C west. This trend is examined in conjunction with butt morphology below. Of the complete blades, 87% had less than 25% of their dorsal surface corticated, confirming that the majority of blades were

Table 20 Condition of blade assemblage (n=3102) in scatter C

	No.	%
Complete	1143	36.9
Proximal fragments	819	26.4
Mesial fragments	456	14.7
Distal fragments	662	21.3
Unclassified	23	0.7
Total broken	1959	63.1
Total complete & broken	3102	

Table 21 Comparison of blade length in scatters C west (n=7161) and C east (n=427)

Scatter	Range	Average	Standard deviation
C west complete blades			
Length (mm)	102–12	43	17
C east complete blades			
Length (mm)	130–13	51	21

57

produced following some decortication and preparation of the raw material.

Table 22 and Fig 56 contain data on the butt types of the complete blades in C west and C east. While plain and abraded plain butts dominate both assemblages, faceting forms a significant component in C east, which is comparable with the pattern in scatter A (Fig 42).

Table 23 shows that in both scatters C west and C east, soft-hammer technique was the preferred method of manufacturing blades. The proportion of hard to soft hammer mode was very similar in both scatters. However, when these data are compared with Table 12, it is clear that scatters C east and A present the closest similarity.

DISTRIBUTION

The distribution of all blades is shown in Fig 54, and together with flakes they form the main constituents of the lithic assemblages in both scatters C east and C west.

Complete blades with plain and abraded plain butts are predominant in all of the major lithic concentrations and sub-assemblage areas. Fig 55 shows that although few in number, complete blades with faceted butts are clearly concentrated in scatter C east.

This clear patterning prompted further investigation into the potential differences between the assemblages in C west and C east by analysing the relationship between blade length and butt type. Both attributes have been explicitly linked to chronology by Barton (1991).

The method chosen was to construct cumulative frequency plots of the lengths of complete blades with different butt types, namely plain, plain with platform edge abrasion, and faceted (Fig 57). (Note that the sample size of faceted blades in C west was too low (n=20) to allow plotting and analysis.) The validity of the visual patterning in size distributions was tested statistically by applying the Kolmogorov-Smirnov two-sample test (outlined by Fletcher and Lock 1991, 100). The null hypothesis adopted was that there was no significant difference in the lengths of the blades with different butt types. The results were as follows (Fig 57).

1) *Within* each of C west and C east, blades with plain and abraded butts formed a single population.
2) There was a significant (at >99% confidence level) difference *between* the C west plain abraded butt assemblage and that in C east. C west and C east statistically formed two separate populations, with the plain abraded blade assemblage in C east being significantly longer than that in C west.
3) The C east blades with faceted butts tended to be the longest of all. This tendency was significantly greater (at >99% confidence level) when compared with the C west plain abraded butt assemblage. However, the difference was not as marked (at 95% confidence level) when compared with the plain abraded assemblage in C east.

Therefore, the scatter C blade assemblage can be divided on the grounds of butt type and length into two sub-assemblages occupying two spatial areas which overlap to some degree. The implications of this will be further discussed below (3.7).

Table 22 Blade butt morphology in scatters C west and C east

Type	C west	C east
Linear	34	16
Plain	233	179
Plain abraded	355	117
Faceted	20	68
Unclassified	75	46
Total	717	426

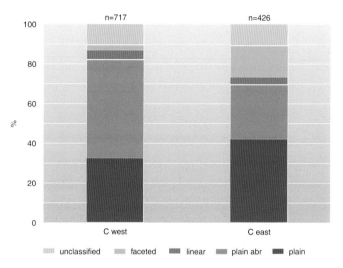

Fig 56 Comparison of butt morphology of complete blades in scatters C west and C east

Table 23 Blade hammer mode in scatter C

Scatter	Hard	Soft	Unclassified	Total
C west (no.)	83	468	166	717
C east (no.)	29	330	67	426
C west (%)	12	65	23	
C east (%)	7	77	16	

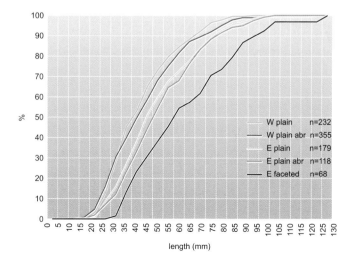

Fig 57 Cumulative frequency curves of blade length in scatters C west and C east

However, it is clear that the requirement for longer blades in C east was met by employing different technological approaches to those used in C west to produce shorter blades. It is considered that this technological difference is clear evidence of a chronological distinction between scatters C west and C east.

Core preparation pieces

Three main classes of core preparation debitage were recognised in the assemblage: crested pieces, core tablets, and other pieces such as cresting flakes and *flancs de nucléus* (Fig 58; Table 24).

CRESTED FLAKES AND BLADES
Most of the 189 crested pieces, which form 1.2% of the total assemblage, were blades. In addition, a further 11 crested pieces were used as supports for formal tools such as scrapers (eg FFN

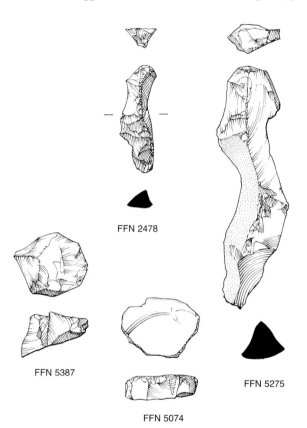

FFN 2478

FFN 5387

FFN 5074

FFN 5275

Fig 58 Core preparation pieces: crested pieces FFN 2478 and 5275; core tablets FFN 5074 and 5387 (scale 1:2)

Table 24 Composition of core preparation assemblage in scatter C

Type	Complete	Broken	Total	(Burnt)
Crested pieces				
– uni-directional	71	76	147	(2)
– bi-directional	20	22	42	(2)
Subtotal	91	98	189	(4)
Core tablets	103	28	131	(8)
Flancs de nucléus	9	1	10	(0)
Misc other types	20	12	32	(2)
Total	223	139	362	(14)

8942) and burins (eg FFN 5470). Cresting was also present on a number of core tablets (below). Uni-directionally crested pieces (eg Fig 58, FFN 2478) outnumber bi-directional pieces (eg Fig 58, FFN 5275) by a factor of *c* 3.6:1, although both types could be produced during the reduction of a single core. The function of cresting is discussed more fully below (3.6, 'Core reduction processes').

The quantitative data for the uni- and bi-directional crested pieces were very similar, and are not discussed further here. However, there were statistically significant differences (Fletcher and Lock 1991, 75–81) in the length range of crested blades between C west and C east, as Table 25 and Fig 58 show. This accords with the analysis of blade lengths carried out in the preceding section, and suggests that the aim was to produce longer blades in C east than in C west.

Table 25 Quantitative data for crested pieces in scatters C west (n=55) and C east (n=36)

	C west	C east
Length range (mm)	103–20	142–14
Average length (mm)	54.0	73.4
Standard deviation (mm)	17.0	26.9

CORE TABLETS
The 131 core tablets form 0.8% of the total assemblage; 103 are complete, with only 28 broken examples, and eight of the 131 are burnt. In addition, core tablets were occasionally used as supports for a number of formal retouched tools such as end scrapers. Most of the core tablets are fairly thick, robust flakes (mean thickness 8.4mm).

Several core tablets have been refitted to each other and also to the tops of blade cores, indicating that knapping took place *in situ*. The presence of cresting on some core tablets has been noted above. It is clear that in some cases (particularly in C east: eg Fig 58, FNN 5387) the removal of a core tablet was used to rejuvenate a platform which had previously been partially faceted. This demonstrates the interchangeability of technique.

FLANCS DE NUCLÉUS
Only those flakes representing removal of all or part of a core flaking face by use of a transverse blow have been included in this category (Barton 1992, 268, fig 7.8). Ten pieces were present in the assemblage, of which nine were complete and none were burnt. In addition, one piece (Fig 70, FFN 1977) was utilised as a support for an end scraper. The low number of *flancs de nucléus* suggests that this technique of rejuvenation was relatively little used.

MISCELLANEOUS PREPARATION PIECES
The 32 pieces in this category include flakes produced during cresting, possible faceting flakes, and other miscellaneous core preparation and rejuvenation pieces. Twenty of the pieces were complete and two were burnt.

DISTRIBUTION

All the core preparation types (crested pieces, core tablets, *flancs de nucléus* and others) are, not surprisingly, closely associated with the densest concentrations of lithic material, indicating that these are the product of *in situ* knapping (Fig 59). However, no further zonation or differentiation is apparent. For example, there was no patterning in the distributions of uni- and bi-directionally crested pieces.

Cores

The assemblage was composed of 87 complete cores and 20 broken cores or fragments (eg Fig 60), representing 0.7% of the total assemblage. Of the complete cores, blade and bladelet cores dominate the assemblage (79), while flake cores form a minor component (8). Table 26 shows the composition of the core assemblage in greater detail.

FLAKE CORES

The eight flake cores are predominantly irregular and globular single and opposed platform types. The three globular opposed platform flake cores were probably blade cores which were reduced to such an extent that flakes became the product (FFN 2436, 5279). It was this factor, together with hinge fractures (as on FFN 5279), that probably led to their abandonment. The irregular forms such as FFN 8418 and 610 seem to represent opportunistic flaking of small broken pebbles or irregular chunks of fragmented nodule.

BLADE CORES

Twin-platform cores are the most prevalent type. Of these, opposed platform types predominate (55), of which one (Fig 89, FFN 8797) was a broken axe (Fig 114) reused as a blade core. One offset and one bifacially worked example complete the twin-platform core assemblage. The twin-platform blade cores were predominantly prismatic in shape (eg Fig 60, FFN 8995) (39), followed by pyramidal (eg Fig 60, FFN 3583) (8), globular (eg Fig 60, FFN 6454) (4) and irregular (4). Most of the globular types represent fully reduced blade or bladelet cores.

Eleven of the 22 single-platform cores were pyramidal in shape (eg Fig 60, FFN 7395), while the remainder were equally spread between prismatic (eg Fig 60, FFN 884), globular (eg Fig 60, FFN 3028) and irregular types. Two of the irregularly shaped single-platform cores consisted of broken axe rough-outs (eg Fig 89, FFN 1727). Fig 61 shows the composition by shape of the single- and twin-platform core assemblages.

OTHER CORE ATTRIBUTES

Other morphological attributes of blade and flake cores were recorded. These were mainly to do with the treatment of the back or sides of the core and were as follows:

FL = transverse flaking to back of core;
CO = unmodified cortex on back of core;
RM = blade removals from back of core (ie continuation of main flaking face to rear of core);
CR = cresting to back or side of core;
FR = core on a broken or shattered nodule;
FK = core on a large flake.

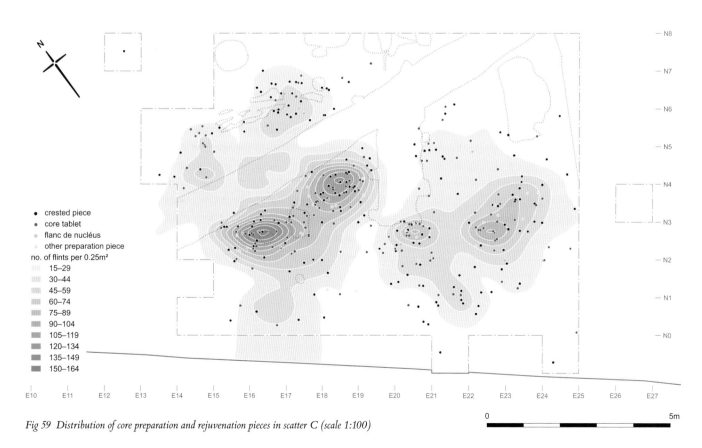

Fig 59 Distribution of core preparation and rejuvenation pieces in scatter C (scale 1:100)

scatter C west

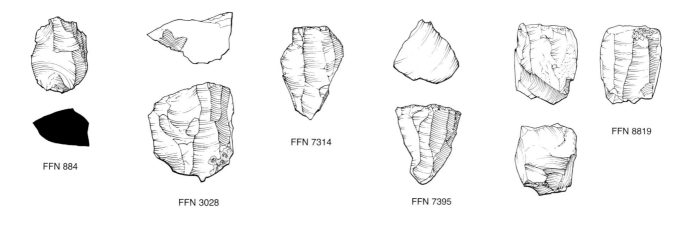

FFN 884

FFN 3028

FFN 7314

FFN 7395

FFN 8819

scatter C east

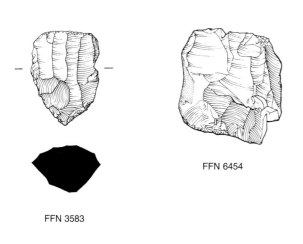

FFN 3583

FFN 6454

FFN 6470

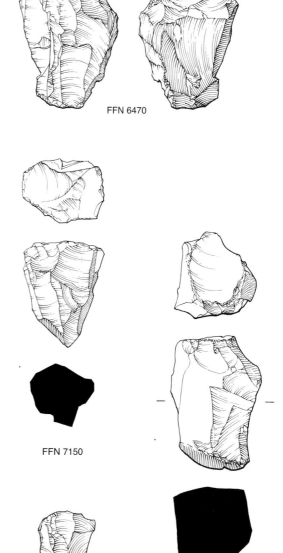

FFN 7150

FFN 7716

FFN 8995

*Fig 60 Cores: scatter C west – FFN 884, 3028, 7314, 7395 and 8819;
scatter C east – FFN 3583, 6454, 6470, 7150, 7716 and 8995 (scale 1:2)*

Table 26 Core morphology in scatters C west and C east (in brackets)

Type	Prismatic	Pyramidal	Globular	Irregular	Total
Blade cores					
1-platform	3 (1)	10 (1)	1 (2)	4 (0)	18 (4)
2-platform (opposed)	22 (17)	4 (4)	1 (3)	3 (1)	30 (25)
2-platform (offset)	0 (0)	0 (0)	1 (0)	0 (0)	1 (0)
2-platform (bifacial)	0 (0)	0 (0)	0 (0)	0 (1)	0 (1)
Total 2-platform	22 (17)	4 (4)	2 (3)	3 (2)	31 (26)
Total	25 (18)	14 (5)	3 (5)	7 (2)	49 (30)
Flake cores					
1-platform	0 (0)	1 (0)	0 (0)	1 (2)	2 (2)
2-platform (opposed)	0 (0)	0 (0)	1 (2)	1 (0)	2 (2)
2-platform (offset)	0 (0)	0 (0)	0 (0)	0 (0)	0 (0)
2-platform (bifacial)	0 (0)	0 (0)	0 (0)	0 (0)	0 (0)
Total	0 (0)	1 (0)	1 (2)	2 (2)	4 (4)

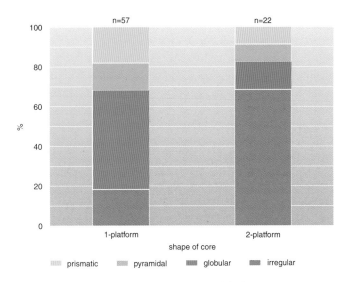

Fig 61 Composition of core assemblage by shape and platform in scatters C west and C east

Table 27 Other attributes of cores in scatters C west and C east

Attribute	C west	C east	Total
FL	16	6	22
CO	17	16	33
RM	5	6	11
CR	4	10	14
FR	5	9	14
FK	11	1	12
Total	58	48	106

Table 27 shows the numbers of complete flake and blade cores which displayed these attributes in scatters C west and C east. It shows that some cores displayed more than one attribute, for example a core could have a transversely flaked back and traces of cresting. Nonetheless, the table does give an indication of certain trends. For instance, transverse flaking of the rear of the core, although present in scatter C east (eg Fig 60, FFN 6470), occurred more often in C west.

The use of broken, smashed nodule fragments was twice as prevalent in C east as in C west. Conversely, the use of flakes as cores (eg Fig 60, FFN 884) was much more frequent in C west than in C east.

QUANTITATIVE ANALYSIS

There was a considerable overlap in the size distribution of single and opposed platform cores (Table 28). Neither was there a clear division in size of single and opposed platform cores between C west and C east. This was somewhat surprising, since a visual inspection of the cores suggested a general increase in size from C west to C east. This can be partly explained by the different composition of the core assemblages in the two areas. While there is no significant size difference in the opposed platform cores between C west and C east, the pyramidal cores are much smaller, with an average length of

Table 28 Quantitative data for blade cores in scatter C

Type	Range	Average	Standard deviation
Single-platform blade cores (n=22)			
Length (mm)	91–20	46.3	15.1
Width (mm)	78–17	37.3	11.9
Thickness (mm)	47–16	27.4	8.2
Weight (g)	230–10	62.2	55.8
Twin-platform blade cores (n=57)			
Length (mm)	94–37	58.0	12.5
Width (mm)	65–23	38.3	9.3
Thickness (mm)	48–12	27.4	8.7
Weight (g)	270–20	77.1	55.1

38.8mm and a standard deviation of 10.3mm. Thus, compared with C east, scatter C west contained a significant component of small single-platform cores.

PLATFORM PREPARATION

In the course of this analysis core platforms have been classed as follows.
1) Plain (eg Fig 60, FFN 7395).
2) Plain with abrasion of the platform edge (eg Fig 60, FFN 8995).
3) Faceted or partially faceted, with evidence of multiple removals from the striking platform (eg Fig 60, FFN 7150).
4) Possible or accidental faceting, where the appearance of partial faceting may have been caused by repeated unsuccessful attempts to remove a single core tablet.

Fig 62 shows the increase in the proportion of faceted to plain striking platforms in C east compared to C west. These data compare very closely with those for the butt morphology of complete blades (Fig 56), suggesting that the majority of blade debitage can be spatially associated with the cores from which they were produced, at least at the level of analysis represented by C west and C east. All the faceted platforms in C east were on twin-platform core types, while in C west two of the deliberately faceted platforms were on twin-platform types and one was on a single-platform core.

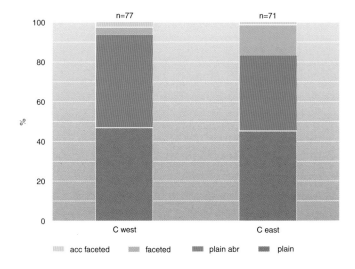

Fig 62 Comparison of core platform morphology in scatters C west and C east

DISTRIBUTION

Fig 63 shows the distribution of single- and twin-platform flake and blade cores together with broken cores and fragments. The cores were generally located in the areas of highest artefact density, except for the small group of cores in the north-east. Fig 64 shows the spatial distribution of all cores and fragments with at least one faceted platform. It can be seen that they were predominantly located in and around the hearth in C east.

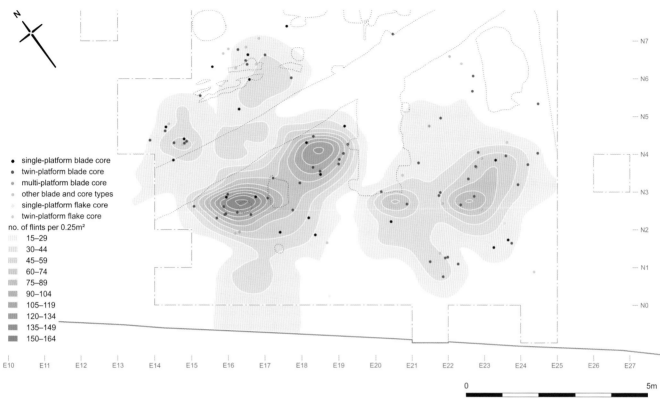

single-platform blade core
twin-platform blade core
multi-platform blade core
other blade and core types
single-platform flake core
twin-platform flake core
no. of flints per 0.25m²
15–29
30–44
45–59
60–74
75–89
90–104
105–119
120–134
135–149
150–164

Fig 63 Distribution of cores in scatter C (scale 1:100)

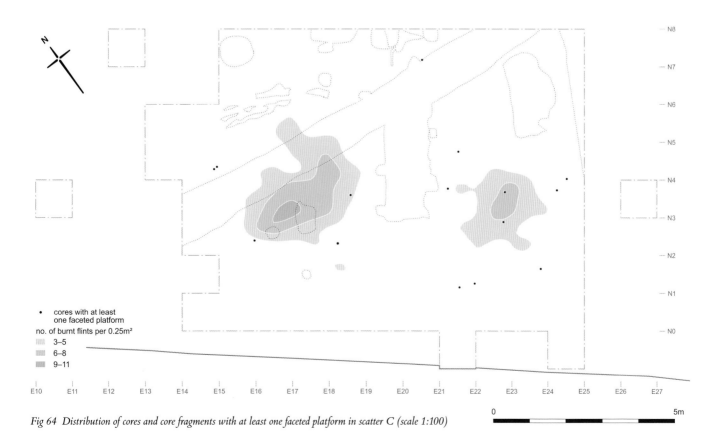

cores with at least
one faceted platform
no. of burnt flints per 0.25m²
3–5
6–8
9–11

Fig 64 Distribution of cores and core fragments with at least one faceted platform in scatter C (scale 1:100)

Unworked and partially worked nodules

A total of 124 unworked and partially worked nodules/pebbles were recovered from scatter C (Table 29). In addition, one smashed nodule fragment (FFN 3277) which is part of refitting group 45 (Fig 48; Fig 103) was located in scatter A.

Overall, the level of burning of the nodules was low, and confined to pieces weighing less than 100g. The unworked nodules which weigh less than 100g are unlikely to have been selected for use as potential raw material. It is possible that the presence of at least some of these small pebbles is unconnected with human activity, and is the result of natural processes. However, there is a cluster of small pebbles in square E21N01 which could be humanly derived (Chapter 1.3, 'Features and structures').

The 30 partially worked pebbles and nodules are in most cases the result of the smashing of larger river flint cobbles into smaller fragments, presumably to test the raw material for flaws and suitability for knapping. Alternatively (or in addition), the smashed fragments may be the result of the deliberate breaking of larger cobbles into a number of smaller chunks, some of which were then selected for knapping.

A number of partially worked and broken fragments have

been refitted to gain some idea of the size of the original nodule. When complete, refitting group 42 would have weighed in the region of 1050g, with dimensions of 150 x 110 x 65mm. It is noticeable that the centre of the nodule and one side are missing, and they may have been selected for further reduction. Several cores (eg Fig 60, FFN 6470) have clearly utilised such shattered nodule fragments.

Alternatively, some of the nodules were utilised as hammer stones, especially those such as refitting group 45 which show signs of repeated blows (Fig 48). These blows caused the nodule to fragment. Refitting group 45 would have had an original weight of *c* 1150g and dimensions of *c* 140 x 90 x 60mm. The similarity in size of refitting groups 42 and 45 suggests the selection of nodules of a standard size.

DISTRIBUTION

Fig 65 shows the distribution of all unworked nodules/pebbles. The two small concentrations in square E21N01 are very apparent. The other nodules are distributed over the rest of the site, in loose association with the main concentrations of flint debitage. However, when only those nodules heavier than 99g are plotted (Fig 65), a grouping of pieces can be seen in the north-central part of the site, around squares E18N04–E18N05, while the concentration in square E21N01 is still present.

Partially worked and smashed nodules were mainly distributed around the periphery of the main flint concentrations (Fig 66), particularly in scatter C east. Fig 66 also shows the refitting groups 32, 42 and 45. The components of refitting group 45 can be seen to be closely spaced, as are the two elements of refitting group 32. Thus, the partially worked

Table 29 Quantification of partially worked and unworked nodules in scatter C

Type	No. (burnt) <100g	No. (burnt) =>100g	Total
Unworked	61 (3)	33 (0)	94
Partially worked	13 (1)	17 (0)	30

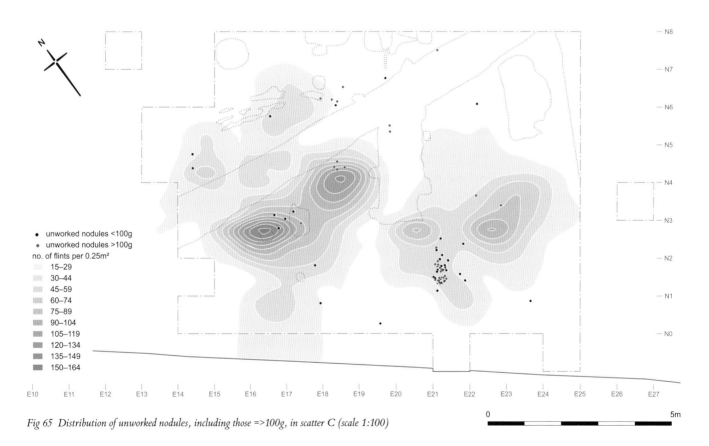

Fig 65 Distribution of unworked nodules, including those =>100g, in scatter C (scale 1:100)

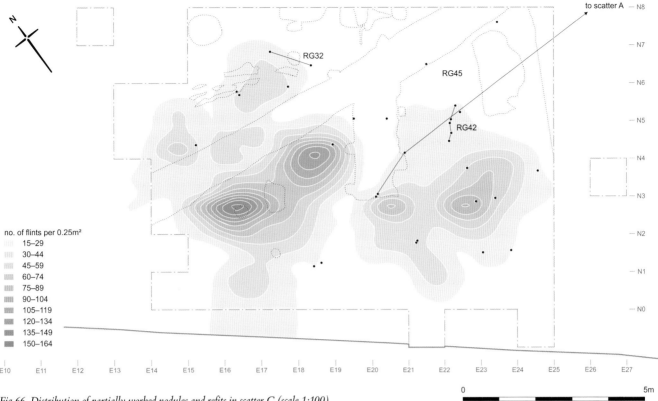

Fig 66 Distribution of partially worked nodules and refits in scatter C (scale 1:100)

smashed nodules seem to represent the rejected debris at the periphery of the hearths and knapping scatters, while the missing parts of the refitted nodules were presumably reduced nearer the hearths and main debitage concentrations. As mentioned above, two of the elements of refitting group 45 were relatively close together, but the third (FFN 3277) was located 16.05m away in scatter A. Possible explanations for this will be discussed below.

Hammer and anvil stones

In total there were nine pieces in the assemblage that appeared to have been used as hammer or anvil stones.

Hammer stones

Six hammer stones were present, five in C east and one in C west. Three consisted of rounded oval flint pebbles, two of fine-grained quartzite oval pebbles, and the sixth was a fine-grained quartzite cobble (Fig 67). This last piece at 620g was significantly larger than the other five, which varied between 85g and 375g in weight. A number of the hammer stones showed signs of damage around their circumference such as pecking and pitting, flaking and fracturing. In addition, a few of the cores showed signs of damage, indicating that they may have been utilised in a secondary capacity as hammer stones.

Anvil stones

Three large cobbles with signs of damage could be interpreted as anvil stones, since they were too big to be used as hammer stones.

One example of yellow flint lay in C west, while the other two, of fine-grained quartzite, lay in C east. One of the eastern examples (FFN 20056) had very extensive pecking over its surface (Fig 68). The anvil stones weighed between 1850g and 1150g.

FFN 20061

Fig 67 Hammer stone FNN 20061 (scale 1:1)

FFN 20056

Fig 68 Anvil stone FNN 20056, showing surface 'pecking' (scale c 1:1)

65

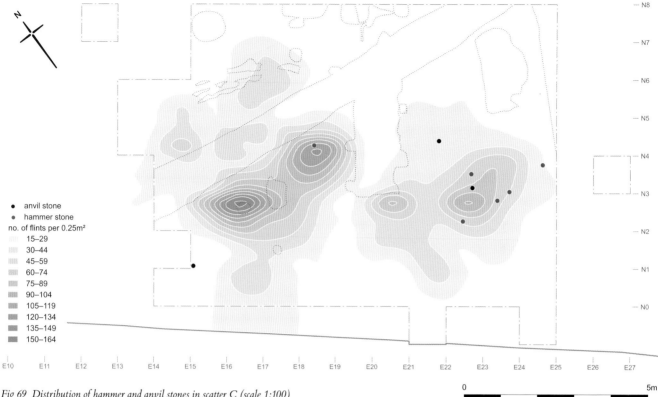

no. of flints per 0.25m²

• anvil stone
• hammer stone

	15–29
	30–44
	45–59
	60–74
	75–89
	90–104
	105–119
	120–134
	135–149
	150–164

E10 E11 E12 E13 E14 E15 E16 E17 E18 E19 E20 E21 E22 E23 E24 E25 E26 E27

N8 N7 N6 N5 N4 N3 N2 N1 N0

Fig 69 Distribution of hammer and anvil stones in scatter C (scale 1:100)

0   5m

Distribution

Fig 69 shows the distribution of the majority of hammer and anvil stones as being around the hearth in scatter C east. This is presumably connected with the greater concentration of partially worked and unworked nodules in C east.

Retouched tools

Scrapers

The 126 scrapers formed the largest single category of retouched tool in scatter C, constituting *c* 0.9% of the retouched tool assemblage; a selection of them is shown in Fig 70. Simple end scrapers dominated the assemblage, but side, double and other scrapers were also represented. Very few scrapers were burnt (Table 30). Scatter C east produced a restricted range of scraper types with slightly more emphasis on blades as supports compared with C west.

In scatter C as a whole, end scrapers characteristically had semi-abrupt or abrupt retouch at the distal end, and usually on the dorsal surface. Only three examples had retouch on the ventral surface, and only two had retouch at the proximal end. Seven examples had some retouch on lateral margins, but not enough to classify them as round scrapers (eg Fig 70, FFN 3485). Almost all the end scrapers had convex scraper edges. Two examples had concave edges (eg Fig 70, FFN 6178), while two others possessed a slight 'nosed' appearance (eg Fig 70, FFN 8682). Many of the end scrapers had a hooked profile, although some were relatively flat.

Of the three side scrapers, two were on flakes (one of which, FFN 1340 (Fig 70), was on a burnt core tablet) and one was on a snapped blade or flake. All had semi-abrupt retouch on the right lateral margin and two were burnt.

All four double scrapers were on flakes, and all were retouched from the ventral surface except for FFN 9009 (Fig 70). The distal scraping edge of this piece was retouched from the ventral surface, but the proximal scraping edge had very abrupt dorsal retouch. The original blank in this case was a core tablet, with additional retouch to shape the proximal scraping edge. Use-wear analysis suggests that both edges had been used.

The scraper/burin FFN 5000 (Fig 70) consisted of an end scraper on a blade with a burin spall removed from its proximal end. Use-wear analysis did not suggest that the burin edge had been used, and so this modification may have been to facilitate hafting or handling.

A single scraper (Fig 70, FFN 7980) had been heavily retouched almost all the way around its circumference, resulting in an irregularly shaped piece.

The eight scraper fragments consisted mostly of scraper edges which had snapped from the original supports (eg Fig 70, FFN 5956). Use-wear analysis shows that at least some of these fragments had been used, and it would seem probable that they were broken during use. FFN 7247 (Fig 70) consisted of an end scraper on a blade which had lost part of its scraper edge in just such a way.

Table 31 and Table 32 show the quantitative data for flake and blade scrapers. They indicate the selection of more robust blanks for scraper supports. Blade supports seem to be of a more standardised size than flakes. Flake supports consist of a range of forms, such as core tablets (including FFN 1977 (Fig 70) on a *flanc de nucléus*) and a broken axe fragment (C west, refitting group 4, FFN 4497 (Fig 94)).

scatter C west

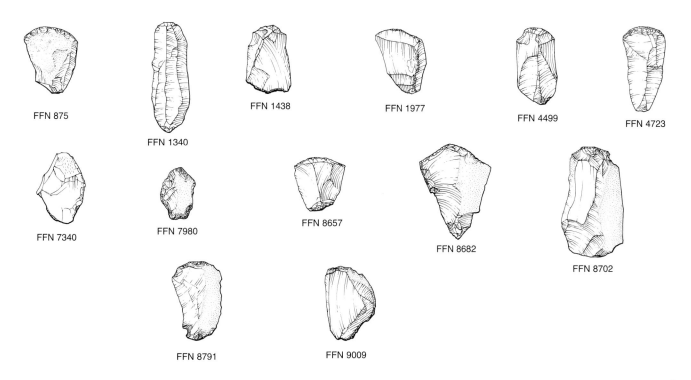

FFN 875

FFN 1340

FFN 1438

FFN 1977

FFN 4499

FFN 4723

FFN 7340

FFN 7980

FFN 8657

FFN 8682

FFN 8702

FFN 8791

FFN 9009

scatter C east

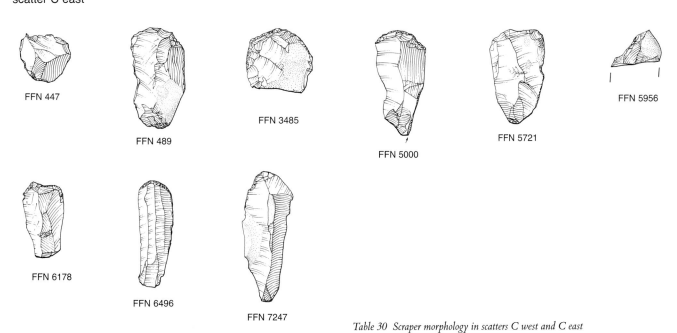

FFN 447

FFN 489

FFN 3485

FFN 5000

FFN 5721

FFN 5956

FFN 6178

FFN 6496

FFN 7247

Fig 70 Scrapers: scatter C west – FFN 875, 7340, 1438, 1977, 4723, 4499, 7980, 8657, 8682, 8702, 8791 and 9009; scatter C east – FFN 447, 489, 3485, 5000 (scraper/burin), 5721, 5956, 6178, 6496 and 7247 (scale 1:2)

Table 30 Scraper morphology in scatters C west and C east

Type	Complete (burnt)		Broken (burnt)		Total
	C west	C east	C west	C east	
End scrapers					
– on blade	12 (0)	7 (0)	6 (0)	1 (0)	26
– on flake	40 (2)	12 (0)	24 (2)	7 (0)	83
Double scrapers	1 (0)	0	3 (0)	0	4
Side scrapers	1 (1)	0	2 (1)	0	3
Other scrapers	1 (0)	0	0	0	1
Scraper fragments	0	0	4 (0)	4 (0)	8
Scraper/burin	0	1 (0)	0	0	1
Total	55 (3)	20 (0)	39 (3)	12 (0)	126

Table 31 *Quantitative data for end scrapers on flakes in scatters C west and C east*

Scatter	Range	Average	Standard deviation
C west			
Length (mm)	79–21	39.2	13.1
Width (mm)	77–16	29.2	12.8
Thickness (mm)	28–4	8.8	4.7
C east			
Length (mm)	52–29	40.3	6.3
Width (mm)	47–22	31.0	6.3
Thickness (mm)	12–5	8.0	2.0

Table 32 *Quantitative data for end scrapers on blades in scatters C west and C east*

Scatter	Range	Average	Standard deviation
C west			
Length (mm)	66–25	47.1	11.7
Width (mm)	26–12	20.5	3.9
Thickness (mm)	16–4	8.3	3.3
C east			
Length (mm)	76–40	56.0	12.1
Width (mm)	31–18	23.3	3.9
Thickness (mm)	10–4	8.1	2.2

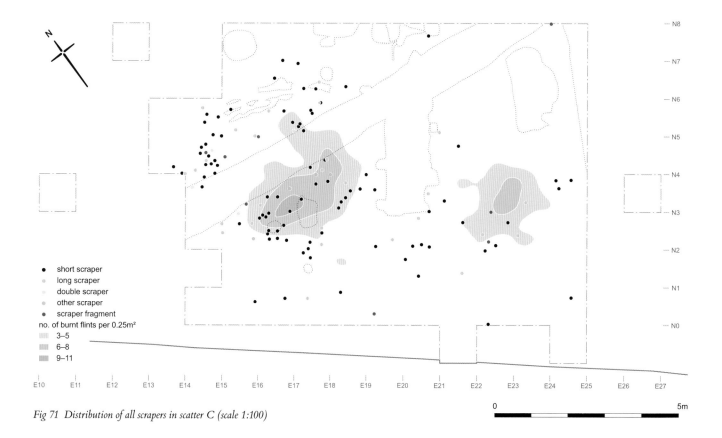

- ● short scraper
- ○ long scraper
- ○ double scraper
- ○ other scraper
- ● scraper fragment

no. of burnt flints per 0.25m²
- ▨ 3–5
- ▨ 6–8
- ▨ 9–11

Fig 71 *Distribution of all scrapers in scatter C (scale 1:100)*

0   5m

DISTRIBUTION

Fig 71 shows that the majority of scrapers were distributed around the western hearth area in C west, with a smaller group to the south-west of the eastern hearth in C east. Both flake and blade scrapers reflect this distribution. However, the four double scrapers were all located close together to the north-east of the western hearth. The three side scrapers (two of which were burnt) were also all located in close proximity to this hearth.

Truncated blades/flakes

There were six truncated pieces in the assemblage (three each in C west and C east), all of them blades with ventral, abrupt or semi-abrupt retouch. In all cases the truncation was at the distal end. FFN 2628 also had abrupt retouch on a proximal lateral margin and on the proximal end itself; the retouched proximal end (FFN 3299) of this piece had snapped off, possibly during use (below, refitting group 38).

One of the truncations was straight and five were oblique (eg FFN 7246, Fig 72); in the case of FFN 3906 (Fig 72) the truncation was also slightly concave. Four of the truncated blades were complete and, with an additional conjoined example (refitting group 38), provided the range of dimensions shown in Table 33.

DISTRIBUTION

Fig 73 shows that three of the truncated blades were located around the southern periphery of the eastern hearth. FFN 7201 was part of refitting group 10, and the blank was thus produced in the vicinity of E20N02. It was recovered 3.5m from its place of origin; it is unclear whether this movement was due to human agency, but it is significant that this is the one piece with clear lateral edge damage and abrasion. Thus FFN 7201 may have been subjected to post-occupation movement.

Truncated blades associated with the western hearth include refitting group 38 (FFN 2628–3299). The flexion break on this piece suggests that the truncated blade broke while in use. This

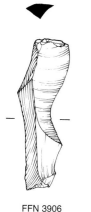

FFN 7246

FFN 3906

Fig 72 Truncated blades FFN 3906 and 7246 (scale 1:2)

Table 33 *Quantitative data for truncated blades (n=5) in scatter C*

	Range
Length (mm)	78–53
Width (mm)	21–17
Thickness (mm)	15–3

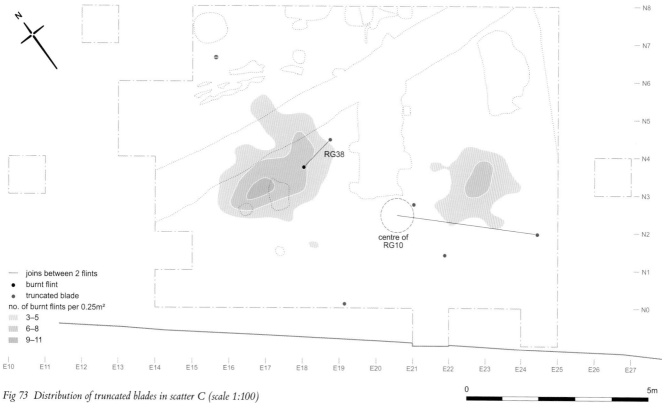

Fig 73 Distribution of truncated blades in scatter C (scale 1:100)

tends to be borne out by use-wear analysis of the broken proximal end (below), and the relatively small distance between the two conjoining pieces (Fig 73).

Microliths and microburins

Microliths totalled 79 pieces (1% of the total assemblage), of which 33 were complete and 46 were broken. Seven microliths were burnt, and only three had cortex on their dorsal surface. Table 34 shows the typological classification of the assemblage, subdivided into C west and C east; in this, Clark's scheme of microlith classification (Clark 1933) was followed where possible. Classification of the broken microliths was difficult; in some cases it was possible to assign a piece to a particular type with some certainty, but in others classification was more problematical, or even impossible. In addition to type, the shape (ie convex, straight, or concave) of the proximal and distal truncations was recorded. The angle of the proximal and distal

truncations was also measured in degrees from the longitudinal axis of the microlith (Fig 74). Type examples of microliths in scatters C west and C east are illustrated in Fig 75 and Fig 76 respectively.

ASSEMBLAGE COMPOSITION

Of the total scatter C assemblage, the 55 'A' type obliquely backed points (Clark 1933) comprised 70% of the microlith assemblage (Table 34). The rest of the assemblage was composed of distinctive obliquely bi-truncated 'C' types (four pieces, 5%), two 'D' type isosceles triangles, ten unclassifiable fragments and seven (*c* 11%) distal fragments which were obliquely backed at their distal end. It is possible that the latter represent the broken distal ends of 'C' type microliths. One proximal tip fragment was refitted to one of the 'C' type microliths (refitting group 40). All the microliths were retouched from the ventral surface, except for three which were retouched from the dorsal surface and two which had bi-directional retouch.

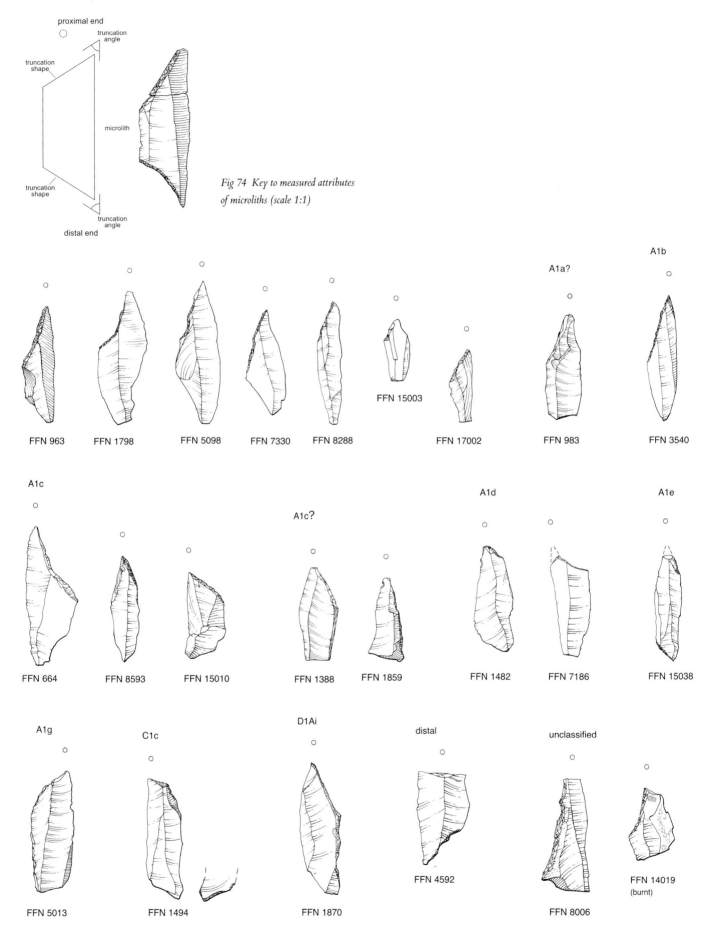

Lithic material

proximal end

truncation
angle

truncation
shape

microlith

truncation
shape

truncation
angle

distal end

Fig 74 Key to measured attributes
of microliths (scale 1:1)

FFN 15003

A1a?

A1b

FFN 963   FFN 1798   FFN 5098   FFN 7330   FFN 8288   FFN 17002   FFN 983   FFN 3540

A1c

A1c?

A1d

A1e

FFN 664   FFN 8593   FFN 15010   FFN 1388   FFN 1859   FFN 1482   FFN 7186   FFN 15038

A1g

C1c

D1Ai

distal

unclassified

FFN 4592

FFN 14019
(burnt)

FFN 5013   FFN 1494   FFN 1870   FFN 8006

Fig 75 Microliths, scatter C west: A1a – FFN 963, 1798, 5098, 7330, 8288, 15003 and 17002; A1a? – FFN 983; A1b – 3540; A1c – FFN 664, 8593 and 15010;
A1c? – FFN 1388 and 1859; A1d – FFN 1482 and 7186; A1e – FFN 15038; A1g – FFN 5013; C1c – FFN 1494; D1Ai – FFN 1870; distal – FFN 4592;
unclassified – FFN 8006 and 14019 (scale 1:1)

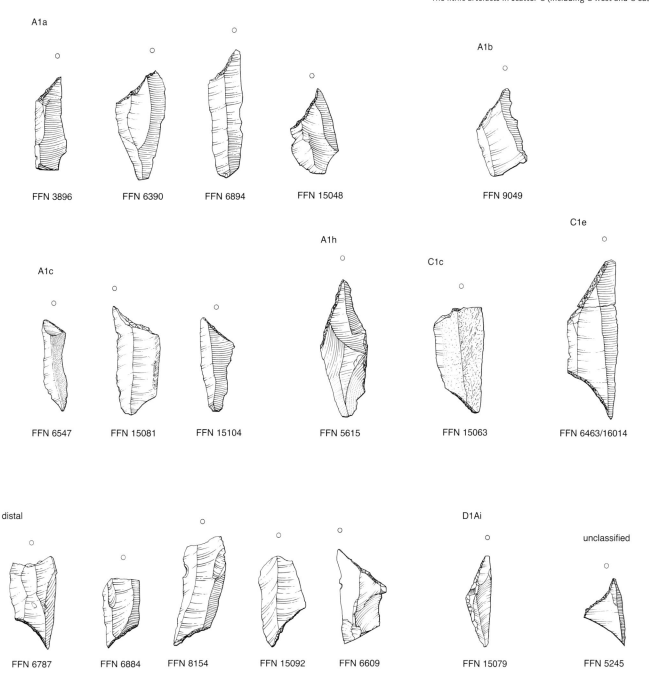

Fig 76 Microliths, scatter C east: A1a – FFN 3896, 6390, 6894 and 15048; A1b – FFN 9049; A1c – FFN 6547, 15081 and 15104; A1h – FFN 5615; C1c – FFN 15063; C1e – FFN 6463/16014; distal – FFN 6787, 6884, 8154, 15092 and 6609; D1ai – FFN 15079; unclassified – FFN 5245 (scale 1:1)

Simple obliquely backed points dominate (classes A1a and A1c (Fig 75; Fig 76), totalling 56. Five examples had additional retouch on the opposite (leading) edge (A1b and A1d; Fig 75; Fig 76). Also, four examples had retouch in addition to the oblique truncations. These consisted of one example with partial retouch on the left distal end (A1e, Fig 75), one with partial retouch at the distal end (A1f), one with retouch on the left distal lateral margin (A1g, Fig 75) and one with retouch on the right distal lateral margin (A1h, Fig 76). Overall the ratio of left-handed to right-handed 'A' types was 1.4:1.

Due to the small number of 'C' and 'D' type microliths (Fig 75; Fig 76), only quantitative data for the 29 complete 'A' types is presented in Table 35.

The dimensions were fairly standardised, particularly thickness. It is also clear that the 'A' type microlith blanks lay just within the bladelet rather than blade size class. There is no significant difference in the quantitative data for right- and left-handed 'A' type microliths.

The four bi-truncated 'C' type microliths included in the assemblage were quite distinctive. Each one had either a proximal or distal concave truncation. FFN 1494 (Fig 75) was dissimilar to the other three 'C' types (Fig 76) in that the distal truncation was achieved with inverse retouch. This piece was, therefore, technically somewhat similar to hollow-based points (Clark's 'F' types); however, it is quite unlike the majority of hollow-based points. In the case of FFN 15063 and 6463 (Fig

Table 34 Composition of microlith assemblages in scatters C west and C east (see Fig 75 and Fig 76 for type examples)

Type	C west				C east				Total C
	Complete	Broken	Total	Burnt subtotal	Complete	Broken	Total	Burnt subtotal	Complete & broken
A1a	9	1	10		5	0	5		15
?A1a	0	9	9	1	0	2	2		11
A1b	1	0	1		1	0	1		2
A1f	0	0	0		0	1	1		1
A1g	1	0	1		0	0	0		1
A1h	0	0	0		1	0	1		1
Subtotal left	11	10	21		7	3	10		31
A1c	5	0	5		4	0	4		9
?A1c	0	10	10		0	1	1		11
A1d	2	0	2	1	0	0	0		2
?A1d	0	1	1		0	0	0		1
A1e	0	1	1		0	0	0		1
Subtotal right	7	12	19		4	1	5		24
Subtotal leading edge	3	0	3		1	0	1		4
Total 'A' type	18	22	40		11	4	15		55
C1a	0	0	0		0	1	1		1
C1c	0	1	1		0	0	0		1
C1e	0	0	0		1	1	2		2
Total 'C' type	0	1	1		1	2	3		4
D1ai	0	0	0		1	0	1		1
D1bi	1	0	1		0	0	0		1
Total 'D' type	1	0	1		1	0	1		2
Distal	0	1	1		0	6	6	1	7
Ref fragment	0	0	0		0	1	1		1
Unclassified	0	5	5	4	1	4	5		10
Grand total	19	29	48		14	17	31		79

Table 35 Quantitative data for 'A' type microliths (n=29) in scatter C

	Range	Average	Standard deviation
Length (mm)	40–21	29.5	5.4
Width (mm)	16–6	11.0	2.5
Thickness (mm)	4–2	2.5	0.6

76), the truncations were very markedly concave, and were identical to the 'C' type microlith FFN 3957 in scatter A (Fig 49). None of the 'C' type microliths in scatter C were complete, although the proximal tip was refitted to FFN 6463 (refitting group 40), restoring this to near completeness.

The very distinctive concave truncation which is present on microliths in scatters C east and A strongly suggests not only a broad chronological link between the scatters, but also demonstrates strong links with the epi-Ahrensburgian of north-western Europe (see eg Taute 1968 and Johansen and Stapert 1997–8 for very similar microliths from Continental sites). Similar examples are very rare in Britain, with the 'long blade' site at Launde, Leicestershire (Cooper 2006), perhaps providing the best comparisons. Cooper has already compared the Launde microliths with those from Three Ways Wharf and stressed the links between the British and Continental examples (ibid).

Given the incomplete state of the 'C' type microliths, it is possible that the seven distally truncated fragments (Fig 76)

represent broken 'C' type microliths. Six of the seven distally truncated fragments had concave truncations of varying degrees, suggesting a stylistic link with the 'C' type microliths. Apart from refitting the proximal tip to FFN 6463 (above), no microliths were refitted to the distally truncated fragments, suggesting that breakage occurred off-site. This implies that the distally retouched fragments and broken 'C' type microliths may represent 'retooling', repairing broken hunting equipment with new projectile points. Another interpretation is that the distally truncated fragments were not broken 'C' type microliths, but 'microliths' produced by snapping off the proximal end of the blank without using the microburin technique.

There were two 'D' type triangles in the assemblage: FFN 1870 (Fig 75), a scalene (D1bi), and FFN 15079 (Fig 76), an isosceles (D1ai). The former had the oblique truncation on the right side, while the latter was truncated on the left.

MICROBURINS

There were a total of 20 microburins in the assemblage; 13 were retouched on the left-hand side (with the proximal end uppermost) (eg FFN 1389 and 3361, Fig 77) and three were retouched on the right. There were two miss-hits (*sensu* Barton 1992, 269) and one distal microburin.

In addition, a single notched piece (FFN 8950, Fig 77) is interpreted as a failed attempt at manufacturing a microlith. Even though use-wear analysis suggests that it had been used for scraping wood, it is included with the microburins.

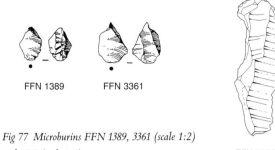

Fig 77 Microburins FFN 1389, 3361 (scale 1:2) and 8950 (scale 1:1)

FFN 1389   FFN 3361

FFN 8950

MICROLITH PRODUCTION

From the distribution of microburins (Fig 79) it is clear that microlith production using this technique was concentrated around the western hearth. Refitting group 3 consisted of a tranchet axe which, having snapped in half, was reused as a bladelet core. A refitting microburin from the broken axe/core illustrates that it provided blanks to produce at least one (probably an 'A' type) microlith (Fig 114).

Only two microburins were found in the east of scatter C, one of which was a miss-hit (FFN 17012). The second (FFN 9063) possibly rejoined an 'A' type microlith (refitting group 9). Refitting group 10 was centred on E20.50N02.50 (SAS 3), and the microlith FFN 15063 (Fig 76) was located only c 1.5m from this point (Fig 106). The blade blank used to produce the microlith was detached at a fairly early stage in the reduction sequence from a large opposed platform core with two prominent crested keels (Fig 104). Refitting shows that the blade blank would have been c 70mm long, and also reveals why the central mid-section of the blade was selected to form the microlith (Fig 104).

Although the microlith has been broken at its proximal end, the original blank was reduced by at least 35mm because of excess thickness, and twist and curvature. The result was a bi-truncated microlith with a thin and flat profile. The 'C' type microlith FFN 15063 (Fig 76) was composed almost entirely of a translucent quartz vein inclusion, a characteristic peculiar to refitting group 10. It is clear from the reconstructed nodule and the number of missing blade blanks that the quartz vein in the nodule was intentionally utilised and exploited to produce blanks.

Although the proximal end of microlith FFN 15063 (Fig 76) was missing, use-wear analysis suggests that the piece was used for cutting hide (Chapter 6.4). Refitting illustrated that in this case the microlith was manufactured, used and discarded within a very confined area. In this instance, the microlith was probably not hafted, given the probably very short production, use and discard time-cycle.

The other important aspect of refitting group 10 is that it also produced a large *lame mâchurée* (FFN 8189, Fig 100; Fig 104, d–e; below, 3.6).

Thus, it can be demonstrated that the distinctive bi-truncated 'C' type microliths present in scatters C east and A were contemporary with *lames mâchurées* which have become almost a type-fossil of the Lateglacial 'long blade' industries (Barton 1989).

Both refitting groups 9 and 10 suggest that microlith manufacture was a minor component of the knapping scatter SAS 3. The lack of microburins east of E19.50 has been discussed above.

DISTRIBUTION OF MICROLITHS AND MICROBURINS

The microliths were distributed across the centre of the excavated area of scatter C, with no discernible difference in the distribution of broken and complete microliths (Fig 78). Since

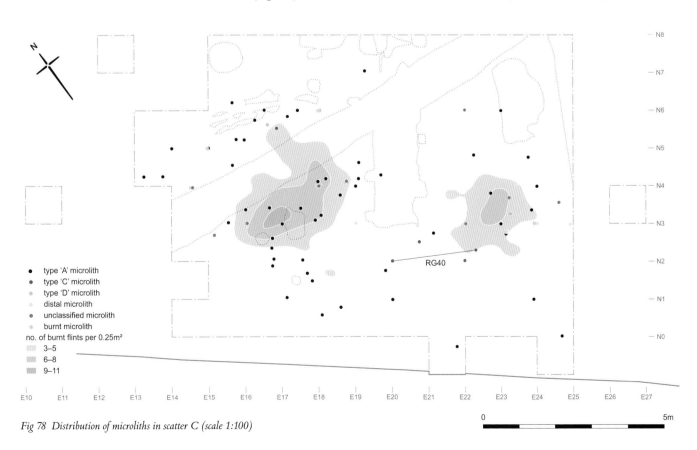

- • type 'A' microlith
- • type 'C' microlith
- • type 'D' microlith
- • distal microlith
- • unclassified microlith
- • burnt microlith
- no. of burnt flints per 0.25m²
- 3–5
- 6–8
- 9–11

RG40

0   5m

Fig 78 Distribution of microliths in scatter C (scale 1:100)

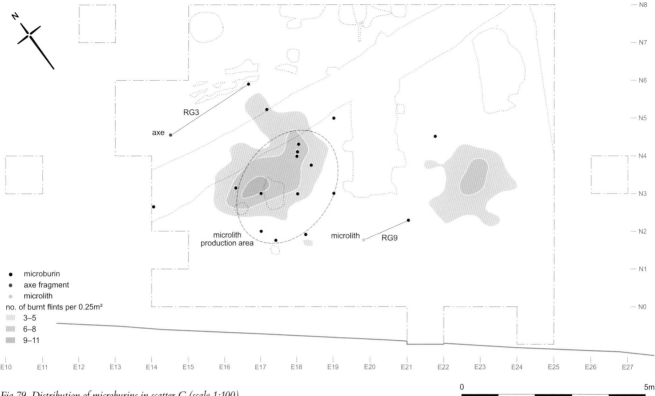

Fig 79 Distribution of microburins in scatter C (scale 1:100)

the 'A' type microliths form the bulk of the assemblage, their distribution determined that of the microliths as a whole.

Three of the 'C' type microliths were located to the south-west of the eastern hearth, while one lay on the northern edge of the western hearth. Of the two 'D' types, the isosceles was located in C east and the scalene in C west. The distally retouched fragments were mainly clustered on the eastern hearth, with a few outliers to the west. Microburins are clearly associated with the western hearth (Fig 79).

SUBDIVISION OF MICROLITH ASSEMBLAGE INTO C WEST AND C EAST

The majority of the microliths in scatter C consisted of broad, obliquely backed 'A' types, with small quantities of triangles ('D' types), bi-truncated 'C' types and distally retouched fragments. Fig 80 shows the main differences between the microlith assemblages in C west and C east.

The 'C' types and distally retouched fragments clearly form a significant component in C east. These are especially important typologically, as they are a very rare form which refitting has shown to have been contemporary with the production and use of *lames mâchurées* (below). The presence of both types of artefact within scatters A and C east suggests activity broadly contemporary with scatter A. The heavily calcined distally retouched piece with concave truncation FFN 6787 (Fig 76) provides a link between the suggested early occupation and the eastern hearth. However, it has to be acknowledged that microliths displaying very distinctive concave truncation, while present in scatters A and C east, also occur in C west (eg FFN 664 and 1798, Fig 75). These probably represent outliers from scatter C east or examples which have

moved due to the horizontal dispersal mechanisms described in Chapter 5.2.

The majority of simple broad-bladed 'A' types in both C west and C east show little difference from those in scatter A. There are some forms of 'A' type which are at variance with this pattern, however.

Fig 81 displays the truncation angles for all microliths as a percentage of all truncations. Among 'A' and 'D' types, truncation angles between 21° and 40° were prevalent, with angles greater than 40° forming a significant component. Truncations of 20° or less were infrequent. However, all the distal truncations of the 'C' types and over half the truncations on the 'distal' pieces were over 40°. Microliths with truncation angles of between 20° and 40° were present in both C west and

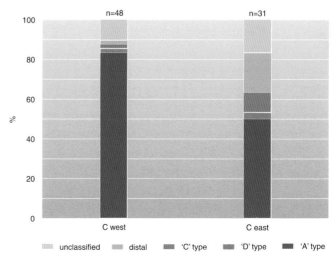

Fig 80 Comparison of microlith assemblages in scatters C west and C east

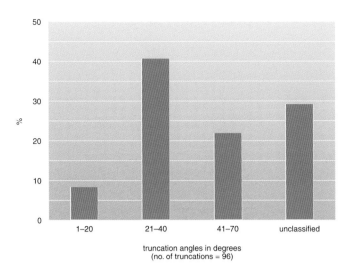

Fig 81 Microlith truncation angles in scatter C

C east. Narrower forms with truncation angles of 20° or less, sometimes with leading edge retouch, were largely confined to C west (Fig 82). In marked contrast, 15 microliths with proximal or distal truncation angles of more than 40° clustered quite tightly around the hearth in C east, while five were located around the periphery of the western hearth (Fig 82).

Burins and burin spalls

The assemblage contained 21 burins (*sensu* de Sonneville-Bordes and Perrot 1956) (Fig 83; Table 36). In addition, there was one

scraper/burin (FFN 5000) which has been discussed with the scrapers (above). Also present were four so-called 'Corbiac' burins (Bordes 1970a). These pieces all had their proximal ends removed by a characteristic transverse blow, probably by striking the blank against an anvil. Refitting group 65 (Fig 84) consisted of a 'Corbiac' burin and the conjoining 'spall', and clearly illustrates the 'Corbiac' technique. Another 'Corbiac' burin (FFN 370, Fig 83) displays spalling to one of the lateral edges probably caused by the 'Corbiac' blow rather than deliberate removal.

In this report, 'Corbiac' burins which had no further burin spall removals are not classed as 'true' burins, and for statistical purposes are included in the category of miscellaneous retouched pieces. However, it is clear that this technique was used in the manufacture or reuse of a number of the 'true' burins discussed in this section.

None of the 21 true burins were burnt. Two of the burins were on the proximal end of the blank (one was on a truncation and the other unclassified). The 19 other burins were all made on the distal ends of blanks. There was a marked preference for using blades (18) rather than flakes (3) as blanks for burin production.

Eight of the burins were complete, although refitting restored FFN 5699 (Fig 83) to its original length, allowing quantitative data to be collected from nine examples. These data are summarised in Table 37, and generally reflect the blade-like nature of the original blanks. As with scrapers, the mean thickness of burins was considerably greater than that of unretouched flake and blade blanks.

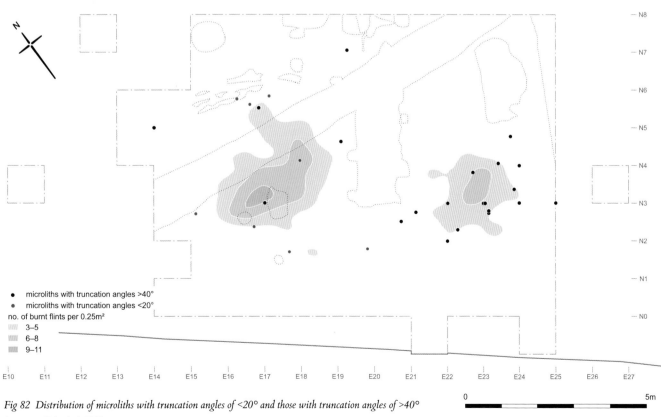

Fig 82 Distribution of microliths with truncation angles of <20° and those with truncation angles of >40° in scatter C (scale 1:100)

Lithic material

scatter C west

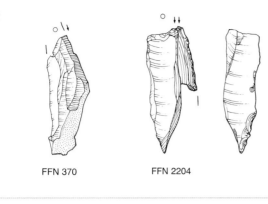

FFN 370   FFN 2204

scatter C east

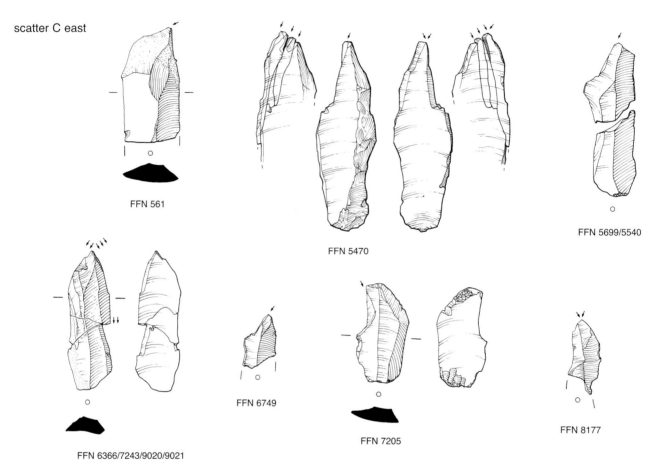

FFN 561

FFN 5470

FFN 5699/5540

FFN 6749

FFN 7205

FFN 8177

FFN 6366/7243/9020/9021

Fig 83 Burins and burin spalls: scatter C west – FFN 370 ('Corbiac') and 2204/4033; scatter C east – FFN 561, 5470, 5699/5540, 6366/7243/9020/9021 (RG7), 6749, 7205 and 8177 (scale 1:2)

Table 36 Composition of burin assemblage in scatter C

Type	C west Complete	C west Broken	C east Complete	C east Broken	Total C Complete & broken
Dihedral burins					
– on break	0	1	1	2	4
– on natural surface	1	2	0	2	5
– symmetrical	0	2	0	2	4
Subtotal	1	5	1	6	13
Truncation burins	1	2	1	1	5
Unclassified burins & fragments	0	0	2	1	3
Total	2	7	4	8	21

'Corbiac' spall

'Corbiac' burin

Fig 84 Refitting group 65: 'Corbiac' burin and spall (scale 1:2)

Table 37 Quantitative data for burins (n=9) in scatter C

	Range	Average	Standard deviation
Length (mm)	99–35	67.2	17.7
Width (mm)	33–16	25.0	5.6
Thickness (mm)	13–5	8.5	2.0

Table 38 Quantitative data for burin spalls in scatter C

Type	No. (with retouch/burnt)
Primary spalls	15 (7 with retouch, 1 burnt)
Secondary spalls	11 (1 with retouch)
Total	26 (8 with retouch, 1 burnt)

Seventeen burins were uncorticated, two had less than 25% and three had 25–50% of their dorsal surface corticated. These observations together with the metrical data would accord with the selection of larger, thicker and more robust blade blanks such as FFN 5470 (Fig 83), a symmetrical dihedral burin supported on a large crested blade.

The only burin on a concave truncation (FFN 1238) was a multiple burin. One of the truncation burins (FFN 2204, Fig 83) had dorsal semi-abrupt retouch on a distal lateral margin.

The dihedral types showed a slight tendency for utilising natural surfaces (Table 36). One of the burins on a natural surface (FFN 7205, Fig 83) had dorsal scalar retouch at both the proximal and distal ends.

The dihedral burin FFN 8177 (Fig 83) was formed at the distal end of a blade segment which itself was a 'Corbiac' burin spall. The use of the transverse blow to break blanks or reuse burins to manufacture other burins is discussed below. It is, therefore, possible that the two unmodified 'Corbiac' burins discussed above may have been intended as blanks for burin manufacture, although in the absence of further modification, this cannot be proven.

BURIN SPALLS

The identification and classification of debitage as burin spalls was rigorous, and there are doubtless some pieces classed as debitage which may have been burin spalls. A total of 26 pieces were regarded as definite, and their composition is shown in Table 38.

Retouch on burin spalls has been recognised as aiding the successful removal of a long spall (Barton 1992, 113), and this feature is more prevalent in the primary spalls from scatter C (eg FFN 4033, Fig 83). In addition to the 'true' burin spalls, there were three 'Corbiac' burin spalls.

BURIN PRODUCTION AND DISTRIBUTION

The majority (13) of burins were located in scatter C east, with a distinct cluster to the east and south-east of the eastern hearth itself (Fig 85). The burins in scatter C west were located to the north-west and south-east of the western hearth, with a single example located centrally. Truncation and dihedral burins occurred in both C west and C east, although symmetrical dihedral burins only occurred in C east.

Seven of the eight retouched burin spalls were located in C

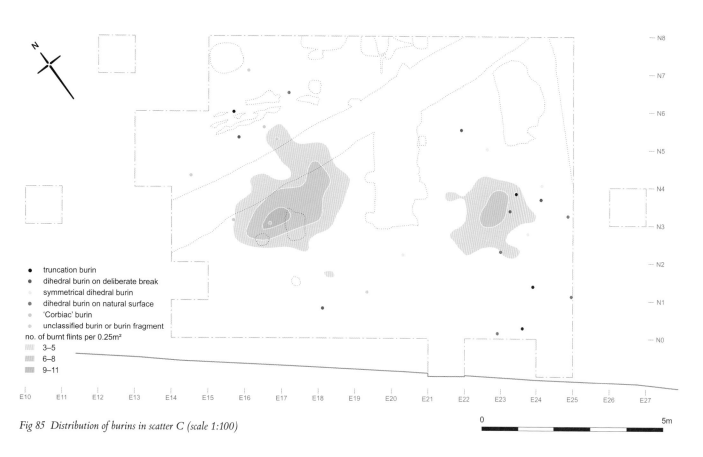

truncation burin
dihedral burin on deliberate break
symmetrical dihedral burin
dihedral burin on natural surface
'Corbiac' burin
unclassified burin or burin fragment
no. of burnt flints per 0.25m²
3–5
6–8
9–11

Fig 85 Distribution of burins in scatter C (scale 1:100)

0   5m

west, revealing a preference for the technique in this area (Fig 86). The majority of secondary burin spalls (seven) were located near the eastern hearth, whereas the primary spalls were predominantly around the western hearth. Numerically,

however, primary burin spalls were fairly evenly distributed between the two hearth areas.

Fig 87 shows that at a small scale of analysis, burins and spalls were slightly offset from each other. This pattern suggests

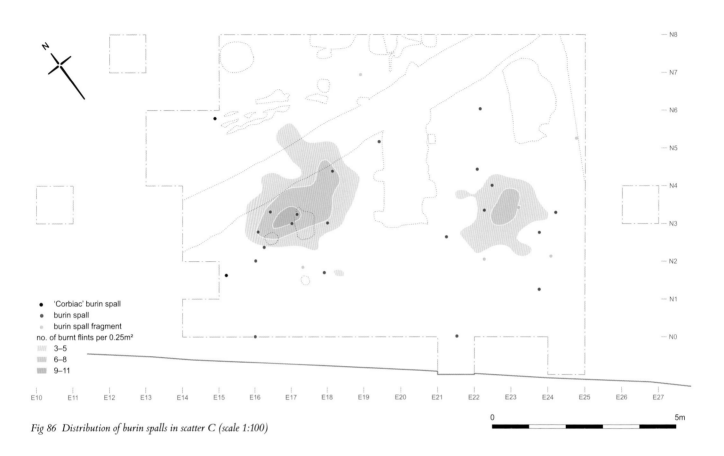

Fig 86 Distribution of burin spalls in scatter C (scale 1:100)

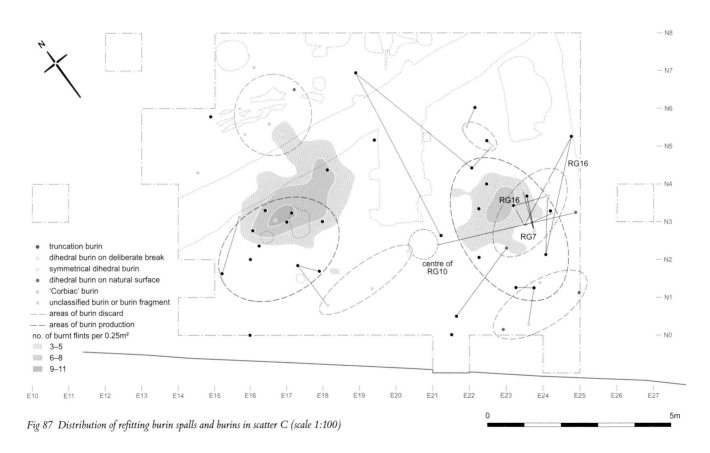

Fig 87 Distribution of refitting burin spalls and burins in scatter C (scale 1:100)

a subtle shift of perhaps a metre or two between the burin manufacturing areas and the utilisation/discard areas. Refitting and use-wear analysis tended to confirm that burins were used and discarded within the space of a metre or two from where they were manufactured. For example, two burins (FFN 561 (Fig 83) and 1238) were refitted back to their original knapping clusters. The double burin on a truncation FFN 1238 (Fig 88) was found within a metre of two large flakes/blades which immediately preceded its removal in the reduction sequence. Also lying within one or two metres of FFN 1238 were three burin spalls which refitted to both the burin facets on the double burin. Use-wear analysis (Chapter 6.4) suggested that both burin facets had been used for scraping bone: thus the process of manufacture, use and discard was very localised.

Burin FFN 561 (a burin on an unmodified surface; Fig 83) was refitted to refitting group 10 (Fig 106), an extensive knapping cluster which also produced a broken 'C' type microlith and a bruised blade (*lame mâchurée*). In this instance, use-wear indicated that the burin was unused, and the piece was found *c* 4m from the centre of the knapping cluster. This relatively large distance may be explained by post-depositional factors such as trampling, bioturbation, water action and the like. However, it is also possible that the burin was deemed unsuitable for use, as the piece was broken in half with the proximal end missing. Its location away from the knapping scatter may, therefore, be the result of 'toss' discard.

Seven other burins were refitted to burin spalls or conjoined to blade segments. Use-wear analysis suggested that multiple removal of burin spalls from a burin occurred during the original manufacture of the piece and did not represent 'resharpening' of the tool, as only two burin spalls showed signs of utilisation.

When 'resharpening' of burins did occur, it took the form of removing the entire end of the blank which supported the burin (often using a 'Corbiac' transverse blow) and manufacturing a new burin on the platform provided on the break surface of the remaining portion of the blank. Refitting group 7 (Fig 83) typifies this approach. In this case a symmetrical dihedral burin on the distal end of a large blade (FFN 9020) was snapped off by the use of a 'Corbiac' blow. The product was a waste blade segment (FFN 6366) and the remainder of the blade blank. The break surface of the remnant blank was then used to support a burin (FFN 7243) which was manufactured by the removal of several burin spalls, one of which (FFN 9021) was refitted. The proximal end of the second burin (FFN 7243) is missing, and from the break pattern there it is clear that this in turn was also snapped off the remaining blank by a 'Corbiac' blow, and the whole process was probably repeated. Use-wear analysis confirms that both burins FFN 7243 and 9020 were utilised for grooving a medium/hard substance, in the case of FFN 7243 antler, while the refitting spall FFN 9021 was not utilised. Refitting group 7, therefore, illustrates a cycle of use, 'resharpening' by deliberate breakage and removal of burin spalls, reuse and probable 'resharpening'. Once again, this cycle took place within a very confined area of *c* 1.5m².

Axes, rough-outs and axe debitage

Table 39 shows the axe and axe debitage component of scatter C. A further broken axe was recovered from above the black humic layer (SU50) in the vicinity of E16N03. Judging by its

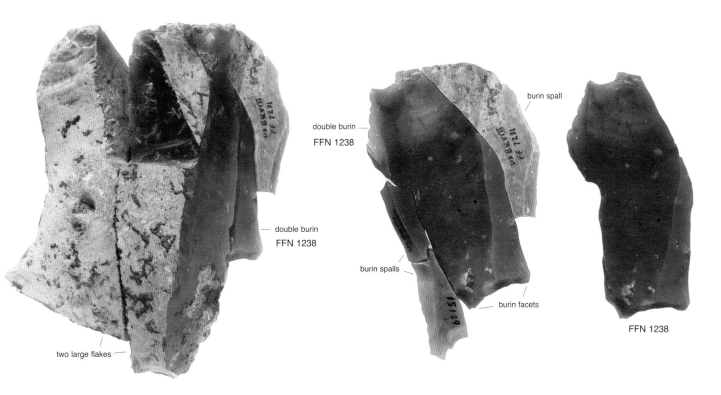

Fig 88 Refitting group 16: large double burin on truncation (FFN 1238), spalls and associated knapping debris (scale 1:1)

Table 39 Composition and condition of axe and axe debitage assemblage in scatter C

Type	Definite	Possible	Complete	Broken	Subtotal C west	Subtotal C east	Total C
Axes	2	0	0	2	2	0	2
Axe rough-outs	1	1	0	2	2	0	2
Unstratified axes	1	0	0	1	1	0	1
Axe thinning flakes	14	72	70	16	70	16	86
Axe sharpening flakes	15	2	14	3	16	1	17
Misc axe flakes	3	0	2	1	3	0	3
Total	36	75	86	25	94	17	111

condition, this axe may have originally been stratified in the main scatter, but was displaced by the cutting of the later prehistoric ditch.

It is likely that many more flakes which have been classed as ordinary debitage were the product of axe manufacture, but they could not be classified as such with any confidence. For example, refitting group 14 consisted of two large flakes (FFN 5462 and 5441, Fig 89) which showed signs of being the product of bi-facial working, possibly the result of producing an axe rough-out. Unfortunately, they could also have been produced as a result of the preliminary shaping and decortication of a nodule which was further reduced as a bi-polar core. Similarly, some of the possible axe thinning flakes

listed in Table 39 could have been the by-product of core reduction, for instance by posterior flaking of an opposed platform core. However, Fig 89 does show four yellow flakes (FFN 1203, 1119, 1072 and 1125) which, due to their curvature, thinness, evidence of previous flake removals of the dorsal surface, and butt morphology, can confidently be attributed to the process of axe-thinning. Table 39 shows that the majority of thinning and sharpening flakes were complete, whereas all the axes and rough-outs were broken.

Two finished axes represented by the fragments FFN 8797 and 2435 (Fig 89) were present in the stratified assemblage, both being broken in half. FFN 8797 had been reused as a blade core, while FFN 2435 was not further utilised as a core, probably due

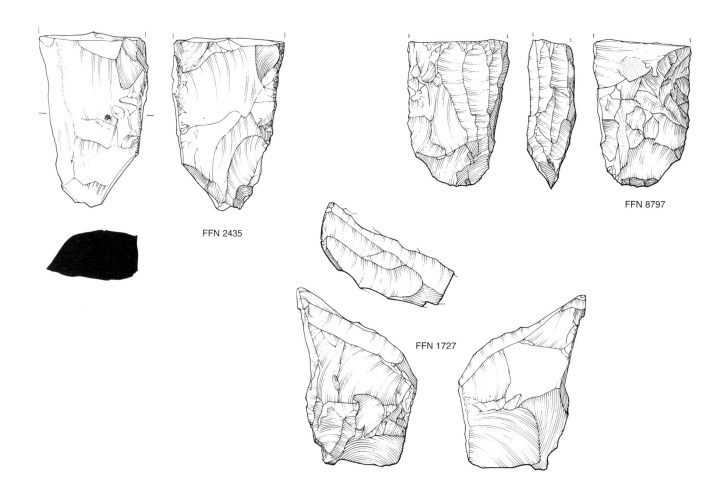

FFN 2435

FFN 8797

FFN 1727

Fig 89 Axes: FFN 2435, 8797 and rough-out FFN 1727 (scale 1:2); axe debitage: possible preliminary axe thinning flakes FFN 5462 and 5441 (RG14); and definite thinning flakes FFN 1203, 1119, 1072 and 1125 (scale 1:1)

to the large chert inclusions. Refitting analysis together with counts of axe debitage flakes strongly suggests that axe FFN 2435 was manufactured on site, while FFN 8797 was not (below). Like axe FFN 2435, the two axe rough-outs (eg FFN 1727, Fig 89) were both manufactured from yellow flint with large chert inclusions. In common with both the axes, the two rough-outs were also broken in half; following breakage, both were reused as cores.

DISTRIBUTION AND PRODUCTION

Fig 92, Fig 93 and Table 39 show the distribution of the entire axe and axe debitage assemblage. The broken axes and axe rough-outs were concentrated in scatter C west. The concentration of thinning and transverse sharpening flakes to the south of the western hearth suggests that this was the main axe manufacturing area, with a small scatter to the south of the eastern hearth.

The large size range of the thinning flakes (Table 40) suggests that the (predominantly yellow) flakes (Table 41) represent the entire process of axe manufacture. For example, refitting group 36 (Table 40; Fig 90), together with pieces such as FFN 7046, was clearly from the early stages of axe thinning. Other, smaller examples and the transverse sharpening flakes were obviously from the latter stages of the manufacturing process. Finally, single thinning flakes were refitted to axe FFN

2435 (Fig 91) and rough-out 1727 (Fig 89), which links these pieces with the manufacturing process and demonstrates the validity of the putative axe manufacturing area (Fig 92). In both

Table 40 Quantitative data for axe thinning flakes (n=67) in scatter C

	Range	Average	Standard deviation
Length (mm)	83–19	42.85	12.68
Width (mm)	138–16	49.35	20.48
Thickness (mm)	20–2	5.91	3.81

Table 41 Colour variations within axe and axe debitage assemblage in scatter C

Colour	Sharpening flakes	Thinning flakes	Misc	Axes & rough-outs	Total
Grey	1	1	0	0	2
Brown	4	19	0	0	23
Mottled brown	4	5	3	1	13
Yellow	5	46	0	3	54
Grey-black	0	1	0	0	1
Grey-brown	1	4	0	0	5
Yellow-brown	2	10	0	0	12
Total	17	86	3	4	110

FFN 5441

FFN 5462

FFN 1119

FFN 1125

FFN 1203

FFN 1072

thinning flake

FFN 2435

Fig 90 Refitting group 36: axe thinning flake cluster from scatter C west (scale 1:1)

Fig 91 Refitting group 66: axe FFN 2435 and conjoining thinning flake from scatter C west (scale 1:2)

cases the refits showed that thinning took place before breakage and abandonment of the piece.

The nature of the utilised raw material is such that a single nodule may produce blanks of varying colours (eg refitting group 10, Fig 104). Nevertheless, Table 41 suggests patterns in the manufacture, use and reuse of axes. These can be summarised as follows.

1) Axes and rough-outs were manufactured in C west (Fig 92). For instance, a single thinning flake refitted to axe FFN 2435 (Fig 91) demonstrates that this piece was manufactured on site, and this accords with the high number of yellow axe debitage flakes. Like axe FFN 8797, the other half of axe FFN 2435 was probably utilised as a core, since it was not present in the assemblage. Fig 93 shows that the yellow flakes were clustered to the south of the western hearth, and manufacture probably took place here. A few possible thinning flakes were situated adjacent to the hearth in C east, suggesting possible axe manufacture in this area (Fig 92). However, as noted above, they are small in number and could have been produced from flaking the posterior of some of the opposed platform cores found in this area.

2) A small number of axes may have been brought on to the site in a complete state, resharpened and then removed. Thus, there remain a low number of sharpening flakes and a few thinning flakes of colours such as the various greys from clearly finished axes but for which no corresponding axes were recovered. For example, two brown refitting sharpening flakes, both of which showed evidence of use (refitting group 14, Fig 89), were located just to the east of the western hearth (Fig 93). As no axe corresponding to this colour was present in the assemblage, it is possible to suggest that following use and

resharpening the axe was removed from the excavated area for use elsewhere.

3) At least one complete axe (refitting group 3, FFN 8797; Fig 89) which was brought to the site broke in half. Refitting demonstrates that many of the mottled brown flakes were the product of this broken axe, and it is possible to suggest that all the axe debitage of this colour was the product not of manufacture but of the reuse of the axe (refitting group 3) as a blade core (Fig 93; Fig 114). No true axe thinning flakes of the same colour as this group were present in the assemblage. Use-wear analysis suggests that axe FFN 8797 had been used, although it is not known if this activity took place prior to its arrival on site. Refitting shows that the axe was originally quite substantial and demonstrated that it snapped in half (perhaps during use?) on the site. Both halves of the axe were then reused as cores. One half remained largely intact, and refitting illustrates the modifications made to turn the axe fragment into a blade core, such as cresting along the axe edge and some thinning. A number of blades and bladelets were produced, including one which served as a microlith blank, as evidenced by refitting microburin FFN 1503 to the core (Fig 114). The other half of the axe appears to have been completely reduced, and apart from the two conjoining flakes (FFN 2285 and 4484) no other fragments of this half of the artefact have been definitely identified. However, one of the small opposed platform cores may represent the worked-out remnants of the original axe fragment. In addition, refitting group 4 (Fig 94), which consists of two axe sharpening flakes and a thinning flake reused as a scraper, may represent the butt end of the worked-down axe fragment. This cannot be confirmed, since there was no join between groups 3 and 4.

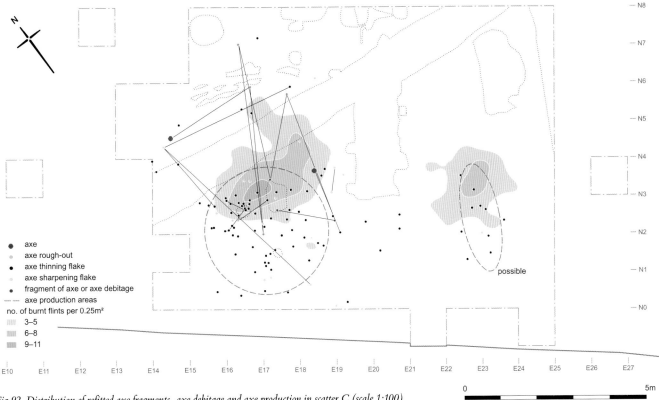

Fig 92 *Distribution of refitted axe fragments, axe debitage and axe production in scatter C (scale 1:100)*

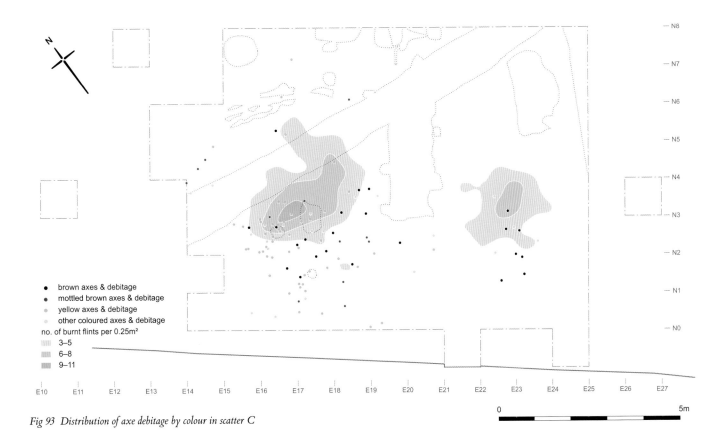

Fig 93 *Distribution of axe debitage by colour in scatter C*

In conclusion, refitting and distribution plots suggest that the area to the south of the western hearth (Fig 92) was the location of the manufacture and resharpening of several (predominantly yellow) axes and rough-outs, of which only three examples were recovered from the site. Complete axes were also brought to the site, sharpened, used and resharpened. At least one of these broke and the fragments were reused as cores, producing at least one microlith and a scraper.

Fig 94 *Refitting group 4: two axe sharpening flakes and a scraper from scatter C west (scale 2:1)*

Notched pieces

The assemblage contained 17 notched pieces, of which seven were flakes, nine blades and one was unclassified. Only four of the pieces were complete. Thus, notched pieces covered a wide variety of shapes and sizes, with probably an equally wide range of functions. Some were used for scraping a hard material such as wood. There were no denticulates in the assemblage, although FFN 2377 (Fig 95) had two contiguous notches at its distal end.

DISTRIBUTION
Fig 96 shows a fairly tight grouping of notched pieces around the southern part of the western hearth. In contrast, the remaining notched pieces had a more dispersed distribution in the eastern part of the site.

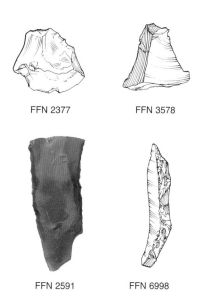

FFN 2377   FFN 3578

FFN 2591   FFN 6998

Fig 95 *Notched pieces FNN 2377 and 3578, awl FNN 2591 and piercer FNN 6998 (scale 1:2, photograph 1:1)*

Awls and piercers

There was only one awl in the assemblage, FFN 2591 (Fig 95). This consisted of a broken blade mid-section with abrupt retouch on both margins, and is similar to the many examples from Star Carr (Clark 1954, fig 39).

Five pieces were interpreted as piercers, although all were atypical. All had abrupt retouch on one rather than two margins. The retouch was not extensive, and all five examples appeared to be opportunistic adaptations rather than the deliberate production of formal tool types. Use-wear analysis indicates that three of the pieces were utilised, two of them for piercing hide and boring wood (eg FFN 6998, Fig 95)

DISTRIBUTION
Fig 96 shows that four of the five piercers were associated with the eastern hearth, while the awl fragment was located near the western hearth.

Miscellaneous retouched pieces

There were a total of 107 miscellaneous retouched pieces in the assemblage (eg Fig 97). This class of artefact includes unclassified retouched tools and fragments, retouched flakes and blades, unclassified retouched fragments and other pieces that do not fall into the preceding categories (Table 42). Possible examples of 'spontaneous retouch' (Newcomer 1976), trample, trowel and post-depositional edge damage have been excluded wherever possible. Nevertheless, there remains a possibility that what appears as retouch on some of the pieces in this category was not deliberately produced.

Unclassified tools, tool fragments and tool debitage

Seventeen of the retouched pieces probably represent broken fragments of formal tool and tool debitage types. For example,

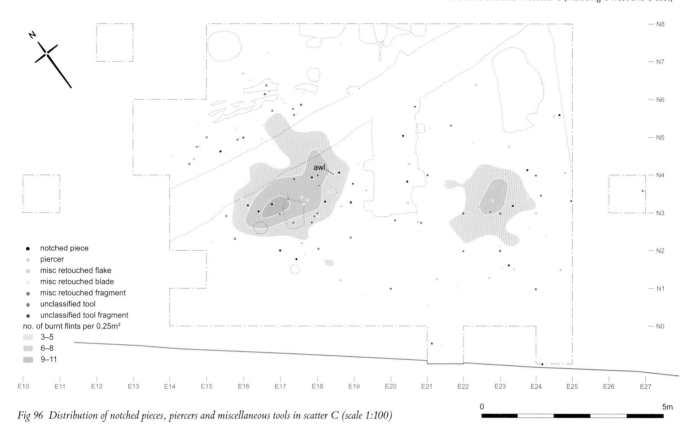

● notched piece
○ piercer
◐ misc retouched flake
○ misc retouched blade
◑ misc retouched fragment
● unclassified tool
● unclassified tool fragment
no. of burnt flints per 0.25m²
▨ 3–5
▨ 6–8
▨ 9–11

E10 E11 E12 E13 E14 E15 E16 E17 E18 E19 E20 E21 E22 E23 E24 E25 E26 E27

Fig 96 Distribution of notched pieces, piercers and miscellaneous tools in scatter C (scale 1:100)

0   5m

FFN 14024 could have been a broken distally retouched microlith (above, 'Microliths and microburins') and FFN 2474 (Fig 97) could represent a large burin spall. However, none of these pieces could be identified with a sufficient degree of certainty to allow these classifications.

Retouched blades and flakes

Sixty-six pieces appeared to have been deliberately retouched and utilised as tools in their own right. In these cases, the retouch was usually ventral, semi-abrupt or abrupt and confined to the lateral margins, for example on FFN 6692, 2732 (Fig 97),

FFN 2474   FFN 2732   FFN 6692

Fig 97 Miscellaneous retouched pieces and unclassified tool fragments: unclassified tool fragment FNN 2474; retouched blades FNN 2732 and 6692 (scale 1:2)

2882 and 8451. Retouch at the distal end of the latter may have served as an aid to hand-holding the piece.

Unclassified miscellaneous retouched pieces and fragments

On 24 pieces the retouch was confined to small areas of the margins or proximal or distal ends. These were difficult to interpret in a functional sense. In addition, there were fragments which were too small to fully interpret.

Within this heterogeneous category of artefacts, breakage rates were high although only three of the pieces were burnt (Table 42). The quantitative data for the above categories of artefacts was similarly wide-ranging, with no discernible standardisation of dimensions.

DISTRIBUTION

The unclassified tools and tool fragments were located around the two hearth sites. The retouched blades and unclassified

Table 42 Composition of miscellaneous retouched tools assemblage in scatter C

Type	Total	Broken	Burnt
Unclassified tools	1	1	0
Unclassified tool fragments	16	16	0
Retouched flakes	23	11	1
Retouched blades	43	24	2
Unclassified retouched fragments	24	24	0
Total	107	76	3

retouched fragments tended to cluster on the western hearth, with a more diffuse distribution around the eastern hearth. Retouched flakes were also more diffusely distributed over the site (Fig 96).

Intentional breakages

Using only the 'contact feature' criteria outlined by Bergman et al (1987), nine pieces could confidently be identified as having been broken intentionally. Features which result from flexion breakage have not been considered, as these can also result from accidental breaks (ibid).

The total excludes tools such as burins which show evidence of deliberate breakage and reuse, but includes the two 'Corbiac' burins which had not been further modified by burin spall removal. This total of deliberately broken pieces is as follows:

2 'Corbiac' burins, one with conjoining proximal end (refitting group 65);
1 distal and 1 proximal blade segment;
2 conjoining blade segments (refitting group 50);
2 conjoining flake fragments (refitting group 52).

Refitting group 65 consisted of a 'Corbiac' burin and conjoining proximal end. The 'Corbiac' technique of breaking blanks has been discussed above ('Burins and burin spalls') and will not be elaborated on here.

Refitting group 50 consisted of two conjoining blade segments which displayed cones of percussion on both the dorsal and ventral surfaces at the break. Hence the piece was apparently broken by a blow from the dorsal surface while resting on an anvil.

Refitting group 52 consisted of a flake intentionally broken by the delivery of a blow to the ventral surface. Some modification to the uncorticated margin at the proximal end was evident, as was the presence of small burin-like facets on the corticated margin of the distal segment at the break. This latter feature has been noted by Barton (1992, 131) among the Lateglacial assemblage from Hengistbury Head, Dorset.

DISTRIBUTION

The intentionally broken pieces were located on the periphery of the two hearths (Fig 98).

Utilised pieces

There were a total of 50 pieces in the assemblage which, although showing little or no deliberate modification, can be classed as *a posteriori* tools (*sensu* Bordes 1970b) on the basis that they show signs of utilisation. Table 43 shows the composition of the utilised assemblage. Two of the broken edge-damaged blades were

Table 43 Composition of utilised debitage assemblage in scatter C

Type	C west	C east
Rubbed pieces	0	5
Edge-damaged blades	16	12
Edge-damaged flakes	4	1
Edge-damaged fragments	1	0
Bruised blades	0	5
Bruised flakes	0	3
Battered pieces	1	2
Total	22	28

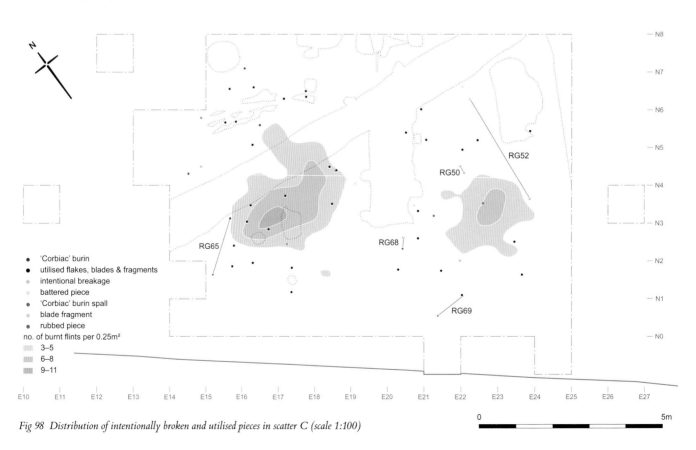

Fig 98 Distribution of intentionally broken and utilised pieces in scatter C (scale 1:100)

conjoined (refitting group 10). Only one of the 50 utilised pieces (a battered core) was burnt.

PIECES WITH ROUNDED OR HEAVILY 'RUBBED' LATERAL OR TERMINAL MARGINS

Five blade fragments had rounded, smoothed and rubbed edges (Fig 99). Four had this feature on a lateral margin, while one had a rubbed proximal and lateral margin. Despite all five pieces consisting of blade segments, it is clear that all were originally of a similar size and shape. The average width of the five was 17.2mm with a standard deviation of 1.5mm, while the average thickness was 4.6mm with a standard deviation of 0.5mm. Only one piece was corticated, and this to a very minor degree. Thus, this category of artefact seems to have required the selection of parallel-sided blades of a standard width and thickness, produced during the main phase of core reduction.

EDGE-DAMAGED PIECES

The edge damage on these pieces took the form of discontinuous, uneven 'retouch' on lateral or break margins. The damage was frequently invasive and localised along a lateral edge.

Edge damage could be confidently attributed to contemporary utilisation on 34 flakes, blades and fragments (Table 43). A great many more pieces (285) had edge damage possibly caused by utilisation; however, the damage on these pieces may also have been caused by post-depositional movement, trampling and trowel damage, and they are therefore treated as debitage.

Among the 34 definite edge-damaged pieces, there was a bias towards blades rather than flakes (Table 43). Breakage was fairly high among the blades, with only 11 complete examples.

When compared with the quantitative data from unretouched blade blanks, Table 44 suggests a tendency towards the utilisation of slightly larger, more robust blades.

BRUISED BLADES AND FLAKES

Five blades and three flakes exhibited very distinctive edge damage. Termed *lames et éclats mâchurés* (Bordes 1967, 30; Barton 1986), the damage on these pieces had a typically 'bruised' and battered appearance. In all cases the damage was localised on the lateral margins of large, thick blanks (below), usually with steep edges. This damage was invasive, stepped and scalar, and was usually (though not always) confined to the ventral surface (Fig 100). Experimental work suggests that such damage can be replicated by chopping bone or antler (Barton 1986). The pattern of damage on the pieces in scatter C is very similar to that on the single example from scatter A.

Seven of the eight bruised pieces were corticated (eg FNN 8135 and 8189, Fig 100), which together with their large dimensions suggests that they were produced during the earlier stages of core reduction (as confirmed by refitting in the case of FNN 8189; Fig 104, d). Three of the bruised pieces (all blades) were incomplete (eg FNN 8364, Fig 100), thus making quantitative analysis difficult. Table 45 contains the metrical data for the five complete examples, and it can be seen that large, thick blanks were preferred. On average, the bruised pieces were larger than those blades with edge damage described in the preceding section (Table 44). If the incomplete examples are included, the length range increases to 108–53mm.

BATTERED PIECES

There were three artefacts in this category, all of them cores (Table 43). A small opposed platform prismatic bladelets core (FFN 5152, Fig 100) shows evidence of crushing and battering on one of the platforms. This is the only one of the cores which is in a slightly rolled condition. Two other opposed platform cores display heavy crushing and step-fracturing along a lateral edge (eg FFN 8243, Fig 100; this core had also been heated). These patterns of damage are not attempts at cresting, and may have been produced by reusing the cores as hammer stones or choppers.

DISTRIBUTION OF RUBBED BLADES AND BATTERED CORES

The rubbed blades formed a small group located just to the west of the eastern hearth (Fig 98). Two of the pieces were situated within a few centimetres of each other.

Two of the rubbed blades were conjoined to their respective broken blade segments (refitting groups 68 and 69). The

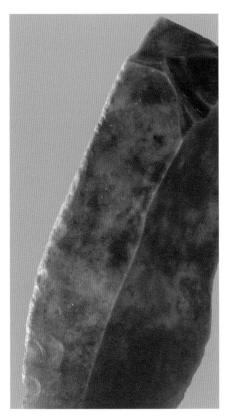

Fig 99 Refitting group 69, close-up view of rubbed edge

Table 44 Quantitative data for edge-damaged blades (n=11) in scatter C

	Range	Average	Standard deviation
Length (mm)	84–31	66.45	15.42
Width (mm)	28–12	20.91	5.68
Thickness (mm)	9–3	6.36	2.06

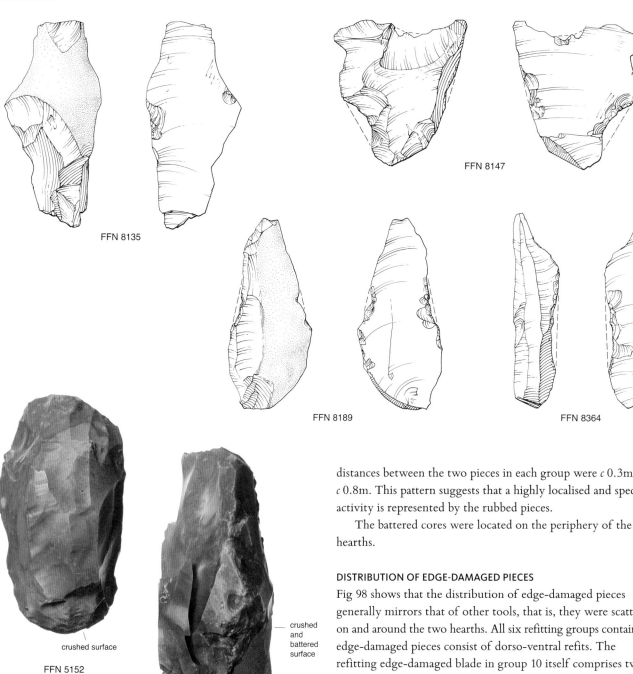

FFN 8135

FFN 8147

FFN 8189

FFN 8364

crushed surface

FFN 5152

crushed and battered surface

FFN 8246

Fig 100 Utilised pieces: lames mâchurées FFN 8135, 8147, 8189 and 8364; battered pieces FFN 5152 and 8246 (scale 1:2, photographs 1:1)

Table 45 Quantitative data for bruised pieces (n=5) in scatter C

	Range	Average	Standard deviation
Length (mm)	98–61	77.40	11.88
Width (mm)	77–26	45.80	17.12
Thickness (mm)	18–11	13.60	2.65

distances between the two pieces in each group were *c* 0.3m and *c* 0.8m. This pattern suggests that a highly localised and specific activity is represented by the rubbed pieces.

The battered cores were located on the periphery of the hearths.

DISTRIBUTION OF EDGE-DAMAGED PIECES

Fig 98 shows that the distribution of edge-damaged pieces generally mirrors that of other tools, that is, they were scattered on and around the two hearths. All six refitting groups containing edge-damaged pieces consist of dorso-ventral refits. The refitting edge-damaged blade in group 10 itself comprises two conjoining edge-damaged blade segments (FFN 7838 and 8245).

The close proximity of the pieces within the dorso-ventral refitting groups suggests that the edge-damaged blades were selected, utilised and discarded very close to where they were knapped. The edge damage on the conjoining blade fragments in group 10 suggests that the break occurred either during use or following discard. There is no evidence that this piece was intentionally broken (*sensu* Bergman et al 1987).

DISTRIBUTION OF BRUISED BLADES AND FLAKES

Four of the seven bruised blades and flakes (*lames et éclats mâchurés*) cluster very tightly on *c* E20.75N02.75, at the centre of SAS 3. The remaining three pieces were more widely dispersed, two *c* 3m to the north and one at the far eastern edge of the excavated area (Fig 101). One *lame mâchurée* (FFN 8189, Fig 100) has been refitted to refitting group 10 (Fig 104), which forms a major part of SAS 3. Refitting group 10 is centred on the concentration of *lames mâchurées*, and it seems that they were

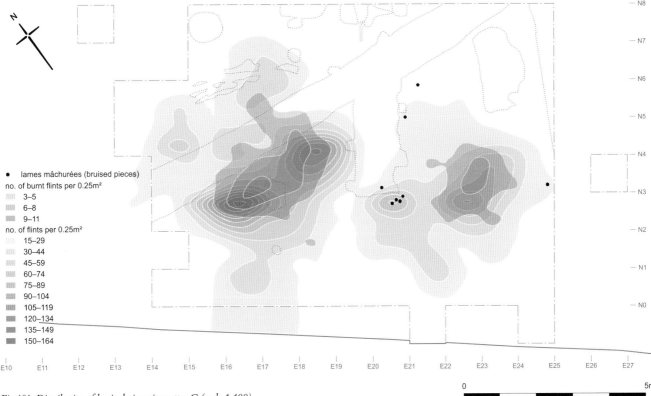

Fig 101 *Distribution of bruised pieces in scatter C (scale 1:100)*

used and discarded in close proximity to their point of manufacture. This contrasts with the burin and 'C' type microlith which were also the products of refitting group 10, but were found a greater distance away from the centre of the knapping scatter. As noted above, seven of the eight bruised pieces were corticated and one of them was crested, suggesting that the blanks derive from the earlier stages of core reduction. FFN 8189 is somewhat anomalous, in that although a large corticated blade, it was produced after substantial reduction of the core had already taken place (Fig 104, c).

3.6 Flint refitting and core reduction processes

It was realised from an early stage in the project that refitting would have a key part to play in the analysis of the Three Ways Wharf assemblages (Chapter 1.4). However, refitting is an extremely complex, time-consuming and therefore expensive exercise. Funding was made available for limited refitting on the strict understanding that:

1) refitting should be aimed at studying the production, use and discard of retouched tools;
2) core reduction sequences were not to be reconstructed;
3) no attempt should be made to establish refits between scatters A and C.

Consequently, of the total of 78 refitting groups from all scatters at Three Ways Wharf, only three contained more than

ten constituent refits. One of the few sequences which reconstructed a large part of the reduction process, refitting group 10 (Fig 104), illustrates the futility of separating the study of the core reduction process from the manufacture of retouched tools. In this instance, it was possible to demonstrate that one of the highly distinctive bi-truncated microliths, a *lame mâchurée* and a burin were all produced from the same block, and were thus contemporary. This is the first time that these three classes of tools have been directly linked, which would never have occurred if the core reduction sequence had not been reconstructed. Nevertheless, sufficient data has been gleaned from the refitting process to allow a significant contribution to be made to the study of the assemblages.

A total of 315 flints were refitted in 78 refitting groups, the spatial distribution of which is shown in Fig 102. Of this total, 20 refitting groups were composed solely of conjoins (ie rejoined broken fragments of artefacts), which are indicative of breakage either during or following the production of the artefact. The remaining 58 groups contained refits between dorsal and ventral surfaces of artefacts, which are evidence of the core reduction and tool manufacturing process.

Refitting data are mentioned and included in numerous sections of this report where it was thought most appropriate, rather than this analysis being dealt with in isolation. For example, refitting data are utilised in the sections on site formation and taphonomy (Chapter 5), retouched tool production and distribution, and the spatial analysis and interpretation of human behaviour (Chapter 6). This section concentrates on the evidence from refitting for the study of core reduction strategies employed at Three Ways Wharf.

Fig 102 *Distribution of all refits in scatters A and C (scale 1:200)*

Core reduction processes

Refitting allows the complete cycle of lithic production, from selection of raw material to core discard, to be reconstructed and provides a further classificatory tool when comparing variability between assemblages (Barton 1992, 139). Thus, general technological similarities and contrasts emerge that may not be visible in individual pieces. Distribution plots of each refitting group mentioned in the following text are used along with photographs to illustrate the points made there.

Raw material selection

SCATTER A

In scatter A large gravel cobbles seem to have been selected in order to produce the larger blade blanks required. Due to the relatively poor quality of the available flint, some testing of the raw material seems to have been carried out. Refitting group 18 (Fig 168) is a large flint nodule which had been struck and shattered into 20 pieces. A few of these, such as FFN 103 and 1317, had been further modified by flake removals and the attempted preparation of striking platforms. However, the poor quality of the flint and the small size of the shattered fragments led to the abandonment of this process. In addition to refitting group 18, a single component of refitting group 45 (Fig 48; Fig 103) was also present in scatter A, while the other two nodule fragments were located in scatter C east.

SCATTER C

The smaller size of blades and crested blades in scatter C west compared to C east, together with variations in raw material colour, suggests that smaller nodules (possibly from a different source) were chosen for reduction in this area. Larger nodules were utilised in C east, as evidenced by refitting groups 10 and 30 (Figs 104–7). In C east the nodules seem to take three main forms: cylindrical, tabular and irregular. The initial preparation of the first two types is discussed below. The distribution of smashed and partially worked nodules suggests that large irregular nodules were commonly broken into smaller fragments in C east. This may represent the breakage of nodules used as hammer stones, but a number of cores were manufactured on these broken fragments, suggesting at least an opportunistic exploitation of raw material and at most a deliberate strategy of testing and selecting raw material.

In C west, a higher proportion of cores utilised large flakes in addition to smashed fragments. The resulting cores were small and often contained inclusions, making them of inferior quality.

Initial preparation

SCATTER A

The amount and type of preparation was dependent on the original shape of the nodule. The original nodule represented by refitting group 21 (Fig 108; Fig 109) would probably have

Fig 103 Distribution of refitting group 45 (scale 1:200)

been tabular in form, and thus suitable for use as a blade core with minimal preparation of the two platforms. The edge of the nodule would have provided a convenient keel, again with minimal need for decorticating or cresting as evidenced by the core retaining cortex over almost the entire surface apart from the flaking face.

More irregular-shaped nodules would have needed more extensive pre-shaping. Refitting group 23 (Fig 109; Fig 110) consists of a large flake with a cortical covering, and illustrates the approach of decorticating and pre-forming the nodule. Soft hammers were preferred to hard hammers for initial preparation, with the latter decreasing in importance as core reduction progressed.

SCATTER C

In scatter C, as with scatter A, the degree and form of initial core preparation differed according to the size and shape of the nodule. The proportions of primary, secondary and tertiary flakes within C west and C east suggest that initial decortication was carried out to a greater degree in C east than in C west, although to a lesser degree in comparison with scatter A (Table 46).

In scatter C east, as in scatter A, soft hammers were preferred for initial core preparation (Fig 40). However, the percentage of hard hammer usage is higher in C east than in scatter A, and remains relatively constant around 20% as flaking proceeds (Fig 53). In C west hard hammer usage is preferred for initial decortication (40%), falling to just over 20% in tertiary

flakes (Fig 53).

There is some evidence in C east of initial core preparation and decortication taking place away from the site. Refitting group 10 (Fig 104; Fig 106) consists of a large nodule containing a distinctive vein of quartz. The refitting nodule was largely decorticated before reduction commenced, yet no cortical flakes containing the quartz vein were located during excavations, suggesting that the nodule was decorticated elsewhere.

Generally, it would seem that the shape of the original nodule determined the degree of initial preparation. In C east, large nodules such as refitting group 10 needed extensive pre-forming, whereas ovoid and tabular nodules such as refitting group 30 (Fig 105; Fig 107) simply needed cresting.

Cresting, platform preparation, blade production and core discard

The main forms of platform preparation and rejuvenation employed at Three Ways Wharf were tablet removal and faceting. In the former the whole of the striking platform was removed by a single flake, while the latter technique employed constant modification to the platform by means of multiple flake removals. In scatters A, C and D these removals are often confined to the front of the platform and have been described as 'partial' faceting (Barton 1989). These techniques resulted in blanks with plain and faceted butts respectively. In addition to plain butts, many blades had the edges of their striking

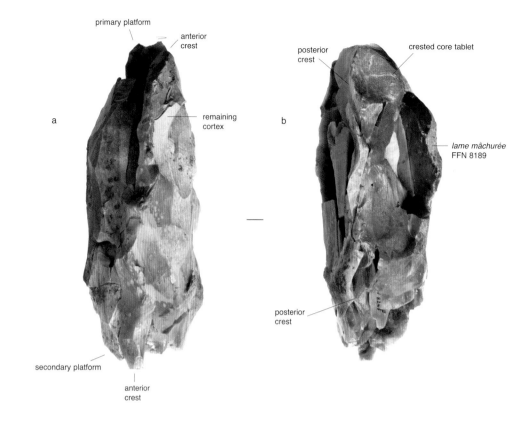

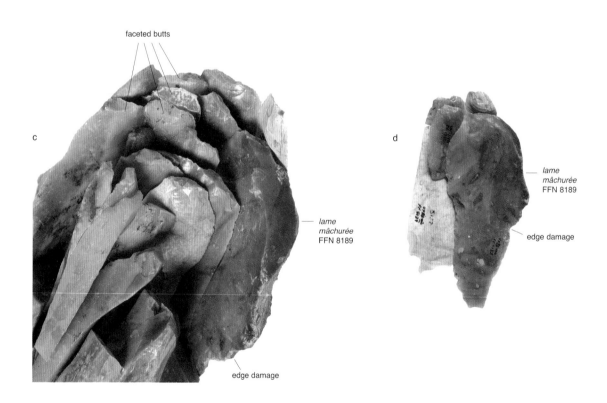

Fig 104 *Reduction sequence of refitting group 10: a – decorticated prepared nodule, showing anterior crest; b – posterior crest; c – blade sequence showing faceted butts and bruised blade (*lame mâchurée*) FFN 8189; d – ventral view of* lame mâchurée *FFN 8189 and dorsal refits; e – blade sequence showing quartz vein and broken microlith FFN 15063; f – blade sequence showing quartz vein and broken burin FFN 561; g – cresting to rejuvenate the face of the core; h – view of faceted secondary platform of core following rejuvenation by cresting; i – abandoned core (scale a–d 1:2; e–i 1:1)*

e

broken microlith
FFN 15063

quartz vein

f

burin
FFN 561

burin facet

missing
burin spall

g

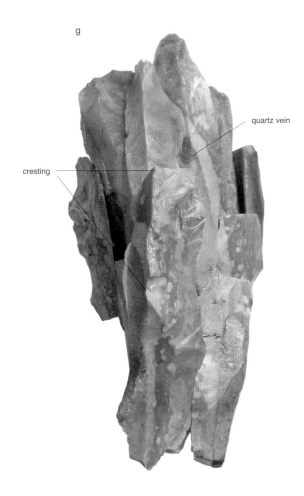

quartz vein

cresting

h

faceted core
platform

blades produced from
secondary platform

i

Fig 105 Refitting group 30 (scale 1:2)

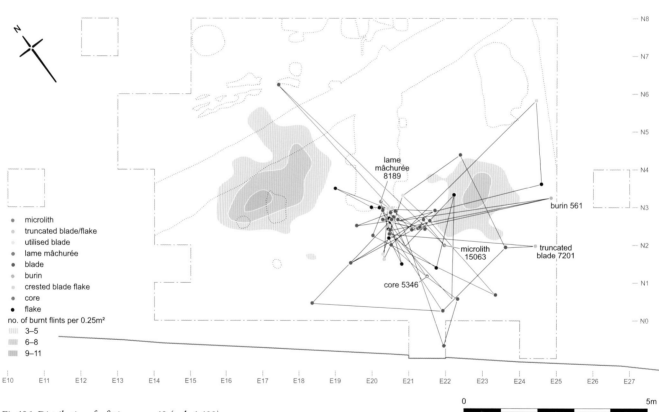

Fig 106 Distribution of refitting group 10 (scale 1:100)

platforms and arêtes modified by grinding or chipping. This abrasion served to strengthen the edge of the platform and improve the chances of producing laminar blanks. Bi- and uni-directional cresting was utilised in scatters A and C, both in initial core reduction stages and to rejuvenate the flaking face of the core. However, cresting was not employed if the initial

shape of the nodule did not require it.

SCATTER A

Blanks with plain butts predominate in scatter A, suggesting that core tablet removal was the main method of platform rejuvenation. However, blanks with faceted butts form a

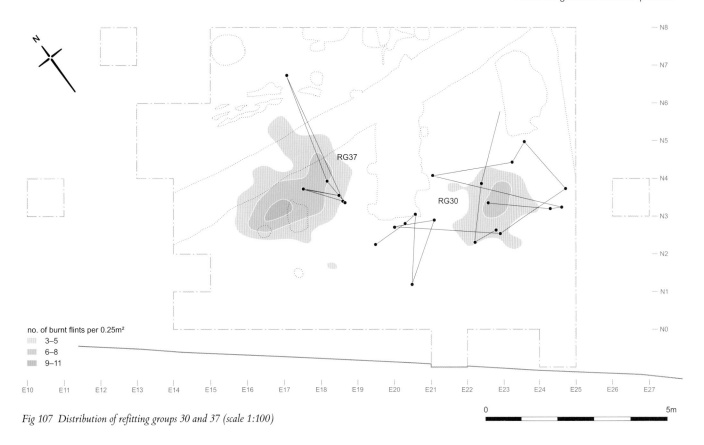

no. of burnt flints per 0.25m²
3–5
6–8
9–11

Fig 107 Distribution of refitting groups 30 and 37 (scale 1:100)

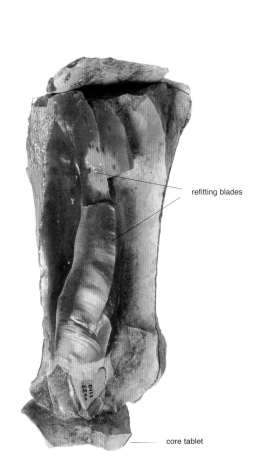

refitting blades

core tablet

Fig 108 Refitting group 21 (scale 1:1)

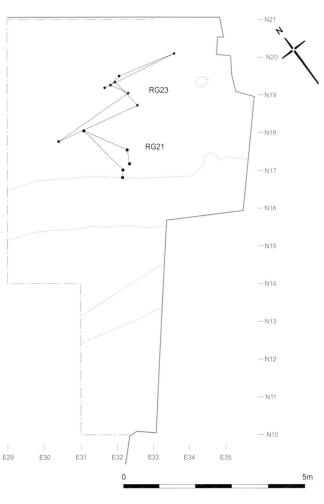

Fig 109 Distribution of refitting groups 21 and 23 (scale 1:100)

95

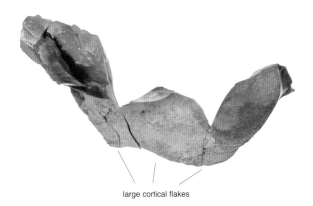

large cortical flakes

Fig 110 Refitting group 23 (scale 1:2)

Table 46 Comparison of complete flakes in scatters A (n=187), C west (n=1065) and C east (n=782)

Type	C west (%)	C east (%)	A (%)
Primary (100–75% cortex)	3.5	5.8	11.2
Secondary (74–1% cortex)	36.5	41.5	38.5
Tertiary (0% cortex)	60.0	52.7	50.3

significant proportion of the assemblage and show that faceting was also important.

Soft-hammer technique was by far the most important mode of blade production in scatter A. It is probable that cresting was used both in the initial stage of blade removal and in rejuvenating the flaking face. The large *lame mâchurée* (FFN 9022) on a crested blade and the corticated crested blade FFN 10282 probably originated during the initial stage. Conversely, refitting group 26 (Fig 111) is illustrative of the removal of a sequence of blades from a natural 'keel' on a nodule with minimal preparation. This refitting sequence demonstrates the rejuvenation of a faceted platform by the removal of a single core tablet, which converted the dorsal platform from faceted to plain. A slight variation in rejuvenation technique is exemplified by refitting group 17 (Fig 44; Fig 112). In this group, a core tablet (FFN 3675) with a plain abraded platform has been refitted to a *flanc de nucléus* (FFN 3676). It is clear that this group was detached from a very substantial core, possibly the same one which produced the large blade FFN 3495 (Fig 43). This piece retains traces of faceting and platform abrasion at its proximal end and extending around the lateral edge, and it is possible that FFN 3495 was intended to rejuvenate the flaking face of the core.

From the preponderance of blade cores it is clear that the main aim was the production of blades and bladelets. The only regular retouched tools in the assemblage are the microliths, and many of the blanks produced would have been ideal for the manufacture of these tools.

The abandonment of three cores while still quite large (FFN 10174, 8977, 8978) may be explained by the poor quality of the raw material, resulting in frequent hinging and plunging.

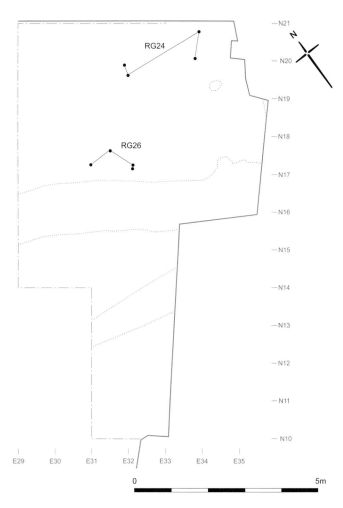

Fig 111 Distribution of refitting groups 24 and 26 (scale 1:100)

SCATTER C

From the proportions of plain to faceted butts it is clear that core tablet removal was the dominant form of rejuvenation in C west and C east, although in the latter area faceting formed an important component, while its incidence in the former was minimal. As in scatter A, in C east it is also clear that faceting and core tablet removal were interchangeable. This is shown by the latter stages of the main striking platform in refitting group 10 (Fig 104) and also on FFN 5387, a faceted core tablet. Soft-hammer technique was again by far the most important mode of blade production in scatter C. In both C west and C east cresting was used in both the initial stage of blade removal and to rejuvenate the flaking face. In C west, refitting group 37 (Fig 107; Fig 113) shows that bi-directional cresting followed initial decortication and preceded blade removal.

C east

Refitting group 30 (Fig 105; Fig 107) illustrates repeated attempts at cresting following initial platform preparation. Once again the poor quality of the raw material thwarted attempts to produce a series of blades from what would have been a large opposed platform core. It is possible that the use of poor raw material and relatively poor craftsmanship indicates the participation of children or apprentices. The nodule was turned around and a bi-directional crest was started on the opposite

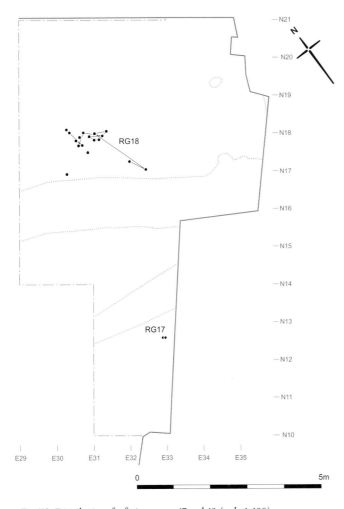

Fig 112 Distribution of refitting groups 17 and 18 (scale 1:100)

Fig 113 Refitting group 37 (scale 1:1)

edge of the nodule. This was abandoned when the nodule was either accidentally or deliberately broken in half. One fragment of the nodule was abandoned, but the other fragment was turned into a smaller opposed platform core, utilising one of the original platforms and the new break surface as the main platform. From this was detached a series of thick and rather poor-quality blades before the piece was abandoned.

Cresting was also employed on the backs and sides of cores in a number of cases, probably to aid the removal of core tablets. Refitting group 10 (Fig 104; Fig 106) combines all these features. Following extensive decortication of this large (*c* 200mm long) nodule, two large bi-directional crests were created, one anterior and the other posterior, resulting in a large 'twin-keeled' nodule (Fig 104, a–b). The removal of the posterior crest resulted in the optimum angle being created for the main striking platform of the core. The removal (in several broken segments) of the anterior crest acted as the guide for subsequent blade removals from the main flaking face. During the first phase of blade removals, the main striking platform was continuously adjusted by faceting, as illustrated by the butts of the refitting blades (Fig 104, c). The aim of this phase of reduction appears to have been to produce blades which contained a large proportion of the highly distinctive quartz vein which was present in this nodule. Many of the absent blades in refitting group 10 would have been largely composed of this translucent quartz (Fig 104, f), and it is tempting to imagine them as being valued on aesthetic grounds. For instance, the refitting 'C' type microlith FFN 15063 (Fig 76; Fig 104, e) was composed entirely of quartz.

Removals from the opposite striking platform were confined to short flakes. These were probably attempts at blade manufacture prevented by hinge terminations. Possibly because of this, it became necessary to rejuvenate the main flaking face of the core, which was achieved by creating a uni-directional crested blade and detaching it from the secondary platform (Fig 104, g). Subsequently the secondary platform played a greater part in producing blades. Judging from the abandoned core (Fig 104, i), this platform was also faceted. However, towards the end of the reduction process the main platform was rejuvenated by the removal of a core tablet or deliberate breakage of that end of the core, producing a plain platform. The large hinging tablet/core fragment was not recovered, but further removals were made from this platform. On abandonment the core was 68mm long, representing a marked reduction in volume from the original nodule.

C west

Fewer blade clusters have been refitted from C west, and none on the scale of refitting group 10. Certain trends are apparent, however, such as the smaller size of cores and the increase in single-platform pyramidal types. Many of these smaller cores are made on large flakes or broken fragments. Also in C west, there was a tendency to reuse broken core tools to produce new blanks and tools. Refitting group 3 (Fig 114; Fig 115) consists of an axe which broke in half and was subsequently reused as a blade core. One half of the axe was completely

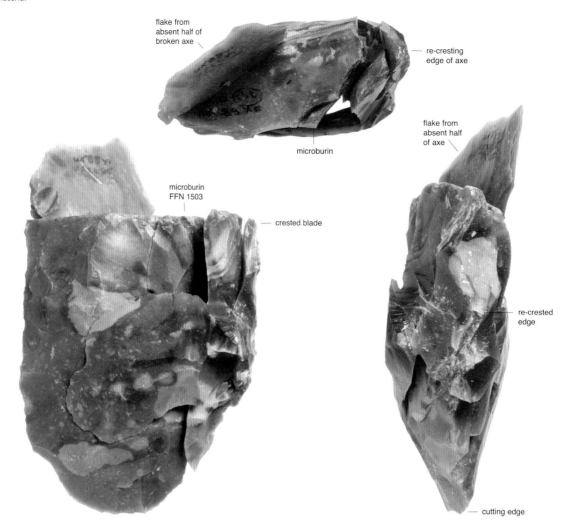

flake from
absent half of
broken axe

re-cresting
edge of axe

flake from
absent half
of axe

microburin

microburin
FFN 1503

crested blade

re-crested
edge

cutting edge

Fig 114 Refitting group 3 (scale 1:1)

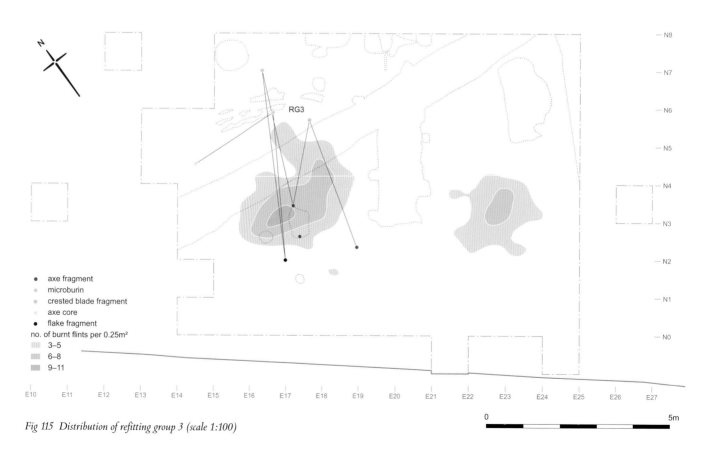

RG3

- ● axe fragment
- ● microburin
- ● crested blade fragment
- ● axe core
- ● flake fragment

no. of burnt flints per 0.25m²
- 3–5
- 6–8
- 9–11

0   5m

Fig 115 Distribution of refitting group 3 (scale 1:100)

flaked down and reduced, but the other half was still recognisable. In this instance it might be expected that the edge of the axe would form a ready-made crest, and the break surface the platform. However, the edge was re-crested which led to a secondary thinning of the axe and the production of a bi-directionally crested blade. A series of blades were removed both from the main platform on the break and from a secondary opposite platform on the blade-end. One of the blade blanks was then turned into a microlith, probably an A1a type, as illustrated by the refitting of a microburin to the axe core. The reason for the abandonment of this core is unclear. Generally in scatter C, core abandonment can nearly always be attributed to either raw material flaws or the exhaustion of the nodule for making suitably long blanks.

Technological trends

It is accepted that the horizontal dispersal of artefacts will have led to some mixing of the Lateglacial scatter C east assemblage with the Early Mesolithic C west material. The presence of a few microliths with distinctive concave truncations in scatter C west illustrates the point. However, as will be shown below (Fig 117), technological aspects of the sub-assemblages suggest that the integrity of scatters C east and C west remains remarkably intact.

The context for some of the general trends revealed in the core reduction discussion above can be seen in Fig 116. The increase in the proportion of blades to flakes, and the decrease in the proportion of core preparation pieces, from scatter A to C west can be interpreted as representing a decline in the

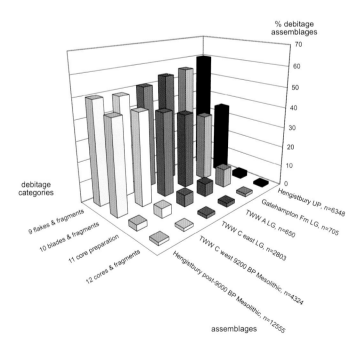

Fig 116 3D histogram of debitage composition of scatters A, C west and C east, compared with Hengistbury Head (Upper Palaeolithic and Mesolithic) and Gatehampton Farm (Lateglacial 'long blade')

degree of initial core pre-shaping and decortication. Coupled with this, in scatter A the concern seems to be with producing fewer but longer blades from larger nodules, with more care lavished on core preparation and maintenance during the reduction cycle. In C west, the focus is is on producing greater numbers of shorter blades from smaller nodules, with less emphasis on core preparation and maintenance through the reduction cycle. In all cases C east forms an intermediary stage between scatters A and C west. These broad changes in technology are what might be expected when the Three Ways Wharf assemblages are compared with other Upper Palaeolithic and Early Mesolithic assemblages. In Fig 116, Gatehampton Farm, Oxfordshire, compares well with scatters A and C east, while the Mesolithic assemblage from Hengistbury Head, Dorset, is comparable with scatter C west. The Late Upper Palaeolithic assemblage from Hengistbury Head (being the earliest assemblage) shows even more pronounced core preparation than the 'long blade' assemblages. On the basis of this limited comparison, scatters A, C east and C west would seem to represent a chronological progression. This does not mean that scatter C east is in some way an evolutionary stage on the way to the true Mesolithic, but rather that C east *may* be a more evolved form of the epi-Ahrensburgian 'long blade' industry, possible associated with changes in climate and exploitation of fauna. Johansen and Stapert (1997–8, 84) have postulated that the epi-Ahrensburgian sites of Höfer, Bedburg and Gramsbergen may represent the end of the final Upper Palaeolithic reindeer hunting tradition, since tanged points and reindeer were absent, but other Upper Palaeolithic traits such as large blades remained. Clearly, the presence of reindeer in scatter C east at Three Ways Wharf demonstrates that this occupation cannot have taken place as late in the Pre-Boreal as Johansen and Stapert have postulated for the sites they have discussed, and as we have suggested, microliths appear to have taken the place of tanged points in the Uxbridge hunter's tool kit.

In summary, a number of core reduction techniques were prevalent in the Three Ways Wharf assemblages.
1) Some irregularly shaped nodules required extensive pre-shaping and preparation, which cylindrical or ovoid-shaped nodules did not require. Alternatively, in scatters A and C east, large irregular nodules were tested or deliberately smashed into smaller fragments.
2) Cresting was utilised in the initial stages of blade production or to alter the angle and trend of the flaking face (as in refitting group 26). In C east cresting was also utilised on the back of some cores, probably to pre-shape the nodule and aid core tablet removal.
3) In scatter A preparation of two opposed striking platforms was the norm. Rejuvenation was by core tablet removal or faceting, with the former more prevalent. Platform edge abrasion was frequently carried out. Refitting group 26 illustrates that tablet removal and faceting were not mutually exclusive. This pattern is similar to that in C east, particularly SAS 3 which included refitting group 10. In C west, opposed platform cores tend to be smaller and there is

an increase in single-platform types. Many of the cores are manufactured on large flakes as well as broken fragments. Plain platforms predominate, again with a degree of edge abrasion.

4) Blade and bladelet production was the main aim of flint working. In scatter A relatively few blade blanks were used for tool production. In scatter C the full range of tools were manufactured on blade and flake blanks.

5) The factors of quality of raw material or length of blade removals dictated core abandonment.

6) Although the quality of the raw material must determine to a large extent the core reduction techniques employed, overall the patterns of core reduction strategy and technology suggest a clear chronological separation of scatters A and C west. They also suggest some differences between scatters A and C east, although their degree and significance is difficult to ascertain.

3.7 Internal variation: spatial and chronological integrity of scatters C west and C east

As mentioned above (3.1), the 11 sub-assemblages which make up scatters A, C west and C east could in theory each represent individual occupations of the site. This obviously has implications for interpreting the spatial distribution of artefacts and the dating of human activity. For instance, does SAS 3 constitute the earliest phase of occupation in C east, with SAS 4 and the hearth representing a later phase completely unconnected with SAS 3?

The depth distribution of artefacts suggests that the sub-assemblages in scatter A had the highest degree of vertical dispersal, followed by C east and C west, although the relative concentration of lithic material may also have had a bearing on this pattern. The depth distribution does not allow detailed comparisons between C east and C west or their constituent assemblages. In this chapter, the morphological, typological and distributional differences between scatters A, C west and C east have been explored. Three methods were used to try to establish the internal consistency of scatters C west and C east:

1) subjective analysis of the spatial patterning of lithic and faunal material;
2) quantification of the butt morphology of complete blades and tools;
3) analysis of burnt lithic material.

Unfortunately, the low frequency of material within SAS 10 and 11 prevents analysis along these lines within scatter A.

Spatial patterning

Detailed spatial analysis of artefacts and faunal material is discussed in Chapter 6. In this section it is sufficient to study the gross distribution patterns. Fig 12 showed that in C west, four of the sub-assemblages (SAS 1, 2, 6 and 7) are tightly grouped around a central hearth. Furthermore, there is a clear relationship between the lithics in C west and the distribution of the skeletal material, particularly the bone waste disposal area (Chapter 6). This relationship is generally exclusive, that is, the bone material is densest where there is no lithic material (eg notice how the bone material runs between SAS 1 and 2). This very tightly defined spatial patterning makes it unlikely that the individual sub-assemblages in C west represent multiple occupations. However, that does not preclude the incorporation within C west of some material from C east due to the proximity of the two scatters.

C east displays different spatial patterning. For instance, the density of artefacts and skeletal material is lower and more diffuse. Nonetheless, the major sub-assemblage (SAS 4) is clearly associated with the concentration of burnt flint representing a hearth. Like the pattern in C west, the densest part of SAS 4 lies slightly to the side of the hearth. Contouring of the debitage in C east shows that SAS 5 and 9 are probably the peripheral zones of the activity represented by SAS 4. This leaves the relationship between SAS 3 and the other sub-assemblages in C east. The centre of SAS 3 lies c 2m from the densest part of the eastern hearth, and twice this distance from the corresponding portion of the western hearth. The skeletal material (predominantly red and roe deer) in the waste disposal area does not respect the presence of SAS 3. In contrast, this later skeletal material does clearly respect the lithics of SAS 1 and 2 in C west. Technological and typological aspects of SAS 3 discussed in the lithics report and below would suggest that SAS 3 certainly pre-dates the activity in C west. However, there is no unambiguous spatial link between SAS 3 and the hearth in SAS 4.

Butt morphology

Table 47 and Fig 117 present a comparison of the butt morphology of complete blades in each sub-assemblage of scatters A, C west and C east. These data show that the constituents of scatter C east, SAS 3, 4, 5 and 9, form an integral unit with a consistent proportion of faceted blade butts which is comparable to that in scatter A. The ratio of plain to faceted butts within the sub-assemblages in scatter C west is fairly constant, suggesting that those sub-assemblages also form an integral unit. These patterns were repeated even when including broken blades in the analysis.

Fig 118 shows that where the butt morphology of retouched tools could be determined, they also show an increase in faceting in C east compared to C west. The pattern would also suggest that if C west and C east represent two chronologically different occupations, then relatively little mixing of the tool assemblage between the two areas has taken place. This would accord with the refitting evidence, which shows that the production, use and discard of tools took place within spatially limited areas.

Table 47 Butt morphology of complete blades by sub-assemblage of scatters A, C west and C east

	SAS 10	SAS 11	Total A	SAS 1	SAS 2	SAS 8	SAS 6	SAS 7	Total C west	SAS 3	SAS 4	SAS 5	SAS 9	Total C east
Linear	2	2	4	16	9	4	1	4	34	4	7	0	5	16
Plain	7	9	16	79	38	23	28	65	233	37	81	29	32	179
Plain abraded	16	4	20	133	103	21	77	21	355	44	41	12	20	117
Faceted	9	3	12	5	8	1	4	2	20	15	29	11	13	68
Unclassified	5	5	10	34	16	7	9	9	75	11	20	4	11	46
Total	39	23	62	267	174	56	119	101	717	111	178	56	81	426

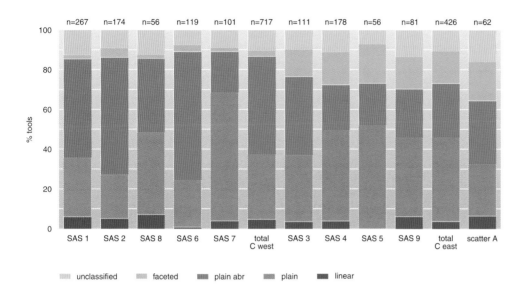

Fig 117 Butt morphology of complete blades by sub-assemblage

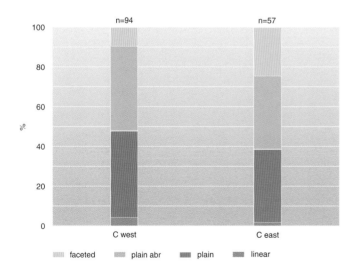

Fig 118 Butt morphology of retouched tools in scatters C west and C east

Burnt lithic material

The only direct evidence of a link between the early phase of activity in scatter C east and the eastern hearth is in the form of the burnt lithic material, which provides three strands of evidence.

1) A broken opposed platform core in SAS 3 (refitting group 5, FFN 8246; Fig 100) showed signs of light heating at one end. One platform is plain, but the other is faceted. Refitting showed that several removals had occurred following the heating of the core, and the core also appeared to have been used as a hammer stone following heating. This may be interpreted in two ways. Either the core reduction sequence and heating (and thus by inference the hearth area) were contemporary, or the heating and further reduction represent secondary reworking which took place much later.

2) It was possible to determine the butt morphology of 37 burnt blades and flakes in scatter C east. Of these, four were faceted (above).

3) Scatter C east contained a single burnt, broken, distally retouched microlith (FFN 6787). This piece is heavily calcined and the distal truncation is deeply concave. It has been suggested above that such pieces represent broken 'C' type microliths, one of which was produced from refitting group 10. This refitting group was centred on SAS 3 and also produced a *lame mâchurée* (Fig 104, d–e), suggesting that on typological and technological grounds SAS 3 pre-dated the occupation in C west.

The presence of the burnt core with faceted platform, the burnt distally retouched microlith, and the burnt debitage with faceted butts suggests a link between SAS 3 and the eastern hearth. However, it has to be admitted that this evidence is slender. Finally, the distribution of refitting material from group 10 suggests an eastward rather than a westward bias, with many pieces seemingly distributed around the periphery of the eastern hearth area.

In summary, the spatial distributions would suggest that C west formed an integral unit, and that SAS 4, 5 and 9 in C east formed a similar unit. The evidence from burnt lithic material and blade butt morphology would suggest that SAS 3 was also associated with the C east spatial unit and thus the hearth.

Summary comparison between scatters A, C east and C west

The main technological, typological and compositional differences between scatters A, C east and C west are summarised below.

Raw material and patination

Scatters A and C east: larger river gravel flint nodules, with significant component of blue-grey pieces partly due to higher degree of patination. Possibly a slightly different source of raw material from C west, or at least exploitation of different types and size of nodules. Increased patination probably due to ground conditions but may also indicate greater age.

Scatter C west: smaller river gravel flint nodules of varied colours, largely unpatinated.

Debitage

FLAKES

Scatter A: increase in incidence of faceting of butts and soft hammer usage as core reduction progresses. Highest proportion of flakes to blades. Evidence of deliberate decortication and pre-shaping of nodules.

Scatter C east: proportion of flakes to blades intermediate between that in A and C west. Evidence of decortication of nodules, sometimes away from site.

Scatter C west: lowest proportion of flakes to blades. Less elaborate preparation of nodules prior to reduction.

BLADES

Scatter A: plain butts dominate, butt faceting a significant (19%) component.

Scatter C east: plain butts dominate, and faceting a significant (16%) component. Significant tendency for blades with faceted butts to be longer than those with plain butts. Significant tendency for longer blades than in C west.

Scatter C west: plain butts dominate, with faceting an insignificant (2.8%) component. Significant tendency for blades with plain butts to be shorter than those with plain butts in C east.

CORE PREPARATION PIECES

Platform abrasion common in all three assemblages.

Scatter A: bi- and uni-directional cresting employed in initial preparation and rejuvenation. Striking platforms maintained by core tablet removal and faceting.

Scatter C east: cresting similar to scatter A. Cresting also used on rear of some cores. Striking platforms maintained by core tablet removal and faceting.

Scatter C west: cresting similar to C east and A, except for little evidence of cresting to rear of cores. Striking platforms maintained predominantly by core tablet removal.

CORES

Blade cores the dominant type in all scatters.

Scatter A: opposed platform prismatic blade cores the dominant type, two examples being particularly large. In addition at least one large nodule smashed into smaller fragments.

Scatter C east: opposed platform blade cores predominate, particularly prismatic types. Very few single-platform pyramidal forms. Cresting present on sides and backs of some cores. Faceting present on 14% of platforms. Some cores made on smashed nodule fragments.

Scatter C west: opposed platform prismatic and single-platform pyramidal blade cores predominate. Cresting rare, but when present restricted to sides of cores. Faceting present on few platforms (2.6%). Some cores made on broken nodule and core tool fragments, and (as an extension of this trend) on large flakes.

UNWORKED AND PARTIALLY WORKED NODULES

Scatter A: single large nodule smashed and attempts made to utilise fragments.

Scatter C east: several irregularly shaped nodules deliberately smashed or broken during hammering. Some fragments converted into cores.

Scatter C west: less direct evidence of deliberate breakage of nodules, but more cores in this area made from large nodule fragments and flakes.

HAMMER/ANVIL STONES

Scatter A: none present, although core FFN 3911 may have fulfilled this function.

Scatter C east: five hammer stones and two large anvil stones, some showing heavy damage and all located adjacent to hearth. A number of cores and possibly broken nodules may also have been used as hammers.

Scatter C west: one broken hammer stone and one anvil stone.

Some of the patterns summarised above can be seen in Table 6.

Retouched tools

Generally, scatter A contained a very restricted retouched tool inventory, while scatter C showed much more variation.

SCRAPERS

Scatter A: single crude example of an end scraper on a flake.

Scatter C east: almost exclusively end scrapers, those on flakes outnumbering those on blades by a ratio of 2.4:1.

Scatter C west: scrapers the dominant class of retouched tool. Preponderance of end scrapers, with flake supports outnumbering blade supports by 3.5:1. Low numbers of side and double scrapers also present.

MICROLITHS

Scatter A: microliths the main class of formal retouched tool. Half of assemblage composed of simple broad 'A' types with truncation angles >40°. Remaining half comprising bi-truncated 'C' types and distally retouched fragments. Deep concavity of truncation a feature of the assemblage. No microburins.

Scatter C east: broad 'A' types form main component of assemblage (*c* 45%), often with truncation angles >40°. 'A' types with retouch on the right outnumber those with retouch on the left. As with scatter A, significant number of large bi-truncated 'C' types and distally retouched fragments. Deep concavity of truncation again a feature of the assemblage. Single 'D' type triangle. Microburins extremely rare.

Scatter C west: 'A' types very prevalent (*c* 80%), some with truncation angles <20°, the majority with angles of 20–40°. 'A' types with retouch on the right slightly outnumber those with retouch on the left. Remainder of assemblage composed of single examples of an atypical hollowed-base 'C' type, a 'D' type triangle and a distally retouched fragment. Occasional presence of deeply concave truncations probably reflects presence of microliths related to activity in C east. Microburins prevalent.

BURINS

Scatter A: none present.

Scatter C east: burins form significant component of retouched tool assemblage (*c* 11%). Dihedral types predominate, truncation burins present. 'Corbiac' technique used in manufacture and resharpening. Burin spalls present.

Scatter C west: burins form low proportion of retouched tool assemblage (2.5%), consisting of truncation and dihedral forms. No symmetrical dihedral burins. Four 'Corbiac' burins with no further modification present. Burin spalls present.

AXES AND CORE TOOLS

Scatter A: none present, but one possible axe thinning flake.

Scatter C east: no core tools present. Low frequency of possible axe thinning flakes.

Scatter C west: four axes/rough-outs present. Evidence of reuse as cores following breakage. Axe debitage prevalent.

AWLS AND PIERCERS, MULTIPLE TOOLS

Scatter A: none present.

Scatter C east: no awls, one burin/scraper; four piercers, all atypical.

C west: a single true awl, one piercer.

MISCELLANEOUS RETOUCHED AND DELIBERATELY BROKEN PIECES

Scatter A: joint largest (with microliths) retouched category. No formal tool types in this category.

Scatter C east: largest category of retouched pieces.

Scatter C west: third-largest retouched category.

Some of the patterns summarised above can be seen in Fig 119, which contains the data for the retouched tool assemblages (excluding utilised pieces) of scatters A, C east and C west divided into sub-assemblages. These figures are also expressed as percentages of the total retouched tool assemblage.

Utilised (unretouched edge-damaged) pieces

Scatter A: low frequency. One *lame mâchurée* with distinctive bruised edges.

Scatter C east: relatively high frequency (18), in addition to eight *lames mâchurées*.

Scatter C west: relatively high frequency (21), no *lames mâchurées*.

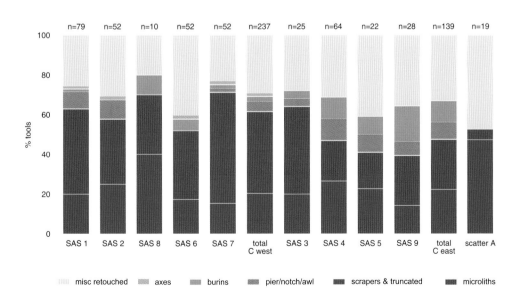

Fig 119 Retouched tool component of scatters A, C east and C west by sub-assemblage

4

Faunal remains

4.1 Introduction

Methodology

The total collection of bones studied comprised over 37,000 fragments (Table 48). We have seen above (Chapter 1.3) that these were recovered by excavation and from sieved soil samples, the latter being sieved at mesh sizes of 3mm, 1.5mm and 0.85mm, thereby producing samples of bone not precisely comparable. Most of the material recovered by hand during excavation was allocated a final bone (FB) number, and these fragments constitute over 80% of the sample by weight, although less than 25% of the actual number of counted bone fragments in the assemblage.

The major part of the identification of this assemblage was carried out by Alan Pipe. Subsequently, further identifications and a few corrections to Pipe's catalogue were made by the author when he laid out all the material to assess possible bone joins, minimum number estimates, and fragmentation and preservation information. This stage was especially useful in the separation of the red deer and reindeer bones, since all fragments of the same skeletal element were laid out together and comparisons across all fragments were thereby made possible.

Table 48 Details of the recorded bone assemblage from Three Ways Wharf

All bone	
Total no. of fragments	37558
No. of fragments assigned to CSZ, SSZ or UNI	35671
Total weight of recorded bone	21509g
Weight of bone assigned to CSZ, SSZ or UNI	10841g
Average fragment weight for whole assemblage	0.57g
FB-numbered bone	
No. of FB nos assigned (ie of excavated bone fragments generally >5cm)	1865
Total no. of fragments	8504
No. of fragments assigned to CSZ, SSZ or UNI	6875
Total weight of bone	18369g
Weight of bone assigned to CSZ, SSZ or UNI	5717g
Average fragment weight	2.16g
Note: see text ('Bone identification') for category codes	

The proportion of this material which could be identified to species or a category that could reasonably confidently be assigned to a single species was very small, and the majority of the useful zoological data derives from the fragments excavated and collected on site (Table 49). As a result of the high level of contamination of the microfauna (Chapter 1.4) a large proportion of the samples that were processed were not studied and recorded for microfauna.

Bone recording and spatial data

The fauna from Three Ways Wharf was recorded in the manner employed at the time by MoLAS, with some modifications. Where fragments were not identifiable to species or bone, a collection of fragments with similar characteristics (ie all shaft

Table 49 Numbers of fragments of mammal and bird identified in the total faunal assemblage studied, with material assigned an FB no. on site separated from the remainder; this includes some elements believed to be contaminants and one or two fragments from intrusive features

Species	FB-numbered	Others
Horse	13	1
?Horse	2	
Reindeer	96	8
cf Reindeer	20	3
Reindeer size	199	7
Red deer	448	30
cf Red deer	34	9
Red deer size	177	18
Red deer or reindeer	105	13
Red deer- or reindeer size	142	7
Cattle size*	4926	1785
Roe deer	53	12
cf Roe deer	5	
Roe deer size	210	21
Sheep size*	314	496
cf Wolf		1
Canid, dog or wolf	1	1
Red fox		1
Fox sp		1
Cat		1
Pine marten		2
cf Pine marten	1	1
?Carnivore	1	
Beaver	7	2
Hare, cf Blue hare		1
Swan	4	
cf Swan	1	
Large ?bird	1	
Duck sp (goldeneye size)		1
cf Swallow		2
Small bird	14	2
Unidentified bird	12	19
Mole		1
Rat sp		1
Rabbit		1
Mouse/vole sp	8	13
Small mammal	1	7
Frog/toad		6
Cattle, domestic	1	
Pig, cf domestic	2	19
Sheep/goat	4	1
Unidentified	1621	25574

*Although fragments were assigned to the categories 'cattle size' or 'sheep size', this does not imply a specific identification. At this site CSZ fragments were similar in size to prehistoric red deer and SSZ to smaller reindeer and roe deer bones

the data were treated in two ways. Where general bulk and distribution of the animal bones is under discussion, the dataset includes all retrieved material presented in $0.5m^2$ blocks, the highest common denominator of spatial information for all categories of find. While the analysis has considered the 3D distribution of the identifiable fragments of bone, those from the excavation and samples that do not carry a 3D coordinate were allocated a point in the centre of the 0.5m square from which they were recovered. These plots, therefore, contain precise 3D coordinates and 'best fit' (within 0.25m) data. Since most of the analysis is concerned with broader distributional patterns than 0.25m, potential error was not felt to prejudice the spatial analysis and discussions.

Bone identification

Owing to the considerable fragmentation of the collection, combined with the quantity of material derived from the wet-sieving programme, it was impossible to identify the majority of the individual bone fragments recovered. However, since the species diversity was relatively low, and many of the research questions concerning the faunal material required a spatial approach to the analysis, bones were assigned to non-specific categories as well as species. These were selected with the research aims in mind but have inevitably led to a certain amount of subjectivity in assignment which must be borne in mind. This assignment of unidentifiable bone fragments to a 'category' was both helped by the low diversity of identified species and complicated by the particular species identified at the site. Apart from intrusive elements which included domestic species, the only ungulates positively identified in the collection were horse, red deer, reindeer and roe deer. Other positively identified species whose fragment size may be considered to overlap with some of these ungulates are beaver, fox and swan, all of whose unidentifiable fragments could be similar in size to those of roe deer. Less confidently identified species with an overlapping size are wolf or canid, whose unidentified fragments might overlap in size with all four ungulate species. All these identified and possible groups are represented by no more than a few bones each (Table 50).

Given these possible alternatives, the unidentifiable fragments were assigned to the following categories.

CSZ – fragments defined as comparable in size to domestic cattle bones, which on this site is equivalent to red deer, but which could also be from horse, elk, giant deer and possibly aurochs (although neither of the latter three were identified at the site) as well as reindeer.

REDSZ – fragments defined as comparable in size to the prehistoric red deer identified at the site and similar sites of this period, including Star Carr.

RorR – fragments whose size was somewhat smaller than those assigned to REDSZ but fell within the possible range of smaller or juvenile red deer on the site and of reindeer, and which could generally be confidently identified to bone element.

RorRSZ – fragments that could not be confidently identified to bone element but fell within the same size range as RorR.

fragments of deer size long bones) could be recorded under the same record with the number of fragments entered in the number field. Hence, although some 37,500 bone fragments were studied, only 5250 records were produced. In many cases the material which derived from the soil samples was so small that identification was impossible, and some single records include up to 100 or more unidentifiable fragments. Although the 3D-recorded finds account for the bulk of the material which was subsequently identifiable to species and bone type (Table 48), other fragments were identified, and in order to consider the spatial distribution of bone material across the site

Table 50 Fragment numbers and weight of species identified from SU30–SU50

Species	Scatter A		Scatter B		Scatter C		Test pits	
	No. frags	Wt (g)	No. frags	Wt (g)	No. frags	Wt (g)	No. frags	Wt (g)
Red deer	-	-	-	-	473	8124.4	4	140.7
cf Red deer	-	-	-	-	41	237.1	2	2.2
Red deer size	1	0.9	-	-	192	1071.2	1	0.9
Roe deer	2	7.4	-	-	63	139.1	-	-
cf Roe deer	-	-	-	-	5	13.1	-	-
Roe deer size	-	-	-	-	231	196.8	-	-
Deer sp	1	0.2	-	-	42	32.7	-	-
Red deer or reindeer	2	11.0	1	3.8	114	429.6	-	-
Red deer- or reindeer size	2	7.6	-		145	221.2	1	0.7
Cattle size*	50	26.5	1	1.2	6590	5952.0	20	10.1
Sheep size*	136	22.7	-	-	673	268.7	3	1.0
Reindeer	36	293.0	-	-	48	764.7	-	
cf Reindeer	3	10.7			21	169.7	-	
Reindeer size	21	22.8	-		183	246.6	1	5.0
Horse	8	460.2	-		6	47.0	-	
cf Horse	2	15.6	-		-		-	
Beaver	-		1	10.6	8	19.2	-	
cf Wolf	-		-		1	0.5	-	
Canid sp	-		-		2	1.3	-	
Pine marten	-		-		2	0.3	-	
cf Pine marten	-		-		2	0.4	-	
Red fox	-		-		1		-	
Fox sp	-		-		1	0.8	-	
?Cat sp	1	0.1						
?Carnivore	-		-		1	1.0	-	
Hare sp	-		-		1	0.1	-	
Rabbit	1	0.1	-		1	0.1	-	
Rat sp	-		-		1	0.1	-	
Mole	-		-		1	0.2	-	
Mouse/vole sp	-		-		6	0.5	7	0.1
Small mammal indeterminate	-		-		7	1.0	1	0.1
Frog/toad	-		-		6	0.6	-	
Swan	-		-		4	40.0	-	
cf Swan	-		-		1	16.4	-	
cf Swallow	-		-		2	0.3	-	
Duck sp	-		-		1	0.2	-	
Large bird	-		-		1	2.2	-	
Small bird indeterminate	-		-		16	5.5	-	
Unidentified bird	2	0.2	-		28	26.8	-	
Unidentified fragments	6682	178.7	122	3.5	18952	1705.7	1690	93.1
Cattle	-		-		-		1	77.0
Sheep/goat	-		1	3.8	2	2.4	-	
Pig	10	4.8	-		12	4.2	-	
Total	**6960**	**1062.5**	**126**	**22.9**	**27887**	**19743.7**	**1731**	**330.9**

* See note on Table 49

SSZ – fragments defined as comparable in size to domestic sheep, which on this site is equivalent to roe deer, possible wolf and some of the other smaller species. The occurrence of many fragments of this category in scatter A indicates that the thinner-walled fragments of reindeer long bone are perhaps more likely to be recorded as SSZ than as CSZ.

ROESZ – fragments comparable in size to those of the identified roe deer bones on the site, and which were generally identifiable to bone element.

REINSZ – fragments comparable in size to those of the identified reindeer on the site.

UNI – fragments which could not be assigned exclusively to any category, generally because the fragments were too small.

There was a marked difference in the size of the red deer and reindeer bones (Fig 120; Fig 158) and confident assignment of identified bone elements was possible, although unidentified fragments, classed as 'long bone shaft fragments', are more doubtfully assigned. Each of these categories, because of their subjective nature, will include fragments which should have been assigned to others, but for the purposes of the analyses these errors are unlikely to result in any substantial distortion in interpretation. The least reliable group is SSZ since this category

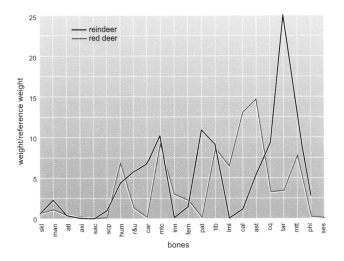

Fig 120 Relative weights of red deer and reindeer bones (figures for reindeer have been multiplied by 10 for ease of comparison)

might also include fragments of the larger bones of beaver, fox and other carnivores, such as wolf, and the large birds such as swan which might be present. A re-examination of some of this material after the initial cataloguing revealed further examples of the large bird species, initially recorded as SSZ.

At the element level complications also arose in the identification. The fragments of different bone elements vary appreciably in the level to which they can be identified. Shaft fragments of tibiae and metapodials display characteristics which generally make many of them recognisable, even when only small fragments are present. In contrast, fragments of humerus and femur shaft are often very difficult to assign and can also be very similar, making it impossible to identify which of the two bones a fragment derives from. With a site of Late Palaeolithic and Mesolithic age the occurrence of particular bone types, and their relative frequency and its subsequent interpretation, is a major aspect of the study, so biases introduced through variations in the ability to identify the material, rather than its presence or absence, can seriously prejudice the analysis. During the cataloguing of this collection some fragments were recorded as, for instance, 'TIB?' or 'HorF' (humerus or femur), while others were identified to specific element. However, a very large proportion of the fragments were catalogued as 'LBF' (long bone shaft fragment) where insufficient characteristics were present on the fragment. It is also clear from a re-appraisal of a proportion of the unidentified collection that a number of fragments were recorded as 'LBF' where it could not even be established conclusively that the fragments were from a long bone shaft. This is likely to have under-represented the contribution of other bone types to the assemblage, although – since none of these fragments could be assigned to any bone type with confidence – it does not affect the overall proportions of the identified elements. Fragments for which no conclusion as to bone type could be drawn were recorded as 'UNI', and it may be that a number of the 'LBF' category should have been assigned to 'UNI'. Since these were fragments which were unlikely to contribute a great deal to the analysis of the faunal sample, their

recording was not as rigorous as that of the identified component, except regarding whether they were burnt or not.

Analytical procedures

It was the intention to spend a major component of the allocated time on the reconstruction of bones from a number of fragments in the same area. However, the experience of reconstructing the long bones of large birds and roe deer from the assemblage suggests that not 'all' the fragments required are present, and neither should the time factor be underestimated, one or two hours sometimes being required for a single bone. This is perhaps the area in which the faunal analysis has been least successful, and has subsequently affected other aspects of the analysis.

Preliminary inspection suggested the possibility of establishing more than one bone from each prey animal in the faunal assemblage, with the objective of plotting the distribution of bones of a single individual and analysing this in terms of the process of butchery of the carcass. This approach turned out to be impracticable for two reasons. Firstly, very few measurable bones were found and most of the rest of the material was too fragmented to compare bone size. Secondly, the number of individuals was greater than originally anticipated and, in the major bone spreads in scatter C, several individuals were represented by a number of bones within a relatively small area, making association impossible.

During the post-excavation analysis it became apparent that the 3D patterns in scatter C and the fragmentation would yield the most data relating to human behaviour, and the focus of the work shifted from the analysis of carcass butchery to other aspects of processing and activity division across the site. The fragmented and unidentifiable assemblage became important, and the fragmentation analysis itself yielded information not anticipated at the assessment stage. The recovery and recording strategies were not directly geared to these re-prioritised analyses, and the author would now employ a more comprehensive and rigorous recording of fragments if afforded a second opportunity to study a site of this type.

Quantification

A number of the individual site bone finds (with FB nos) were found to join with other fragments, with individual bones being represented by up to four identified bone fragments and probably many more. Since the individual fragmentation of the various bone elements is variable, the fragment numbers are not a good guide to the frequency of individual bones, or the different species. Other quantification methods are required in order to answer some of the questions posed of the faunal assemblage. Three quantification methods were used: minimum number of individuals (MNI); minimum number of elements (MNE); and a relative frequency based upon the weight of fragments assigned to particular bone elements.

MINIMUM NUMBER OF ANIMALS
The MNI was calculated using the data obtained from the

minimum number of elements, and was based upon the most frequent element from one side plus any from the other side that were clearly of a different age or size. This differs from the method proposed by Binford (1978b, 69–72), but where the bones derive from a limited number of animals it more accurately represents the actual number of animals than dividing the total of left and right side by two (cf ibid, 70). However, this measure is not felt to reflect either the quantity of meat brought on to the site or the frequency of parts of the various animals. It can nevertheless give an indication of loss factors, in other words what did not reach (or subsequently left) the site, when considered in conjunction with the minimum number of elements. In comparing the frequency of different parts of the skeleton, Binford recommends the division of the MNE by the frequency of that element in the skeleton, in order to normalise the data for bones that occur in differing frequencies (ibid, 71–2).

MINIMUM NUMBER OF ELEMENTS

The minimum number of animals was calculated by laying out all the fragments of each type of element of a species. These were then compared for part, side, size and age in order to establish the minimum number of different bones they derived from. The minimum number of elements (MNE) was the sum of the left and right sides of each individual element identified. In some of the analyses this method was reduced further to consider the frequency of particular parts of an element, for instance the distal end, shaft and proximal end of a long bone.

WEIGHT

The considerable fragmentation means that much of the bone is not identified to species although many fragments can be identified to element. In order to establish the relative proportions of these different elements, the total weight of fragments assigned to an element and classified to a collection of comparable species categories (ie red deer, cf red deer and red deer size) is divided by the weight of that element in a control reference skeleton (Fig 120). This normalises all the weight data, reducing each element to a figure that represents its total abundance at the site relative to all the other elements of that group of species categories, and utilises all identified fragments irrespective of whether they contributed to the MNE or MNI figures. This removes some of the bias that might have been introduced by differential fragmentation, although it may create a new bias associated with the ability to recognise small fragments of some elements more easily than others. It should also be recognised that figures resulting from this exercise are not an estimate of the numbers of animals, since the prehistoric animals were in some cases much larger than the reference animals used, but rather an indication of the relative proportions of the bones and their degree of fragmentation.

Introduction to the assemblage

Animal bones were recovered from the whole area of the site, although, as we have noted above, much of this material was concentrated in scatter C. The entire sample also includes, in addition to the Lateglacial and Early Holocene collections, material from stratigraphic contexts of later date and the intrusive material discussed in Chapter 1.4. This chapter deals only with the bones recovered from the early prehistoric levels at the site that can be positively or probably associated with the contemporary human activity.

Species occurrence and frequency

The species recovered from SU30–SU50 are listed in Table 50. The samples from scatter B and the 1.0m² test pits are small and will not be discussed further. Red deer dominate the assemblage from the site and comprise over 40% of the total weight of bone studied (Table 50). Interestingly, there is no evidence for either aurochs or elk at the site despite these species being present in numbers at the broadly contemporary sites of Star Carr (Legge and Rowley-Conwy 1988) and Barry's Island (P Rowley-Conwy, pers comm) in North Yorkshire and also represented at Thatcham, Berkshire (Wymer 1962). One or two of the 'cattle size' fragments were large but not impossibly from large red deer and, considering the frequency of bones of the major prey species, it is extremely unlikely that no identifiable bones of either elk or aurochs would have survived on site if they had been present. An argument will be advanced later that the site constitutes a fireside camp where bones may have been heated and cracked for their marrow. It is possible that the more robust bones of elk and aurochs were processed elsewhere as part of some spatial organisation at the site, but this seems to be special pleading and neither aurochs nor elk appears to have figured in the hunting activities of the occupants.

A minimum number of 15 red deer is indicated. A considerable proportion, if not all, the 'cattle size' fragments and those of 'red deer size' can probably be safely assumed to have derived from red deer. The total weight of the red deer bones and these categories is over 15kg (75% of the collection) but, since a single (modern!) red deer skeleton weighs more than 7kg, even with all this material assigned to red deer there is no necessity for any more individuals to be represented even if the heads and vertebrae never arrived on site (Chapter 6.3). Reindeer, although from a different time period, are the next most frequent species, comprising 4.9% of the total weight of bone and represented by at least four animals (Table 49; Table 50). A proportion of the unidentified fragments must also derive from these reindeer bones but unfortunately the assignment of unidentifiable fragments to one or other large deer species would in many cases be purely speculative. Nevertheless, an attempt has been made to recognise the difference in size between the red deer and the reindeer, and some fragments have been divided on the basis of size, particularly shaft circumference and cortical bone thickness. Roe deer is the only other mammal species occurring with a frequency greater than 1 (Table 51). The bones of this species are particularly fragmented, and many small bone fragments were assigned to either 'roe deer size' or 'sheep size'. In contrast to the larger species it is possible that this unidentified component includes further individuals not recognised among

Table 51 Fragments, weights and MNI in scatters A and C

Scatter:	No. frags		Wt %		MNI	
Species	A	C	A	C	A	C
Red deer		514		87.3		15
Reindeer	40	69	38.6	9.8	2	3
Roe deer	2	68	0.9	1.6	1	2
Horse	10	6	60.5	0.5	1	1
Beaver		8		0.2		1
Fox		1		<0.1		1
cf Wolf		1		<0.1		1
Pine marten		4		<0.1		1
Swan		6*		0.6		3*
Total	52	677	787g	9573g	4	28

* Includes a humeral shaft probably but not certainly assigned to swan

the specifically identified bones. Fragments assigned to either roe deer size or sheep size weigh over three times as much as specifically identified roe deer fragments (Table 50), a pattern quite different from the reindeer and red deer where the identified components exceed in weight those unidentifiable fragments of comparable size, even if some of these elements derive from other species (above). Since the fragmentation level is also high, with the 63 identified roe deer fragments weighing no more than two intact modern humeri, it seems likely that more than two individual roe may be represented at the site. The remainder of the species are represented by single fragments or two or three pieces. A number of unidentified bone fragments from large birds may derive from the swans already identified, and a number of other bird species are definitely present although it is unfortunately impossible to identify them because of the fragmentation and condition of the bones. A duck of the size of a goldeneye is represented by a single bone, and a number of other fragments are from a similar sized bird although, as discussed above (Chapter 1.4), they could be intrusive in the deposits. Beaver, fox and marten are specifically identified, and a canine probably of a wolf and three canid fragments are also present. The other small bones of small mammal and fish have been considered above to be probable and certain contaminants, although some of the freshwater fish species may be contemporary with the formation of the deposits (Chapter 1.4).

Separation of the three archaeological scatters

In Chapter 5.1 at least two different archaeological episodes are recognised at the site. Radiocarbon dates of 10,060 BP and 10,010 BP (Table 1) on a horse tooth and a mandible fragment from scatter A suggest a Lateglacial phase of occupation which can be associated with the reindeer bones in scatter A (Fig 167) on the basis of their close association in the bone scatter, while three radiocarbon assays on roe and red deer from scatter C have given dates of 9280 BP, 9265 BP and 9200 BP (Table 1), indicating an Early Holocene occupation. This separation in date between the

horse material and the red and roe deer, combined with the occurrence of reindeer and the generally poorer preservation of this species and its deeper distribution in the deposits, supports the ecological distinction between the species, with horse and reindeer deriving from an early phase of the site and the red and roe deer from the subsequent Mesolithic occupation. It is, therefore, considered that the distributions of the identified bones of red deer and reindeer are likely to reflect the contemporary occupation areas during these two phases of the site (Fig 121). In scatter A (Fig 167) the bulk of the material can be assigned to the early phase since no red deer remains were identified in this area, while horse, a typical Lateglacial species, does occur in association with the reindeer bones. The only element out of place are two roe deer bones, and in the absence of other temperate species this would appear to be an outlier from scatter C or represent an adjacent undiscovered scatter.

The data allow us confidently to accept the presence of two faunal assemblages in scatter C, although the separation of these two assemblages is much more problematic. The reindeer and red deer scatters can only be confidently separated spatially where specific identifications were made. It is not, therefore, possible to separate the unidentified fragments from the different areas. The two horse teeth and the tibia fragment in the north-east of scatter C (Fig 128) barely contribute to the earlier assemblage and may even be related to the remains in scatter A, rather than the reindeer concentration here. These are the only two species that can confidently be assigned to the earlier scatter, even though other species occur in the assemblages that might be contemporary, including a fox astragalus (below).

In summary, then, the Lateglacial assemblage is defined by the distribution of the identified reindeer bones, and apart from the horse teeth and bones no other fragments can be positively associated with this period.

In scatter C east the bones that can be associated with the early phase of occupation (Fig 121) are dispersed over an area largely in the east and south of the scatter and are relatively more numerous lower in the stratigraphic unit (Table 60). The bones show a higher concentration in this area than in scatter A and, despite the absence of reindeer bones from the test pits in between scatters A and C, material may have continued across the intervening unexcavated part of the site. It is unknown whether these two reindeer scatters are contemporary or from different phases of occupation perhaps separated by a few or even hundreds of years. None of the reindeer material from scatter C that was submitted for radiocarbon dating contained sufficient collagen to produce a result (Table 1). However, we can probably assume a broadly contemporary date for this second scatter of bones, particularly since the reindeer bone in both areas was distributed across a similar depth of deposit and had suffered significantly more erosion than the red deer bones (Figs 156–8).

The main scatter of bones in C west is dated by radiocarbon analyses of red and roe deer teeth to *c* 9200 BP (Table 1). This scatter is composed of two concentrations which may have been artificially divided by the intrusion of a later prehistoric ditch (Fig 121). The closeness between the radiocarbon dates from the

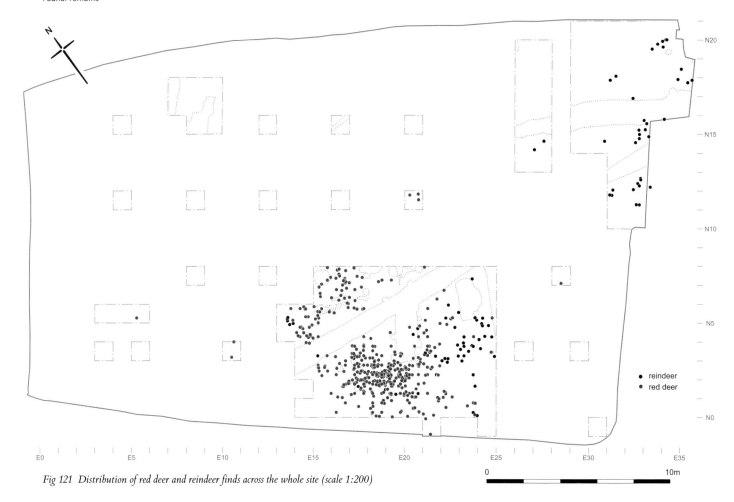

Fig 121 Distribution of red deer and reindeer finds across the whole site (scale 1:200)

main concentration and those obtained from a roe deer mandible from E16N06/E16N07 (Table 1; Fig 19) in the north-west concentration suggests that these two groups are contemporary and represent the same phase of occupation. This conclusion is reinforced by the distributional data considered in Chapter 6. There is a positive association between the distribution of red deer in scatter C and the bones of roe deer and swan (Fig 163; Fig 164; Fig 143), but the other species found in this area cannot so securely be tied to the Early Holocene occupation rather than the Lateglacial. The beaver occurs in scatter B and across scatter C, overlapping with both the red deer and reindeer distributions. Ecologically it is more credible in an Early Holocene than in a Lateglacial context, and in this report it is treated as such. The probable wolf, fox and canid bones occur in the region of overlap between the Lateglacial and Early Holocene distributions, while the fragments of pine marten occur within both the red deer and reindeer bone scatters. The distribution of these species in Europe today includes northern areas of Scandinavia and Russia. None can be confidently assigned to one or other of the phases of occupation, although the fox astragalus which was found in the middle of the eastern hearth suggests that this species is contemporary with the reindeer scatter. As we shall see (Chapter 5.1) bones also occur in other areas of the site. Identified red deer bones have been found to the north, east and west of the excavated scatter C (Fig 121). Beaver is identified from scatter B, while a number of unidentified bones including

red deer size fragments were found in a number of the test pits. These may represent outliers from the occupation phases in scatters A and C, or similar sites beyond the limits of excavation, or perhaps indicate a low level of peripheral activity on the site that did not produce the volume of material found around the hearth in scatter C west. The presence in scatter B of a red deer size humerus fragment that had passed through a carnivore gut perhaps suggests that some of this distribution may have been a result of limited scavenging activity. Each of the three identified scatters occupies a relatively large area and their distributions suggest that they extend beyond the limits of the excavated area, even though the majority of the assemblages on the site have probably been recovered. Whether these scatters represent just one area of an occupation site which extends beyond the limits of the trench is considered in Chapter 6.

Human association

It has tacitly been assumed above that the bones at this site are largely the result of human activity. The spatial association of flints and bone in such a marked concentration is probably sufficient to justify this assumption, but for the rarer species and the reindeer perhaps something more is required to prove that these remains result from human actions. While there may be little argument with the conclusion that the roe and red deer remains are the result of human activity, this is reinforced by the occurrence of marks attributed to butchery. In scatter C, 15 red deer bones bear marks that appear to be due to butchery. Unfortunately, the condition of the bones is such that the scanning electron microscopy carried out on a number of these marks was inconclusive, although their appearance (Fig 122) is consistent with butchery. One roe deer phalanx also exhibits a cut mark on its distal end (Fig 153). Burnt fragments of both these species have been identified, which is further evidence in support of a positive association between the bones and flints. Of the rarer species probably associated with the Mesolithic scatter, only swan bears cut marks (Fig 146; Fig 149) illustrating a positive link between this species and the occupants of the site. For the other species the association is less positive, although a fox astragalus, a duck coracoid, an unidentified bird bone and a fish bone were burnt, and a fragment of an unidentified bird long bone carried a knife cut. There is little room for doubt that all these species are positively associated with the human occupation at the site, although accidental burning of bones derived from elsewhere remains an outside possibility. Despite the association of the reindeer fragments in scatter C with the flint scatter to the east of the area and a possible second focus of burnt flint and bone, there is perhaps more doubt concerning the human origin of these remains. Nevertheless, three reindeer bones and one probable one in this area bear possible cut marks. A metacarpus and metatarsus show possible evidence of butchery, while a distal humerus exhibits convincing evidence (Fig 123), with the cut marks located at a

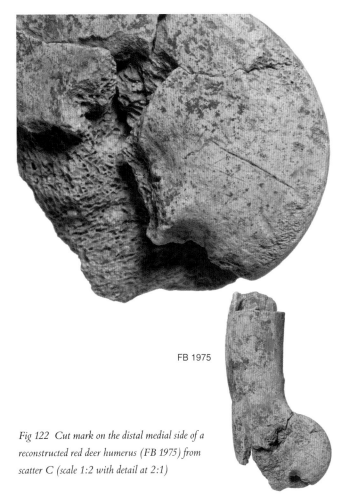

FB 1975

Fig 122 Cut mark on the distal medial side of a reconstructed red deer humerus (FB 1975) from scatter C (scale 1:2 with detail at 2:1)

a

b

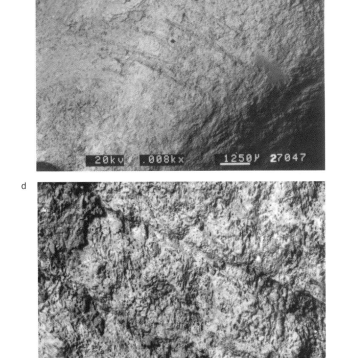

c

d

Fig 123 Cut marks on a reindeer distal humerus (FB 1577)

point typical of the dismemberment of the elbow joint and cutting of the ligament that holds the humerus and radius together (below, 4.6). One of these bones, a metacarpus, shows wear (Fig 124) suggesting that it may have been used as a tool of some sort. Further bones in scatter A also display probable cut marks, although none of these are so convincing. Although no burnt reindeer fragments were identified, small fragments of burnt bone were recovered from many of the samples processed from scatter A (Fig 125). This evidence and the pattern of skeletal representation, and the association of this scatter of bones with a flint assemblage with distinct Late Palaeolithic characteristics, seem sufficient to conclude that the bone distribution is in part the result of human action.

4.2 Species composition of Lateglacial scatter A

The Lateglacial scatter of bones in this area is not complicated by the superimposition of a later phase of occupation, and only a roe deer astragalus and a pisiform indicate the intrusion of later material into the scatter. This scatter was also more dispersed (Fig 126), although a considerable number of small, mainly unidentifiable, bone fragments were recovered throughout the area from the soil samples. Most FB numbers refer to a single bone, although many had broken up, and there is no indication of the bone or 'midden' deposits found in the Early Holocene scatter or the concentration around the eastern hearth in the contemporary deposits in scatter C east. The identification of this scatter as being the result of human activity is not as clear as in scatter C. Burnt bone is distributed throughout the deposits (Fig 125) with no concentrations. The weight of bone from the area was concentrated mainly in four 0.5m squares around E32N14 (Fig 127) where fragments of femur and tibia from more than one reindeer limb and parts of

FB 1691

Fig 124 Wear on the distal articulation of a reindeer metacarpus (FB 1691) (scale 1:1)

Fig 125 Distribution of burnt bone in scatter A, by grid-square quadrant (scale 1:100)

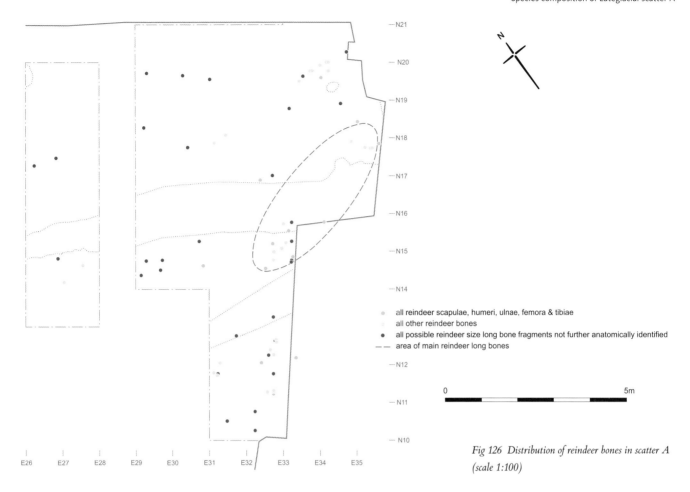

Fig 126 Distribution of reindeer bones in scatter A (scale 1:100)

a horse mandible occurred, but there is no evidence for this concentration being due to human behaviour. Unlike the Lateglacial scatter in C east, none of the bones bear any evidence of butchery. The most positive evidence is the association of a Lateglacial 'long blade' lithic industry with these bones (below, 6.5). Only two species, reindeer and horse, can confidently be ascribed to this episode on the site.

Reindeer

Thirty-seven fragments from this scatter have been specifically identified as reindeer, three more are comparable with this species and a number of other bone fragments probably also derive from reindeer bones, although specific identification is not possible (Table 52). Many of these fragments are further broken, but have been recorded as single pieces even though, in some cases, not all the broken bits could be included in the reconstruction. Unlike the red deer assemblages in scatter C there is no evidence for multiple bone elements among these fragments. Preservation is poor as well as fragmentation being quite severe, and most of the bones show severe etching of the surface (Fig 159).

Frequency and skeletal part representation

The assemblage is summarised in Table 53. The only skeletal element that clearly indicates the presence of more than one individual is the intermediate carpal, of which two occur from

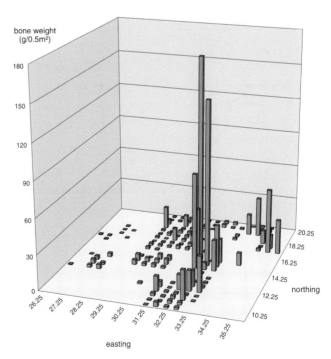

Fig 127 3D histogram of bone weight across scatter A

the right side. Allowing for some variations in proportion within the species, there is no indication from this exercise that more than two animals are represented. It could even be argued that most of the bones derive from a single individual somewhat

113

Table 52 Reindeer fragments and weight in scatter A

Bone	Reindeer		cf Reindeer		Reindeer size		RorRSZ		Deer sp		Cattle size		Sheep size		Unidentified	
	No. frags	Wt (g)	No. frags	Wt (g)	No. frags	Wt (g)	No. frags	Wt (g)	No. frags	Wt (g)	No. frags	Wt (g)	No. frags	Wt (g)	No frags	Wt (g)
Maxillary tooth	2	2.1														
Mandibular tooth	1	0.1														
Tooth									1	0.2	4	0.6	4	0.3	2	0.2
Mandible	1	20.0									4	7.4				
Cervical vert							1	1.5								
Vertebra													1	0.1		
Rib	1	3.9											1	0.1		
Costal cartilage													1	0.1		
Scapula	1	29.5														
Humerus	1	1.2														
Radius	1	12.1	1	1.5												
Radial carpus	1	3.1														
Intermediate carpus	2	5.3														
Carpus 2+3	1	3.1														
Metacarpus	1	18.0											1	0.8		
Femur	2	27.3	1	5.7												
Tibia	4	52.0	1	3.5												
Calcaneum	2	22.2														
Astragalus	2	16.1														
Tarsus	1	1.5														
Metatarsus	7	54.5														
Phalanx 1	2	8.6														
Phalanx 2	1	2.4														
Phalanx 3	1	0.4														
Metapodial	2	9.6														
Long bone frag					17	10.1	1	6.1			32	12.6	69	18.2	20	1.8
Unidentified					4	12.7					8	3.4	60	3.2	6723	177.4

Key: RorRSZ = red deer or reindeer size

larger than the reference Swedish bull reindeer used for comparison, with an intermediate carpal and possibly the scapula deriving from a second individual that may be represented by bones in scatter C.

Most skeletal elements are represented by very few fragments, but examples of most of the limb bones are present. No skull, vertebrae, ribs or sternal bones were recognised, although a fragment of cervical vertebra could be reindeer, and at least one maxillary tooth and a fragment of mandible were found. Given the number of bones in the axial and thoracic region, their absence from the sample is interesting. If the collection derived from the natural death of an individual, then the absence of the spine, thorax and head would be unexpected. Even if the carcass had been scavenged, it is these elements rather than limb bones that would tend to get left at the site (Binford 1984; Binford and Bertram 1977; Brain 1981). It could be suggested that scavengers or animal predators had dragged the archaeologically recorded material from a carcass beyond the limits of the excavation, or even the limbs of more than one carcass if the site was a habitual feeding area. This is a possibility, and it could be argued that the condition of the bone explains the absence of visible gnawing marks and other evidence. However, this pattern is also one that would be expected if humans had hunted the animal. In such circumstances the hunters may have butchered the animal at the kill site, removing the limbs and meat for transport back to a hunting camp and leaving the unwieldy head and thorax. In his study of Nunamiut reindeer hunting, Binford (1978a) records the caching of carcasses during the winter and spring months, with the head and antlers often being left as a marker for the meat store. Such practices could also result in the separation of the head, thorax and spine from the limbs. Another behavioural practice documented by Binford (ibid, 98–9), that of drying the rack or bones of the spine and rib cage in spring, could also account for the absence of these elements from the assemblage. Therefore, the supposition that the assemblage may largely derive from only one carcass may be incorrect, and limbs from more than one animal may be present on the site.

Age and sex

Very little information is available to give an indication of the age of the animal or animals represented by the sample. Only five fragments carry an epiphysis: a distal tibia, a distal metacarpus, two fragments from a distal metapodial, a proximal radius and a proximal phalanx. All these fragments exhibit the

Table 53 Summary of fragment numbers, weight, left, right, MNI and relative weight of different elements of reindeer and cf reindeer in scatter A

Element	No. frags	Wt (g)	L	R	MNI	Rel wt*
Antler						
Skull						-
Maxillary teeth	2	2.1	I	I	I	
Mandible	I	20.0	I		I	0.20
Mandibular teeth	I	0.1	I		I	
Atlas						-
Axis						-
Cervical vert						-
Thoracic vert						-
Lumbar vert						-
Sacrum						-
Caudal vert						-
Sternum						-
Rib	I					
Scapula	I	29.5		I	I	0.23
Humerus, p	I	1.2			I	0.03
Humerus, d				I	I	
Radius, p	2	13.6	I	I	I	0.12
Radius, d						-
Ulna						-
Carpals	4	11.5	I	2	2	0.55
Metacarpus, p	I	18.0			I	0.29
Metacarpus, d				I	I	
Innominate						-
Femur, p	3	33.0			I	0.14
Femur, ms			I	I	I	
Femur, d						
Patella						-
Tibia, p	5	55.5	I		I	0.24
Tibia, ms			I	I	I	
Tibia, d			I		I	
Lateral malleolus						-
Calcaneum	2	22.2	I		I	0.72
Astragalus**	2	16.1	I	I	I	1.46
Tarsus 3	I	1.5		I	I	0.75
Metatarsus, p	7	54.5	I		I	0.48
Metatarsus, ms			I		I	
Metatarsus, d			I		I	
Metapodial	2	9.6		?I		
Phalanges	4	11.4			I	0.24
Sesamoids						-

Key: d = distal; ms = midshaft; p = proximal

*For definition of relative weight, see Chapter 4.1, 'Quantification – weight'

**An astragalus was sent for ^{14}C dating in 1986; side and weight were not recorded, but weight has been entered as the same as the second astragalus, and side has been taken to be the opposite

fused condition, and all the bones in question (except the radius, which fuses earlier) generally fuse at about 2–3 years of age (Egorov 1967) and could therefore have come from an animal of any age older than this. A permanent maxillary PM3 shows fairly heavy wear indicating an adult, and a second tooth, a permanent mandibular PM3 or 4 (Table 54), is worn but the enamel of the cusps has not yet joined up, suggesting a youngish adult, probably aged over 2.5 years (Spiess 1979). Whether or not these two teeth could have come from the same individual is a problem, since limited reference material is available for comparison and the teeth of the fossil reindeer

appear much larger than those on comparable modern specimens. One mandibular fragment included the M1, M2 and M3. All three of these teeth were well worn, with the dentine surrounded by a ring of worn enamel. The M3 has normally erupted by 2.5 years of age (Spiess 1979) and the condition of wear on the teeth in this jaw indicates an animal somewhat older than this. Sturdy (1972) records the state of tooth wear on a cull of Greenland reindeer. Animals with their molar cusps well worn, with the cusp rounded or nearly worn flat (a condition similar to the scatter A specimen), were 4–5 years old. This would suggest an age of at least 4–5 for our specimen, although variation can be expected between populations. The mandibular premolar mentioned above could derive from the same jaw as these teeth despite being less worn since the premolars erupt at a similar age to the M3, or even after the M3 (Spiess 1979), and these teeth can still show an unflattened wear on the cusps when the molars have worn flat.

The only clue to the sex of the reindeer in this sample is their size. Unfortunately, no antlers or skull fragments are present that would allow an anatomical distinction. Most of the bones derive from animals slightly larger than the modern mature bull used for comparison. The problem with this approach is the lack of data on the variability in relationship between the bones from a single skeleton. All bar two or three of the fragments in the sample could have derived from a single adult bull reindeer a little larger than the reference animal, with a few fragments coming from one or more other individuals of slightly smaller size. Attribution of sex on the basis of the size comparison of the Three Ways Wharf specimens with reindeer from Midglacial Interstadial environments may be a mistake since two ecologically distinct types are generally recognised, a woodland and a tundra reindeer (eg Murray 1994; Gordon 1988). Any comparison of these different samples without first establishing the ecological group to which the reindeer belong may be misguided. With such a small sample and the absence of well-documented comparative modern or ancient assemblages, we must question the reliability of the sexing of the reindeer in these samples.

Seasonality

The anatomical data from this collection provide no information on the time of year when the animals died. The individuals represented are all subadult or adult, and therefore too old for dental or epiphyseal data to suggest a season, and no antlers were found that might otherwise have provided some information.

Horse

The distribution of the horse bones and teeth in scatter A is plotted on Fig 128. Two specimens from this scatter produced radiocarbon dates, one of 10,270±100 BP (OxA-1778) from a maxillary tooth from E32N15, and the second of 10,010±120 BP (OxA-1902) from bone of the anterior mandible from the same square (Table 1). (The horse tooth from scatter C

Faunal remains

Table 54 Tooth wear, all species

a) Red deer [3 animals (probably 4), various ages]
Mandibles

FB no.	Side	Square	INC	PM2	PM3	PM4	M1	M2	M3	Comments
1790	R	15/2/C/2							WJJ	same jaw – used for ¹⁴C dating; up to 3 years of age
1930	R	15/2/C/3				W	FWFW	WJ		
1771	R	15/2/A/2	sl							very slight wear , I 1 or I 2
1772	R	15/2/A/2		J						
1788	R	15/2/D/2							?U	cusp only
605	R	18/2/B/3	no							I 3, no wear
2058	R	19/1/A/3					JJ?>			2 fragments of same tooth; approx I year old
1371	R	19/1/A/4					JJ?>			
1377	R	19/1/B/4					?>>			broken tooth, 3 fragments
1326	R	19/1/C/3				<U				just up, ²/₃ of tooth, no wear on posterior cusp; ? just over 2 years old
	R	19/2/D/5	no							no wear
127	R	20/11/A/5					JU>			very slight wear, possibly in 1st year

Maxillae

FB no.	Side	Square	INC	PM2	PM3	PM4	M1	M2	M3	Comments
282	L	16/1/A/3							JJ	
281	L	16/1/A/3						WJ		same jaw, used for ¹⁴C dating; possibly same animal as FB 1906 below
280	L	16/1/A/3				FW	WW			
280	R	16/1/A/3				?				
454	L	16/2/C/3	?sl							
459	?	16/2/C/3					?U>>			cusp fragment, unworn
1236	L	17/3/C/2				<FW				
1906	R	20/0/B/5					JJ>			M1 or M2
	L	20/4/B/2						WW		broken M2
1675	L	21/0/C/4							JJ	probably M3
1572	R	21/1/D/2			FW	??				PM4 ?lost
1982	L	21/1/D/5						<WW		probably M2
1026 (1020)	R	21/4/C/3					WW>			M1 or M2

b) Reindeer [at least 3 animals]
Mandibles

FB no.	Side	Square	INC	PM2	PM3	PM4	M1	M2	M3	Comments
286	L	16/1/A/3		U		WJ				
1533	R	22/3/B/3							JJU	
1702	R	23/5/B/3					FWW>			
1576	R	23/5/B/3		U	UJJ	JJJ				
1171	L	33/15/C/3					HWHW	HWHW	HWHW	
1396	L	33/15/D/2			WW>					

Maxillae

FB no.	Side	Square	INC	PM2	PM3	PM4	M1	M2	M3	Comments
	L	20/2/B/6					WW>>			
F314	L	32/14/A/-			HW>					

c) Roe deer [2 animals, probably both 2 years old or thereabouts, possibly late spring or summer kill]
Mandibles

FB no.	Side	Square	INC	PM2	PM3	PM4	M1	M2	M3	Comments
302	R	16/0/C/3	no							I 3, no wear
587	R	16/6/B/5				WW	WW	WW		same jaw; I year old
588	R	16/6/B/6		U						
67	R	16/7/B/4							WWW	possibly same jaw as FB 587/588

Table 54 (cont)

FB no.	Side	Square	INC	PM2	PM3	PM4	MI	M2	M3	Comments
911	L	17/2/A/3			WFW	WW				probably same animal as below
	R	17/2/A/5			WFW					same jaw, probably same animal as above; ?2 years old
	R	17/2/B/4				WW				
491	R	18/3/A/2							?WW	same tooth, broken; ?2 years old
486	R	18/3/A/2							?WW	
	?	18/3/C/3					W?>>			cusp fragment

Maxillae

FB no.	Side	Square	INC	PM2	PM3	PM4	MI	M2	M3	Comments
406	L	16/0/A/3		?W						
794	L	16/2/A/4		?W						
455	L	16/2/D/3					WW>>			
471	L	18/4/B/2					WW>			

Notes:
Letter coding after Legge and Rowley-Conwy 1988
> or < indicates that the specimen could be the tooth in the next column to the right or left respectively; >> indicates that the specimen could be either of the teeth in the next two columns to the right; in all cases the wear categories have been placed with the preferred identification

produced insufficient carbon for dating.) The scatter A sample comprises five maxillary teeth, the symphyseal region of a mandible with incisors and one canine (fragmented), a degraded and fragmented piece of mandible with two fragments of a tooth, and a lateral metapodial. Two further fragments are probably horse: a shaft fragment from a thick-walled bone comparable with a metapodial and a thick-walled shaft fragment probably from a tibia. All the maxillary and mandibular teeth and the mandible occurred together in E32N15 and E33N15 and probably derive from the same animal. The radiocarbon dates should, therefore, be seen as two dates on the same item. The absence of the mandibular premolar and molar tooth row suggests that these parts of the jaw were never present or were removed from the site. The maxillary teeth include ones from both the left and right sides of the maxilla. The whole tooth row has erupted, with substantial wear on the PM2 but only slight wear on the M3 and with the enamel of the cusps not yet joined up. The mandibular incisors show a level of wear that Habermehl (1961) records as occurring on animals up to 11 years old, although the lack of wear on the M3 suggests a younger age. In any event, the animal was adult and can say nothing about the season of the year in which it died. The presence of postcranial bones is indicated by three fragments, only one of which is certainly identified. All of these lay some distance from the maxilla and mandible. None of these bones bear any evidence of butchery and, except for the spatial association of the maxilla and mandible with a group of reindeer bones, there is no evidence for the horse having been exploited by man. The occurrence of so few of them on the whole site might suggest that the horse bones are background material resulting from natural death and dispersal by floods and scavengers along the stream margin. On the other hand, the location of most of them in areas where other evidence suggests human activity

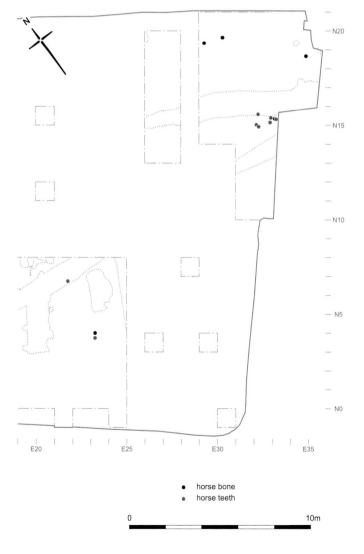

Fig 128 Distribution of horse bones across the whole site (scale 1:200)

provides at least some indication that they may be related to the human activity at the site, although there is no evidence for the scale of treatment afforded to the reindeer.

4.3 Species composition of Lateglacial scatter C (C east)

Reindeer

This was the densest and largest concentration of reindeer bones on the site. They were spread across more than 32m² of the site with a concentration in the eastern half in and around the hearth (Fig 129). The bone distribution exhibits a similar relationship to the C east hearth as the 'midden' does to the hearth in C west, although in the absence of burnt reindeer or horse bones this association cannot be proven.

Frequency and skeletal part analysis

The frequency and weight of fragments of reindeer bone and the less specific categories are presented in Table 55. The sample size is small and hence less reliable than the data for red deer. Some of the bone elements are only represented by a few grams of bone and, as with the red deer, a number of fragments in the 'reindeer size' and 'red deer or reindeer' categories almost certainly derive from this species. In the summary table (Table 56) only fragments assigned to reindeer, cf reindeer and

reindeer size (and not 'red deer or reindeer') have been used, since the latter follow the scatter sufficiently closely for this material to be reasonably confidently included; the 'red deer or reindeer' category fragments are distributed across the whole area.

The most frequent fragment is the proximal end of the left metacarpus, representing three individuals, and the proximal posterior shaft (with foramen) of the tibia, also indicating three individuals. Most of the other bone fragments represent a minimum number of two animals, with a few suggesting only one (Table 56). The consistency of these data in such a small sample suggests that many of these fragments derive from the same two animals. The spatial pattern (Chapter 6.3) supports this inference, with bones from the same side and joint lying near each other (Fig 182).

Although there is a marked absence of vertebrae and innominates, most of the other parts of the skeleton indicate the presence of both the individuals and there appears to have been little selectivity or selective disposal of parts of the carcass. The absence of more bones of the third individual might be attributable to the partial excavation of this scatter. Unlike the red deer in scatter C west, the reindeer bones are concentrated towards the edge of the excavated area, and the scatter may have extended fractionally to the east of the excavation limits; however, the presence of a medieval ditch in this area has obscured this distribution.

Little comment can be made upon the fragmentation of this material. Proportionally the sample includes significantly more epiphyseal ends than the red deer sample and, considering its greater antiquity, it appears to have undergone less destruction,

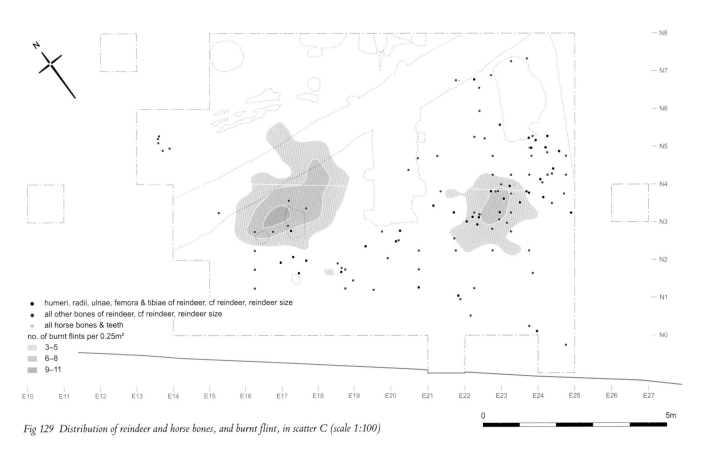

● humeri, radii, ulnae, femora & tibiae of reindeer, cf reindeer, reindeer size
● all other bones of reindeer, cf reindeer, reindeer size
● all horse bones & teeth
no. of burnt flints per 0.25m²
▨ 3–5
▨ 6–8
▨ 9–11

0   5m

Fig 129 Distribution of reindeer and horse bones, and burnt flint, in scatter C (scale 1:100)

Table 55 Reindeer fragments and weight in scatter C east

Bone	Reindeer No. frags	Reindeer Wt (g)	cf Reindeer No. frags	cf Reindeer Wt (g)	Reindeer size No. frags	Reindeer size Wt (g)	RorR No. frags	RorR Wt (g)	RorRSZ No. frags	RorRSZ Wt (g)	Deer sp No. frags	Deer sp Wt (g)	Sheep size No. frags	Sheep size Wt (g)
Antler	7	134.2	2	20.2			27	50.0						
Skull & horn	1	58.5												
Skull			1	6.2			1	21.7	3	6.3				
Maxillary tooth	1	4.4					5	3.3			1	1.0		
Mandibular tooth	2	9.5						0.5	2					
Tooth							8	2.0	1	0.2	6	2.1	2	1.6
Mandible	2	12.1					1	1.2	1	3.8				
Atlas					2	8.2								
Cervical vert							1	11.6						
Lumbar vert											1	0.4		
Sacrum							1	19.2						
Caudal vert									1	0.1				
Vertebra			1	0.6					1	0.3				
First rib							1	2.6						
Rib							3	2.1	3	3.3			4	1.5
Scapula	1	9.2	1	2.6					5	5.6				
Humerus	2	67.7	1	10.5	5	16.5	10	55.5	2	6.4	1	1.4	3	2.3
Radius	7	108.1					2	3.7						
Ulna	1	2.4			1	1.2	2	9.2						
Radial carpus	2	6.1												
Ulnal carpus	2	3.8												
Carpus 2+3	1	1.6	1	1.9										
Metacarpus	8	62.1	2	17.1			15	33.3						
?Metacarpus					1	2.0								
?Innominate									1	2.2				
Femur	2	15.2			2	17.0	7	31.7	2	6.4	1	16.1		
Patella	1	12.0												
Tibia	4	101.7	4	71.2	7	36.8	17	145.8	4	34.1	1	3.4		
?Tibia									4	19.3				
Calcaneum	1	3.0					1	4.0						
Astragalus	1	12.1												
Centroquartal	1	9.6	1	2.2										
Tarsus			1	1.4	2	1.9								
Metatarsus	7	118.6	4	31.0	1	4.1	4	13.9						
?Metatarsus			2	4.7	1	3.0			1	2.0				
Sesamoid			1	0.7			3	3.2					1	0.1
Phalanx 1	2	12.8												
Phalanx									1	0.6				
Humerus or femur					3	13.1			5	12.8				
Metapodial							3	15.1	1	0.6	1	2.2		
Long bone frag					152	139.2			74	100.4			449	188.2
Unidentified					6	3.0			35	16.6	29	5.8	213	72.6

Key: RorR = red deer or reindeer; RorRSZ = red deer or reindeer size

although its physical condition is poorer. The relative weight shows a marked variability in the proportions of the different elements present (Table 56), with fragments of skull, vertebrae and girdle poorly represented or absent, while the metacarpi, tibiae and metatarsi are the best represented. This pattern appears in part to be one of survival rather than selection, with the more robust and recognisable fragments producing the largest relative weights. However, the complete absence of vertebrae, ribs and sternal fragments below the atlas indicates that these bones either never arrived on site or were removed. A comparison of these data with the red deer relative weights shows a marked difference (Fig 120). In this figure the weights for reindeer have been multiplied by ten for ease of comparison. There is a fairly pronounced inverse relationship between parts

of the two datasets, with elements which are particularly lacking in the red deer sample – carpals, radius and ulnae, patella, centroquartal and tarsus 3 – being better represented (by weight), while innominates and the upper bones of the tarsal group are lacking.

Age and sex

Most of the epiphyseal fusion data indicate the fused condition; however, one distal radius was not yet fused, which normally takes place at 4 years of age (Egorov 1967), while a second was fused and clearly represents a second individual of different age. These results are in part supported by the dental data which include the right mandible of an animal in which the M3 is only

Table 56 Summary of fragment numbers, weight, left, right, MNI and relative weight of different elements of reindeer, cf reindeer and reindeer size in scatter C east

Element	No. frags	Wt (g)	L	R	MNI	Rel wt*
Antler	9	154.0	2	2	2	
Skull	2	65.0	2	2	2	0.016
Maxillary teeth	1	4.0			1	
Mandible	2	12.0	1	1	2	0.22
Mandibular teeth	2	9.0			1	
Atlas	2	8.2			1	0.07
Axis						
Cervical vert						
Thoracic vert						
Lumbar vert						
Sacrum						
Caudal vert						
Sternum						
Rib	1					
Scapula	2	12.0		2	2	0.09
Humerus, p	8	94.0		1	1	0.42
Humerus, d			2	2	2	
Radius, p	7	108.0	2	1	2	0.57
Radius, d			2		2	
Ulna	2	4.0	1	1	2	nc
Carpals	6	14.0	1	1	1	0.67
Metacarpus, p	10	79.0	3		3	1.01
Metacarpus, d			1	2	2	
Innominate						
Femur, p	4	32.0	2	1	2	0.14
Femur, ms						
Femur, d			1	1	1	
Patella	1	12.0			1	1.09
Tibia, p	15	210.0	3	1	3	0.91
Tibia, d			1		1	
Lateral malleolus						-
Calcaneum	1	3.0		2	2	nc
Astragalus	1	12.0	1	1	1	0.54
Centroquartal	2	12.0	1	1	1	0.92
Tarsus 3	3	3.0		2	2	1.5
Metatarsus, p	12	154.0	1	2	2	1.24
Metatarsus, ms			1	2	2	
Metatarsus, d			1		1	
Phalanges	2	13.0	1	1	1	0.27
Sesamoids						

Key: d = distal; ms = midshaft; p = proximal; nc = not calculated

*For definition of relative weight, see Chapter 4.1, 'Quantification – weight'

recently in wear and may correspond to the juvenile radius (Table 54). One right and one left mandible carry a PM4 at slightly different stages of wear (Table 54), which suggests a different individual, but otherwise all the mandibular teeth could have derived from a single animal.

Reindeer are sexually dimorphic for size, and fully mature animals can be expected to be sexed on the basis of size differences on some bones within a known single population (Spiess 1979). Very few bones from the Lateglacial scatter were measurable, but single measurements were taken on a distal humerus and a distal metacarpus, and two on the distal radius. Measurements were taken on modern reference specimens and collected from fossils (Murray 1994; Rackham 1982) to use for comparison, and the Three Ways Wharf data plotted on a

histogram with this material (Figs 130–2). The fossil samples include reindeer from a Middle Devensian context at Isleworth, an undated Pleistocene sample from Sandford Hill (Murray 1994), a collection of juvenile animals from Inchnadamph, Highland, of Late Devensian or Lateglacial age (ibid), and modern reference material in the Natural History Museum and the author's own collection. One specimen (Fig 130) is clearly smaller than most of the comparative specimens, including both adult male and female specimens; it is at the lower limit of the range and suggests either a female or a juvenile. The metacarpus measurement (Fig 131) is similar in size to a modern Swedish male but the samples are too limited for determination. The final measurements on the radii show the Three Ways Wharf specimens to be of equivalent size to an adult female reference specimen and a little smaller than the Swedish male. The larger of these two specimens had an unfused distal epiphysis and is thus from an immature animal, almost certainly a male. There is a significant size range above these Uxbridge specimens among

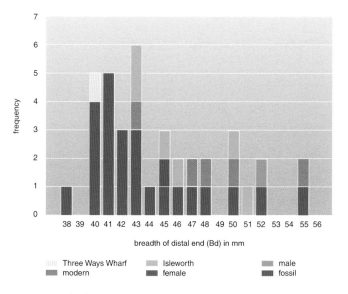

Fig 130 Reindeer humerus measurements

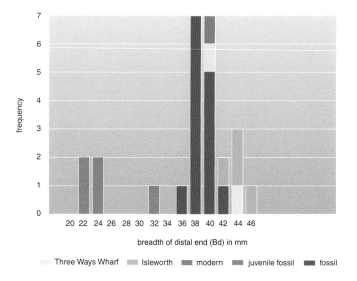

Fig 131 Reindeer metacarpi measurements

both modern and fossil specimens (Fig 132). Collectively these specimens suggest an adult male, a possible immature male, less than 4 years of age, and perhaps an adult female; since the distal radius is a late-fusing epiphysis, the smaller of the two radii must have derived from an adult animal aged over 4 years (Egorov 1967).

Seasonality of the Lateglacial scatter

Only one fragment provides any clue to the season of the year when the site was occupied. This is a fragment of reindeer skull with pedicle and antler base attached. In order to establish the season it is first essential to determine the sex of a specimen. Bouchud (1966) and Sturdy (1975) considered that measurements of the diameter of the beam above the brow tine could be used to distinguish adult males from juveniles and females, although Sturdy believed that separation of females from juvenile males was not possible purely upon this

measurement. Rackham (1982) measured the maximum diameter of the pedicle below the corona or burr and showed that Devensian reindeer could be separated into adult male assemblages and female and calf groups. Spiess (1979) felt that season of death from any but clearly large adult male antlers should be ignored. Owing to the condition of the surviving fragment from Three Ways Wharf, only the diameter of the pedicle (taken at the point where signs of shedding were visible) could be measured, and this measurement was compared with the data from a male-dominated sample (Isleworth) and a female/calf-dominated sample (Tornewton) from Rackham (1982). The size of the antler indicates that it lies on the boundary between the female and the male range, although occurring within the male range (Fig 133). It could, therefore, derive from a very large adult female or a subadult or young male. The data against which it is compared come from reindeer populations several thousand years older than the Three Ways Wharf sample, but a comparison with Sturdy's results from his study of Lateglacial reindeer from German and Swiss Magdalenian sites suggests that the size of the Uxbridge specimen would be consistent with the lower range of his adult males (Sturdy 1975, fig 3), although the measurements are not directly comparable. The shape of the antler does not help the deliberations much, since antler shape is very variable, but a subadult male is perhaps most likely indicated.

The sex is an important consideration if the time of death is to be established, since the cycle of growth and shedding differs between adult males and females, and juvenile and adult males (Spiess 1979; Sturdy 1975; Bouchud 1966; Kelsall 1968). One important characteristic of the Three Ways Wharf fragment is that the antler is beginning to suture and break off from the pedicle. This process had only just begun but separation would probably have taken place in only a few weeks. If the animal was a young male or a barren female then this bone would indicate death between January or February and May, but if it was a female with calf then death may not have taken place until June or July, the animal dying shortly before it would

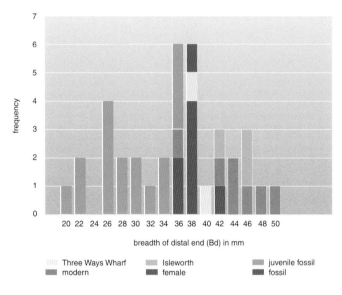

Fig 132 Reindeer radius measurements

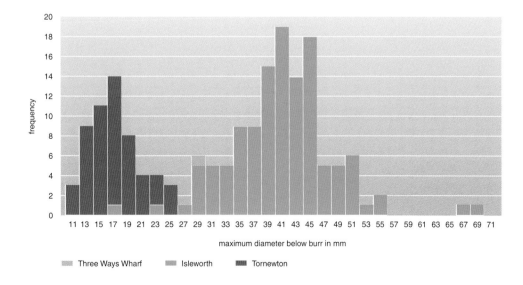

Fig 133 Reindeer antler measurements

have shed its antlers. A further complication is that in old age the antlers of males regress, that is to say they develop smaller antlers. If this specimen derived from an aged bull then it could have been due to shed in November, with the animal being killed a little before this. This latter scenario appears to be the least likely, and a late winter or spring date seems the most likely, with early summer a possibility. A second antler may contribute to the picture. A small group of thin iron-stained antler fragments occurred in E18N01, SU30 and SU40, together with a skull fragment with the base of a small pedicle. The condition of the material is poor and it cannot be established for certain whether the pedicle fragment had an unshed or a shed antler, although the broken surface may actually be the suture. The species determination is also uncertain, but if the broken surface is the suture then the fragment is almost certainly reindeer, since this species has a much shorter pedicle on the skull than does red deer. The juxtaposition of the two small antler fragments with this skull (Fig 182) may suggest that they had broken off it. The fragments indicate a very small, poorly formed antler beam typical of reindeer calves or young females. Although the sex cannot be determined, such antlers are generally shed between January and May. If the identification is correct, this would suggest death in the winter or early spring, which would accord with the inference of a young male from the other fragment. One mandibular fragment, since destroyed for radiocarbon dating, had an unworn PM2, and a PM3 and PM4 just in wear on their three cusps (Table 54). Although the state of eruption of the M1 and M2 and the presence of the M3 are uncertain, this mandible derives from a juvenile animal; however, the data are not sufficient to determine the season of death.

Horse

Three horse bones or teeth were identified from scatter C (Fig 128). Two of these, a fragment of robust tibia shaft with pronounced muscular ridges, and a fragmented molar cusp with no wear, occurred in the area of the eastern hearth at the heart of the reindeer scatter, both in SU30. The tibia fragment shows no evidence of erosion and the broken edges are reasonably sharp. The absence of any other postcranial fragments of this species suggests that horse was not actually a component of the fauna hunted by the people associated with this scatter, unless most of the bones were left at the kill site. Given the relatively high frequency of reindeer bones, the horse fragments in this area may be derived from material exploited in scatter A or an unexcavated part of the site. A maxillary PM2 was recovered 2–3m to the north-west of the hearth. There is no evidence other than their location to indicate that these bones relate to the occupation phase responsible for the reindeer.

Red fox

A single astragalus of fox was recovered from the area of scatter C east. This specimen is burnt and completely calcined, and must have undergone some shrinkage. Even allowing for this,

the bone is larger than the specimens of arctic fox with which it was compared, and it has been assigned to red fox. The assignment of this specimen to the Lateglacial phase of scatter C east is based entirely upon its location within the area of the eastern scatter and the fact that it had been burnt. There are also two possible cut marks across the proximal end of the bone, but these have not been studied under a scanning electron microscope and the nature of the marks cannot be confirmed.

4.4 Species composition of Early Holocene scatter C (C west)

The bone debris from this area of the site is very concentrated and represents over 90% of the whole assemblage (Fig 161). This concentration, while closely associated with the flint scatter, is offset to the south-east of the major concentration of flint (Fig 12) in the western half of the area. The only species which can confidently be associated with this phase of activity are roe deer, red deer, beaver and swan, with the cf wolf, other canids and bird species possibly belonging to it.

Roe deer

Apart from one isolated astragalus and a pisiform carpal in scatter A, the whole roe deer assemblage is located in scatter C. Although 'sheep size' fragments occur in scatter A, there is little to indicate that these derive specifically from roe deer rather than small reindeer or other species. The number of specifically identified roe deer bones is small (Table 57), largely due to the fragmentation levels of these less robust bones. However, a considerable number of fragments can be assigned to animals of a size which means the majority are likely to be roe. The distribution of these categories is presented in Fig 134. Roe deer bones are distributed across most of scatter C, and do not appear to depart from the general concentration of bone material on the site. The minimum number of animals represented by the bones of roe and roe-sized animals is given in Table 57. From most of the skeletal elements the MNI is only one individual, but from the mandibles (and teeth), humeri, innominates and tibiae at least two animals are represented. There may be more individuals that have not been recognised because of the high fragmentation. One of the roe deer was clearly a large buck. An innominate indicates a large animal and one of the distal tibiae, as well as being quite large, shows pronounced ridging of the ligament seating on the distal shaft, suggesting an older animal; a second, not so large, has no such development, but both distal tibiae are fused. A fragment of basi-occipital indicates an animal as large as the largest roe deer skulls in the Natural History Museum collections, again suggesting a buck. The unfused epiphysis of a proximal humerus, probably of roe, testifies to an animal not fully mature, while the jaws from two individuals (Table 54) suggest an age of approximately 2 years by analogy with the data

Table 57 Roe deer fragments and MNI in scatter C west

Bone	Roe deer	cf Roe deer	Roe deer size	Sheep size	MNI
Skull	I			I	
Maxillary teeth	8				
Mandibular teeth	10				2
Tooth				6	
Mandible	5				
Rib			3	6	
Costal cartilage				I	
Humerus	3	I	9	3	2
Radius	4		3		I
Ulna	I				I
Accessory carpal	I				I
Metacarpus	6	2		I	I
?Metacarpus			I		
Innominate	4				2
Femur	2		12		I
?Femur		I			
Tibia	6		8		2
Calcaneum	I				I
Astragalus	2				I
Centroquartal	I				I
Metatarsus	6	I			I
Sesamoid	I			I	I
Phalanx I	I				I
Humerus or femur			10		
Metapodial	3				
Long bone frag			179	520	
Unidentified			6	274	

presented by Legge and Rowley-Conwy (1988). This evidence suggests that the assemblage includes an individual of approximately 2 years of age and a second animal of similar age, with the possibility that the large tibia fragment may derive from an animal older than either of the mandibles.

Despite the very small size of the sample it is clear that most, if not the whole, of the roe deer carcasses were brought to the site. Fragments of skull, maxillary teeth, long bones and feet have been identified, although there is a marked absence of fragments identified as vertebrae and scapulae, while few rib fragments were recognised. The total weight of specifically identified bones is no more than the weight of two complete modern roe deer humeri, although material of roe deer size and fragments catalogued as 'sheep size' amount to over four times that weight (Table 50).

There is little evidence to indicate the season during which these animals were killed. No antler that could be assigned to roe deer was recovered. The teeth, although suggesting 2-year-olds similar to the putative 2-year age group at Star Carr, do not permit any close estimate of the season of their death. However, by analogy with the data of Legge and Rowley-Conwy (1988), one of the individuals may have been killed in spring or summer as it turned 2 years of age.

Although a number of the bones assigned to the roe deer size or sheep size categories were burnt, only two fragments exhibited any evidence of butchery. One long bone fragment of sheep size appeared to bear a 'knife' cut, and the distal lateral side of a roe deer first phalanx has an oblique score mark, probably a humanly derived cut mark (above, 4.1; Fig 153).

Red deer

The red deer was by far the most abundant animal at the site and, apart from a very few fragments, all the identified red deer

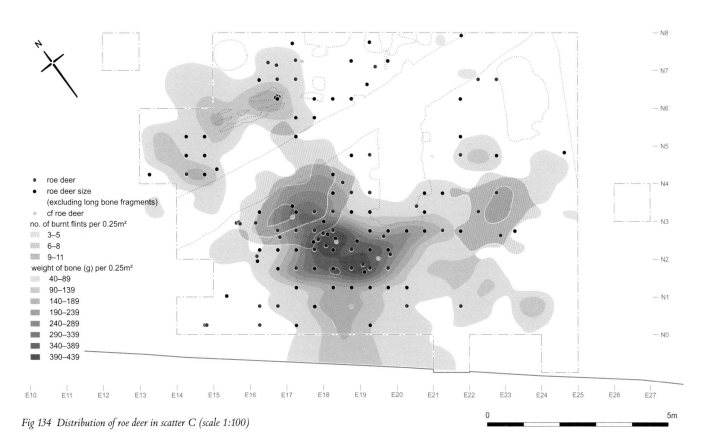

Fig 134 Distribution of roe deer in scatter C (scale 1:100)

material occurred in scatter C. The pronounced concentrations of bone noted above can be largely attributed to fragments of red deer (Fig 163).

Frequency and skeletal part analysis

Table 58 presents the data for the number of fragments and weight of red deer bones and the various other categories to which unidentified material was assigned. It shows that a relatively large proportion of fragments could be identified to bone element, but not positively to species. In the apparent absence of either elk or aurochs, there is little reason to doubt that most if not all of these fragments are red deer. Nevertheless, in the detailed consideration of the frequency of different parts of the skeleton, only fragments assigned to red deer or cf red deer have been utilised (Table 59). This table also contains the minimum number of elements, in some cases divided into proximal and distal, for each side of the body, the actual MNI (above, 4.1) and a figure for the relative weight of the different elements as described above (4.1). The most frequent element is the proximal tibia, with an MNE of 26. This estimate was based upon fragments of the anterior proximal spine of the tibia and the posterior proximal foramen. No intact or fragmented proximal epiphyses were recovered,

Table 58 Red deer fragments and weight in scatter C west

Bone	Red deer		cf Red deer		Red deer size		RorR		RorRSZ		Deer sp		Cattle size	
	No. frags	Wt (g)	No. frags	Wt (g)	No. frags	Wt (g)	No. frags	Wt (g)	No. frags	Wt (g)	No. frags	Wt (g)	No. frags	Wt (g)
Antler	6	297.5	2	13.1			27	50.0						
Skull & horn	1	125.8												
Skull	13	369.7	1	1.0	1	1.5	1	21.7	3	6.3			9	13.0
Petrous													1	0.3
Maxillary tooth	15	56.2	1	0.5			5	3.3			1	1.0		
Mandibular tooth	19	73.0	5	0.9			2	0.5						
Tooth			1	0.5	4	1.4	8	2.0	1	0.2	6	2.1	5	1.3
Mandible	8	85.7	1	3.3			1	1.2	1	3.8			1	6.4
Atlas	1	5.0	1	5.9										
Axis	1	1.4												
Cervical vert					1			11.6						
Lumbar vert											1	0.4		
Sacrum								19.2	1					
Caudal vert									1	0.1				
Vertebra											1	0.3	1	0.1
First rib	1	11.2					1	2.6						
Rib							3	2.1	3	3.3			8	14.7
Scapula	2	38.7							5	5.6			1	0.2
Humerus	43	1097.7	8	92.9	50	290.1	10	55.5	2	6.4	1	1.4	20	75.4
?Humerus					2	5.5								
Radius	14	165.1	1	5.9	1	19.7	2	3.7						
Ulna	6	35.2			3	12.9	2	9.2						
Radial carpus	1	5.7	1	2.9										
Metacarpus	95	994.8	2	3.5	10	34.8	15	33.3						
?Metacarpus													3	6.2
Innominate	14	355.7			2	4.5								
?Innominate									1	2.2				
Femur	37	379.9	5	25.3	22	115.3	7	31.7	2	6.4	1	16.1	2	22.0
Tibia	71	1886.3	8	74.3	36	349.3	17	145.8	4	34.1	1	3.4		
?Tibia					4	27.1			4	19.3			5	24.4
Calcaneum	18	530.8					1	4.0						
Astragalus	15	450.9	2	3.4										
Centroquartal	2	55.8												
Tarsus	2	7.1			2	2.8								
Lateral malleolus	7	18.6												
Metatarsus	79	1072.9	1	3.0	7	19.9	4	13.9					1	3.6
?Metatarsus									1	2.0				
Sesamoid			1	0.7			3	3.2						
Phalanx 1	1	3.9												
Phalanx										0.6	1			
Humerus or femur					11			43.9	5			12.8	9	32.2
Metapodial	2	3.4	0		8	31.1	3	15.1	1	0.6	1	2.2	1	2.7
Long bone frag					24	108.2			74	100.4			6038	5581.5
Unidentified						3.2				16.6		5.8		156.6

Key: RorR = red deer or reindeer; RorRSZ = red deer or reindeer size

Table 59 Summary of fragment numbers, weight, left, right, MNI and relative weight of different elements of red deer and cf red deer in scatter C west

Element	No. frags	Wt (g)	L	R	MNI	Rel wt*
Antler	8	310.0	I	I		
Skull	15	496.0	2	I		0.22
Maxillary teeth	15	49.0	2	I		
Mandible	9	89.0	I	4	4	1.3
Mandibular teeth	21	73.0				
Atlas	2	10.9			I	0.07
Axis	I	1.5			I	0.02
Cervical vert	(4)	(39.0)			I	-
Thoracic vert						-
Lumbar vert	(I)	(0.4)				-
Sacrum	(I)	(19.2)			I	-
Caudal vert	(I)	(0.1)			I	-
Sternum						
First rib	I (I)	11.2 (2.6)		2	2	-
Rib	(13)	(6.2)		I		-
Scapula	2	38.7		I	I	0.3
Humerus, p	51	1191.0	5	4	5	6.8
Humerus, d			10	13	13	
Radius, p	15	171.0	3	2	3	1.2
Radius, d			2		2	
Ulna	6	35.0	2	4	4	
Carpals	2	9.0	I	I	2	0.4
Metacarpus, p	97	999.0	7	6	7	9.1
Metacarpus, d			7	5	7	
Innominate	14	356.0	4	2	4	3.0
Femur, p	42	405.0			5	2.1
Femur, ms			11	11	11	
Femur, d			15	7	15	
Patella						
Tibia, p	78	1865.0	12	14	14	8.6
Tibia, d			12	6	12	
Lateral malleolus	8	21.7	4	4	6	7.2
Calcaneum	17	483.5	8	8	8	11.8
Astragalus	18	488.1	11	6	11	15.7
Centroquartal	2	56.0	I	I	2	3.1
Tarsus 3	3	9.1	I	2	2	3.0
Metatarsus, p	80	1076.0	6	7	7	7.7
Metatarsus, d			7	4	7	
Phalanges	I	4.0		I	I	0.07
Sesamoids	I	1.0				-

Key: d =distal; ms = midshaft; p = proximal

*For definition of relative weight, see Chapter 4.1, 'Quantification – weight'

although the proximal end of one of the spine fragments carried the fused end. Although these fragments were the most numerous, the MNI (15) was indicated by the distal femur. Once again no fragments of the epiphyseal ends survived, and the estimate was based upon the occurrence of the muscle seating on the distal posterior lateral end of the shaft. It was a characteristic of this assemblage that most of the epiphyses were either absent or destroyed beyond recognition, with only the distal tibia and the distal humerus surviving with any regularity, both of which are very robust pieces. Since fragments of the shaft adjacent to these ends survived on the site, and with sufficient frequency to exceed the more robust epiphyses, one must assume that the epiphyses themselves were present on the site at some stage. The epiphyses that are particularly missing,

while adjacent shaft fragments are abundant, include the proximal humerus, proximal femur, distal femur and proximal tibia. These are all very cancellous ends and, with the exception of the femur head, particularly susceptible to canid and mechanical destruction. Nevertheless, the complete absence of parts that might have been present in numbers as high as 30 seems improbable given the lack of direct evidence for canid scavenging and the presence of other intact long bone ends. It is possible that these large-volume cancellous ends were utilised for the nutrients they contained and were actually ground up or destroyed during 'cooking'. The humerus, femur and tibia occurred with greater frequency than any of the other bones of the skeleton, and even the intact astragali, which survived in good condition, were less frequent. There is a marked concentration on the long bones, with few girdle fragments and almost no elements of the axial skeleton. While metacarpi and metatarsi were reasonably abundant, the feet and the carpals and tarsals were rare. This cannot be due to recovery efficiency, given the circumstances of the excavation. By far the greatest proportion of the unidentified component is also accounted for by fragments of long bone shaft. While the accuracy of these latter attributions cannot be guaranteed in all cases, the superabundance of fragments of limb long bone (Table 58) suggests that the hollow long bones have been preferentially collected, or preserved, at this site. The exception to this pattern is the radius, the only 'long bone' which is relatively absent. The proximal end of this bone is one of the most robust and easily recognisable fragments in the skeleton and, as the Kuiseb data show, is one of the pieces that survives canid attrition. One is inclined to view its absence as indicative of its non-arrival on, or removal from, the site; however, with a preference being shown for long bones, the reason for its absence is not immediately obvious. A comparison of the data with those from Star Carr serves to illustrate the differences between the sites (Fig 135).

Mandibles, scapulae and radii are particularly lacking at Three Ways Wharf, while all are very common at Star Carr along with maxillae. Distal metapodials are also frequent at Star Carr while proximal ends are relatively uncommon. This contrasts with Three Ways Wharf where both proximal and distal ends of the metapodials were deposited. Femora, proximal tibiae and proximal humeri are the most abundant fragments at Three Ways Wharf, while these pieces are virtually absent in the Star Carr assemblage.

Since the data from Star Carr are based upon epiphyseal ends rather than shaft fragments, they may not be directly comparable with those from Three Ways Wharf, and if the recovered sample was 'winnowed' or only the larger fragments collected during the excavation (Chapter 7.2), then these absences in the Star Carr data may be an artefact of the recovery or analytical procedure. After all, such a policy at Three Ways Wharf would have resulted in no femora, no proximal humeri and no proximal tibiae, a pattern identical to that at Star Carr.

However, some of the differences described above, and particularly the relative absence of antlers at Three Ways Wharf, which were the most frequent finds at Star Carr (Fraser and

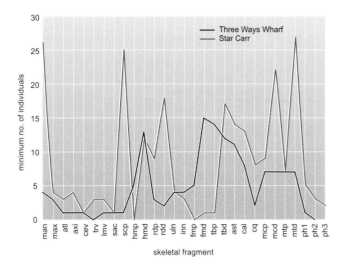

Fig 135 *Comparison of red deer bones from Three Ways Wharf and Star Carr*

King 1954), serve to illustrate that the assemblages are different irrespective of any recovery or selection biases.

Legge and Rowley-Conwy (1988) interpret the Star Carr assemblage as a hunting camp on the basis of a comparison with the caribou collection from a Nunamiut hunting camp (ibid, fig 37), arguing that the pattern of skeletal representation does not match that of a base camp or kill site (ibid, figs 35–6). However, it is those very elements that are common at Three Ways Wharf and absent from Star Carr that are responsible for this failure to match the base camp pattern, and although the patterns for the two Nunamiut base camp assemblages do not match precisely the sample from Three Ways Wharf, there is a similar pattern of abundance of the major long bones (Fig 136; Fig 137).

Rather than viewing the sites at Star Carr and Three Ways Wharf as hunting and base camps respectively, which is the inference from these analyses, their evidence could equally reflect different parts of the same type of site, with the Star Carr assemblage high in antlers, mandibles, scapulae and metapodials representing discard from butchery, antler

working, bone working and other processing activities from which marrow and grease bones were removed to a hearth like that at Three Ways Wharf. Instead of seeing these two assemblages as representing two different site types, they might equally, or even more plausibly, be seen as complementary samples representing the same type of site complex where function and disposal are related to activities and 'facilities' such as a fire or hearth, or water supply. For instance, Gronnow (1985) suggests that the reindeer antler in the lake at Stellmoor was cached there to soften it, and the different preservation of the cortical (worked!) antler at Three Ways Wharf may reflect such a soaking. Legge and Rowley-Conwy (1988) have alluded to just such behaviour being responsible for the concentration of antler in the Star Carr assemblage.

Pattern of skeletal fragmentation

In order to confirm this abundance of hollow long bones, all the identified fragments were used by dividing the gross weight of each element by the weight of that element in a control reference specimen. This reduced the fragments to a measure that was comparable for all elements. The results closely follow the MNI data (Fig 138) but allow us to consider the variation in treatment of the individual elements. Where the MNI line lies above that of the 'relative weight', the MNI is seen to be disproportionately high by comparison with the total weight of bone from that element. The converse is true when the relative weight line lies above that of the MNI. For instance, the low fragmentation of the tarsals is reflected in their higher 'relative weight' in that most of the bones were complete or nearly complete. In contrast, the very high MNI as against relative weight for the femur, and to a lesser extent the humeri and tibiae, shows that many of the fragments of these bones have failed to be recognised or that some parts, such as the cancellous ends, are completely missing, thereby depressing the total weight. The metapodials on the other hand show a very close relationship between the relative weight and the MNI, which

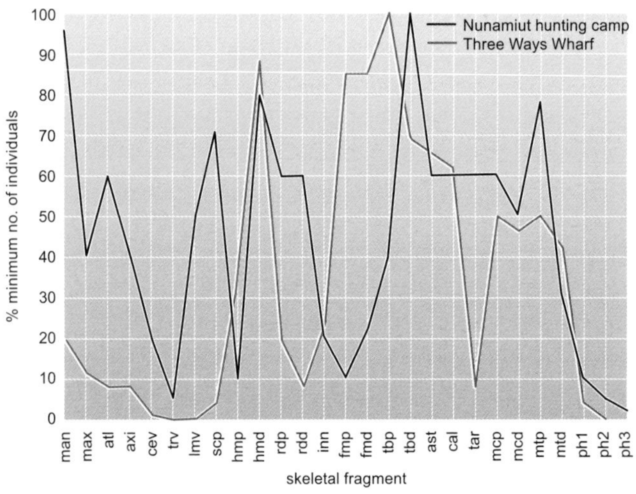

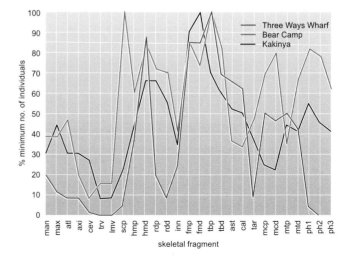

Fig 136 *Comparison of red deer bones from a Nunamiut hunting camp and Three Ways Wharf*

Fig 137 *Comparison of red deer bones from Bear Camp, Kakinya and Three Ways Wharf*

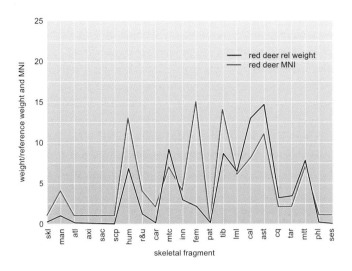

Fig 138 *Red deer MNI and relative weight*

Fig 139 *Partially burnt long bone fragments FB 149 (top) and FB 912 from scatter C (scale 2:1)*

perhaps suggests that many, though not all, of the fragments deriving from these elements were present and recognised.

It is clear from Fig 138 that the bones found on site and which have undergone the most extensive fragmentation are the humerus, radius, femur and tibia. The spatial analysis (Chapter 6.3) will consider the distribution of these remains across the area, and a concentration of identified and unidentified shaft fragments is responsible for most of the focus of bone in the south-western half of the site. It appears that not only are the hollow long bones preferentially located in this area but they are also preferentially fragmented, including the destruction of the softer epiphyses. This, combined with the location in relation to other features on the site (below), suggests a specific process reflecting human behaviour, and perhaps most easily explained as the smashing of long bones for marrow extraction and other cooking processes. The Kakinya assemblage in Fig 137 includes a bone cache collected for the manufacture of grease (Binford 1978b) and this group most closely resembles the Three Ways Wharf sample. The occurrence of occasional bones whose ends have been charred or burnt (Fig 139) may reflect roasting on the bone or heating of bone fragments to melt the marrow fat. The occurrence of the bones in this position, just beyond the flints and perhaps 2–3m from the fire (Fig 17; Fig 219), and their very smashed character in contrast to many of the bones around the periphery of the scatter (Fig 162), is perhaps indicative of a 'midden' deposit. If this is the case, it also serves to show that the site was occupied for an extended period of time rather than merely a few days, since the accumulation of a 'midden' of this size and associated with only one hearth is unlikely in such a short time.

Age and sex

The information on the age of the red deer exploited at the site is derived from the tooth data and the epiphyseal fusion of the postcranial skeleton. Of the latter all identified epiphyses were fused. Most of these were distal humeri, proximal radii, distal tibiae and distal metapodials, all of which fuse in immature and subadult animals, fusion being complete by 3 years of age (see eg Lewall and Cowan 1963 on black-tailed deer). This would suggest that none of the postcranial material represents juvenile animals. However, that need not be entirely true since a number of 'small' bones showing limited development of muscle ridges are represented by their shafts but not their ends. These have been recorded as 'red deer or reindeer' since many of the characteristics which might permit specific identification are not fully developed in juveniles, and fragments such as the midshaft region of a femur cannot be assigned with confidence to either species. The dental data are more informative, but since they only represent a small proportion (*c* 25%) of the total number of animals identified, they cannot be viewed as representative. The wear on the teeth has been recorded in the manner described by Legge and Rowley-Conwy (1988) for Star Carr. The mandibular dataset (Table 54) suggests one animal possibly in its first year, one *c* 1 year old, a third just over 2 years old and a fourth up to 3 years old. These latter two could be accounted for among the postcranial elements, but the 1-year-old and the younger animal have left no recognisable parts of the postcranial skeleton. The maxillary data (Table 54) indicate two animals similar in age to the oldest mandible.

The sex of the red deer has been established from the four innominate bones, being recognisable from the morphology of the tuberosity on the pubic bone. Of the four examples from scatter C, three are females and the fourth is a male. The presence of antler fragments of red deer indicates male animals, but only one definite individual is present; other fragments may have derived from shed antler.

Measurement

Large wild ungulates such as red deer are sexually dimorphic in terms of size, although age is also a contributory factor. The dimorphism is most marked in fully mature animals. The measurements from the tibia and humerus were taken on bones with fused epiphyses, but, as Legge and Rowley-Conwy (1988) have shown, some growth continues after fusion. However, the skeleton of an adult male red deer aged perhaps 5–6 years, of Neolithic date, was excavated at Seamer Carr, North Yorkshire (Tooley et al 1982), and furnishes a specimen of known sex and approximate age against which to compare the Three Ways Wharf and Star Carr bones. The Seamer Carr specimen is in the upper size range of the Early Holocene examples (Fig 140), suggesting little or no change or diminution in size during the Mesolithic and Neolithic periods. Both Star Carr and Three Ways Wharf clearly include adult males, but no pronounced division in the distribution allows the definition of a female and a male group. It is possible that the presence of immature males is obscuring any clear dimorphic pattern in the fully mature animals. Legge and Rowley-Conwy (1988) obtained a possible division from measurements on the distal humerus. These are plotted with the Three Ways Wharf specimens in Fig 141 and immediately suggest an inconsistency in the measurements. This

might be due to a discrepancy in the measurement location, but might equally result from a layer of PVA on the Star Carr bones, or erosion on the Three Ways Wharf specimens, which could account for measurements 1–2mm greater than those of the latter. Legge and Rowley-Conwy (ibid) tentatively suggested a division of the Star Carr sample into nine males and 12 females. If this is the case then all the Three Ways Wharf specimens fall within the male size range. These measurements derive from at least five of the 15 individuals recorded at the site and might suggest a preponderance of males in the cull. The third bone for which measurement data are available is the astragalus (Fig 142). This bone has a strong correlation with body weight (Noddle 1973) and increases in size throughout the growth of the animal. Since it carries no morphologically recognisable ageing characteristics, clear separation of the sexes is unlikely unless the sample is composed of mature animals. The Three Ways Wharf specimens are all smaller than the Seamer Carr male and fall within the lower half of the Star Carr range. If both sexes were present among the bones from Star Carr, then the Three Ways Wharf assemblage must also include females or young immature males. Unfortunately, the data do not permit any firm conclusions regarding the proportions of males and females among the Three Ways Wharf individuals, although some male animals are clearly present.

Beaver

The beaver is represented by nine bones on the site, eight of which were found in scatter C and the ninth in scatter B. They occur across both the Lateglacial and Early Holocene bone concentrations in SU30 and SU40, and cannot be positively linked to either scatter. The present-day distribution of beaver would not rule them out as fauna of a Lateglacial stadial with birch woods and other trees along the river margins, but it is probably more appropriate to envisage them within the later Holocene wooded environment. The fragments include two teeth, an innominate bone, a humerus, a femur, two tibial

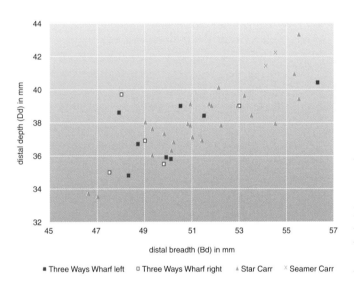

Fig 140 Red deer tibia size

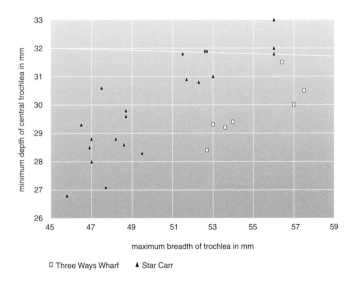

Fig 141 Red deer humerus size

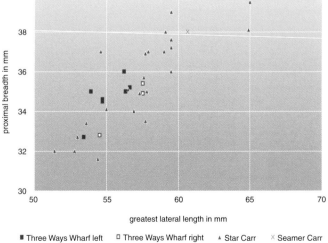

Fig 142 Red deer astragalus size

fragments, and a second and a third phalanx. None bears any evidence of butchery or burning, so no positive connection can be made with the human occupation of the site, although beaver is a frequent find on British and European Mesolithic sites (Coles 2006, 76–84).

Carnivores

Five fragments of canid were recorded from scatter C. One of these, a burnt astragalus of fox, has already been discussed (above, 4.3). A second fragment, a mandibular incisor, is assigned to fox and a third, an upper canine, is comparable with the wolf, *Canis lupus*. Two fragments of rib are carnivore in character, with one polished proximal end being equivalent in size to a wolf or large dog rib. The fox astragalus is only tentatively associated with the Lateglacial scatter and similar problems apply to the wolf and canid remains which are distributed across both scatters. Neither exhibits any evidence of human exploitation, and they may have arrived naturally on the site. One bone in scatter B looks as if it may have passed through a carnivore gut and may testify to the presence of scavenging canids, at least on the periphery of the occupation or after its abandonment. Two pine marten teeth, probably from the same jaw, lay to the east of the main bone concentration, and two further teeth, an upper canine and maxillary tooth almost certainly from this species, lay on the periphery of the major bone concentrations. The postcranial skeleton of this species may have been too small to survive intact on site, and a number of the fragments listed as unidentified bird long bone could plausibly derive from it. While an association between the

pine marten and the Early Holocene occupation is probable, there is no clear evidence of exploitation and the material may have arrived on the site naturally.

Swan and other birds

Although very few bird bones could be specifically identified, the incidence of thin-walled long bones with a large medullary cavity relative to the shaft circumference, which were recorded as 'unidentifiable bird', 'small bird' or 'large bird', was relatively high, and they were distributed across much of scatter C (Fig 143). The possibility that some of these fragments may have derived from the smaller carnivores has been raised (above) but the assignment to the category 'roe deer size' of fragments of bone which upon reconstruction could be identified as swan is illustrative of the subjective character of the unidentified recording classes used. A few at least of the unidentified fragments could be assigned to bone element and allow their positive determination as bird bones. The only species that can confidently be related to the Early Holocene occupation is the swan, on the basis of its distributional association with the red deer bone scatter but also because two of the bones have positively identified butchery marks (above, 4.1; Fig 145; Fig 148). The swan is represented by two humeri shaft fragments and two distal tibio-tarsus shafts, with a fifth bone, a humerus, being comparable with swan. Yet another large humerus shaft that required reconstruction is probably also swan. If the latter is the case, then three individuals are represented at the site, and at least two of them were butchered. All the fragments were compared with specimens in the Natural History Museum Bird

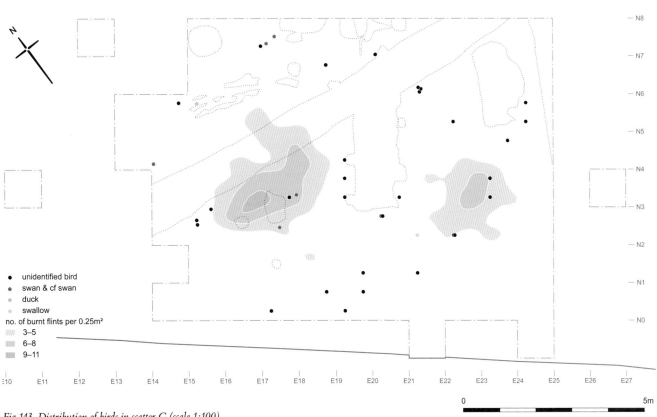

Fig 143 Distribution of birds in scatter C (scale 1:100)

Section collections at Tring, and two of the individuals were found to be as large as or slightly larger than the largest mute and whooper swans. Unfortunately, the fragments included insufficient characters to allow a positive distinction between *Cygnus olor* and *Cygnus cygnus*, although the best-preserved humerus (Fig 145) has been identified as *Cygnus* cf *cygnus*, the whooper swan. Exploitation of swans is not uncommon on European sites of Mesolithic date, although no such finds have previously been made in the British Isles.

4.5 Seasonality of the Mesolithic occupation

Among the Mesolithic material the data relating to the seasonal use of the site are sadly deficient. Only two pieces of direct evidence are present. Firstly, the red deer mandibular teeth suggest the presence of animals in their first year, and aged *c* 1, just over 2 and up to 3 years. The oldest of these four is of little use, but given that the red deer probably gave birth in May or early June (Legge and Rowley-Conwy 1988) an animal possibly in its first year is likely to have been killed perhaps in the spring or later, with the *c* 1-year-old animal being killed in the late spring or early summer. The 2-year-old would be indicative of the same period. Estimation from this dataset is somewhat nebulous, but one skull fragment carrying an antler was recovered from the site and affords a second piece of direct evidence. The skull clearly indicates an adult animal but there is no sign that the antler was due to be shed. Since the antlers of the red deer are shed sometime in April or May, but progressively earlier as the animal gets older, around the beginning of March in 8-year-olds (Taylor-Page 1971), this adult would perhaps have shed in March or April, and the shedding line would have been visible for a period before the antlers were lost. The condition of the antler on this animal therefore suggests that it was killed before early March. Since the animals grow their antlers between casting and early July or August, when they fray the velvet, the further likelihood is that this individual was killed between August and March. A small fragment of skull and pedicle from an individual whose species is not certainly identified has been discussed above as coming from a reindeer, but if it was a red deer then this animal would be a juvenile, with a small pedicle and the antler apparently shed. It was probably the first-year antler or spike which in modern animals is shed in late April or May, with the new antler growing over the subsequent two months. If the attribution to red deer is correct, this fragment would suggest death in late April or May, soon after shedding of the antler, and would be consistent with the mandibular data for an animal aged approximately 1 year. The latter part of this season would be consistent with two of the other mandibles but it is not possible to be more precise than this.

The potentially hunted birds provide no clue to the season since they are not species subject to significant seasonal movements and can be found in Britain all year round. If a more positive identification of whooper swan could be made it might indicate a winter occupation of the site, although whooper may have been breeding as far south as Britain during the Pre-Boreal.

One other suggestion might be considered. We have seen that there is a tendency to high fragmentation of the long bones or 'marrow bones'. This is particularly true of the concentration around E18N02, but is much less so for the concentration in the north-west of the scatter. Speth discusses the importance of fats and non-protein food in the human diet (Speth 1991) and has used this to illustrate the importance of sex selection in the cull (Speth 1983). The marrow fat in particular is a non-protein food resource when the meat is lean and the condition of the hunted animals poor, a situation that might be expected to pertain at the end of winter and in early spring. Such intensive processing of the long bones may be attributable to the exploitation of this resource at a time of dietary deficiency. Late winter to early spring, extending into the late spring and early summer, is, therefore, a possibility for the period of occupation at the site, although this must remain decidedly speculative.

4.6 Taphonomic modifications and cut marks

Peter Andrews and Barbara Ghaleb

Eight bones were submitted for study. These were selected by Alan Pipe from among several thousand bones from all levels of Three Ways Wharf as being the ones showing the most positive evidence of human activity in the form of cut marks or other modification. Only five were found to have definite evidence of butchery, and their locations are shown in Fig 144.

Specimen FB 1604 consists of most of the shaft of the humerus of a swan (Fig 145). This is a robust bone 98.2mm in length and of 17.2mm maximum midshaft diameter. Both articular ends are missing, with angular and irregular breaks. At the proximal end there is a spiral break, but there is no evidence of crushing or any marks to indicate how either this break or the one at the distal end occurred. The projecting points of the distal break are edge-rounded, indicating that the breaks are old, and although the proximal break lacks this feature, its colouration and degree of surface modification indicate that this break too is old. The entire surface of the bone, including the broken ends, is modified with slight pitting and manganese deposition. Towards the distal end of the shaft is a prominent cut mark (towards the right in Fig 145) which is shown in more detail in the photo-mosaic of Fig 146. The cut starts with a V-shaped profile, becoming more flattened and trough-like in the centre, with a strongly asymmetric profile (shown enlarged in Fig 147) and tapering off to a narrow V-shaped profile again at the end. The mark is 10.8mm in overall length, and the shape of the profile and the presence of minor striations along parts of the cut show that it was made by a sharp stone blade. Also

Fig 144 Location of cut-marked bones (scale 1:100)

no. of burnt flints per 0.25m²
- 3–5
- 6–8
- 9–11

Fig 145 General view of the lateral side of swan humerus FB 1604, showing the diagonal cut mark towards the distal end (right) (scale 1:1)

Fig 146 Composite SEM micrograph showing the full length of the cut mark on FB 1604 (×16)

apparent from the SEM micrographs (Fig 146; Fig 147) is the superficial damage to the surface of the bone, with one pit almost 1mm in diameter at the end of the cut mark and another slightly smaller one above the middle. In addition, the cut mark is interrupted at several points by post-depositional shallow pitting. Exactly how this bone became broken is not known,

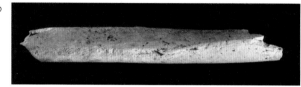

Fig 147 Enlargement of the central part of the cut mark on FB 1604, showing its asymmetric outline and U-shaped profile (×110)

Fig 148 General view of swan tibia FB 1605 (a – posterior view; b – lateral view) (scale 1:1); one of the V-shaped spiral breaks is shown on the posterior view (a, right) which also shows the long cut mark running diagonally across the posterior surface of the bone; the lateral view shows additional marks cutting across the lateral ridge of the bone, interpreted here as trampling marks

although human activity cannot be ruled out. The cut mark is certainly the result of human action. The edge-rounding of the broken ends and the pitting of the surface of the bone all took place after the breakage and the cut. Neither is recent, and it is probable that they occurred at or soon after the time of burial. The presence of a cut mark in this position on a swan humerus can probably be related to butchery, specifically cutting off the flesh of the wing.

Specimen FB 1605 is part of the shaft of a swan tibia, with both articular ends and the ends of the shaft missing. Both ends have truncated spiral breaks, leaving V-shaped notches cut into the ends (Fig 148). Most of the broken surfaces are edge-rounded, but one projecting fragment has been chipped more recently, probably during collection (the upper right projection of bone in Fig 148). The surface of the tibia shaft is lightly pitted (Fig 149) in the same way as described for FB 1604, and this is consistent with the damage to the broken ends. On the posterior surface of the tibia there is an extremely long (26.8mm) cut mark running diagonally across the surface, which can be seen on the general view of the tibia (Fig 148, a,

right) and on the composite SEM micrograph in Fig 149. This shows that the mark is a complex one, and although it appears continuous it consists of marks made in at least two operations since the two ends have different directionality, out from the centre in both cases. Fig 150 shows one end of the mark, with multiple striations merging into a single cut which ends at the broken end of the bone, and the other end of the cut mark is very similar except for the opposite direction of the cut. The profiles are V-shaped and asymmetric.

There are two other cut marks, with similar morphologies but much shorter, on this tibia as well as a series of marks across two of the lateral ridges (Fig 148, a, on the ridge above the long cut mark; Fig 148, b). These are shallow transverse marks (Fig 151, a), very numerous and all in similar positions across the

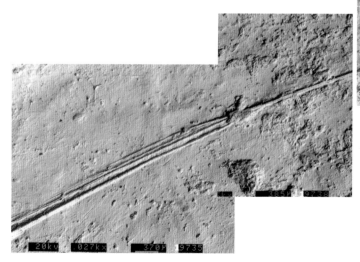

Fig 149 Composite SEM micrograph showing approximately 10mm of the long diagonal cut mark on FB 1605 (×27)

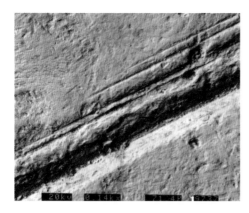

Fig 150 Enlargement of the multiple striations at the bottom left in Fig 149 (×140)

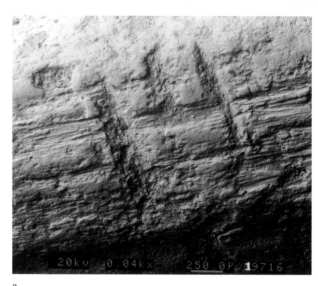

a

b

c

Fig 151 a – Three transverse trample marks from the right side of FB 1605 (×40); b – enlargement of trample mark that mimics a cut mark (×70); c – enlargement of trample mark that mimics a scrape (×70)

lateral angle of the bone, and bearing superficial similarities to shallow cut marks (Fig 151, b) or scrapes (Fig 151, c). They are very eroded and their morphology is difficult to interpret, but from their number, position all along the shaft of the tibia, and superficial nature it is unlikely that they are cut marks, and they are interpreted here as trampling marks. The presence of pitting superimposed on both the trampling marks (Fig 151) and the cut marks (Fig 149) indicates that both occurred before burial. There is no evidence to show whether the cut marks preceded the trampling or vice versa. The presence of three cut marks on a bone that carries almost no flesh in the living bird is hard to explain, and it would seem probable that a simple skinning operation is indicated by the marks rather than butchery.

Specimen FB 1623 is a roe deer phalange which is complete and lightly pitted in common with other bones from this site. There are gouges, scrapes and uni-directional apparent cut marks towards the distal end of the bone (Fig 152), but their interpretation is uncertain. One of the marks on the palmar surface is a single, moderately deep cut with a V-shaped and asymmetric profile (Fig 153, a), and it is probable that this is a human-derived cut mark. The other marks positioned more laterally and dorsally are more superficial, multiple and shorter, and have a rounded profile (Fig 153, b). It is also apparent that they have the striated profile seen in stone-worked cut marks (Fig 153, b), but it seems more likely in this case that these are cut mark mimics resulting from trampling after deposition. If the one mark is correctly interpreted as a cut mark, it would appear to be the result of butchery producing dismemberment of the foot.

Specimen FB 1304 is a fragment of humerus from a species of deer. It is extremely fragmentary and consists of a short section of the shaft. At one end of the fragment is an area of battered bone with numerous striations and grooves (Fig 154). These have a preferred orientation transverse to the long axis of the bone and, although in most cases the marks have little apparent structure, some have the appearance of chop marks. One such is shown in Fig 155, which is an enlargement of the central mark on Fig 154. This has a strongly asymmetric cross-section, with one side almost vertical and lacking a raised rim, and the other side smoothly angled. Other marks have varying

Fig 152 *General view of roe deer phalanx FB 1623, showing ?cut marks near the distal end; there is a single complex of marks on the upper lateral surface and a single mark located more ventrally (scale 1:1)*

a

b

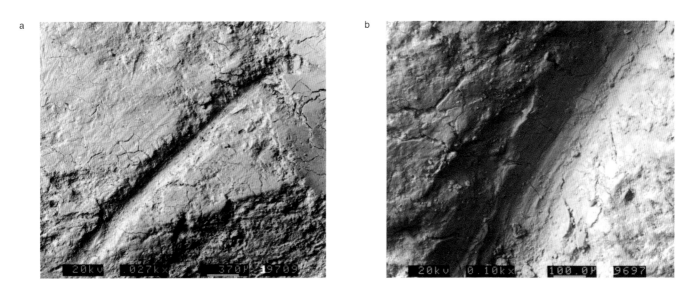

Fig 153 *a – SEM micrograph of the single ventral mark on FB 1623 (×27); b – enlargement of a bifurcating upper lateral mark (×100)*

Fig 154 *Composite SEM micrograph of the battered region of deer humerus FB 1304, showing the distribution of the marks (×13)*

Fig 155 *Detail of the groove in the middle of the cluster of marks in Fig 154 (×60)*

degrees of similarity to this 'chop mark', and since they are so strongly associated in terms of distribution, it is concluded that all were the product of the same process, although clearly that process was not one of consistent chopping. A tentative conclusion is that this fragment of humerus was used as a soft hammer for reworking stone tools, and that this damaged portion of the bone was the working area, so that with varying degrees of force being applied the observed variation in the marks would be produced.

Specimen FB 1577, the distal end of a reindeer humerus, exhibits definite cut marks across the anteriomedial ridge of the distal humerus. These marks are very much altered by subsequent corrosion and little detail can be seen (Fig 123). This is an area of muscle attachment and cuts in this region have the highest frequency (0.83) of anywhere on the (bovid) skeleton (Bunn 1983).

A number of other bones were examined for evidence of human activity. These all have the same degree of surface pitting and edge-rounding of broken ends, which makes it difficult to see any cut marks that may have been present. In many instances the surfaces are too poorly preserved as a result of these post-depositional processes for there to be any expectation of the earlier marks being preserved.

Additional specimens were received for examination as possibly bearing cut marks, although most marks proved to be of natural origin. One other specimen, FB 935, is a red deer metacarpal with apparent scrapes extending along the length of one side of the nutrient foramen. It is not known what caused this effect – it does not look like any form of natural break, but equally it would not appear to have any significance in terms of butchery or any other human activity.

In conclusion, there is evidence at Three Ways Wharf of human butchery and skinning of animals, but the evidence is slender and based on a very small number of specimens. This precludes any generalisations concerning butchery practices. The generally poor state of preservation of all the specimens, with surface pitting and edge-rounding obscuring the detail of many of the surface modifications, probably means that there may have been many more butchery and skinning marks left on the bones, but which are now obscured or destroyed.

4.7   Ecology of the identified species

Alan Pipe

This short appraisal attempts to summarise the ecological characteristics of the macro-faunal species recovered in terms of their habitat requirements, and to speculate on the techniques involved in their exploitation. The current British distributions of the birds discussed are given by Lack (1993) and Sharrock (1987), and those of the mammals (except for reindeer, horse and wolf) by Arnold (1993). The indigenous mammal fauna of mainland Britain is summarised by Currant (1989, 24).

Red deer (*Cervus elaphus*)

The red deer is the largest species of deer extant in the British Isles and is indigenous throughout temperate Europe (except Iceland and northern Scandinavia), western North America, and areas of North Africa and Central Asia.

Although the preferred habitat is open deciduous woodland, the species is able to exploit open mountainous and moorland country, as for example in much of upland Scotland. They feed by grazing on grass and moss, and by browsing on berries, shoots and buds (Lawrence and Brown 1973, 131), as well as feeding on heather and conifers during the winter (Corbet and Ovenden 1980, 202). Their distribution is effectively limited by snow deeper than 0.5–0.7m (Gamble 1986, 108).

Considerable variation is shown in body weight, group size and migratory behaviour, depending upon the habitat; as a general rule larger, sometimes migratory herds are formed in open mountainous country, and much smaller, less mobile groups in woodland. Indeed, the core unit in forest may be as small as a family group of one hind and her young, with stags usually solitary or in loose temporary groups (Ahlen 1965). The basic herd size has been suggested as four to ten individuals (Gamble 1986, 108) although groups of a few hundred may occur in open country (Ratcliffe and Staines 1982).

The animals graze mainly at dawn and dusk, spending the day resting in woods or on hills. They may undertake altitudinal migrations and tend to move down to more sheltered areas during bad weather. Body weight tends to be greater in forest than in open country, and it is speculated that the mean body weight in unstressed prehistoric populations may have exceeded that attained by modern animals (Smith 1992, 66).

This species is of obviously very great value as a food source; males may weigh 100–250kg and adult females 70–150kg (Gamble 1986, 108), with 50–60% of this being edible meat. It also provides a range of materials for use in the manufacture of a wide variety of products, such as hides (clothing, boats, tents, containers, lashings), sinew (sewing thread, bindings, bow reinforcement), guts (containers), bone (projectile points, needles, skates, tools), hooves (glue) and antler (bows, projectile points, tools, gaming pieces, toggles, pegs). Antler may have been obtained from killed stags or collected after shedding.

The rut occurs from mid September until the end of October, with birth of the young in May and June. The antlers are only present in males and are shed between mid March and mid May (Taylor-Page 1971, 36). This species may have been hunted using pitfall traps, or by archery from ambush positions at drinking points, or at natural or manufactured obstacles.

Reindeer (*Rangifer tarandus*)

This species is also diurnal and gregarious. It is currently extinct in the British Isles except for one introduced herd of domestic reindeer living semi-wild in the Cairngorm Mountains of Scotland. They now occur in the mountains of southern Norway, in Spitzbergen, Finland and through eastern Siberia, and are the 'caribou' of arctic America.

Their preferred habitat is montane and arctic tundra, although they may also occur in open woodland (eg in Finland). Their distribution is limited by snow of greater than 0.6m depth and by the distribution of an important dietary component, the tundra lichen ('reindeer moss'), *Cladonia rangiferina* (Cornwall 1968, 48). Their feet are broad and the toes spread easily to allow efficient movement over snow (Lawrence and Brown 1973, 145). In general they are grazers, particularly on lichen, and also browsers on willow and birch shoots (Gamble 1986, 108).

As with red deer, there are behavioural differences linked to habitat. In open country the usual herd size is 30–40, and in woodland 15–20 (Gamble 1986, 108). Open-country reindeer may form very large groups of thousands of individuals, and migrate many hundreds of kilometres between the summer calving and feeding grounds and the wintering areas at the forest margins, while woodland reindeer tend to remain in small groups and undertake only small altitudinal migrations, moving down to shelter in bad weather (Smith 1992, 67; Lawrence and Brown 1973, 145). Body weight is 120–150kg in adult males and 80–100kg in adult females. The young are born in late May to June. Both sexes sport antlers.

The exploitation of this species at Three Ways Wharf would have been determined by the local habitat and the corresponding behavioural patterns. Larger groups of animals could have been hunted by driving and then killed with harpoons, spears or arrows at an obstacle such as a river crossing or a manufactured corral; smaller groups of woodland animals could have been stalked, shot from hides ('bow-rests') or caught in pitfall traps (Davis and Reeves 1990, 293–5). The central Inuit preferred to hunt this species after the spring thaw and during the summer as the hides were then most suitable for manufacture into clothing (Boas 1888, 93–5). The animals were shot using broad-headed arrows fired from bows made of wood and sinew, or reindeer antler. This was preferably done while the animals were swimming or wading across a water obstacle. When this was impossible, the deer were stalked, or driven past a hunting stand or hide and shot from there. More rarely, pitfall traps were used. The economic value of this species compares closely with that of red deer.

Roe deer (*Capreolus capreolus*)

This species is indigenous and still abundant in the British Isles (except Ireland) and throughout Europe and northern Asia. Unlike red deer and reindeer, these animals are shy, largely solitary and tend to feed at night. They are essentially a species of open deciduous woodland, particularly where there are rivers or streams, secluded clearings and considerable undergrowth; they may also be found in coniferous woodlands, particularly in the winter (Tegner 1951, 23). They are mainly browsers feeding on berries, shrubs and broad-leaved trees. For much of the year these deer are solitary, although they may form small groups in winter. As with red deer and reindeer, when this species does occur in more open areas, herd size and migratory tendencies increase.

Roe deer are very much smaller than red deer or reindeer,

the adult males attaining a body weight of 25–30+kg and the adult females a body weight of 20–25kg (Tegner 1951, 29). The antlers are also small and do not show the extensive branched pattern seen in the two larger species (Taylor-Page 1971, 32). The rutting season is in mid July to mid August and the kids are born in late April to mid June (ibid, 53). The antlers are shed in November to December (Lawrence and Brown 1973, 140). These small and elusive deer could have been hunted using the techniques suggested for red deer, which would possibly have been easier during the winter months when the deer formed groups and there was little or no foliage to restrict archery.

Horse (*Equus ferus*)

This species is currently extinct in the British Isles and only occurs in the wild as a relict population of the eastern race, *E f przewalskii*, in Central Asia. Most races of this species were adapted to open grassland, steppe or parkland with a continental climate and hard winters. Cornwall (1968, 48) states that at least one race, *E f robustus*, was present in temperate forest. In general, the distribution of this species was probably limited by human predation and the spread of forest. They were predominantly grazers eating grasses and possibly grubbing for acorns and tubers (Smith 1992, 65).

Horses were large animals attaining a body weight of up to 350kg. They may have been caught in pitfall traps, driven into corrals or shot from hides as with the other large ungulates.

The minor species

These species are each represented at Three Ways Wharf by only a few bones. They are probably to be regarded as minor dietary components, possibly hunted on an opportunistic rather than a planned basis.

Swan (*Cygnus* spp)

This genus of large aquatic birds is represented by three non-introduced species in the British Isles and north-west Europe. These are the mute swan (*Cygnus olor*), whooper swan (*Cygnus cygnus*) and Bewick's swan (*Cygnus columbianus bewickii*). Mute swans are the most abundant and commonly seen species in the British Isles. They are fully resident, and occur and nest throughout mainland Britain in a wide range of freshwater habitats, including marshes, pools, rivers, lakes and the upper reaches of estuaries, usually below the 300m contour line (Sharrock 1987, 102). They may move towards coastal habitats during the winter months. Although this species is indigenous and truly wild, it was brought into semi-domestication during the medieval period, particularly in southern Britain. It is the largest and heaviest British bird, attaining a beak-to-tail length of 1.52m (Peterson 1993, 49) and a body weight of up to 15kg. The flesh and eggs are palatable, and the wing plumage provides large, straight, strong feathers very suitable for arrow fletching.

Whooper swans are currently mainly winter visitors to the British Isles and north-west Europe, breeding mainly in the taiga zone of Eurasia. This species is the same size and build as mute swan. Most of the British wintering birds probably derive from the Icelandic breeding population (Lack 1993, 66). They formerly bred in the Orkney Islands, perhaps regularly down to the 18th century (Sharrock 1987, 447), and a few individuals remain for the summer on isolated lochs in Scotland, particularly in the Outer Hebrides, and in Ireland. In Britain the majority of birds occur north of the Wirral–Humber line in a range of aquatic habitats including standing water and intertidal mudflats; they are usually present from mid October to mid April.

Five swan bones, humerus and tibia mid- and distal shafts, were recovered from scatter C; two of them bore fine, well-preserved flint cuts (Andrews 1995; above, 4.6) and may, therefore, have come from deliberately killed birds. The large midshaft width and general large size and robustness of these bones suggest that they derive from adult mute or whooper swan. The lack of articulations prevents further identification to species level and therefore precludes any comments on seasonality.

These birds may have been hunted using a variety of techniques including thrown or slung stones, archery, or snares. The central Inuit tribes of arctic Canada are recorded as having caught swans using lines of 'whalebone' nooses arranged in shallow water to snare feeding birds, or at nesting sites; the birds were also speared, stoned, or shot during the moult when unable to fly well (Boas 1888, 103–4). Similar techniques may be presumed to have been available to the hunters of Three Ways Wharf.

Duck sp

One duck bone, a charred coracoid fragment, was recovered from scatter C. This may be presumed to have derived from a consumed individual, possibly taken using one of the techniques described for swan.

The exploitation of the birds has been demonstrated at Maglemosian sites (Cornwall 1968, 113), although it is impossible to specify the hunting techniques employed. The development of archery during the ?later Palaeolithic and its subsequent refinement during the Mesolithic allowed accurate, rapid discharge of a projectile without the sudden noise and movement involved in use of a stone, spear or dart (ibid, 111), and this may have resulted in an increase in exploitation of such alert and mobile prey.

Beaver (*Castor fiber*)

The European beaver is the largest rodent species in north-west Europe. Although currently extinct in the British Isles, it has been recovered from a range of prehistoric sites and is thought to have survived at least into the Anglo-Saxon period (Rackham 1986, 34). It is aquatic and feeds on a wide range of vegetation in the summer, but is chiefly reliant on bark and twigs (eg of poplar and willow) during the winter (Corbet and Ovenden 1980, 150). They may create ponds with a constant water level by damming streams, or may simply burrow into a river bank. They are effectively confined to lakes and rivers with deciduous

forest margins and a boreal climate (Cornwall 1968, 48). Beaver are highly esteemed for their meat and are still an exploited fur species in Russia and northern North America and Canada.

Beaver was represented at the site by nine fragments, most or all of which could have derived from the same individual. No butchery marks were noted, so these remains may represent a deliberately hunted animal or a chance local casualty. The animals could have been acquired by a variety of techniques including trapping and the use of projectiles.

Pine marten (*Martes martes*)

This indigenous species is a shy, active, elusive diurnal carnivore which is able to climb and swim at great speed. It still occurs in mainland Britain, particularly in the Scottish Highlands but with isolated populations in England, Wales and Ireland, as well as across much of Europe as far as western Siberia (Corbet and Ovenden 1980, 183–4). The preferred habitat is coniferous or mixed forest but it is also found in deciduous woodland and occasionally on open rocky ground up to the 2000m contour line. Its prey includes fish, frogs and a range of small birds and mammals, and insects and berries are also occasionally taken (Lawrence and Brown 1973, 58). The marten is solitary and tends to keep to regular runs and resting places. Although this is not an esteemed food species, the pelt is particularly attractive and the remains may derive from an animal killed – probably snared or trapped – for this purpose.

Red fox (*Vulpes vulpes*)

This species is very widely distributed, occurring throughout Europe (except Iceland, but including Britain and Ireland), North Africa, temperate Asia and much of North America (Corbet and Ovenden 1980, 179). Although definitely preferring deciduous woodland, foxes may occur in open moorland and mountains. They are highly versatile and adaptable carnivores, able to exploit carrion, refuse, insects, earthworms, eggs, birds and the smaller mammals, as well as fruit and berries in the autumn. They are not currently esteemed as food, although their fur is decorative and the animals are still hunted and farmed for this purpose. Two fragments, an unworn canine tooth and a calcined astragalus, were recovered from scatter C, implying an anthropogenic reason for the presence of this species. This may indicate deliberate hunting or trapping of the animal perhaps for its fur, or less premeditated killing of an animal scavenging on discarded deer remains. The central Inuit employed a sophisticated and ingenious variety of baited pitfall and deadfall traps to acquire these animals (Boas 1888, 102).

Wolf (*Canis lupus*)

This species is currently extinct in the British Isles but still occurs in Russia, several European countries, Arabia, India and North America. It is a very adaptable carnivore able to exploit a range of prey including carrion, birds, small mammals and large ungulates. Its occurrence, distribution and abundance are functions of prey availability rather than climate. In Europe the preferred habitat is open woodland and tundra, with some occurrence in dense forest. Wolves are exploited as a fur species and have invariably been killed when coming into contact with man, although they are almost certainly the wild precursor of the domestic dog. The central Inuit used pitfall traps, a variety of snares and hunting 'in ambush' to catch this species when individuals were becoming troublesome near to villages or dog teams (Boas 1888, 102). Wolf was represented by a fragment of canine tooth from scatter C at Three Ways Wharf.

4.8   Summary and conclusions

It is clear from the analyses of the bone distributions that the excavated part of the site represents two, or possibly three distinct phases of occupation. The first two involved a Lateglacial occupation with the hunting of reindeer, with one at least possibly taking place in late winter or early spring.

Neither of these two phases of occupation seems likely to have lasted for any substantial length of time, and the foci of the two reindeer bone scatters were *c* 8m apart. Horse bones and teeth are associated with both these phases, but it is not possible to establish whether these remains occurred on site through human action or merely accidentally as a result of natural agencies. The occupation in scatter C east appears to be associated with a hearth, since there is a concentration of burnt bone in this area, including a burnt fox astragalus which suggests that this species was also hunted at this time.

The third period of occupation must have been several centuries later and the hunting during this phase was directed towards red deer, with more rarely roe deer and swan also being taken. Other faunal remains included pine marten, beaver, a duck and a possible wolf, but none of these can be directly associated with the human occupation. At least 15 individual red deer are represented among the bones; most of the latter are heavily fragmented long bones which appear to have been processed for the extraction of their marrow and then thrown on a 'midden'. It is probable that the season of occupation during this phase was late winter or early spring.

5

Site formation processes and taphonomy

In order to study how human behaviour is reflected in the artefact and faunal distributions, the effects of non-anthropogenic 'natural' and non-intentional human agents had first to be assessed. The study analysed the horizontal and vertical distributions of artefactual and faunal material and tried to model the site formation processes. In addition, the vertical distributions of artefacts and fauna were analysed to try and elucidate a relative chronology for the different phases of occupation at Three Ways Wharf.

5.1 Faunal material: horizontal and vertical trends in distribution, weathering and non-human taphonomy

The condition and distribution of the faunal material on the site (Chapter 4) were the result of a considerable number of taphonomic factors in which both human behaviour and natural processes played a part.

Differential preservation

Preservation across the site varied. Much of the material in scatter C, particularly most of the red deer material, was reasonably well preserved. This bone was somewhat chalky and had lost all its protein content, but showed relatively slight surface erosion (Fig 156) and frequently quite sharp broken edges. Such preservation applied over most of scatter C, but to the east, where the levels in which the bones lay dropped slightly (Fig 31), many of the bones were more brittle, tended to flake and had been to a lesser or greater extent impregnated by iron salts or bore iron-rich surface deposits. The possibility that this difference may have been related to material from the earlier bone scatter in this area (Chapters 4.3 and 6.3) is not entirely consistent with the evidence, since red deer as well as reindeer bones were found in this condition.

A third state of preservation was found in scatter C. This is particularly well illustrated in Fig 157. In the fragments in this state the bone surface is severely etched and exhibits a fibrous texture as well as some smoothing and 'wear' on the bone protuberances or broken edges. Fig 158 illustrates two bones from square E18N01 in the centre of the bone concentration in scatter C. The first, an astragalus of a reindeer, was found in spit 4, SU30, and the second, a red deer astragalus, in spit 2, SU40. The reindeer astragalus exhibits the fibrous etched surface pattern, while the second fragment shows much more limited surface damage to the bone. A number of bone fragments exhibit this pattern of preservation in the east part of scatter C, and of these none can be confidently assigned to red deer, but in fact are more closely comparable with reindeer material. It would appear that while the iron-impregnated material reflects its burial environment (presumably at a level most influenced by

FB 1964

FB 774

FB 748

Fig 158 Reindeer FB 774 (left) and red deer FB 748 astragali from square E18N01 in scatter C, showing differences in surface preservation; the reindeer bone has lost its posterior articulating surface; both bones also show deposition of iron salts on the surface (scale 1:1)

changes in water table) and cannot be attributed to the age of the material, the etched surface pattern, occurring both in areas of the site where iron salts do not affect the bones and in those where they do, is more confidently attributable to the greater age of these bones in the deposits. The occurrence of both red deer and reindeer bones throughout the same sequence (Chapter 6.3) suggests that burial of the site largely post-dates the later occupation at the site. The earlier bone must, therefore, have lain around on the surface and within the top soil layer for considerably longer than that from the Mesolithic scatter, before the whole site was buried beneath the black alluvial sediments represented by SU50. This appears to have been responsible for the greater degree of erosion on these fragments. Some of the reindeer bone appears as if subjected to water erosion (P Andrews, pers comm), although this could equally have been caused by repeated fluctuations in water table while in the topsoil.

In scatter A the bones exhibited yet another state of preservation. The fragments in this area retained some of their surface but exhibited clear signs of rootlet and surface etching (Fig 159). Breaks were, however, still relatively sharp, which

Fig 156 Distal end of red deer tibia FB 1964 from scatter C, showing the average state of preservation and surface condition of the bones from the Early Mesolithic scatter (scale 1:1)

FB 1870

Fig 157 The heavily etched condition of a fragment of reindeer tibia FB 1870 from scatter C (scale 1:1)

FB 1012

Fig 159 Reindeer femur fragment FB 1012 from scatter A, showing heavy surface root etching and iron salt deposition in the superficial layers of the bone (scale 1:1)

suggests that much of the fragmentation may have taken place after burial. The fragments from this area include very chalky pieces and some where salt deposition may have taken place in the bone. This material is in general a little better preserved than the reindeer material in scatter C east but still poorly by comparison with most of the red deer fragments deriving from C west.

The poorer condition of the reindeer bones in both scatters is reflected in the fact that, despite equivalent or larger sample sizes, insufficient carbon was obtained from their teeth for a radiocarbon assay, while the teeth of both red and roe deer produced dates (Table 1).

The preservational aspects can largely be attributed to natural processes, as discussed above, the variations in condition of the bone across the site being related to the degree of or length of time that the bones underwent aerial weathering, and subsequently sub-aerial erosion within the topsoil. Water movement in the soil caused leaching of minerals and destruction of the organic fraction of the bone, as well as salt deposition within the bone matrix and upon its surface.

Fragmentation

The generally high level of fragmentation has been noted above, but some of this can be attributed to post-depositional factors. Many of the bone fragments were lifted during excavation still within their clay matrix. A considerable number of these bone fragments had fractured and split *in situ*, probably as a result of freezing and thawing, or drying and wetting, of the clay sediments. This fracturing was clearly visible where the bone fragments were lifted with the clay matrix, with individual pieces still juxtaposed with their adjacent fragments. Unfortunately, washing of these finds often resulted in a heap of fragments which it was often very difficult to reconstruct, and complicated by the occurrence of unrelated fragments in the same sediment lump. The breaks were generally sharp and in many cases the fragments could be stuck together to reconstruct the bone. Whether this fragmentation took place shortly after burial, while the sediments were still relatively exposed, or happened since, as a result of seasonal drying-out of the buried clay sediments, is unlikely to be determined. The impact of this factor on the assemblage is substantial and, although the database did not routinely record the number of fragments which fitted back together, this type of fragmentation occurred across the whole site and on a significant proportion of the finds. Probably no more than half of the reconstructable pieces were recognised, and with considerable time and perseverance further pieces could be joined. Even a number of fragments with obviously modern breaks did not find their counterparts.

Nevertheless, despite the level of post-depositional fragmentation it is clear from the detailed faunal analysis that much of the fragmentation was caused by past human activity. In addition to the fragmentation of individual lifted bone finds, a number of joins were made between two or more individual FB-numbered pieces. These were occasionally

adjacent finds which were lifted independently but more rarely occurred up to 20cm or more apart. It seems unlikely that these latter fragments are the result of post-burial fragmentation, and a proportion (although not quantifiable) of the bone finds probably derive from post-depositional, but pre-burial, destructive agencies such as frost or trampling. Even greater dispersal is suggested for bones probably from the same joint or adjacent bones in the limb. For example, a left astragalus and left centroquartal of reindeer in squares E18N01 and E19N02 probably derive from the same ankle. With an assemblage so fragmented there is considerable difficulty in seeking to establish this level of association, but this aspect of the study will be considered in more detail below.

These aspects of the fragmentation of the assemblage are unrelated, except perhaps indirectly, to any human activities. Other aspects may more properly be seen as a consequence of human behaviour and related to aspects of carcass processing, food consumption, or disposal behaviour. This is dealt with in detail above (Chapter 4.6) but here we can briefly draw attention to a general indication of the fragmentation across scatter C. Figs 160–2 present the weight of individual bones per 0.5m², the number of individual bones per 0.5m² and the average weight of the fragments in each 0.5m². Apart from the distributional information these figures contain, it is clear that the level of fragmentation is higher within the area of greatest bone density, with many fragments weighing on average less than 5g, while fragment size increases towards the periphery of the scatter. There are minor differences in preservation, but these are insufficient to account for this distributional pattern which in the discussion below is attributed to human behaviour. These figures contain only the 3D-recorded bones since the sieved material is not

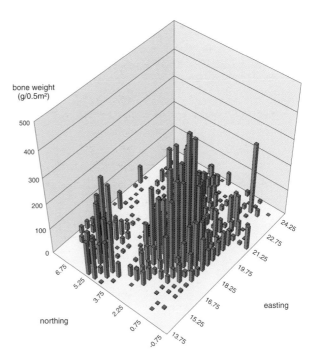

Fig 160 3D histogram of bone weight per 0.5m² in scatter C

comprehensive for the site; but average fragment size diminishes sharply when this element of the sample is considered.

The bulk of the bone from the site derives from SU40, the unit producing most of the larger bone fragments. SU30 contained both fewer and smaller fragments, with only a few identifiable bones coming from SU50 immediately above the main artefact-bearing layer.

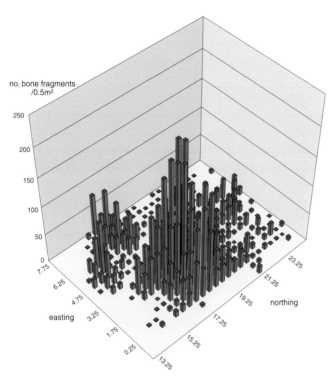

*Fig 161 3D histogram of number of bone fragments (FB-numbered) per 0.5m²
in scatter C*

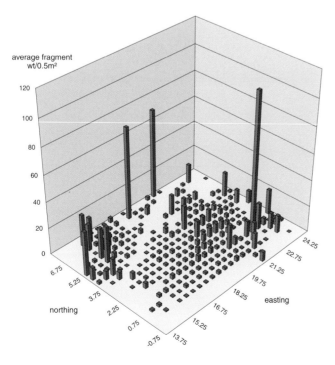

Fig 162 3D histogram of average weight of bone fragments per 0.5m² in scatter C

Evidence for scavenging and carnivore damage

Although the damage to the faunal material is considerable and the more fragile ends of many of the elements – particularly humeri and femora – have been totally lost, there is absolutely no evidence for carnivore damage to material in scatters A and C. There is no physical evidence in the form of gnawing marks on any of the fragments, and none of the complete long bone ends in the collection exhibit any sign of canid damage or the like. Only one bone from the whole site presented any positive evidence for carnivore damage. This was a humeral shaft fragment from scatter B, probably of red deer, displaying tooth indentations and the surface erosion characteristic of bones that have passed through the carnivore gut (P Andrews, pers comm). The dimensions of this fragment suggest an animal the size of a wolf as the candidate. On no other material from the site were such signs observed, suggesting that little or none of the fragmentation or erosion can be attributed to scavenging animals.

There is carnivore material in the sample, including fox and possibly wolf/dog (Chapter 4), but there is nothing to indicate that the human occupation included domestic dogs or 'pet' wolves, and unless their access to the waste bone was rigorously controlled it seems unlikely that the people at the site kept any.

Recognition of two or more episodes on the site

One of the most marked patterns on the site is that of the bone distribution. This can be presented in two ways, in terms either of numbers of fragments or of weight of bone. Since many fragments derive from the samples, but not all the samples have been sorted for bone, a plot of fragment numbers cannot be considered satisfactory unless only the FB-numbered fragments are plotted (ie only hand-excavated bone, Fig 14). On the other hand, the weight of bone lost through not sorting some of the residues is much less significant and a plot of total weight of bone (Fig 15), irrespective of unsorted samples, or weight of FB-numbered bone, is likely to give a good indication of bone distribution across the site.

Areas of the site

Two major concentrations of bone occurred in scatter C (Fig 14; Fig 15) where the quantity of bone rose to a level of nearly 400g per 0.5m² in the southern centre of the area and up to 140g per 0.5m² in the north-west corner. A much smaller assemblage was located in scatter A (Fig 9; Fig 10) where the bone fragments were more dispersed and in far lower frequencies. The major concentration in scatter C occupied an area of c 8m², with weight of bone falling off rapidly towards the periphery of this area (Fig 15; Fig 160). The somewhat smaller bone concentration to the north-west may be a continuation of this scatter that had become separated by the cutting of a later intrusive ditch, although aspects of the bone assemblage indicate both similarity and some slight differences between these two areas. There are minor concentrations of low bone density in scatter C east, in the vicinity of the hearth. For a variety of reasons considered in detail below, it is apparent that these concentrations in scatter C are anthropogenic and cannot be attributed to natural mortality or fluvial mechanisms. The distributions in scatter A could potentially be the result of natural mortality but even here the data suggest that this represents an occupation site. The occasional incidence of bones distributed much further afield over an area of at least 500m² suggests that similar small clusters of bone, indicated by finds in the test pits, may also represent small-scale occupation events either contemporary with or independent of the occupation episodes represented by the major collections in scatters A and C.

This variable density of 3D-recorded bone fragments across the site (Fig 8) suggests that between the two scatters and the other peripheral areas the level of human activity, if such it was (Chapters 3 and 4), was much less on the outskirts of the site than in scatter A, and much less in scatter A than in scatter C. The excavated areas of the site are illustrated in Fig 3 and Fig 8. The bulk of the report and discussions deal with the faunal assemblages from scatters A and C, although a number of bone fragments were recovered from scatter B and several of the test pits; the latter lie beyond the foci of material identified in scatters A and C. In the discussions below, scatters A and C are dealt with independently. This is because the flint and faunal assemblages in the two areas and the radiocarbon dating suggest that they represent distinct sites separated in time (Chapter 1.3,

'Dating'). Furthermore, within scatter C there is good evidence for two chronologically distinct sites which is considered in more detail in Chapter 6.3.

General period and spatial division of the site

The analysis of a mixed assemblage would limit the opportunity to interpret the faunal samples so the general distribution of the major species is addressed first.

The distribution of finds of red deer, roe deer and reindeer in scatter C are plotted in Figs 163–5. The red deer fragments are concentrated in the areas already noted as containing the majority of the bone by weight (Fig 15); the roe deer, although occurring with much less frequency, tend to show a concentration in the same areas. In contrast, the reindeer bones are centred to the east of the area and the majority of specifically identifiable fragments lie outside the concentration of red deer and roe deer fragments. This discrepancy in the distribution, while potentially interpretable as due to some species-specific spatial organisation, is more plausibly explained as two chronologically distinct bone scatters, the later of which overlay to some extent the scatter of reindeer bones.

Working on this premise, the depths of red deer and reindeer bones in scatter C below the upper surface of SU40 (Table 60) were plotted as a histogram (Fig 166). It is apparent that the reindeer bones tend to be distributed at a greater depth

Fig 163 Point plot of red deer, cf red deer, red deer size, red deer or reindeer, red deer or reindeer size, deer sp and cattle size bone across the whole site (scale 1:200)

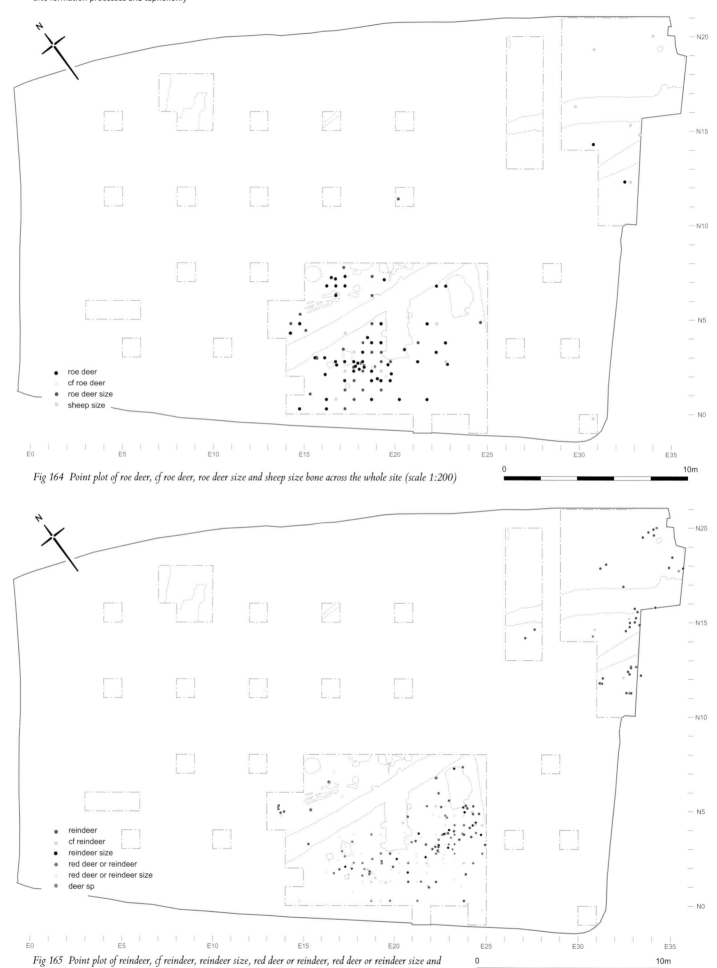

Fig 164 *Point plot of roe deer, cf roe deer, roe deer size and sheep size bone across the whole site (scale 1:200)*

Fig 165 *Point plot of reindeer, cf reindeer, reindeer size, red deer or reindeer, red deer or reindeer size and deer sp bone across the whole site (scale 1:200)*

Table 60 Depth of red deer (n=440) and reindeer (n=89) bones below the surface of SU40 in scatter C (based only on 3D-recorded fragments)

Depth (cm) below SU40 surface	Red deer frags no.	Reindeer frags no.	Cumulative % red deer	Cumulative % reindeer
-6	1		0.2	0.0
-4	5		1.3	0.0
-2	12		4.1	0.0
0	47	1	14.8	1.1
2	107	6	39.1	7.9
4	89	9	59.3	18.0
6	81	6	77.7	24.7
8	50	30	89.1	58.4
10	30	19	95.9	79.8
12	5	6	97.0	86.5
14	4	8	97.9	95.5
16	6	1	99.3	96.6
18	1	2	99.5	99.0
20	1	1	99.8	100.0
22	1		100.0	

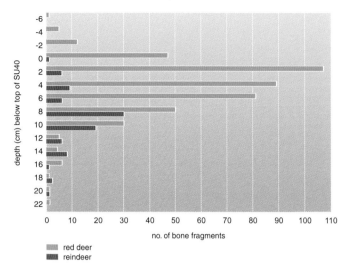

Fig 166 Frequency histogram of depth below the surface of SU40 of red deer and reindeer bones across the whole site

than those of red or roe deer. A Kolmogorov-Smirnov two-sample test rejects the null hypothesis at P<0.001, indicating that the two distributions are different. Despite the absence of radiocarbon dates for the reindeer in this scatter, it can be concluded that they represent an earlier occupation of the site than that associated with the red deer.

In scatter A this problem of superimposition of two sites is not apparent. The faunal assemblage is dominated by reindeer and horse (Fig 167) and, although some of the unassigned fragments may derive from red deer, there are no specifically identifiable red deer finds and only two roe deer bones in this scatter. Even the sheep size fragments are probably very

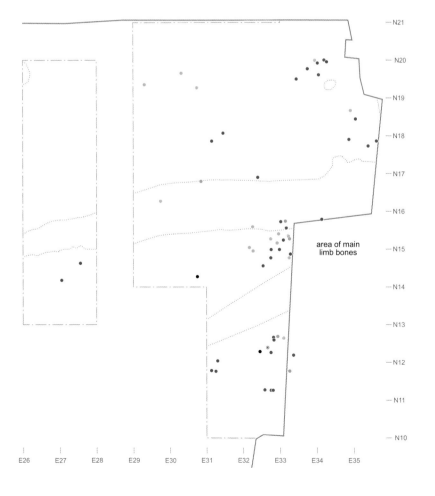

Fig 167 Distribution of identified bones in scatter A (scale 1:100)

fragmented reindeer bones. This concentration of bones from the species associated with the earlier period of occupation at the site is consistent with the lithic evidence and confirms the association with the earlier radiocarbon date on the horse teeth from this scatter.

A Kolmogorov-Smirnov two-sample test on the depth below the top of SU40 of reindeer bones in scatters A and C supports the null hypothesis at P>0.05, suggesting that these scatters are distributed over a similar depth in the soil and may, therefore, be broadly contemporary.

5.2 Lithic material: horizontal and vertical dispersal, and taphonomy

Horizontal dispersal

Introduction

When attempting to assess the degree of post-depositional movement within a lithic scatter, one of the most difficult aspects is to separate movement due to anthropogenic factors from that relating to post-depositional natural taphonomic processes.

In Chapter 1.3 it was demonstrated that both scatters A and C are composed of clearly defined, discrete concentrations of lithic material arbitrarily subdivided into sub-assemblages (SAS 1–11) (Fig 9; Fig 12). The flintwork is unrolled and in excellent condition. In a number of cases refitting burin spalls and burins were in very close proximity (Chapter 3.5). Together with the clustering of burnt flint and bone on two foci (Fig 16) and the strong spatial patterning of the faunal material (above, 5.1), it is clear that the scatters had undergone little non-anthropogenic horizontal disturbance.

Quantitatively, Barton has demonstrated at Hengistbury Head, Dorset, that refitting is one of the most important aids to characterising the nature and degree of lithic artefact movement (Barton 1992, 79–90). Unfortunately, the constraints placed on the refitting programme at Three Ways Wharf precluded the reassembling of large clusters of blades to cores. For instance, the largest refitting groups in scatters A and C contained 20 and 44 pieces respectively, with only one other group attaining double figures. Thus it was impractical to produce 'centroid' diagrams (ibid, fig 3.10) which would have allowed some distinction between anthropogenic and non-anthropogenic movement of artefacts. Nevertheless, four of the larger refitting groups were selected in an attempt to quantify the degree of dispersal of material. Based on Barton (ibid, 79, 160–1), the following data were calculated:

1) Distribution centre = the point which is the mean measurements of the X and Y coordinates (eastings and northings) of all the flints in the refitting group.
2) Group radius = the sum of the standard deviation of the X and Y coordinates of all the flints in the refitting group.

Table 61 Horizontal dispersal data for four refitting groups

Refitting group	No. in refitting group (n)	Distribution centre (mean X+Y)	Standard deviation of X & Y	Group radius (Std X + Std Y)	% Dilation (group radius/ 1.0m)
18 (A)	17	X = 30.95 Y = 17.71	X = 0.56 Y = 0.34	0.90	-
10 (C east)	58	X = 21.10 Y = 02.41	X = 1.40 Y = 1.14	2.54	254%
30 (C east)	17	X = 22.28 Y = 03.30	X = 1.58 Y = 1.07	2.65	265%
37 (C west)	7	X = 18.04 Y = 04.06	X = 0.58 Y = 1.10	1.68	168%

The product-moment correlation coefficients for the X and Y coordinates of the four refitting groups were calculated using the methods outlined by Fletcher and Lock (1991, 105–10). These showed that there were no preferred orientations of the scatters, which could thus be summarised by circles to show their dispersion (Barton 1992, 160).

Experimental knapping data (Barton 1992, 87) suggests that maximum dimensions of undisturbed knapping scatters would rarely exceed 200 x 200cm (ie a radius of 1.0m) and would often lie below 100 x 100cm (ie a radius of 0.5m). Thus it would appear from the data in Table 61 that refitting groups 10, 30 and 37 have undergone some horizontal movement, as all have group radii which exceed a theoretical maximum radius of 1.0m. Even refitting group 18 in scatter A is close to the theoretical limit.

By dividing the theoretical radius limit of 1.0m into the actual group radii, the percentage dilation for each scatter can be produced (Table 61). These factors, ranging from 0–265%, compare favourably with results from Hengistbury Head, where the Late Upper Palaeolithic scatters had dilation factors of 500–600% (Barton 1992, 92). At Hengistbury, however, the lithic material was located in coarse-grained sandy deposits, whereas SU40 and SU30 at Three Ways Wharf were fine-grained clay/silts.

The theoretical scatter dimensions and techniques of analysis, such as the centres of production and group radii referred to by Barton, may be affected by anthropogenic factors such as tool selection and use, or abandonment of unsuitable raw material. This latter factor is present in refitting group 18, which has the smallest group radius (Fig 168). This group comprised a large gravel cobble which had been tested and shattered into many pieces, only one or two of which were further modified by a few flake removals. There is thus a small element of anthropogenic disturbance in this scatter. In addition, the relatively large size of most of the constituent pieces would have required a fairly substantial water current velocity to disperse them.

In contrast, the three refitting groups in scatter C have much wider group radii. Fig 169 illustrates that some of the products of the knapping episodes represented by refitting groups 30 and 37 are widely dispersed. For example, in refitting

group 37, six of the seven pieces lie within a radius of 0.95m of the distribution centre, with one outlier 2.83m away. The single

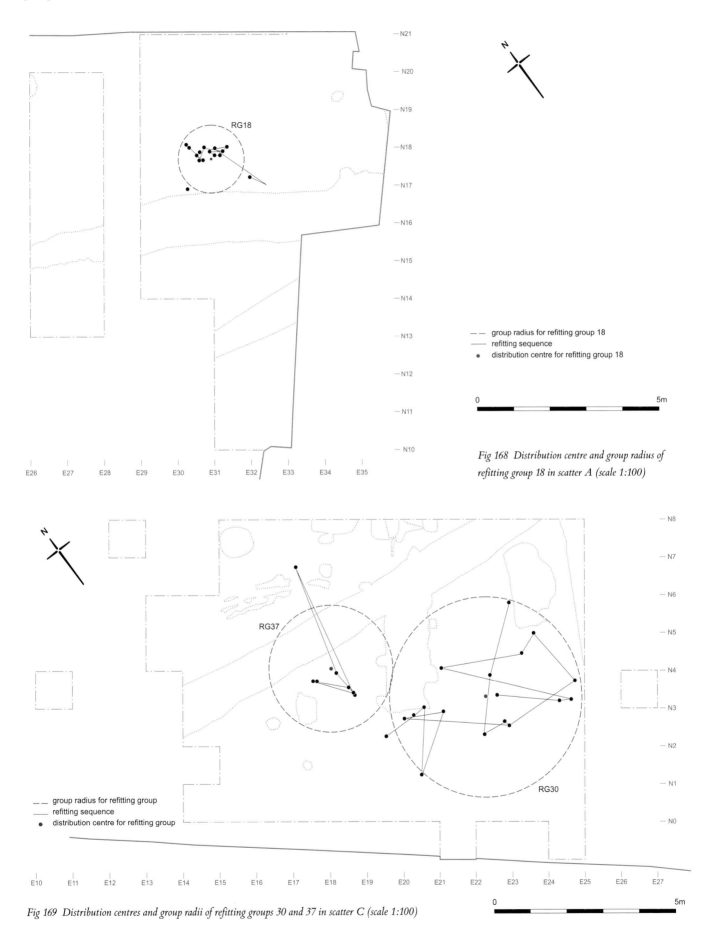

— — group radius for refitting group 18
——— refitting sequence
● distribution centre for refitting group 18

Fig 168 Distribution centre and group radius of refitting group 18 in scatter A (scale 1:100)

— — group radius for refitting group
——— refitting sequence
● distribution centre for refitting group

Fig 169 Distribution centres and group radii of refitting groups 30 and 37 in scatter C (scale 1:100)

outlier thus has the effect of widening the group radius to 1.68m when the majority of pieces lie within 0.95m. This renders attempts to assign a sub-assemblage, let alone individual pieces of flint, to a particular phase of occupation on distributional grounds problematic.

Analysis of the distances from the distribution centre suggests that anthropogenic factors played a part in the distribution pattern of refitting group 10 in scatter C east. This refitting group consists of a large cluster of blades knapped from a fully opposed platform core (Table 62). Fig 170 highlights the distribution of the tools, utilised pieces and core preparation pieces, and when this is considered along with the

data in Table 62, it is possible to suggest certain patterns in the dispersal of material in refitting group 10.

Firstly, the debitage element has an average distance to the centre of production of 1.27m, plus the standard deviation (1.11m), giving a total of 2.37m. Using the theoretical maximum scatter radius of 1.0m, this suggests that the scatter has undergone a horizontal dilation of the order of 237%. However, it should be noted from Fig 170 that most of the debitage is tightly clustered well inside the theoretical scatter radius of 1.0m.

The utilised pieces and the core preparation pieces are much more tightly clustered near the centre of production, at the heart of SAS 3. Both groups of artefacts have a single outlier to the south of the scatter, but these do not influence the pattern, as Table 62 shows remarkably low standard deviations for these groups of artefacts. In contrast, the average distance from the centre of production of the retouched tools is much greater, reflecting their distribution to the east of the main concentration of knapping debris.

This pattern is interpreted as the product of non-anthropogenic and anthropogenic factors. The scatter as a whole reflects the debitage distribution which has been affected by non-anthropogenic factors. However, the core preparation material is located where expected, at the heart of the knapping scatter. Certain blanks are selected for *ad hoc* utilisation (or, in the case of the *lame mâchurée*, heavy chopping) close to the knapping centre. In contrast, the retouched tools seem to have been carried away from the production centre for utilisation around the periphery of the scatter.

Table 62 *Horizontal dispersal data for refitting group 10: composition and average distances to group distribution centre (n = 58, group radius = 2.54m)*

Artefact group	Artefact type	Distance (m) to distribution centre for artefact group	
		Mean	Standard deviation
Retouched tools	1 microlith 1 truncated blade 1 burin	2.74	1.54
Utilised pieces	2 blades 1 *lame mâchurée*	1.02	0.09
Core & core preparation pieces	1 core 7 crested & other prep pieces	1.54	1.39
Debitage	44 blades & flakes	1.27	1.11

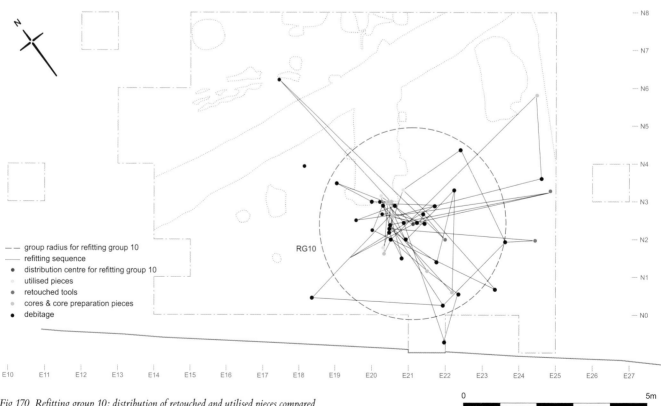

group radius for refitting group 10
refitting sequence
• distribution centre for refitting group 10
  utilised pieces
• retouched tools
  cores & core preparation pieces
• debitage

RG10

Fig 170 *Refitting group 10: distribution of retouched and utilised pieces compared to distribution centre and group radius (scale 1:100)*

0   5m

Importantly, this interpretation suggests that despite horizontal dilation factors of up to *c* 2.3 times, the integrity of spatial patterning caused by anthropogenic factors is maintained.

Mechanisms of non-anthropogenic horizontal movement of lithic material

At Three Ways Wharf the relatively close proximity to an active water source suggested that channelled or surface water flow resulting from overbank flooding was of potentially major significance in non-anthropogenic horizontal movement of lithic and faunal material. This was investigated by studying the orientation of laminar flints.

The basic hypothesis adopted was that the orientation of artefacts would be expected to be random following knapping. If significant trends in orientation were present, this could suggest that the laminar pieces had been reorientated and become aligned with low-energy current flows across the palaeo-land surface (ie minor flood events). The gradient and direction of dip of the local microtopography could also be expected to have had an effect on flint orientation, perhaps in combination with current flow.

In order to test this hypothesis, the orientations of the longer blade-like pieces from five 1.0m squares were selected for analysis, four in scatter C and one in scatter A. The data were those recorded on the orientation sheets described in Chapter 1.3. Where possible the squares were chosen to coincide with the highest densities of flintwork.

No visually or statistically significant patterning in the orientation of the flints was present, and the results are not discussed further. Thus there was little evidence of current flow across the site which might have contributed to horizontal movement of the flintwork. When the angle of dip of artefacts was analysed, it was found that the predominant angle was 15° or less. This would suggest that, although the artefacts were distributed through *c* 20cm of the profile, they had not undergone redeposition or reworking by high-energy forces such as channelled water action, agreeing with the findings of the orientation study. These data would be best interpreted as indicating a gradual burial caused by biological action.

Vertical dispersal

Introduction

The stable land surface/bioturbation model outlined in Chapter 2.2 and above is important, since the degree of vertical movement of artefacts could provide a key to understanding the chronological sequence of occupation and deposition of the lithic scatters and constituent sub-assemblages at Three Ways Wharf. This is supported by the results of the depth analysis of the reindeer and red deer skeletal material presented above (5.1). For this reason, detailed quantified analysis of the depth distributions of artefacts was carried out. This section deals with the vertical distribution of flint tools and debitage greater than 10mm in

size and microdebitage of less than 10mm but greater than 3mm in size.

Artefacts under 10mm in size (microdebitage)

Microdebitage less than 10mm in size was not analysed by stratigraphic unit due to the bias caused by uneven sample sorting between the two scatters. Instead analysis concentrated on the vertical distribution of microdebitage by spit for specific squares.

Six squares were selected for analysis, one each from SAS 1, 2, 3, 4, 10 and 11 (Fig 9; Fig 14). The material collected by sieving and from excavation of microdebitage 3–10mm in size was totalled for each spit within the squares. Due to differential sorting of samples the results for the black humic clay (SU50) were not included. Comparison between squares was complicated by variation in the relative depth of spits within and between squares (Chapter 1.4). This was overcome by plotting the percentage of the total microdebitage collected in each square against the depth of each spit below the top of SU40 and displaying the result as an X–Y graph (Fig 171). This allowed basic comparisons to be made of the vertical distribution of microdebitage between the squares.

The high density of microdebitage in each square confirms that the lithic scatters were the product of *in situ* knapping. The two squares in scatter A (E32N12 and E30N17) show a bi-modal distribution of microdebitage, with peaks occurring at roughly 6cm and 12cm depth (Fig 171). In contrast, two squares in scatter C west (E16N02 and E18N03) and one square (E20N02) in C east (Fig 171) all display a similar general trend showing a distinctly uni-modal distribution, with the greatest concentration *c* 5–7cm below the surface of SU40. This upper 5–7cm of SU40 probably represents the bioturbated palaeo-land surface. There is a fall-off in microdebitage concentration below this point; nonetheless, significant quantities of material occur through the remainder of the profile. Only E22N02 in scatter C east shows a peak concentration slightly lower down the profile, although it remains a uni-modal distribution.

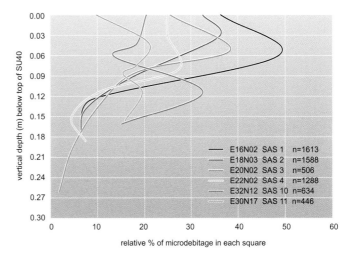

Fig 171 Vertical distribution of microdebitage (artefacts less than 10mm in size) in six selected squares

The differences in the patterns of microdebitage distribution between scatters C and A may be interpreted as indicating that scatter A was exposed to bioturbation for a greater length of time compared to scatter C. This would result in greater movement of material down-profile, and confirm that scatter A is chronologically earlier than either scatter C west or C east. However, if this assumption were correct, one might expect to find the distribution patterns in the squares in C east to be similar to those in scatter A rather than C west. That this is not the case suggests either that the assumption of greater downward movement of microdebitage indicating relatively greater age is incorrect, or that other factors are influencing the patterns in scatter C. The most obvious such factor would be the proximity of scatters C west and C east leading to the distribution pattern of C east being cloaked by that of C west. The slightly different distribution curve for square E22N02 could be interpreted as showing a lower degree of cloaking, since it lies 2.0m further away from scatter C west than E20N02.

Artefacts over 10mm in size

The majority of flintwork in both scatters A and C was contained in SU40 with a fall-off down-profile into SU30. A small proportion of the assemblages was also present in the base of SU50, suggesting some very limited upward movement of artefacts.

Refits occurred across different stratigraphic units, proving that the stratigraphic units cannot be used to define chronologically and stratigraphically independent lithic assemblages. Although the maximum depth of a refitted artefact was greater in scatter A, the average depth of refitted pieces together with the standard deviation was almost exactly the same in scatters C west, C east and A. Thus, in all scatters *c* 65% of refitting artefacts were located within 0.09m (9cm) of the surface of SU40.

In addition, one refitting group (45) contained parts from a shattered nodule, two of which were located in scatter C and one in scatter A, all three pieces being contained in SU40.

Detailed quantified analysis of depth distribution of 3D-recorded artefacts

Due to the relatively small size of the refitting groups, quantified depth analysis was based on the quantity of all artefacts at given depths beneath the surface of SU40. Depth was calculated by subtracting the Z coordinate in metres OD for each 3D-recorded artefact from the level in metres OD of the surface of SU40 for the appropriate 0.25m². This produced some anomalies for squares in which SU40 sloped by a few centimetres, giving results which purported to place flints above the surface of SU40. This was remedied by summing all the flints down to a depth of 0.06m (6cm) and continuing the analysis at a frequency of 6cm.

In order to compare the vertical distribution of the various sub-assemblages and scatters, the absolute values for each 6cm depth interval were converted into relative percentages. Analysis showed that although there was variation between the 11

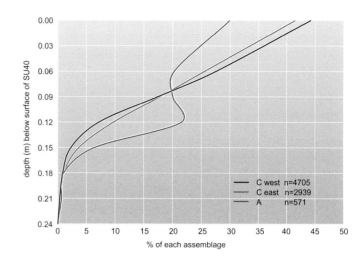

Fig 172 Vertical distribution of artefacts beneath surface of SU40 in scatters A, C west and C east

individual sub-assemblages, this was not significant. The results are, therefore, presented in terms of scatters C east, C west and A as X–Y charts in Fig 172.

From this graph it is clear that the degree of down-profile artefact movement was greatest in scatter A and smallest in C west. Scatter C east corresponds closely to C west, broadly agreeing with the findings of the microdebitage analysis.

Mechanisms of vertical movement

The ratios of broken to complete blades and flakes for scatters A, C west and C east were calculated. The underlying hypothesis in this exercise was that areas which show significantly higher proportions of broken artefacts might indicate greater trampling. However, the ratios of complete to broken blades and flakes were standardised and overlapped to a great extent.

The fairly standardised range of breakage ratios suggests that some factor may have acted on the scatters as a whole, such as weight loading from the overlying later prehistoric and historic period deposits. This may have been a major contributor to the pattern of breakage. It may also have led to a smoothing of the vertical distribution of artefacts through SU40 and SU30 between the various sub-assemblages.

Mechanisms of anthropogenic and non-anthropogenic horizontal and vertical movement have recently been reviewed in the context of the Upper Palaeolithic and Mesolithic site at Hengistbury Head by Barton and Collcutt (Barton 1992, 90–5, 69–78). There seems to be some agreement between the model proposed there and the Three Ways Wharf data. However, there are a number of caveats to be borne in mind.

1) The geology of the Hengistbury Head site was sand, allowing a greater degree of both vertical and horizontal movement of artefacts than the fine-grained alluvial clays at Three Ways Wharf.

2) There was no correlation between high artefact dip angles and depth at Three Ways Wharf.

3) Other factors directly affecting vertical dispersal, such as

trampling and weight loading of later deposits, may be present but masked.

4) Similarly, other factors such as sediment porosity (see 1) above) and hydrology may have indirectly affected the vertical dispersal of artefacts and produced varying patterns across the site.

5) The proximity of two scatters of different dates (C west and C east) may have led to a blurring of the vertical distribution patterns. The analysis of horizontal dilation suggests that some Lateglacial lithic material from scatter C east will be located within the area occupied by scatter C west and vice versa, while technological and refitting analysis, as well as spatial patterning, suggest that this mixing of material would not be great enough to disrupt patterning in vertical movement of artefacts.

6) The density of flintwork within a given area may have had an effect on the degree of vertical movement that material underwent. For instance, in SAS 1 in C west, c 1800 3D-recorded flints were present in an area of 7.5m². Given the assumption that the majority were produced during one phase of occupation, then this material would have lain as a thick mass on top of the palaeo-land surface represented by SU40. It is possible that this mass of lithic material acted as a form of inhibitor of the effects of rooting and worm sorting in moving the material down the profile. In contrast, where the density of lithic material was far less (in scatter A in particular), this may have posed proportionately less of a barrier to bioturbation.

5.3 Summary and conclusions

The data presented thus far suggest that following deposition on a stable land surface, the predominant mechanism causing vertical movement was bioturbation, that is to say vegetation rooting, earthworm and other burrowing animal activity. This would accord with the micromorphological study (Chapter 2.2).

The horizontal dilation factor of c 2–2.5 times indicated by the refitting clusters also indicates that the lithic material lay exposed on a land surface for a period of time and was not immediately cloaked by alluvium deposited by gentle overbank flooding. If the latter scenario had occurred, one might expect more regular patterning in the orientation of the artefacts, as well as increased dip angles, combined with a higher horizontal dilation factor. The degree of dispersal is relatively small and the spatial patterning of the lithic and faunal material remains intact. It is possible that the vegetation cover itself helped to restrict the degree of horizontal movement of the artefacts as the material 'bedded in' to the grass cover of the land surface.

Anthropogenic factors played a large part in the horizontal distribution of material, and in Chapter 6.2 concepts of use and 'drop and toss' discard zones are explored. Refitting group 10 suggests that, despite the effects of non-anthropogenic movement, anthropogenic spatial patterning of artefacts is preserved. Trampling would also have played a part in the vertical and horizontal dispersal of artefacts, but this is much more difficult to quantify and assess.

Depth analysis of reindeer and red deer finds confirms the assumption that the former would be the older (and thus more vertically dispersed) assemblage. Ordering of the lithic scatters by degree of vertical dispersal suggests that, broadly speaking, scatter A would be the oldest phase, although it was difficult to distinguish between C east and C west. However, other factors such as the density of artefacts in a given area may have affected the relative degree of vertical dispersal between sub-assemblages. In this respect, vertical dispersal of artefacts would not seem to be as clear an indicator of relative chronology as faunal material.

6

Human-related (anthropogenic) taphonomy: spatial analysis and interpretation

6.1 Introduction

This chapter deals with the anthropogenic taphonomy of the site, that is, aspects of human behaviour as reflected in patterns of lithic and faunal material; and it thereby seeks to draw inferences about the human use of space during each phase of occupation. The chapter is in four main parts. Sections 6.2 and 6.3 deal with the spatial analysis and interpretation of the lithic and faunal assemblages respectively. Section 6.4 combines elements of those discussions with the use-wear analysis of the lithic material. The final section (6.5) consists of a narrative synthesis of the activities carried out in each phase. It needs to be stressed at the outset that Chapter 6 contains analysis and interpretation of the spatial patterning of the assemblages, and in many cases several possible interpretations are discussed before one is preferred. It is acknowledged that, given the nature of the material and the dearth of knowledge of human behaviour during this period of British prehistory, many different interpretations are possible.

The wider implications of spatial patterning and use, both within the Three Ways Wharf scatters and within the broader landscape, will be discussed in Chapter 7.

6.2 Spatial analysis of lithic material

Methodology

Refitting and microdebitage analysis have shown that the main lithic concentrations in scatters A and C were the product of *in situ* flint knapping, and not dumps of refuse. The distribution of some of the artefact categories (such as axe and microlith debitage, burins and scrapers) and faunal material suggests that humanly produced spatial patterning is present at Three Ways Wharf. The most pressing question during this analysis was to what degree of refinement could the analysis be taken, given a number of limiting factors? These factors included:
1) the very close proximity (and inevitable overlap) of two chronologically distinct scatters (C west and C east);
2) the destructive effects of major intrusive later features;
3) the relatively small area of the landscape that was totally excavated;
4) uncertainty regarding the extent of the scatters – for instance, scatter A extended to the east beyond the site boundary, while scatter C may have extended to the south;
5) uncertainty regarding the place of the Three Ways Wharf scatters in a much wider landscape of possible task- or multi-task-specific activity 'sites'.

Bearing these factors in mind and after reviewing the pertinent literature, it appeared that two approaches to spatial analysis could be adopted, which can be summarised as follows.
1) Visual inspection of artefact distributions from which are drawn subjective inferences. Critical to this approach is the

format chosen to display the artefact distributions, a subject that has been reviewed by Blankholm (1991, 24). One of the most commonly used methods in Britain consists of gradations of shading or dot densities to represent numbers of artefacts by grid unit, for example at Star Carr, North Yorkshire (Clark 1954), Hengistbury Head, Dorset (Barton 1992), and Pointed Stone, North Yorkshire, sites 2 and 3 (Jacobi 1978), among many others. Unfortunately, such displays are relatively difficult to analyse and assimilate visually. Blankholm has emphasised that density contouring of artefacts represents a fast and elegant way of displaying the general nature of artefact distributions, but that this procedure should be handled with care (Blankholm 1991, 25). For example, contour intervals and size of grid must be chosen carefully so as not to obscure some patterns or over-emphasise others. With the advent of surface-generating computer software such as SURFER, the production of density contours has been much simplified. Furthermore, many combinations of contour interval and artefact type can be tested until a suitable display results. Such an approach has been adopted by Grøn (1995) to analyse the spatial patterning within Maglemosian huts. However, in Grøn's analysis very low densities of artefacts (such as microliths) are contoured and compared with very high-density categories such as debitage. One is left wondering whether contours representing such low densities are valid (given that the software will always produce contours), and if not, then the comparisons with high-density artefact types must be suspect.

2) Such subjective approaches have been roundly criticised by Blankholm (1991, 24) as being variable in capacity, relevant consistency, rigour and replicability. Blankholm may be regarded as one of the leading proponents of what may be termed the 'quantitative' approach to spatial analysis, a group of techniques which arose from developments in the 'new archaeology' of the 1960s and 1970s. This approach required the rigorous formal statistical testing of theories and hypotheses. One of the earliest pioneers of this form of spatial analysis was Whallon, who developed the idea that categories of artefacts would be spatially distributed over sites and that clusters of associated tool types would form 'tool kits' (Whallon 1973, 117). However, the problems inherent in this approach soon became apparent, notably that tool typologies do not represent original tool function, and that anthropogenic and non-anthropogenic taphonomic factors will have 'blurred' the spatial distribution. Thus by 1978, Whallon had concluded that '["activity areas" would be] ... generally uninterpretable by inference or by arguing back from the nature of the activity areas to the activities involved, except under certain relatively unusual and restricted circumstances' (Whallon 1978, 33). Blankholm acknowledges many of the problems associated with quantitative spatial analysis, yet argues that modern methods and techniques are much more powerful and suited to the nature of the data encountered, and can provide powerful insights into human behaviour (Blankholm 1991, 47). However, one cannot help feeling that with every advance in statistical analysis comes a new drawback, and such statistical

approaches have been criticised by Olausson (1985–6) and (perhaps unsurprisingly) by Grøn (1995).

Although funding did not allow extensive experimentation with the Three Ways Wharf data, local density analysis (Blankholm 1991, 101) was carried out on the data for scatter C, using the LDEN module of the Arcospace spatial analysis package (Blankholm and Price 1991). The results were then compared against visual plots of the artefact distributions.

Local density analysis (LDA) did reveal certain trends in the association of different artefact categories. For instance, there was a relatively high correlation between scrapers and axes, higher even than between scrapers and scrapers. However, the distribution plots showed that the core tools were located within the densest area of scrapers ringing the hearth in C west. Since there were only four core tools, this would obviously produce a higher correlation than that between all scrapers, which were more widely distributed. Furthermore, this pattern could be easily seen from the distribution plots. In addition, most of the LDA coefficient curves produced simply showed increasing associations between artefacts as the search radius around each artefact increased. The spatial patterning at Three Ways Wharf would appear to be one of the 'unusual and restricted circumstances' alluded to by Whallon (1978, 33). Three Ways Wharf would certainly provide an excellent dataset for testing quantitative methods, but the restrictions mentioned at the beginning of this chapter would have to be borne in mind.

Yet another approach has been developed by Stapert (the 'ring and sector' method) and used to re-analyse the flint scatters at Pincevent among others (Stapert 1989). This approach was also briefly attempted for Three Ways Wharf, but the problems outlined above, in particular the distortions in the scatters caused by the later archaeological features, meant that it was not pursued. The ring and sector method has been used to analyse the Lateglacial lithic scatter at Launde, Leicestershire (Cooper 2006); however, the disturbance caused by an archaeological evaluation trench and the relatively low densities of artefacts present severely limited this attempt.

In this report, then, subjective visual analysis of spatial patterns has been employed. High-density artefact types such as debitage have been contoured, as well as bone and burnt flint, and are displayed as shaded contours. Against these backgrounds, the lower-density artefact types such as retouched tools and refitting clusters are displayed as point data.

The spatial analysis of 'function' is incorporated in the use-wear report (below, 6.4). No attempt will be made to attribute function to the tools or to associate 'tool kits' with certain areas for the reasons outlined above. What is attempted here is to examine the evidence for activity areas using techniques and models which consider how the archaeological record was formed (eg Delpech and Rigaud 1974; Rigaud 1978; analysis of level VII at Le Flageolet I). Such approaches have been usefully summarised by Gamble (1986, 272–7). Fundamental to 'activity area' approaches are a number of elements, perhaps the most important of which can be summarised as the correspondence between tool types and activity areas. Critical factors affecting this correspondence are the degree to which artefacts are recycled within the system and the mode and pattern of discard of artefacts. In the first instance, expedient technologies produce tools which are manufactured on the spot and then abandoned following use, whereas in curated technologies, tools are manufactured in anticipation of future use, and are often repaired and maintained. In curated technologies, it would be expected that there would be little correspondence between location of use and location of discard of artefacts (ibid, 275). Similarly, modes of discard of artefacts will affect spatial patterning; for example, whether artefacts are dropped at their location of use or 'tossed' into a discard zone away from the activity area (Binford 1978a).

The individual artefact sections of the lithics report in Chapter 3 deal with the detailed distributions of artefacts and the production–use–discard cycle for each artefact category. In this section, evidence from the distributions of debitage, tools, tool debitage (the by-products of tool manufacture) and refits will be combined to assess the effects of curation and mode of discard on the spatial patterning of artefacts, before attempting to define the presence of activity areas. This will also be of importance for the definition of activity areas based on use-wear analysis (below, 6.4). However, while attempting this exercise the effect of the horizontal dispersal of artefacts by non-anthropogenic factors should be borne in mind. In Chapter 3 this was estimated to be in the order of *c* 230–260%, which, although relatively small, will nonetheless lead to a blurring of anthropogenically produced spatial patterning.

To begin with, the nature and spatial patterning of the burnt flint assemblage will be considered.

Burnt flint and hearth areas

Chapter 1.3 has described the distribution of burnt lithic and faunal material, the interpretation of this material as representing two hearths, and the relationship of the unburnt lithic and faunal material to the hearths (Figs 9–17). In addition, the evidence for linking the lithic material in scatters C west and C east to the corresponding hearths is presented in Chapter 3.1. This section concentrates on the composition of the burnt lithic assemblages.

Fig 173 displays the percentage of each main assemblage category which was burnt within scatters A, C east and C west. Many more pieces of burnt debitage were recovered in the

sieving programme, especially those <10mm in size, but these were not differentiated from unburnt microdebitage. This does affect the calculation of the percentage of total debitage which was burnt. Even when the percentage of burnt debitage is calculated against the total of 3D-recorded debitage, the relative percentages between the scatters remain the same. Thus the pattern of the data is unaffected.

Scatter A

Fig 173 shows that the amount of burnt debitage in scatter A is low. The burnt flint in scatter A shows very weak spatial patterning (Fig 10), and its low density may simply reflect the low density of flintwork in general in scatter A.

Scatter C

Deposits of charcoal, stone settings and 'fire pits' were all absent from both the C west and C east hearths, although a possible small subrectangular pit in C west may have been associated with the hearth in this area (Chapters 1.3 and 6.3). The quantity and spatial extent of the burnt flint forming the hearth in C west is greater than that in C east. In part this reflects the greater quantity of lithic material in C west, but is probably also the result of a longer duration of occupation and/or the resetting of the fire in slightly different locations within a single central area.

It is argued in Chapters 3, 4 and 5 that there is a chronological division between the occupations represented by scatters C west and C east, and possibly between C east and scatter A. The lithic and faunal material is spatially arranged around both hearths, which would appear to have acted as foci of activity. There is no evidence of deliberate selection of certain categories of artefact (eg partially worked or broken nodules) to be burnt. It is therefore assumed that lithic material became burnt due to accidental incorporation or casual discard in the fire.

Fig 173 shows a distinct difference between the patterns of burning between scatters C east and C west. The low percentages of burnt debitage are roughly similar between C east and C west, supporting the accidental burning model. The marked increase in burnt tool debitage in C west probably represents two factors: the greater prevalence of tool debitage in that area, but also the manufacture and maintenance of tools being carried out in closer proximity to the hearth than in C east. This contrast is even more striking with retouched tools, where the percentage burnt is over three times greater in C west than in C east, although the number of tools is less than twice as great in the former as in the latter. Again this suggests that tasks requiring retouched tools were carried out in much closer proximity to the hearth in C west than in C east.

Artefact production, use and discard

Scatter A

The spatial distribution of material in scatter A has been interrupted by the presence of medieval ditches, thus making

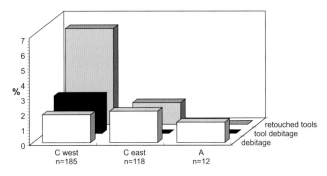

Fig 173 3D histogram of percentage of burnt lithic material in each artefact category in scatters A, C west and C east

interpretation difficult. In scatter A dorso-ventral refits between flints were associated with the main concentrations of knapping waste, demonstrating *in situ* production of debitage. Retouched tools in scatter A were mainly located around the periphery of the higher densities of debitage and the putative hearth area (Fig 174). Only two refitting groups within scatter A contained formal retouched tools. One of these (refitting group 12) consisted of a conjoining broken microlith. The other (refitting group 24, Fig 111) consisted of a single scraper and refitting cortical flakes, and, like the majority of the tools, was located on the periphery of the scatter. However, the proximity of the scraper to the other constituents of the group illustrates that the discard of the artefact took place in close proximity to its production.

Scatter C

Although this scatter can be divided into two chronological phases, the spatial distributions will be considered for scatter C as a whole, with a discussion of similarities and contrasts between C west and C east.

Fig 175 displays all the refits in scatter C and shows that there are only seven refits which cross the arbitrary line dividing scatters C east and C west. The main refitting trends in C west and C east are around and across the hearths rather than between them, thus supporting the division of scatter C into two distinct chronological phases. It will be noted that there is a single refit between SAS 3 in scatter C east and the highest

density of flintwork in scatter A. This refit consists of a fragment (FFN 3277) of deliberately shattered nodule (refitting group 45) in scatter A, separated by a distance of *c* 14m from the other two fragments in scatter C. Although suggestive of a link between the activity in scatters A and C east, a single refit cannot be regarded as strong evidence of contemporaneous occupation.

SCATTER C CORE REDUCTION

The distribution of the main debitage concentrations around the two hearths is discussed in Chapter 3 and above. In Fig 175 it is clear that the contouring of material in C west and C east is affected by the presence of the large later ditches. In particular the material around the western hearth was probably distributed in the form of two arcs, with a decrease in density of material towards the north. However, the presence of the large ditch now gives the appearance of four distinct clusters of debitage. Similarly, the shallow post-medieval feature running north–south in the centre of the site more sharply defines the separation of C west and C east than probably was originally the case.

Fig 65, Fig 66 and Fig 69 show the distributions of unworked nodules, all partially worked nodules (with refits) and hammer stones. These classes of object are predominantly located in C east, where the partially worked and unworked nodules tend to be located on the periphery of the main scatters, while the hammer stones – which presumably were used to shatter the nodules – tend to be situated close to the

Fig 174 Distribution of tool refits in scatter A (scale 1:100)

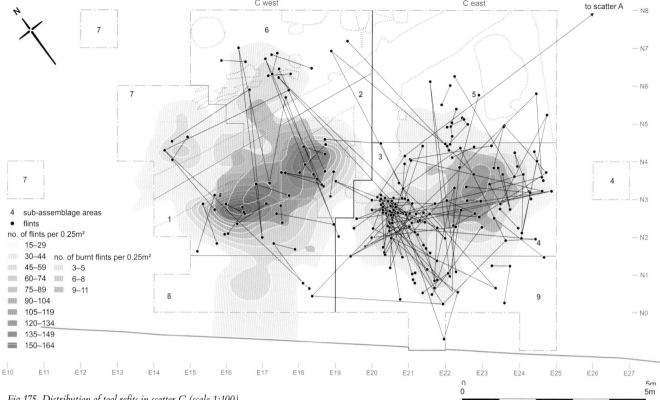

Fig 175 Distribution of tool refits in scatter C (scale 1:100)

hearth. Refitting suggests that some of these nodules were broken where they lay, while others, such as refitting group 45, were dispersed over a considerable area. It is clear that the contrasts in distributional patterns of nodules and hammer stones cannot entirely be ascribed to discard of unsuitable raw material around the periphery of the scatters, since some breakage took place in these areas.

Fig 63 shows that the distributions of cores broadly accord with the debitage contour patterns. However, there are a number of cores, particularly in C east, which lie on the periphery of the areas of highest debitage density and, therefore, some distance from the hearths. These peripheral cores thus have relatively little debitage associated with them when compared with the cores in the main debitage concentrations, and it is possible that their peripheral locations were the result of discard rather than *in situ* knapping.

SCATTER C TOOL PRODUCTION, USE AND DISCARD

Scraper production does not produce easily diagnostic tool debitage, making it difficult to trace the production sequence of these tools. However, given the opportunistic manufacture of the example in refitting group 4 (part of a broken axe, Fig 94) and the use of core preparation pieces as supports in a number of instances, scraper production and use is likely to have been closely related spatially to the main concentrations of knapping debitage. Drawing on the detailed distribution plots for each tool category presented in Chapter 3, Fig 176 shows broad areas of production and discard of three categories of tools: axes, burins and microliths. The tool debitage distributions define the production areas, while the distributions of the tools define the discard areas. The time and spatial segment between production

and discard of an artefact is commonly that which is archaeologically least visible, but which is also the most interesting. This is because as archaeologists we seek to study past human activity and behaviour, and if we could define the period of time when an artefact was in use we could start to understand something about the humans who used them. By comparing the spatial arrangement of the production and discard zones, it is hoped to be able to assess the probability of where the tools were used in the intervening period.

From Fig 176 it is clear that production and discard of the majority of burins took place within very tightly defined areas. In C west, burin spalls are located near the centre of the hearth with burins on the periphery. The burin distribution also corresponds to the areas containing the greatest quantity of bone by weight (Fig 176). In conjunction with use-wear evidence (below, 6.6), this suggests that burins were moved from their place of manufacture to the periphery for working bone. In C east, refitting shows that many burins underwent a prolonged life of use and reuse prior to discard. It is concluded that the close correspondence of production and discard areas, together with the use histories of some burins and the use-wear evidence, suggests that the entire production, use and discard cycle of burins took place in very spatially confined areas.

In the case of axes, Fig 176 represents the production and discard of axes but not necessarily their use. In Chapter 3 it is argued that some axes may have been manufactured on site and then removed, while others, such as FFN 87967, were brought to the site and probably broke during use there. This axe was then reused as a core, one product of which was a microlith. Similarly, the three other core tools seem to have broken or been abandoned during manufacture and some reused as cores. Thus,

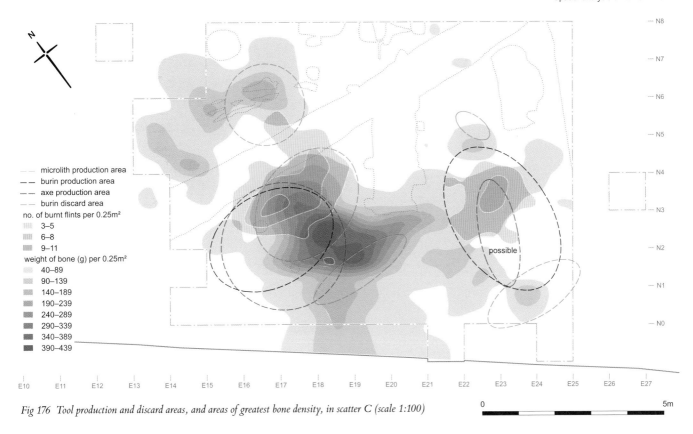

Fig 176 Tool production and discard areas, and areas of greatest bone density, in scatter C (scale 1:100)

some of the axe refitting patterns in Fig 92 refer to initial production and subsequent reuse and discard of core tools as cores, since curation of axes seems to have distorted the use segment of the life cycle of this class of artefact. Nevertheless, the presence of axe debitage suggests that some axe manufacture (or attempted manufacture) did take place around the western hearth. In addition, refitting group 41, consisting of two used axe sharpening flakes, attests to use and resharpening in this area.

Fig 78 shows that the microlith distribution is fairly general across the site. In contrast, microburins (and hence microlith production) are concentrated on the hearth in C west (Fig 176). Although difficult to achieve, one tentative conjoin was obtained between the two types of artefact, and that was in C east. It is, therefore, possible that most of the microburins in scatter C were the waste from microliths which subsequently were removed from the site, while the microliths present on site may have been manufactured elsewhere. The exception to this pattern is the bi-truncated microlith from refitting group 10 in C east, which appears to have been manufactured, used and discarded within a small area.

SUMMARY

It is apparent that major core reduction took place at discrete locations around the two hearth areas, with much of the debitage being discarded immediately on production. The patterning of partially worked and unworked nodules and hammer stones suggests that some of the material was worked *in situ* around the edges of the main scatters while other nodules and fragments were discarded in this peripheral zone. Similarly, the majority of cores correspond to the highest densities of debitage. Particularly

in C east, however, there are a number of cores located on the periphery of the main debitage concentrations, which could be the result of discard in the peripheral zone.

In scatter C east the majority of the retouched tools appear to have been manufactured and discarded within very localised areas. The exceptions to this generally expedient technological patterning are axes and microliths, where transportation and curation may have affected spatial patterning. However, even these artefacts tend to follow the distributional pattern of other classes of tools in clustering around the two hearth areas. Therefore, in the majority of cases, discard locations of tools generally reflect the areas of production and use of those tools. These patterns are illustrated in Fig 177 which shows the dorso-ventral refits in scatter C, with the large cluster of refitting group 10 omitted for clarity.

Three patterns may be discerned in Fig 177. Firstly, as in scatter A, many of the refits are over short distances and are confined to the areas of knapping waste; in addition, the high-density clusters of debitage signify very well-defined spatial areas which were the scene of *in situ* core reduction. Secondly, a number of refits are longer-distance and are distributed either across or around the hearths. This pattern is composed of both unmodified blank and tool production, and resharpening. It is thus likely to be a product of both anthropogenic (such as tool use) and non-anthropogenic factors. This pattern of refits (together with the tool distributions described above) suggests a very well-defined activity zone around the hearths, consisting of core reduction and tool production, use and discard. Finally, the longer-distance refits away from the hearth suggest discard of material on the periphery of the main lithic scatters.

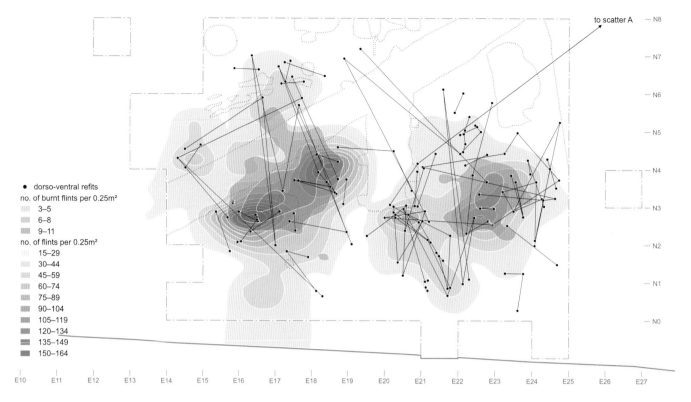

Fig 177 Dorso-ventral refits in scatter C (omitting refitting group 10 for clarity) (scale 1:100)

This model of artefacts dropped near hearths and other artefacts tossed away from the hearth is provided by Binford's study of the Mask site, a Nunamiut hunting stand (Binford 1978a). This model will be referred to again below (6.5), but here the difference in artefact size between the drop and toss zones will be explored further. The model suggests that smaller artefacts would be dropped in the immediate vicinity of a seated human, while larger artefacts would be tossed (frequently over the shoulder) to the periphery of the site. In Fig 178, debitage density is contrasted with the average volume of complete flints per 0.25m². It is evident that the two distributions are largely mutually exclusive, with the largest material on the periphery of the densest artefact concentrations. This pattern would tend to support the interpretation of the periphery of the scatters, particularly in C east, as having been formed at least in part by the tossing of larger material to the edge of the hearth-centred activity areas, which in turn are composed of smaller material dropped adjacent to the human occupiers.

Having established the nature of anthropogenic taphonomic factors affecting artefact distribution, the distribution of artefacts and activity zones can be studied in further detail. Fig 179 employs contours to display the distribution of the formal retouched tool classes (excluding miscellaneous retouched types) discussed in Chapter 3. In order to clarify the distribution, the minimum contour value is 1.5 artefacts per 0.25m², equivalent to six tools per square metre. Fig 179 also compares the point distribution of miscellaneous retouched tools and utilised *a posteriori* tools with the formal tool contour distribution.

The contours generally reinforce the picture of hearth-centred activity involving formal retouched tools. In C west, the

spatial distribution is very well defined around the hearth. Clearly, the southern side of the hearth is of greatest importance, since this area has the greatest concentration of debitage and tools, and also axe debitage and microburins. In C east, the main concentration of tools runs across the southern side of the hearth, with more dispersed material to the north and south. This mirrors the generally more diffuse nature of the scatters in this area. The contouring suggests an increase in the concentration of retouched tools to the south of the site, a pattern also suggested by the debitage distribution. It is, therefore, possible that the site extends southwards downslope towards the active stream margin and beyond the limits of the excavation.

Although broadly in accord with the formal tool distribution, the miscellaneous retouched and utilised pieces are more widely distributed away from the hearth areas in C east when compared with the formal tools. As noted in Chapter 3, the bruised blades and flakes form a notable concentration to the west of the hearth in C east, in the heart of the knapping scatter in SAS 3, with two outliers to the north and east.

In conclusion, in scatter C most of the formal retouched tools appear to have been utilised and discarded close to their place of manufacture, forming a discard drop zone. In most cases the locations of retouched tools correspond closely with the areas of activity for which they were manufactured. These activity zones are predominantly hearth-centred. In C west, the activity zone surrounds the hearth, while in C east the zone runs across the southern side of the hearth, with a more dispersed element around the periphery. This accords well with the analysis of burnt material from the respective hearths (above) which suggests a more intensive utilisation of the

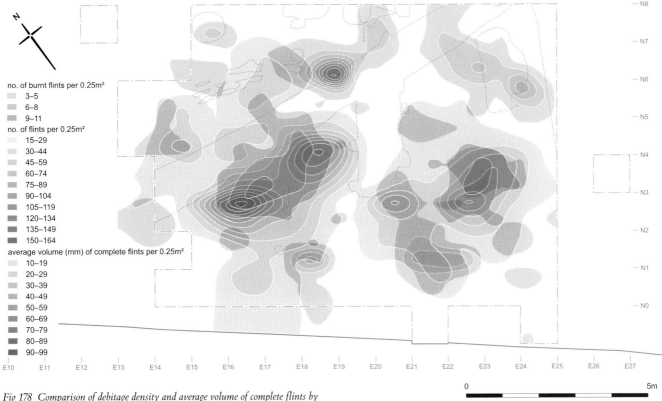

no. of burnt flints per 0.25m²
- 3–5
- 6–8
- 9–11

no. of flints per 0.25m²
- 15–29
- 30–44
- 45–59
- 60–74
- 75–89
- 90–104
- 105–119
- 120–134
- 135–149
- 150–164

average volume (mm) of complete flints per 0.25m²
- 10–19
- 20–29
- 30–39
- 40–49
- 50–59
- 60–69
- 70–79
- 80–89
- 90–99

Fig 178 Comparison of debitage density and average volume of complete flints by 0.25m square in scatter C (scale 1:100)

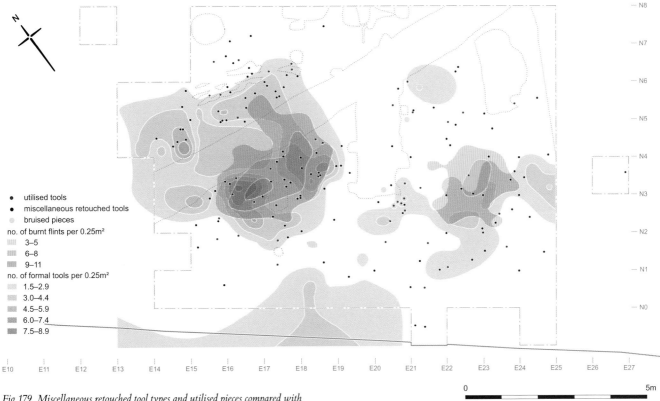

- utilised tools
- miscellaneous retouched tools
- bruised pieces

no. of burnt flints per 0.25m²
- 3–5
- 6–8
- 9–11

no. of formal tools per 0.25m²
- 1.5–2.9
- 3.0–4.4
- 4.5–5.9
- 6.0–7.4
- 7.5–8.9

Fig 179 Miscellaneous retouched tool types and utilised pieces compared with contoured formal tool distributions in scatter C (scale 1:100)

immediate area surrounding the hearth in C west when compared with C east. The majority of debitage also appears to have been discarded where it was produced. These zones of core reduction and high debitage concentration compare well with the distribution of retouched tools, and are again hearth-centred. Thus the manufacturing, use and drop-discard zones

159

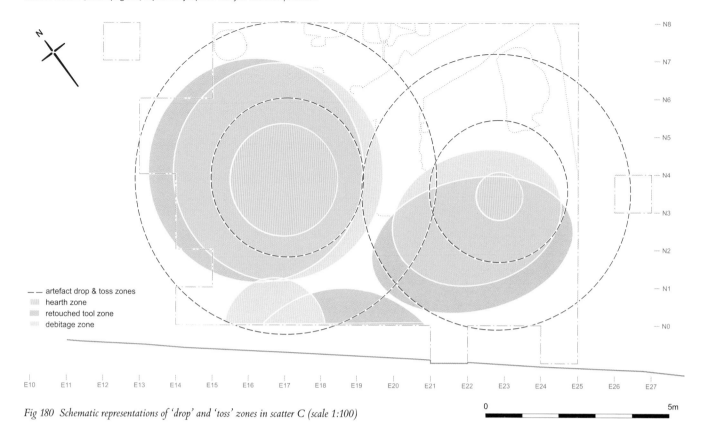

Fig 180 Schematic representations of 'drop' and 'toss' zones in scatter C (scale 1:100)

are largely congruent with one another. The possible exception to this pattern concerns some of the cores, partially worked nodules and larger artefacts. This material appears to have been discarded on the periphery of scatters C west and C east, but particularly the latter, forming a so-called 'toss' zone.

This spatial patterning is schematically summarised in Fig 180, with the core reduction, tool use, and 'drop' and 'toss' zones derived from the data presented above. This is of course a generalised picture, and is based on density distributions of different artefact types. Artefacts lying outside these zones are also of importance, particularly in relation to the distribution of the faunal material, since the spatial distribution of faunal and lithic material is in many cases largely mutually exclusive. The spatial relationships between artefacts, faunal material and functional activity areas will be discussed further below (6.5), but first it is necessary to address the spatial analysis of the faunal material in its own right.

6.3   Spatial analysis of faunal material

The treatment and use of the faunal material by people is represented in two ways within the dataset: firstly, the patterns that derive from the selection and processing of the different parts of the carcass, and the nature of or reasons for this exploitation; and secondly, the subsequent physical distribution of the bone fragments once they have ceased to be useful. These data yield different types of information. The first type allows

the analyst to attribute purpose and behaviour to the prehistoric people at the site by defining the patterns in terms of the processing activities that may have generated the bone assemblage. The second allows consideration of the use of space in the settlement, perhaps permitting identification of the areas within which particular activities were or were not taking place. In plotting the distribution of burnt bone and flint on the site, we have already defined the locations of two hearths. These have been assigned to different phases of occupation on the site on the grounds of lithic typology and technology, and by reference to the distribution of the bones of reindeer and red deer around them. The C west hearth occurs within the middle of the red deer scatter (Fig 163) while the C east hearth lies within the highest concentration of reindeer bones (Fig 165). The association of a slightly different flint typology (Chapter 3) with both the eastern hearth and the reindeer scatter, and burnt flints of this latter type, serves to confirm this separation. This straightforward spatial pattern allows a relatively elegant division of the phases of the site and, for the purposes of the remainder of this section, the red deer bones will be treated as defining the Early Holocene occupation at the site and the reindeer bones the Lateglacial activity.

Lateglacial

Scatter A

The distribution of the recovered bones from scatter A has been seriously disturbed by later archaeological features cutting through the Lateglacial occupation horizon. This has yielded a distribution that at first appears discontinuous, but when these later intrusions are taken into account it need not in reality indicate such discrete scatters of animal bone (Fig 181). There appears to be a focus at E33N15, where a few bones of reindeer occur with a mandible and teeth of horse, the latter yielding a radiocarbon date of 10,200 BP. This focus includes a mandible, teeth and tibial and femoral fragments of reindeer but is completely separated from the adjacent faunal material by later ditches cutting through the archaeological layers to the north and south. The presence of further fragments of the main long bones just to the west, and to the north and north-east, suggests that a scatter of 'marrow' bones may have originally spread from E30N14 to E35N18 (Fig 181). The reindeer bones beyond the limits of this central scatter are exclusively fragments from the lower limbs or feet, if the distal tibia is included. One small group of bones from the hind feet of reindeer centred on E34N19 almost certainly derives from a single articulated ankle joint, from the distal tibia to the metatarsus. At the south side of the trench a group of foot bones including fragments of both fore- and hindlimbs, and phalanges, is centred on E32N12. The only fragments from the axial skeleton are the mandibular fragment, and mandibular and maxillary teeth from the central area of the scatter, as well as a rib from the north-eastern part of the central scatter and a cervical fragment, possibly of reindeer, from E33N12.

The majority of the material in scatter A could all derive from a single animal (Chapter 4.2). Only a right carpus in E27N14 is definitely from a second animal, while the scapula fragment in E35N17 appears to be from a somewhat smaller animal than is suggested by the other bones in the scatter. If we accept that the majority of this reindeer scatter derives from only one animal then the relative weight (Table 53) shows that the carpals, tarsals and metapodials have the best proportional survival, followed by the phalanges, tibia and scapula, while the humerus, radius, femur and skull make up the smallest identifiable component. This may reflect both the fragility and consequent recognisability of the bones and their fragments (ie even small metapodial shaft fragments can be identified) and the scale of processing carried out on the bones. The dispersed foot bones around the periphery of the scatter were presumably discarded with minimal processing and remained partially intact despite several hundred years of superficial erosion in the soil. The long bones and skull, in contrast, may have undergone breakage for marrow extraction or brain removal, thereby reducing these bones to a number of fragments prior to discard. The general dispersal of metapodial bones with the other foot bones suggests that these bones may not have been broken for marrow extraction, but were discarded after removal of the meat or skins.

The possibility that a substantial part of a second animal or more is present in the scatter cannot be excluded. This would not seriously change the interpretations of the distribution of the bones, but would indicate that there has been a much greater loss of bone than would otherwise be the case. The presence of both left and right fragments, and an even

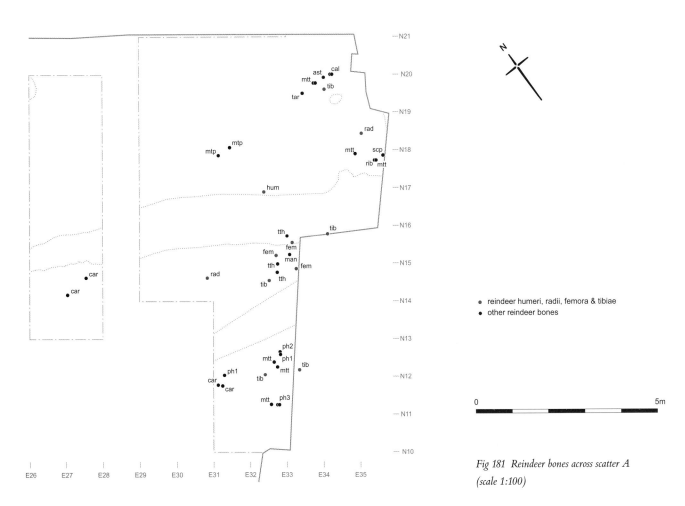

reindeer humeri, radii, femora & tibiae
other reindeer bones

0   5m

Fig 181 Reindeer bones across scatter A
(scale 1:100)

occurrence of many skeletal elements, would support the interpretation of just one animal, and the relative dearth of flint tools and waste does not indicate any great length of time spent by people at the site.

This pattern of survival suggests that the vertebrae and ribs were left at the kill site (Street 1991), with perhaps some cervical vertebrae being removed with the head, and one of the anterior ribs with the scapula and forelimb. The pelvis is absent and may have been left attached to the sacrum at the kill site. Of the bones which came to form scatter A, only a few fragments of mandible and maxilla, including teeth, have survived from the head, and the ulnae are missing, but parts of most of the remaining elements were recovered. There is little or no suggestion that bones with attached meat or hides were removed from the site. It appears that most of the processing of the animal, after initial butchery at the kill site, must have taken place here, with possible treatment of the skin and breakage of the humerus, radius, femur and tibia for the extraction of marrow fat and grease.

This interpretation has a number of implications. The site represents the camp set up after the hunting and killing of a single adult reindeer, perhaps aged 4 years or older and possibly male. The season of kill cannot be determined and, although teeth are present in the sample, the likelihood of being able to recognise annual growth patterns in the cementum of these specimens as a way of deducing the season of kill is extremely small owing to their poor condition; and the molars are no longer available, having been used, unsuccessfully, for radiocarbon analysis.

The pattern of skeletal representation indicates that the vertebrae, ribs and pelvic bones were probably left at the kill site, where skinning and initial dismemberment took place; as has been suggested above (Chapter 4.2), however, the rack of ribs may have been hung up to dry (Binford 1978b, 112–13). Since part of the maxilla arrived on site, the skull (with or without antlers) was presumably also brought to the site, although the antlers (if present) may have been taken along with part of the skull when the site was abandoned. The limbs were probably still articulated when brought to the site and it seems probable that the hindlimbs were broken above the distal end of the tibia, since the distal end, calcaneum and astragalus of the left foot all occur very close together, suggesting that they were deposited in an articulated state. The proximal end and a shaft fragment of a left metatarsal occur c 7m away in square E32N12; if these derive from the same animal it suggests that the limbs were disarticulated above the metatarsus, as the latter was found with a first phalanx rather than the ankle bones. Fragments of the shaft and distal shaft of a left tibia occur in the centre of the scatter; it is possible that this bone was smashed here for the extraction of the marrow, before the ankle joint, with little meat or marrow potential, was tossed away (Binford 1983, 153). A distal fragment of the shaft of a left femur also occurs in this central area of the scatter, as does a fragment of the right femur, but the only identifiable fragment of a right tibia, a shaft fragment, occurs in E33N12 some 2.5m to the south. The only identifiable foot bones of the right hindlimb are a tarsus 3 with the ankle of the left foot in E33N19 and an astragalus recovered

during the 1986 excavations within the central area of the scatter. Unsided metatarsal fragments occur in E34N17, E34N18 and E33N19; these may derive from a right metatarsus and are spatially associated with the other foot bones.

The forelimbs are not so well represented. A right scapula, with an adjacent rib fragment, occurs in E35N17, and a right humeral fragment c 3m to the east in E32N16 and the proximal end of a right radius in E35N18, within a metre of the scapula. No ulnal fragments were recovered but a right intermediate carpal occurs with the group of foot bones in the south of the scatter; a second right intermediate carpal and a right carpus 2+3 were found in E27N14. Since the distal end of a right metacarpus was found in E32N12, a little over a metre away from one of the intermediate carpals, the two carpals in E27N14 probably belong to a second individual, and possibly derive from one of the reindeer in scatter C east. A distal fragment of a right phalanx, almost certainly from the front foot, was found less than a metre from the metacarpus. No fragments of left scapula or humerus were recognised, although the proximal end of a left radius was recovered in E30N14 just to the west of the central scatter. A left radial carpus occurs with the other foot bones in the southern part of the bone scatter, and a possible left proximal metacarpal fragment that may be reindeer was found in E29N17, just to the west of a group of unassigned metapodial fragments.

The spatial relationships between the different bones, while by no means anatomically consistent, do suggest that most of these fragments derive from the same animal. It seems likely that much of the material apparently missing, such as the upper left forelimb and a number of the phalanges, may have been removed when the later ditches were originally dug. The only other possibility is that the foot bones centred on E32N12 and E34N20, over 8m apart, derive from different animals further bones of which lie in unexcavated deposits under the road to the east of the site. Whatever the case, it seems probable that at least some elements of the scatter still lie unexcavated in this area.

If we accept the single animal model and, further, that apart from those axial elements of the skeleton left at the kill site all other bones were discarded within scatter A and any immediately adjacent, unexcavated part of the site, then it follows that the carcass was completely processed at this site. A male animal of medium body size may have weighed about 110kg (Kelsall 1957) of which 22kg was fat and 50kg edible meat if killed in late September, but by late December and later this would have diminished, with potentially a complete loss of the fat content (Spiess 1979) from all but the marrow bones. Since we cannot deduce the season of the kill, using Spiess's figures for the lower carcass weight in winter means that this one animal may have provided sufficient food for an adult for 15 days, assuming an intake of 3000kcal/day at a consumption rate of 3.25kg of meat per day. It seems unlikely that the whole carcass would have been consumed at the site, since a supply would be needed when the camp was abandoned for the next hunt, and unless the transported food was the left shoulder, this meat must have been stripped off the carcass and possibly dried. Scatter A could, therefore, represent the processing and consumption of a whole carcass, or most of it, by a small group or family for between two and four days before the party moved on for the next hunt.

If we were to apply figures for the Nunamiut used by Binford (1978b, 136–9) the results are slightly different. He gives estimates of 2.63lb (1.19kg) and 2.66lb (1.21kg) of caribou meat daily as an average for the whole population, including children. These figures do not include a proportion of the food intake (16%) that was not caribou, and the mean daily consumption of all food for one group of four households was 4.4lb (2.01kg) for adults over 20 years old and a mean of 3.08lb (1.40kg) for the whole group including children. Binford's observed butchery of a 4-year-old caribou bull taken in August, in a good nutritional state and with a live weight of 110.5kg, produced 43kg of meat and fat, 14kg of tongue, heart, brain and liver, and 6.2kg of blood. This would approximate to a maximum of 40 days' supply at the average family rate of consumption or 28 days' supply at the adult rate, assuming consumption of all parts except the blood. With a group size of four adults this would give a maximum of seven days' supply, or for a two-family group of four adults and two children approximately five days' supply.

Yet other figures could be obtained using the estimates of Legge and Rowley-Conwy (1988) based on the approximately 2.2kg of meat needed to meet the 3000kcal/day requirement, but it is not intended that these figures should be applied precisely. Since we do not know the season of death and, therefore, the condition of the animal, or its size, the weight estimates are imprecise at best. We know little of the butchery process or how much meat may have been left at the kill site, and there are numerous possibilities regarding the hunters' group structure and size. What is important is the possible scale represented by the site. An occupation of two to four days represents a different type of site to one occupied overnight or for one day. A variety of activities may be expected to have taken place other than just the butchery of the carcass and some food consumption. The skin was almost certainly processed during that time, if it was in a suitable condition (Spiess 1979), probably at the southern edge of the site. Meat could have been

hung up to dry in order to create a supply for when the group moved on, and marrow bones were certainly broken and the marrow extracted. There are nevertheless relatively few flints distributed around the site, and only a narrow range of types, which would argue against any extended period of stay or wide range of activities. There is no antler in scatter A so perhaps the animal had no antlers or only unsuitable antlers, or no new tools were needed, although the antlers may have been removed and taken when the group left.

Whether this site should be construed as a hunting camp for a group with a more permanent camp elsewhere, or the camp of a nomadic, or seasonally nomadic, hunting group is considered below (Chapter 7.2).

Scatter C east

The reindeer scatter in the east of scatter C appears more extensive than that in scatter A, but although it occupies a greater number of square metres it is only slightly more widely dispersed. To some extent this is because it has not been disrupted to the same extent by later intrusions, but is also because at least three animals are represented among the bones. The bones indicating three animals include the proximal left metacarpus and the proximal left tibia. The possibility exists that the fragments from the third animal derive from the individual in scatter A, so it is necessary to establish whether there is a minimum number of three or four reindeer in both areas.

Table 63 summarises the information pertaining to the possible individual reindeer in scatters A and C east. The juvenile in scatter C east is clearly a different animal from the individual in scatter A. The two probably male adults could be the same animal, and were only separated on the basis that bones of equivalent size from the same element and side occur in both scatters. However, this is very difficult to establish since the material is so fragmented and so few bones include measurable fragments.

A distal left humerus deriving from the larger animal in scatter C east has no counterpart in scatter A. A distal left tibia was found in both scatters. In both cases the bone, unfortunately poorly preserved and not intact, appears to be as

Table 63 Information for possible individual reindeer in scatters A and C east

Scatter A	Scatter C east		
Larger than ref specimen*	Larger than ref specimen*	Slightly smaller than ref specimen*	Similar size or smaller than scatter A individual
Probable male	Male	Probable male	
4–5 years old	Adult	Juvenile <4 years old	Represented only by proximal left tibia and
Worn teeth	Distal radius fused	Distal radius unfused	proximal left metacarpus
	PM4 wear equiv 4–5 years	Wear equiv 30 months approx	
	Distal humerus larger than ref specimen	Butchered distal humerus	
	Measured metacarpus	Measured metacarpus	
	Antler shedding		
	Shedding antler fragments could be from any of the above three individuals; the possible skull and antler fragment could derive from either the juvenile probable male or the individual represented by only two bones		
*reference specimen = adult male aged 4 years from Sweden			

large or larger than the reference specimen and could have come from either of the animals in scatter C east. A left mandible with a PM4 and PM2 from the older animal in scatter C east clearly derives from a different individual to that in scatter A, since a left PM3 from this area does not fit neatly with the wear pattern on the other two teeth. We can, therefore, conclude that a large adult, probable male from scatter C east and the animal from scatter A are different individuals.

The final question concerns whether the bones that indicate a third animal in scatter C east may derive from scatter A. We have already established that the carpals from a second animal in scatter A could derive from the animals in scatter C. The only bones indicating a third individual are a proximal left metacarpus fragment and a proximal left tibial shaft fragment. There is a possible left metacarpal fragment in scatter A but this has not been positively identified to either reindeer or the left side, and apart from this fragment no proximal metacarpals were recognised in scatter A. This bone cannot, therefore, be positively identified as representing another individual. There is a fragment of proximal left tibia shaft in scatter A which is smaller than a similar fragment in C east. The three individuals in C east are recognised on the basis of the nutrient foramen on the proximal posterior shaft; the fragment in scatter C is just proximal to this point and, although it is unlikely that it derives from the same bone as one of the two fragments comparable in size, this cannot be shown conclusively. On balance there is a possibility that the three individuals identified in scatter C east are distinct from the animal represented in scatter A. One of these scatter C animals is significantly bigger than the scatter A individual, while the other two are similar or slightly smaller in size, and one is a young animal, probably a male of *c* 2.5 years of age.

It is unfortunate that a more definite conclusion cannot be reached because the occurrence of bones of the same animal in the two scatters would suggest the possible contemporaneity of the two Lateglacial scatters, while ruling out such a link would perhaps support the idea of two independent occupations of the site during the Lateglacial. The lithic refitting evidence is insubstantial (Chapter 3; above, 6.2). The obvious loss of material from scatter A, as a result of the ditches cutting the site, would also militate against the bones in scatter C deriving from the animal in scatter A, since the absences in the latter area are more easily attributed to these disruptions than to discard or removal to scatter C east.

For the purposes of discussion the scatter in C east will, therefore, be treated as an independent site from scatter A. The pattern of the bones in this scatter is less easily assessed because at least two and probably three animals are represented. Nevertheless, unlike scatter A there was little later disturbance of this area, although it is clear that the scatter continues a very short distance to the east beyond the limits of the excavation. The pattern is very similar to that identified in scatter A. There is a central area with a relatively high density of reindeer bone fragments centred around E23N04, with a more widely dispersed scatter of bones surrounding it, particularly to the west (Fig 182). This central area also has an associated scatter of burnt bone and flint, with some of the latter suggesting an affiliation with the Lateglacial rather than the Mesolithic scatter. It suggests a hearth area at the focus of the bone scatter. The majority of the bones within this focal area are marrow bones, and most of those dispersed around the scatter are foot and skull fragments (Fig 182).

The bones of the forelimb, including the metacarpals, are

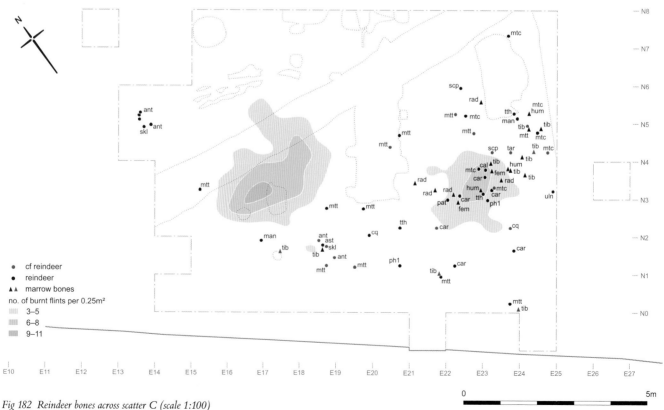

Fig 182 Reindeer bones across scatter C (scale 1:100)

more positively associated with the hearth area than those of the hindlimb, which, apart from the femora, show a much more dispersed scatter particularly to the south and west. The juxtaposition of a left distal tibia and an astragalus in E18N01, and of a centroquartal and proximal metatarsus from the same side a metre to the east, may indicate an ankle joint that was discarded articulated. Mandible fragments are also associated with the hearth area, although antler, skull fragments and maxillary teeth are found several metres from the hearth. Vertebrae, ribs and pelvic fragments are almost completely absent, and those that can probably be ascribed to reindeer are atlas fragments, suggesting removal of the head with the atlas attached. This pattern is very similar to scatter A and indicates that the vertebrae, ribs and pelvic bones were probably left at the kill site. The concentration of marrow bones, including the mandible, around the hearth and their fragmentation indicates breakage for marrow extraction, while bones of little use were discarded ('tossed') to the periphery of the site (Binford 1983, 153). The wider scatter of this material than that in scatter A can presumably be explained by a longer time and greater intensity of use, and a larger body of faunal material to dispose of. Phalanges are relatively under-represented, which may indicate that skins were dealt with outside this area or not kept from all the animals; and, if the third animal is a different individual from that in scatter A, then there is a much greater loss of bone from this site than is suggested there. Bones as well as meat may have been taken away when the site was abandoned.

The few fragments of horse (despite some being located at the hearth site) cannot be linked to this occupation and may derive from scatter A or be an 'accidental' inclusion in the site. The fox astragalus is less easily explained since it is burnt, possibly butchered, and lay within the hearth area. It seems to imply hunting of fox as well as reindeer although, as suggested earlier, it could also represent the casual killing of a scavenging animal.

If we consider scatter C east in a similar manner to scatter A, then this scatter must represent a more substantial occupation. The hearth survived long enough to be visible in the archaeological record. At least three reindeer and a fox were killed, with two of the reindeer being hunted between late winter and late spring (Chapter 4.3). The carcasses of two of the reindeer are likely to have been completely processed and consumed at this site while the third may have formed part of the supplies taken when the site was abandoned. The associated flint scatter is denser and the refitting groups indicate production and usage of a number of tools. Using the Binford (1978b) figures presented above, and assuming reindeer with a low fat content, this occupation could have lasted three times as long as that in scatter A, or a similar length of time for a much larger group. According to these figures a small family group (four adults and two children) could have occupied the site for just over two weeks, while a group of four adults could have been sustained for three weeks. These figures assume consumption of the whole carcass resource, and such a maximum is probably unlikely; but, even allowing for significant errors in the calculations and a consumption of only

part of the third animal, an occupation period of several days is indicated.

These arguments have assumed single periods of occupation, largely from the integrity of the material, but where more than one animal is present it may involve repeat visits with different durations and possibly even site character. Brief stays at the site with material removed to a different camp may only have left behind one or two bones from the hunted animal, while more was transported away. This pattern of occupation could even account for the occasional horse bones and the third reindeer individual in scatter C east.

Early Holocene

In the area of scatter C ascribed to the Mesolithic occupation, bone density and fragment numbers are several orders of magnitude greater than for the preceding Lateglacial sites. A single square metre within the main concentration produced more bone than both Lateglacial sites combined.

The animal bones are not distributed uniformly across the site, but show a marked concentration of bone over perhaps 7–8m^2 centred upon E18N02 and lying just to the east and south of the western hearth. This concentration, although exhibited by all the bone fragments whether identified or not, can be attributed mainly to the bones of red deer (Fig 163) and suggests, in the absence of any candidates of similar size, that the majority of the unidentified material in this area probably also derives from red deer. This concentration of bone is not only offset from the hearth, but also from the major flint concentrations around the hearth (Fig 17). Within any one 0.5m^2 it may be composed of up to 225 hand-collected bone fragments (Fig 161) from a number of different skeletal elements, themselves from a number of different individuals. There is a very rapid fall-off in both numbers and weight of bone (Fig 160; Fig 161) away from this concentration and, apart from a rather less dense spread of bone in the north-west of the trench, over 40% (by weight) of the collection occurs in less than 10% of the excavated area. Clearly this is a bone pile or 'midden' upon which the unwanted waste bone was finally thrown. All 15 of the red deer individuals estimated from the fragments of distal femur shaft occur within or on the immediate periphery of this concentration (Fig 183), and the two left tibia fragments of roe deer, which identify the two roe deer individuals recognised, also occur in this midden. This indicates that the midden received material from all the exploited animals individually recognised in the Early Holocene scatter, except perhaps one of the swans.

This conclusion is of some importance since it indicates that the distinct scatter in the north-west of the trench is part of the same occupation event, despite its apparent separation largely created by the excavation of a later ditch, the hypothesis being that the femora of whichever carcasses this scatter represents were being disposed of in the midden. Fig 183 shows very few identified femoral fragments within this 'separate' scatter, a pattern that is not repeated for the humeri, tibiae or metapodials (below). While it may be that this area includes bones from

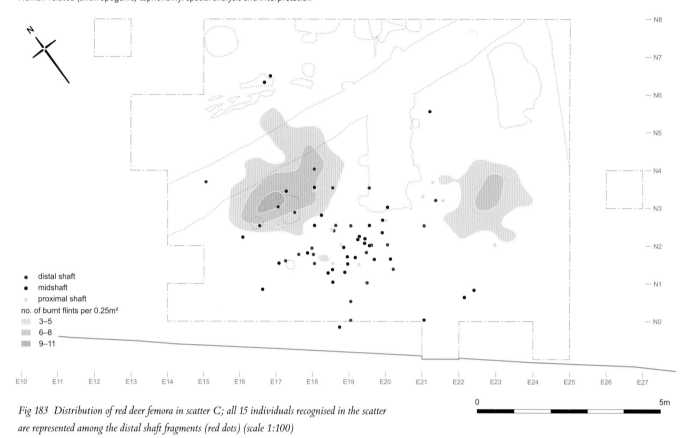

Fig 183 Distribution of red deer femora in scatter C; all 15 individuals recognised in the scatter are represented among the distal shaft fragments (red dots) (scale 1:100)

individuals other than the 15 identified red deer, it is more plausible to conclude that these two concentrations are contemporary and that the 'separate' scatter reflects a less concentrated disposal area to the north-west of the western hearth. The bones have, therefore, defined a major midden to one side of the hearth and a second, apparently contemporary scatter on the opposite side of the hearth. They also indicate an apportionment of the bones which presumably reflects contemporary behaviour (below).

Having established the existence of patterns in the gross distribution of bones across the site, we can consider whether variations occur in the anatomical distribution of the red deer bones. It was decided to use the individual skeletal elements as the unit of analysis, and include in each spatial study the divisions into which each bone was generally fragmented to see if the parts of any bones exhibited independent patterning. The femoral distribution plot (Fig 183) shows the distribution of fragments of the proximal shaft, midshaft and distal shaft. Since all these are shaft fragments and no epiphyseal ends of femora were found on the site, it might be argued that these units are unlikely to be distributed independently, and certainly the plot does not indicate any independence. The tibia may be a more appropriate bone to analyse, with breakage of the bone above the distal end being a potential butchery practice, and given the occurrence of intact distal ends in the assemblage. Fig 184 plots the distribution of tibial fragments across the trench. The 14 identified individuals are recognisable, but what is clear is that there is no particular patterning of the tibial fragments other than their concentration within the midden. The pattern is the

same for the humeri, radii, innominates and metapodials, with no indication of differential distribution of parts of the same skeletal element. In fact these analyses showed that all the long bones of the limbs and the tarsal bones were concentrated within the midden and the less dense scatter to the north-west of the western hearth. A further plot of epiphyseal ends (Fig 185) to test for larger fragments being in a 'toss zone' (Binford 1983) continues to reinforce the concentration to the south-east and north-west of the hearth, with no evidence that the larger waste bones from the processing were being discarded further away than the smaller fragments. The frequency of the major tarsal bones and the distal tibiae (Table 59) suggests that these bones may well have arrived at the hearth still articulated, and possibly also with the metatarsus attached. The concentration of femur fragments in the midden and their absence elsewhere, while the adjoining tibia occurs more widely spread across the site, suggests that this bone may have arrived disarticulated from the tibia. A similar conclusion can be drawn for the humerus because of the very few examples on the site of the radii, ulnae, or scapulae with which they would have articulated.

While the major bones of the limbs were being disposed of in the midden and the scatter to the north-west, certain rather less abundant skeletal elements do not display this spatial pattern. The few scapulae occur more widely, while fragments of vertebrae and rib occur to the east of the midden (Fig 186). The specific identification of some of these latter bones is a problem; but since this distribution includes all the identified vertebrae and rib fragments within the trench, it at least indicates that these bones are largely absent from the midden. The last

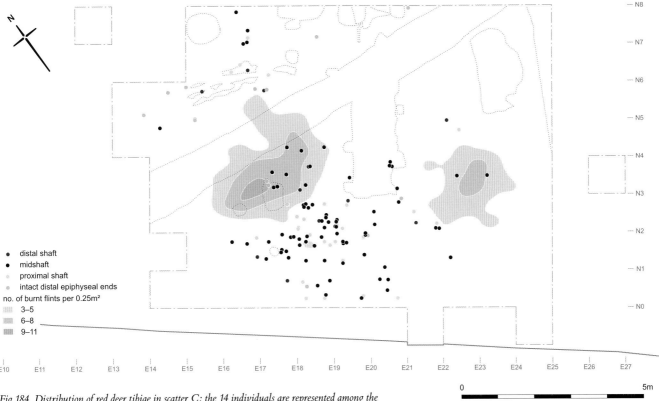

Fig 184 Distribution of red deer tibiae in scatter C; the 14 individuals are represented among the proximal shaft fragments (blue dots) (scale 1:100)

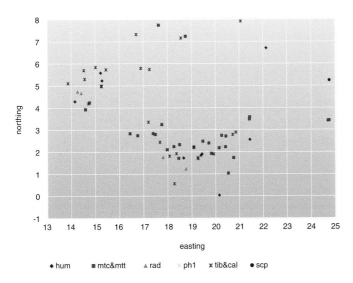

Fig 185 Red deer epiphyseal ends in scatter C

category, skull, teeth, mandibular fragments, phalanges and sesamoids (Fig 186), appears to follow a similar pattern with many of the bones occurring in a dispersed scatter on the eastern edge of the midden. These latter distributions contrast with those of the limb bones and indicate a completely different disposal pattern. It is possible that the distribution of skull fragments follows a pattern governed by the working or use of antler. Fig 187 shows the distribution of antler and skull fragments across the trench, including those of reindeer. Antler is not very common at this site, in contrast to the contemporary

sites at Star Carr (Legge and Rowley-Conwy 1988), Thatcham (King 1962) and Barry's Island (P Rowley-Conwy, pers comm), but what there is shows an interesting spatial pattern. The antler occurs either as tine or beam fragments in the round, or as cortical fragments. These latter fragments cluster in and about E22N02, with a small scatter east of the midden. The splitting of the antler cortex and its further fragmentation into pieces of the sort recovered at Three Ways Wharf (Fig 188) is difficult to attribute to natural processes such as freeze-thaw or trampling; in any case, they are concentrated within a small area of little more than 2m². This spread would appear to indicate small-scale antler-working debris 2–3m west of the midden. A major problem with these fragments is that they have not been specifically identified. They suggest antler beams of sufficiently large circumference to rule out most reindeer beams, but some of the spatulate parts of a reindeer antler could produce fragments of this size. One or two pieces also show the ridged pattern more reminiscent of red deer, but a not dissimilar feature can occur on the distal parts of reindeer antlers. This material is not as well preserved as the other antler from the site, but while this could be due to its being more ancient, it might also reflect any processing or soaking the antler underwent before working. It does not show the evidence of root etching found on some of the reindeer bones. On balance, not least because of the different character of the Lateglacial occupation (below), this group can probably be placed within the Early Holocene occupation. The remaining tine and beam fragments occur on the periphery or beyond the major bone scatters.

We have revealed distinct spatial distributions within the

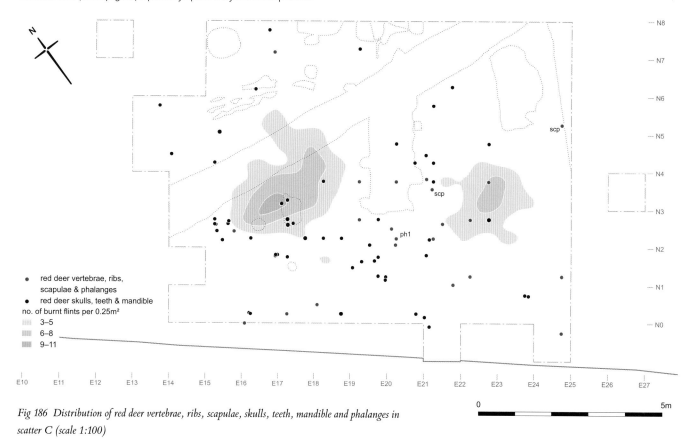

Fig 186 Distribution of red deer vertebrae, ribs, scapulae, skulls, teeth, mandible and phalanges in scatter C (scale 1:100)

Fig 187 Distribution of red deer and reindeer skull and antler across scatter C (scale 1:100)

bone assemblage and drawn attention to the behavioural activities that might have been responsible for some of them. To consider these aspects further, the collection was divided into three groups: the north-west scatter, the central midden, and the remaining areas not covered by these two groups. The considerable fragmentation of the assemblage would mean that many of the fragments would not enter the analysis if minimum number of elements (MNE) or minimum number of

FB 1659

FB 1460

Fig 188 Cortical fragments of antler FB 1659 and 1460 from square E22N02 in scatter C, suggesting antler working in this area (scale 1:1)

can be attributed to their treatment prior to discard.

Before considering this in detail, it is necessary to look at the bone selection that is apparent on the site. Most bones from the metacarpus to the humerus, and from the metatarsus to the femur, occur in the midden. Of these, the cylindrical bones are broken up while the bones of the carpal and tarsal region remain relatively intact. Binford (1978b, chapter 1) devised an index for assessing the utility of the individual bones of a caribou skeleton to the Nunamiut, taking into account meat weight, fat content, marrow, grease and ligaments among other things. A modified version of this index, the modified general utility index (MGUI), taking account of the transportability of bones and their articulation with elements of lower or higher value, was then developed (ibid, 74, table 2.7). Binford studied the bones from a number of recent Inuit sites using the index and found that the frequency of bones at his sites was related in broadly linear fashion to their MGUI. He used a normalised element frequency in his study, dividing the total number of observations of the identification unit by the number of occurrences of this unit in the whole animal. Despite the extensive fragmentation at Three Ways Wharf the assemblage has been considered within observation units similar to those used by Binford; the maximum frequency of a particular skeletal element could only be estimated by laying out all the identified fragments and comparing them, in order to estimate the minimum number (MNE) represented. To create a minimum number of individuals (MNI) for this aspect of the study, the total of the MNE calculated by this method was divided by the number of the element in the complete skeleton or, where paired, by the most frequent side (see Table 59). To produce a unit comparable to that of Binford's minimum number of animal units (MAU: Binford 1984, 50; see also Lyman 2008, 234–5), the total MNE of paired elements has been divided by two and the total MNE of other elements has been divided by their number in the red deer skeleton (ie skull divided by one; non-atlas or axis cervical vertebrae by five; lumbar vertebrae by six; etc). The resulting plot of these red deer MAUs against the MGUI is presented in Fig 190. There is no clear linear relationship between bone element frequency and Binford's MGUI. A number of the bones that have a fairly high MGUI and carry appreciable amounts of meat are poorly represented, for instance the scapulae, sternum and ribs. We have already observed that there is a high level of fragmentation of the long bones which could be due to the extraction of marrow (Binford 1978b, 152; Spiess 1979; Speth 1983; 1991). The data are therefore compared with Binford's marrow index and also his grease index (Fig 191; Fig 192). The plot of MAU against marrow index (Fig 191), while not showing any sort of curvilinear relationship, has clearly separated the bones into two groups – a collection of bones with low marrow content that is poorly represented, and a relatively high frequency for most of the bones with a high marrow content.

A similar picture is indicated by the plot of MAU against grease index (Fig 192). Binford describes an example of the preparation of grease by the Nunamiut. He records their selection and amassing of the articular ends of the long bones,

animal units (MAU) were used, so the total weight of bone of each skeletal element is used to compare the different areas (Fig 189). This graph shows that the long bones and tarsals tend to dominate all the assemblages, indicating that these constitute the main component of the sample across the whole site. There are two main differences between the areas apparent from the graph. Firstly, cranial and axial parts of the skeleton make a contribution only in the areas outside the midden, as the preceding plots have shown. Secondly, the size of the long bone shaft fragment component is very high within the midden, more than twice that in the north-west scatter; a calculation of average fragment weight in these areas based on the data in Fig 189 is 4.3g in the north-west scatter, 2.1g in the midden and 1.9g on the rest of the site. The bones within the midden appear to have undergone a greater level of destruction than those in the north-west scatter. This may be the result of post-depositional disturbance such as trampling or the freeze-thaw effect discussed in Chapter 5.1, although a more severe impact in the midden compared to the north-west part of the trench is difficult to explain. It is possible that this greater fragmentation of the bones within the midden group and to the east of the site

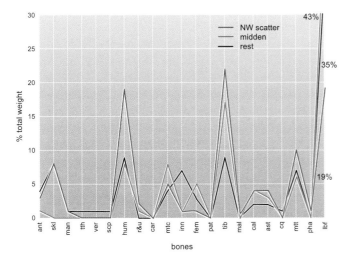

Fig 189 Weight of red deer bones in three areas of scatter C

169

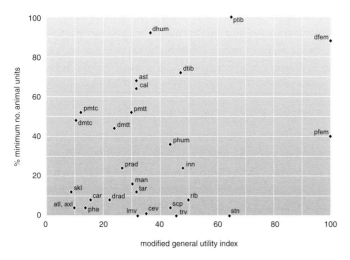

Fig 190 Red deer MGUI plot

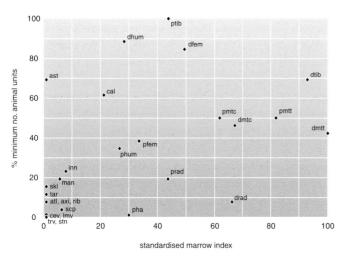

Fig 191 Red deer marrow index plot

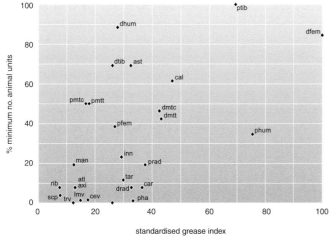

Fig 192 Red deer grease index plot

which are then pulverised prior to being immersed in boiling water, from which the grease is skimmed off after the bone has boiled for a while (Binford 1978b, 158). We have seen in Chapter 4.4 (Fig 137) that of the base camp samples reported by Binford

(ibid), that at Kakinya, which includes an unprocessed cache of bones for grease extraction, most closely resembles the Three Ways Wharf collection. One of the characteristics of the Three Ways Wharf sample is the complete absence of the articular ends of the femora and the proximal ends of the humerus and tibia. Epiphyses are generally poorly represented for all the long bones, with only the distal tibia and distal humerus occurring with any frequency. Given that at least 22 femora were present in the midden and surrounding area, the complete loss of the 44 articular ends that were originally present, including the fairly robust femur heads, is difficult to attribute to natural processes of erosion or scavenging discussed in Chapter 5.1. A similar situation pertains to the proximal tibia, of which 24 different examples were recognised on the basis of the proximal anterior spine and the proximal posterior foramen, and also the proximal humerus, of which 23 different examples were identified. This loss of nearly 50 proximal articulations, while fragments of the shaft immediately distal to the epiphysis survive, is also difficult to reconcile with the general condition and survival of the other bones. To a lesser degree, losses may have occurred to the proximal and distal metapodials. The frequency of individual metapodials in the collection is lower than for the upper limbs (excepting the radius), but this may in part be due to the greater difficulty of recognising them as distinct individual fragments of the shaft of these bones, since they carry fewer diagnostic features than the femur, tibia and humerus. Metapodials may have been as frequent on the site as the other bones and undergone equivalent loss of articular ends.

With such a pronounced selection of the long bones of the limbs and their immediate neighbours, and the positive relationship between marrow index and frequency, the conclusion that this midden represents the waste from marrow extraction seems inescapable – even if the assemblage as it was collected prior to processing had been devoid of meat, the butchery of the carcasses for meat having taken place elsewhere. The interpretation can be taken even further. If the absence of the articular ends of the major long bones can be attributed to human activity rather than natural agencies, then the extraction of grease after the manner described by Binford (1978b) seems the only credible explanation for the assemblage. Both processes would result in heavy fragmentation of the bone, and juxtaposition with the hearth would be essential for both marrow and grease extraction. Nevertheless, three problems cast some doubt on these conclusions.

Firstly, in Binford's account he makes a point of noting the large quantity of wood gathered in order to fuel the fire during the grease processing (Binford 1978b, 157). This might have been expected to leave a visible trace at Three Ways Wharf, but little evidence for charcoal in any quantity was recorded during the excavation (although some may have been removed by flooding, and the identification of the hearth only followed from the plotting of the burnt flint and bone). However, the extensive post-depositional soil micromorphological changes which have affected the palaeosol might have removed any trace of charcoal concentrations (Chapter 2).

Secondly, any boiling would have required the heating of

stones, and as Binford (1978b, 159) has suggested, one might have expected a scatter of pot boilers around the hearth or on the midden. There is a small 'pit' feature, just to the west of the bone concentration and adjacent to the hearth, which could have formed a suitable hollow for the use of a skin as a boiling container (Speth 1991), but whether this can be stratigraphically related to the occupation is problematic (Chapter 1.3).

Thirdly, although there is little evidence of butchery on these bones, the sorts of tools that might have been used for smashing bone shafts to extract the marrow and pulverising their articular ends were hammer stones or large pebbles. Few such finds were made in scatter C west, but these tools at least may have been taken away when the site was abandoned. They are, by contrast, prevalent in scatter C east. Binford, in describing the Nunamiut method of extracting marrow, indicates that the periosteum is scraped off the shaft of the bone (Binford 1978b, 153). It is possible that the marks observed on the metacarpal shaft FB 935 may have been caused by such action, and the humerus fragment FB 1304 interpreted as being used as a soft hammer for working stone tools (Chapter 4.6) could also have functioned as a hammer for cracking open marrow bones. The possible seasonal character of this marrow extraction has been mentioned above, and Binford notes that the Nunamiut tended not to store marrow bones in summer because they spoilt fairly rapidly (ibid, 163).

This discussion has centred on the red deer, for obvious reasons, but the roe deer bones show a very similar distribution (Fig 193), and although the frequency of non-marrow bone fragments suggests that other carcass or food processing was taking place, treatment was clearly similar to that of the red deer.

In the preceding discussions of the Lateglacial scatters, we considered the length of time that the site was occupied and the group size involved. These are much more problematic questions in relation to the Mesolithic assemblage. Because the bones represent the last stage of processing and, as alluded to above, may have carried no meat, the dietary value of the bones on the site might be restricted simply to the value of the marrow and

grease contained within them. This is a very much smaller resource than the meat and fat that the animals carried. Spiess (1979) records a marrow yield of 520g from the femora, tibiae, humeri, radii and metapodials of a 2-year-old, July-killed male caribou, of which 70% by weight was fat. This might provide sufficient calories for one adult for a day (c 3240 calories). No figures are available for red deer but, given an adult body weight of a Mesolithic animal of about 1.5 times that of the caribou and a correspondingly greater bone size, the marrow fat value of 15 red deer might contribute sufficient calories for 22.5 days for one adult. This, compared to a potential 1350kg of meat from the 15 carcasses (using the Legge and Rowley-Conwy 1988 estimates), or c 600 days of adult calorie requirement estimated at 3000 calories per day, does not amount to much, although it does show that the site represents the final processing stages of a substantial food resource. The relative absence of the bones which would give an indication of the season of kill of the animals (although a late spring and early summer occupation is suggested) makes estimates of the length of occupation problematic; but assuming that the butchery of these carcasses was taking place elsewhere, and their consumption was by the same group processing the bones for marrow and grease, then this site represents part of a relatively long period of occupation by a group significantly larger than that indicated by the Lateglacial scatters. If we were to use the group size of four families (eight adults and 12 children) proposed by Clark (1972, 27) for Star Carr, then the total resource from the red deer alone would permit occupation for c 40 days. As mentioned earlier, it is not useful to treat these figures as anything other than a general estimate. It is extremely unlikely that the excavated site represents that occupied by four families for 40 days. It is as likely that the excavated site formed but one component of a larger site, most of which was not excavated, where other processing and craft activities were taking place. A site of this scale may have encompassed a wide range of activities and might be expected to yield a full tool kit, and yet the spectrum of finds is more restricted than that recovered from Star Carr. In fact, scatter C west would fit very well as the hearth and settlement area of Star Carr, since many of the patterns at the two sites are complementary. In Chapter 7 the problem of whether these different settlement elements existed contemporaneously within the landscape, or whether they represent seasonal adjustments to subsistence patterns, will be addressed more fully.

6.4   Use-wear analysis of the lithic assemblages

Roger Grace

Methodology

The use-wear analysis was carried out using the multi-dimensional approach to functional analysis. This approach involves the recording of morphological variables of the

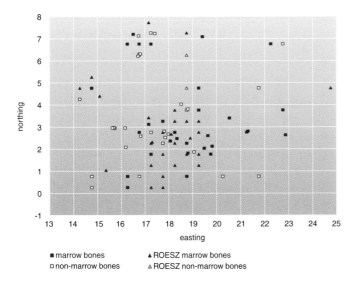

Fig 193 Plot of roe deer and roe deer size marrow and non-marrow bones in scatter C

working edges of stone tools (eg edge angle, profile etc), and the observation of use-wear at both macro (by eye and use of hand lens) and micro (microscopic examination at magnifications from x50 to x200) levels. All these variables are correlated in order to eliminate uses of the tools until the most probable function of the tool is arrived at. Because this process involves the simultaneous consideration of the interaction of some 33 variables, an expert system has been developed in order to process the data. This computer program, FAST (functional analysis of stone tools) is described by Grace (1993; in prep). Detailed explanations of the methods used for this analysis can be found elsewhere (Grace et al 1988; Grace 1989; 1990; Healey et al 1992; Newcomer et al 1986; 1988. The lithics are analysed for motion of use, relative hardness of worked material, and precise worked material where possible.

Results

Scatter A

Only 19 pieces from scatter A were analysed. Of these, 14 were unused and 5 used:

2 for cutting fish in adjacent squares;
1 for whittling wood;
1 for boring antler;
1 for ?scraping.

This constitutes too small a sample from which to draw any conclusions.

Scatter C

From the sample from scatter C, 507 edges were examined, of which 283 were unused, 38 had insufficient data, and 186 were used. Insufficient data refers to pieces that were probably used but where there is insufficient information on which to base an analysis, often because of natural alteration of the flint surface. As there is evidence that the scatter may represent two occupations, the use-wear results will first be considered for the whole site and then as two separate areas.

The results of the use-wear analysis show a wide range of activities. Various motions (cutting, scraping, whittling, boring, grooving, piercing etc) were carried out on wood, hide, bone, antler, meat and fish. A number of tools were used for butchering; that is, the evidence suggests that the tools came into contact with a combination of meat, hide and bone. There is no evidence for the use of tools for processing vegetables (below, 'Influence of sample'). Only two projectile points were found and two other possible ones that were not used.

The two projectile points were microliths (obliquely blunted points). The use of microliths as barbs is difficult to detect as impact is not directly on the microlith and the short duration of contact is unlikely to produce polish. Most of the microliths, particularly in scatter C east around the hearth, have use-wear from contact with other materials, so they were not used as barbs.

Of the eight microliths considered 'pointed' and perhaps suitable as projectile tips:

2 were projectiles;
2 were possible projectiles but unused;
2 were used for boring;
2 were used for cutting with lateral edges.

The general functional configuration of scatter C suggests a 'home base' (Grace 1990; Healey et al 1992). The functional configuration is produced by a histogram of the major motions (cutting, scraping, rotational, percussive and projectile) (Fig 194), with the used material in terms of hardness (soft, soft/medium, medium, medium/hard, hard). This allows the tools that could only be identified to relative hardness rather than precise worked material to be included and gives an overall pattern of activities.

This pattern, for example, is similar to that from the Norwegian Mesolithic site of Farsund (Ballin and Jensen 1995), which is interpreted as a temporary 'home base' (Fig 195). Three Ways Wharf is considered less temporary than Farsund because of the wider range of activities and the size of the site and number of artefacts (Farsund yielded a total of 1235 pieces, 22 of which were retouched and 48 used). The main difference is in the relative

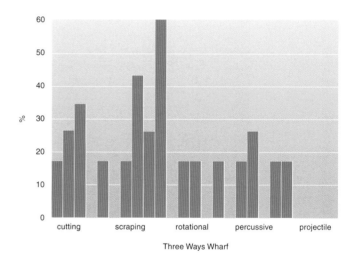

Fig 194 Functional configuration of lithics from scatter C

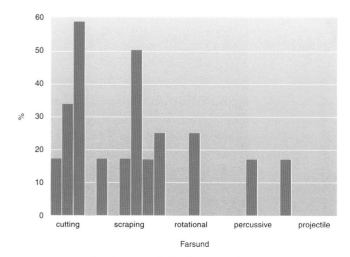

Fig 195 Functional configuration of lithics from Farsund

percentages of tools used on the harder materials (bone and antler) at Three Ways Wharf. However, this may be a product of the influence of the sample as most of the unretouched pieces were not analysed (below). This difference is illustrated more clearly by

the histogram of precisely identified used materials (Fig 196). The higher percentage of tools used for scraping relative to cutting motions is for the same reason (Fig 197).

These 'home base' sites can be contrasted with more specialist sites where the activities are limited. An example is the site of Kvernepollen in Norway (Grace in prep), where the activities are limited to working wood, cutting fish and making projectile points (Fig 198; Fig 199).

Influence of sample

Sixty-six out of 186 used edges are unretouched. Seventeen of these are on burins, particularly burin facets. The remaining 49 were used for the following:

18 for cutting wood;
2 for whittling wood;
2 for boring wood;
1 for scraping wood;
7 for cutting fish;
4 for cutting hide;
4 for cutting meat;
1 for scraping antler;

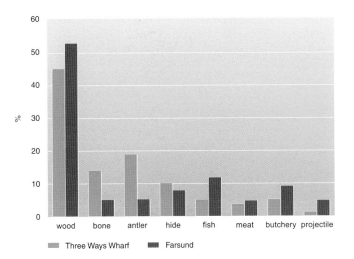

Fig 196 Uses of lithic material at Three Ways Wharf and Farsund

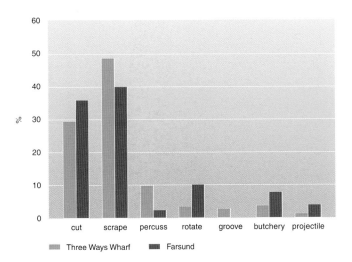

Fig 197 Use motions of lithics from Three Ways Wharf and Farsund

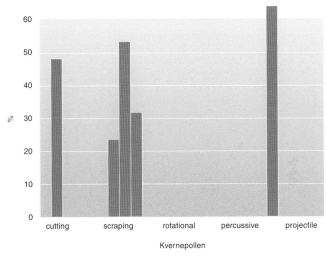

Fig 198 Functional configuration of lithics from Kvernepollen

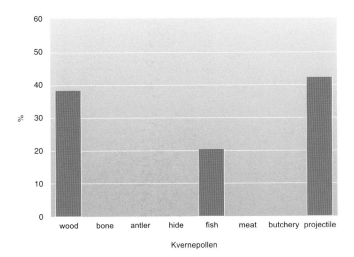

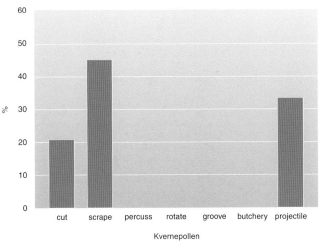

Fig 199 Uses and use motions of lithics from Kvernepollen

1 for whittling antler;

5 for butchering;

?1 for scraping;

?1 for piercing;

?1 for boring;

1 as a projectile.

All edges used on meat and fish, and four out of five edges used for cutting hide were unretouched. Many of the tools had retouch which was for backing or to facilitate hafting while the used edge was unretouched. The truncated blade/flake, for example, was retouched on the distal end but the right lateral unretouched edge was used for butchering. The majority of microliths fall into this category. Therefore, analysis of more unretouched pieces might increase the number of tools used for cutting wood, fish and meat, and for butchering.

It is suggested that the cut marks on the humerus of a swan were made by 'a sharp stone blade' (Chapter 4.6; Fig 145). This kind of mark would most probably have been made with an unretouched edge, so that analysis of a larger number of unretouched pieces might well result in an increase in butchery tools related to such cut marks. This would increase the percentage representation of tools used on softer materials and thus lower the percentage used for antler and bone working, so that the configuration would probably be more similar to that expected of a domestic 'home base' site. This could also influence the spatial distribution, so that the apparent separation of hide working from bone working and chopping and adzing wood would no longer be the case. It is expected that analysis of more unretouched pieces would have little influence on the distribution of bone and antler working.

ACTIVITY AREAS

The concentration of tools used for chopping and adzing wood (Fig 200) can only be an activity area, as the pieces used for adzing wood are of various types comprising:

1 broken axe;

2 axe/adze resharpening flakes;

8 flake end scrapers;

1 blade end scraper.

There are more end scrapers towards the west (Fig 71) but they are distributed throughout the site, so that the concentration is only related to the activity of chopping and adzing wood. The analysed axe/adze flakes are distributed towards the west (Fig 92), but spread over a wider area, including a cluster of three in the south and an outlier in the east. The other axe, which has not been analysed, also falls within this concentration.

Bone-working tools are concentrated in three main areas, to the west, south and east, around the centre of the site (Fig 201). When considering the distribution of bone fragments in relation to the bone-working tools it is interesting to note that in the western area there is a high concentration of bone fragments (Fig 201), thought to represent waste products from bone working. The bone-working tools are distributed around that concentration, and may represent an activity area, not by virtue of being clustered but because they are on the periphery of the concentration of waste products. It is suggested below (6.7) that these distributions may represent a number of people working bone around the area in which they were discarding the waste products.

The distribution of hide-working tools shows no significant concentrations (Fig 202), as is also the case with antler-working

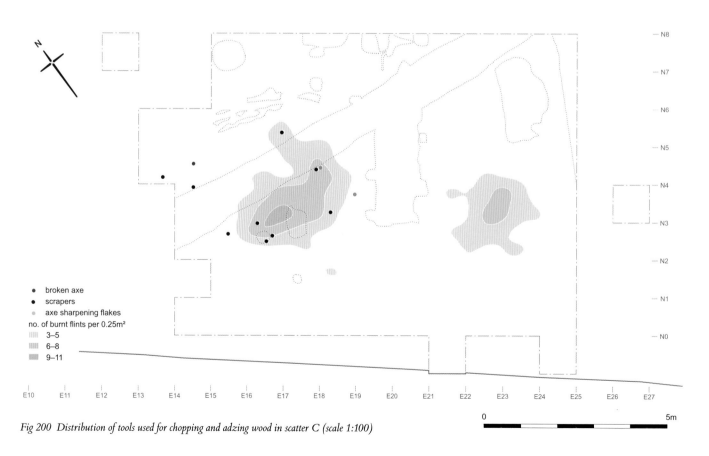

Fig 200 Distribution of tools used for chopping and adzing wood in scatter C (scale 1:100)

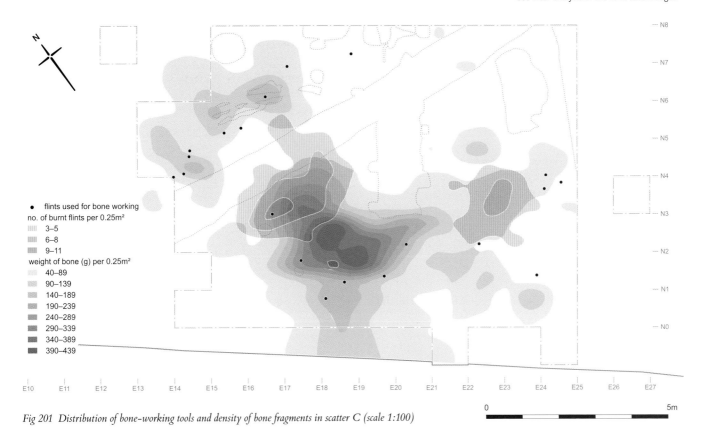

Fig 201 Distribution of bone-working tools and density of bone fragments in scatter C (scale 1:100)

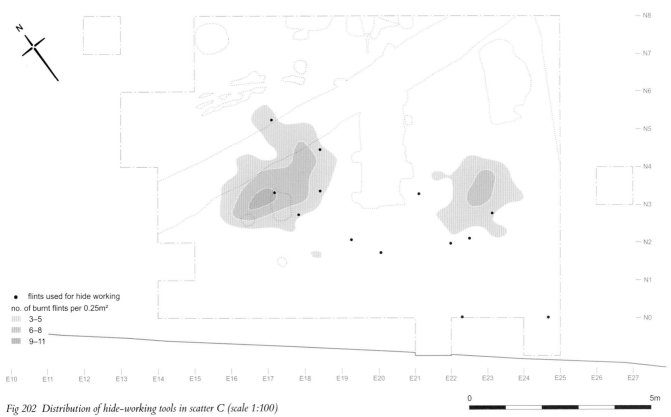

Fig 202 Distribution of hide-working tools in scatter C (scale 1:100)

tools. As the use-wear analysis is of a sample of the material, further investigation might reveal spatial patterning among these tools.

Though these distributions overlap, the degree of separation is of significance. Compare, for example, the distributions at

the Three Ways Wharf site with Farsund, a site that has been disturbed (Fig 203).

Only five tools are identified as having been used on fish, four on meat and seven for butchery in this area. These do not show any concentration (Fig 204).

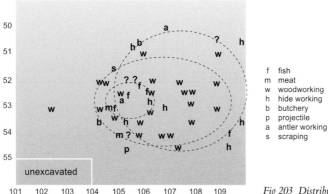

f fish
m meat
w woodworking
h hide working
b butchery
p projectile
a antler working
s scraping

Fig 203 Distribution of used pieces at Farsund

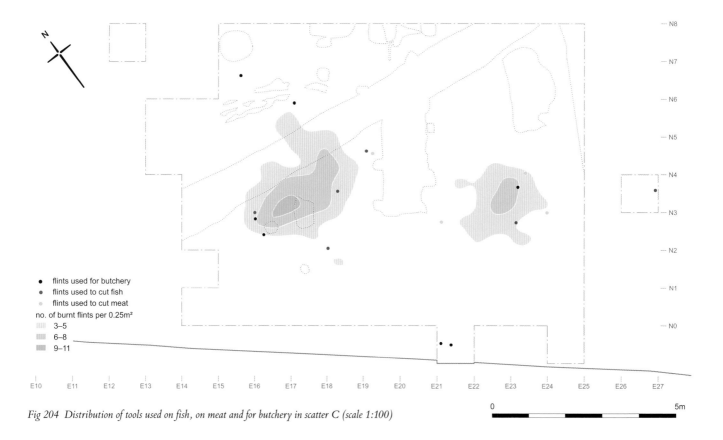

• flints used for butchery
• flints used to cut fish
• flints used to cut meat

no. of burnt flints per 0.25m²
▦ 3–5
▦ 6–8
▦ 9–11

Fig 204 Distribution of tools used on fish, on meat and for butchery in scatter C (scale 1:100)

0   5m

Tools used on wood, that is adding tools used for scraping, cutting, whittling and boring wood to the tools used for chopping and adzing, are distributed throughout the site (Fig 205).

When viewed together, the groups of tools for wood chopping and adzing, and bone and hide working are seen to indicate different activity areas (Fig 206).

Antler-working tools are distributed in the same area as the hide-working tools and they completely overlap when seen together (Fig 206). A good deal of antler working seems to have taken place, and the absence of antler artefacts or waste material could be due to preservation factors and also to removal. If the beams have been removed, then some differential removal of specific antler parts was being practised. There are only two tools used for grooving antler, so that groove and splinter technique was not a major activity, as it was at Star Carr for example. There are two tools used for cutting and two for

chopping antler, and these could relate to the removal of the beams. Scraping antler is a generalised activity that could be pre-processing prior to the manufacture of artefacts (points, harpoons) which may have been carried out elsewhere (ie wherever the beams were transported to).

Use-wear analysis and scatter C as two phases of occupation

The lithic and faunal evidence suggests that the site may represent two chronologically distinct occupations grouped around hearths, one in the west and the other to the east. The use-wear results can be assessed by separating the sample into material occurring in the west and in the east, and treating the two areas as different sites.

The overall functional configurations illustrate a general spread of activities in the west, suggesting a 'home base' (Fig 207). The functional configuration for the east is more

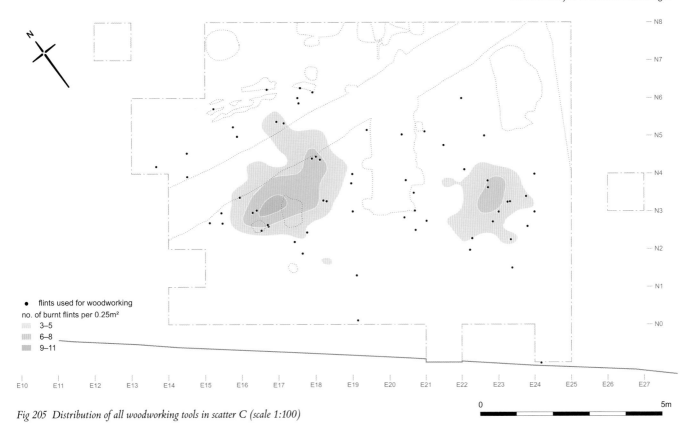

Fig 205 Distribution of all woodworking tools in scatter C (scale 1:100)

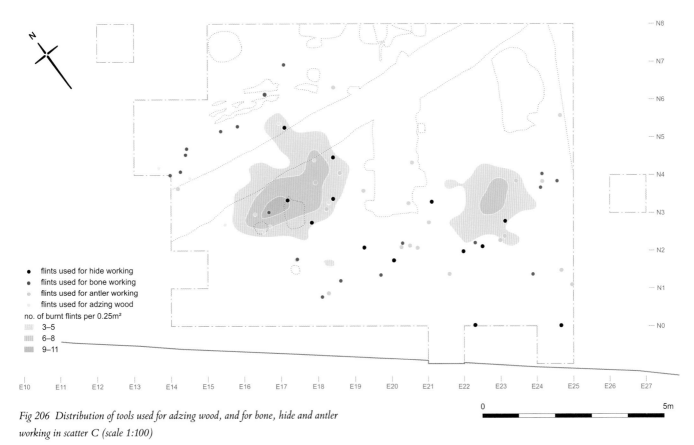

Fig 206 Distribution of tools used for adzing wood, and for bone, hide and antler
working in scatter C (scale 1:100)

specialised, consisting of mainly cutting and scraping activities (Fig 208). However, the range of worked materials is the same for both areas, except that the east has no projectile points, and more antler was worked there than bone (Fig 209).

In terms of motions of use of the tools, the main differences are the higher percentage of cutting motions in C east and the lack of percussive motion (because of the concentration of chopping and adzing wood) in C west that has already been

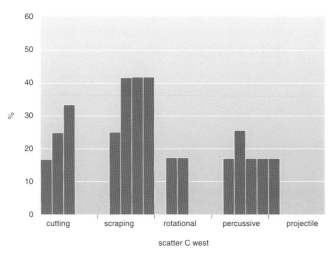

Fig 207 *Functional configuration of lithics in scatter C west*

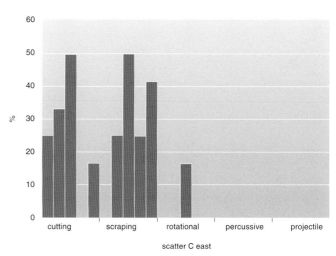

Fig 208 *Functional configuration of lithics in scatter C east*

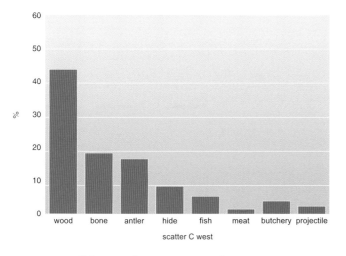

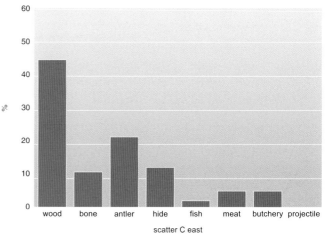

Fig 209 *Uses of lithic material in scatters C west and C east*

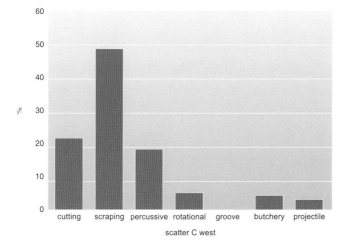

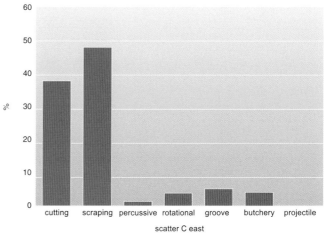

Fig 210 *Use motions of lithics in scatters C west and C east*

mentioned (Fig 210). Also, the hide and antler working was predominately in C east.

There is a difference between C west and C east in terms of intensity of use within tool types. The distribution of microliths,

for example, shows that most of the used ones are in C east, whereas the majority of unused microliths are in the west. With a single exception all the microliths in the north-west are unused (Fig 211).

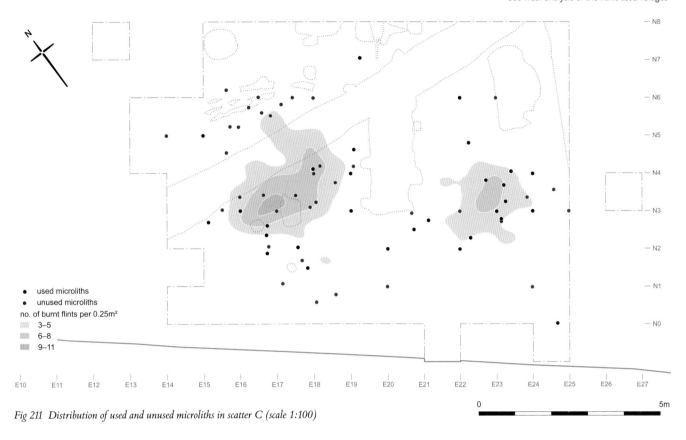

Fig 211 Distribution of used and unused microliths in scatter C (scale 1:100)

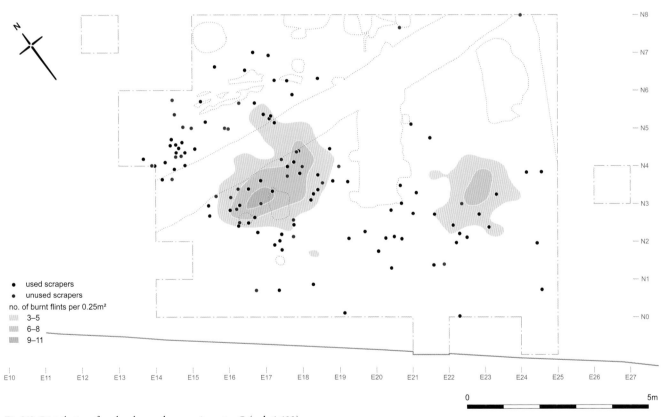

Fig 212 Distribution of used and unused scrapers in scatter C (scale 1:100)

The same trend is followed by the scrapers. Most of the scrapers were used, but the unused ones are overwhelmingly in C west. With only a couple of exceptions the scrapers in C east are used (Fig 212).

The difference in body parts in the faunal assemblage between C east and C west, particularly the lack of toes in C west, giving rise to the suggestion that these were still attached to the hide, supports the interpretation that hide working was

179

being carried out predominantly in the east, based in the first instance on the distribution of hide-working tools. The suggestion of butchery being carried out around the hearth in C east is difficult to correlate with the tools as there are so few butchery tools and they do not cluster (Fig 204). There is a cluster of microliths around the hearth but these were used on a variety of materials (wood, fish, meat and hide). There are relatively few scrapers around the hearth and none of them used on hide, so hide scraping was being carried out away from the hearth. Hide cutting, in the form of skinning, may of course be related to butchery.

Conclusions

Although both the Early Mesolithic scatter C west and the Lateglacial scatter C east could be characterised as 'home bases' (allowing for influence of sample), there appear to be significant differences between them. The two occupations differ both in the types of activity and in the intensity of utilisation. In C west the people were making tools and using some of them, predominately for chopping and adzing wood and on bone. By inference, it is highly likely that the woodworking was associated with the manufacture of wooden artefacts. In C east nearly all the tools were used, predominantly on hide and antler, and with butchery also taking place.

6.5 Comparison of the Three Ways Wharf lithic scatters with other assemblages

Stratigraphic (Chapter 2.2) and radiocarbon (Table 1) dating suggest that all the *in situ* material at Three Ways Wharf dates from the Lateglacial to the early Boreal period. Current archaeological perceptions of this period are discussed in Chapter 7.2. In this section, the Three Ways Wharf assemblages will be compared with other British sites of the same period.

The publication by Wymer and Rose of a lithic assemblage from Sproughton, Suffolk, drew attention to a lithic industry which was 'very different from Mesolithic industries ... or Late Upper Palaeolithic industries' (Wymer and Rose 1976, 10). The term 'long blade' industry was used to describe the assemblage and was assigned on typological and stratigraphical grounds to pollen zone IV, the Pre-Boreal. The work of Barton (1986; 1989; 1991; Barton and Froom 1986) has done much to shed light on the place of the 'long blade' industry in the archaeology of the final Lateglacial and early Postglacial. This section is a summary based almost entirely on that body of work, supplemented by data from Three Ways Wharf and other recent publications.

Definition of the 'long blade' industry

Barton has defined the 'long blade' industry on technological and typological grounds which link it with Late Upper Palaeolithic flintwork from southern Britain. At the same time,

elements of the 'long blade' industry, such as the appearance of microliths, seem to look forward to the true Early Mesolithic. A summary of 'long blade' industries and contrasts with Early Mesolithic assemblages is given below. It should be remembered that this is based on relatively few excavated and (even fewer) published assemblages. The combination of the elements described should be taken to define 'long blade' sites, and not the presence of any one of them in isolation (Cook and Jacobi 1994, 81).

Technology

Raw material

Sites often coincide with the main rich flint-bearing chalk deposits of southern England, and the raw material utilised is usually of excellent quality.

Core preparation and reduction

This is essentially Upper Palaeolithic in technique, with the preparation of one or sometimes two crests and the reduction of blades from two opposed platforms. During core reduction, maintenance of the striking platform was achieved by detaching core tablets and/or partial faceting. In southern British Mesolithic assemblages, preparation is usually confined to a single crest, and core rejuvenation is achieved by core tablet removal, with faceting being very rare or absent.

Blade blanks

These are characteristically long, with a high proportion greater than 120mm in length. The percentage of faceted blade butts in 'long blade' assemblages varies from *c* 48% at Avington VI, Berkshire (Barton and Froom 1986, 81), to *c* 12% at Gatehampton Farm, Oxfordshire (Barton 1995, 56). Faceting is rare in Early Mesolithic assemblages, and average blade lengths are much smaller.

Retouched tool typology and assemblage composition

Retouched tools typically form a low percentage (*c* 2% or less) of the total assemblage, and the inventory is restricted. Scrapers are usually on the ends of large flakes or blades.

Burins show a slight preference for dihedral over truncation types. Avington VI has produced an unequivocal example of a tanged point (Barton and Froom 1986, 83).

These 'Upper Palaeolithic' traits are balanced by the presence in a number of assemblages (such as Sproughton, Suffolk (Wymer and Rose 1976), and Springhead lower floor, Kent (Burchell 1938)) of broad microliths, often obliquely truncated and sometimes with additional modification.

However, microburins are usually rare or absent, and some microliths and backed pieces retain their proximal ends, again a feature with similarities in the Upper Palaeolithic. Also absent are typically Early Mesolithic forms such as drill bits (*mèches de foret*), microdenticulates, axes and adzes, and core tool debitage. The largest proportion of the retouched tool element at most of the British sites seems to consist of miscellaneous retouched flakes and blades, which do not fall within formal tool types.

Utilised pieces

One of the most distinctive forms of *a posteriori* tools within 'long blade' assemblages are the so-called 'bruised' blades and flakes (*lames et éclats mâchurés*) (Bordes 1967, 30). These usually consist of large robust flakes and blades (sometimes crested) which display signs of very heavy edge damage in the shape of stepped, invasive scalar scarring, usually confined to the ventral surface (Barton 1986). Experiments suggest that this distinctive form of damage could be achieved by heavy-duty chopping of material such as animal bone and antler (ibid).

Dating and typological affinities of 'long blade' industries

Dating of British 'long blade' sites has been problematical and based mainly on relative stratigraphic and environmental evidence, together with Continental parallels. For example, on bio-stratigraphic evidence Avington VI, Berkshire, seems to post-date the Windermere Interstadial and is contained within sediments dated to Late Devensian zone III/Pre-Boreal zone IV (Barton and Froom 1986, 80). The assemblage at Sproughton, Suffolk, has been dated to pollen zone IV (Pre-Boreal) on the basis of stratigraphic and environmental evidence (Wymer and Rose 1976, 13). The assemblage recovered at very low tide at Titchwell, Norfolk, was stratified beneath peat, which began to accumulate at the end of pollen zone V or the start of zone VI (ie the Boreal) (Wymer and Robins 1994). Finds analogous to those in Britain occur in north-west Europe, notably in northern Germany, the Netherlands and north-west France (Barton 1991). The tanged points from Avington VI can be paralleled with Ahrensburgian points from Stellmoor (Rust 1943) and other sites in northern Europe. Recent radiocarbon dates from Stellmoor suggest activity at the end of the Younger Dryas, 10,100–9900 BP (Fischer and Tauber 1986, 7). Once again the problem of the 10,000 BP radiocarbon compression prevents truly accurate dating (Bratlund 1991, 196). The Stellmoor assemblage also contains very large blades and examples with 'bruised' margins.

The similarities between British and Continental sites have led Barton to suggest an extensive Ahrensburgian technocomplex spanning the North Sea basin (which in the Lateglacial/early Postglacial would of course have been dry land) (Barton 1991). Most importantly, this technocomplex would also seem to straddle, chronologically, the traditional Late Upper Palaeolithic to Early Mesolithic transition. It has also been suggested that subtle changes occur within this Ahrensburgian technocomplex both chronologically, between the Loch Lomond Stadial and the early Pre-Boreal, and

spatially, between northern Germany, through the Netherlands and into northern France and Britain (ibid). These changes can be summarised as follows.

During the Loch Lomond Stadial (pre-10,000 BP) 'long blade' lithic assemblages contain tanged points as well as microlithic and non-microlithic backed points, with few microburins occurring. However, the frequency of tanged points would seem to decrease south-westwards from Germany into northern France and Britain, where the microlithic element appears to have been more important, possibly on cultural or stylistic grounds (Gob 1991). In Britain, Avington VI would fit this type of assemblage profile, while in France sites of presumed Younger Dryas age such as Les Blanchères (Rozoy 1978) lack tanged pieces but contain backed points and oblique points. Indeed, the Avington VI assemblage includes a Blanchères or Malaurie point (Froom 2005, 15–16).

During the early Postglacial (*c* 10,000–9700 BP) the microlithic/non-microlithic backed point element becomes more important at the expense of tanged points. The truncations of the obliquely backed points are often very oblique (ie truncation angles are high). They often combine an oblique truncation at the tip with additional basal retouch; Taute (1968) describes these as 'Zonhoven points without or with basal retouch' respectively (Johansen and Stapert 1997–8, 10). Although rare, microburins do occur; however, the tool kits remain restricted, with bruised pieces still prominent. Technologically, the core reduction process is still one of Upper Palaeolithic character with pre-shaping of cores, elaborate cresting and faceting. These changes seem to have occurred even in Germany, where the tanged point was most prevalent. For example, a series of north German sites such as Immenbeck III, Giffhorn and Minstedt were originally classified as Ahrensburgian (Taute 1968), but lack tanged points and are dominated by Zonhoven points, which means that they may just pre-date the British sites (Barton 1991, 239). Gob has termed these assemblages 'epi-Ahrensburgian' and dates them to the first three quarters of the 10th millennium BP. He defines this industry as including classic Ahrensburgian common tools, with a trend towards smaller pieces and a reduction in burins; a scarcity or lack of tanged points; a predominance of Zonhoven points; and the presence of atypical geometric microliths derived from tanged points (triangles and small irregular trapezes) (Gob 1991, 229). Clearly scatters A and C east at Three Ways Wharf fall within these definitions, although Gob also included sites such as Star Carr, North Yorkshire, and Thatcham, Berkshire, which are clearly Early Mesolithic. However, Gob also saw the 'long blade' industry of southern England and the Somme valley in France as an atypical workshop facies of the classic Ahrensburgian (that is, dating to before the Pre-Boreal at 10,000 BP).

The scarcity of reliable radiocarbon dates associated with lithic and faunal assemblages in Britain and on the Continent has led to a reliance on the typological comparisons described above. Cooper has recently discussed the various differences between the 'bruised blade' industry of Britain, the 'Belloisian' of Picardy and beyond the Paris basin, the epi-Ahrensburgian of

Belgium and the Netherlands, the Ahrensburgian of the northern Netherlands and Germany, and the Brommian of Denmark (Cooper 2006, 55–7, fig 2).

From the foregoing summary of 'long blade' industries and the summary of the Three Ways Wharf assemblages, it is clear that scatter A and elements of scatter C east have clear parallels with 'long blade' industries, while scatter C west has clear affinities with Early Mesolithic assemblages.

Scatters A and C east

The presence of *lames mâchurées* links scatters A and C east to the 'long blade' industries of Britain and north-west Europe. For instance the 'long blade' sites of Sproughton, Suffolk (Wymer and Rose 1976), Avington VI, Berkshire (Barton and Froom 1986), Gatehampton Farm, Oxfordshire (Barton 1995), Church Lammas, Staines, Surrey (Lewis in prep) and Belloy-sur Somme, France (Fagnart 1991) have all produced similar artefacts. In addition, several of the larger cores have no equivalents from British Mesolithic sites (Cook and Jacobi 1994, 81). Microlithic and non-microlithic backed points from British 'long blade' sites tend to be simple, broad, very obliquely backed 'Zonhoven' points, sometimes with the truncation at the distal end (eg Sproughton: Barton 1991, fig 22.2, no. 6). Many of the obliquely backed points from Three Ways Wharf scatters A and C east can be paralleled with these Zonhoven points. However, absent from the earlier Three Ways Wharf scatters are tanged points, Blanchères points and narrow, slightly obliquely backed points which are present at sites such as Avington VI (Barton and Froom 1986). The very distinctive bi-truncated 'C' type microliths (often with very concave truncations) from scatters A and C east have few British parallels, perhaps the most notable being those from Launde, Leicestershire (Cooper 2006, 73). However, together with the broad obliquely backed points from these assemblages, they can be compared with similar examples from the Continental Ahrensburgian technocomplex (Taute 1968, pls 70, 83; Cook and Jacobi 1994, 81; Johansen and Stapert 1997–8, 41).

If the variations in typology do reflect chronological development (above), then both scatters A and C east could date to the early Pre-Boreal, just prior to the appearance of 'true' Early Mesolithic industries. It is, therefore, unsurprising that the earlier Three Ways Wharf assemblages display many traits common to both the Upper Palaeolithic and the 'Mesolithic'. For instance, refitting group 10 in scatter C east demonstrates for the first time that *lames mâchurées* and the distinctive bi-truncated 'C' type microliths are in fact contemporary, and were produced by a typically 'Upper Palaeolithic' core reduction strategy (Chapter 3.6). This has great typological significance: thus, for example, these distinctive microliths can now be considered along with tanged points as typological markers for this period. Furthermore, when the trial work first uncovered scatter A it was assumed that the lithic material was Mesolithic in date. It is mainly the association with other artefacts, such as *lames mâchurées*, and reindeer fauna, which demonstrates that both scatters A and C east precede traditional

Early Mesolithic industries. It is therefore highly likely that there exist many examples of large opposed platform cores, *lames mâchurées*, and bi-truncated and distally retouched microliths in collections which in isolation and out of context would be categorised as Mesolithic.

Assemblage composition

Having demonstrated the technological and typological affinities of Three Ways Wharf scatters A and C east with 'long blade' industries, the composition of the assemblages needs to be considered. As mentioned above, a low incidence of retouched tools and a generally restricted retouched tool inventory is one of the characteristics of 'long blade' industries (Barton 1989). Scatter A falls within this pattern, but the composition of scatter C east is clearly different (Fig 119). Scatter C east contains a wider range of tool types compared with scatter A, and is in many ways closer in assemblage profile to C west, except for a lack of axes and a greater proportion of burins. This variation might be explained in a number of ways.

1) The composition of scatter C east has been influenced by the later occupation which resulted in scatter C west. Thus C east is a mixed assemblage of two different periods. This must be accepted to a certain degree: for instance, C east contains a small quantity of axe debitage which may be contemporary with this scatter or, more likely, associated with C west.

2) The differences in tool composition between scatters A and C east could be attributed to functional variability. The tool assemblage could, therefore, indicate that a wider range of activities was carried out in C east than in scatter A. The presence of a hearth in C east is unusual at 'long blade' sites, and could signify functional differences between C east and other 'long blade' sites. However, faunal analysis suggests a similar range of activities in both areas, but with C east representing a longer occupation than scatter A.

3) The contrast between scatters A and C east could be due to chronological difference. In this model, tool diversity would increase with time from the Younger Dryas, through the early Pre-Boreal and into the Early Mesolithic of the mid to late Pre-Boreal. This model has been implicitly suggested by other researchers (eg Barton 1991, esp table 22.4). Typologically, then, scatter A could be seen as earlier than C east. In this instance the paucity of tool types in scatter A might mask a diversity of activities as wide as those in C east.

4) The model proposed by Barton of the 'long blade' industry is too general in nature and does not accommodate all the complexities of human activity over a period in excess of one thousand years and witnessing rapidly changing climate. This must be acknowledged, given the very few excavated and published British sites of this period.

These points will be discussed further in Chapter 7 following the spatial and functional analysis of the assemblages in this chapter. It is worth considering that Gob (1991) has included 'long blade' industries within the Ahrensburgian technocomplex. He also notes the chronological trend towards assemblages with smaller pieces, fewer tanged points and more numerous

Zonhoven points which he terms the 'epi-Ahrensburgian'. Certainly the microliths from scatters A and C east compare very closely with those of the epi-Ahrensburgian site of Gelderop III-2 (Rozoy 1978, pl 17; Gob 1991, fig 21.2, no. 3). The evidence from scatters A and C east at Three Ways Wharf would tend to support the notion of an epi-Ahrensburgian phase which would equate with Barton's early Pre-Boreal phase of the 'long blade' industries. In fact, this argument could be extended to suggest that, on the grounds of assemblage composition, scatter C east dates to a later phase of the epi-Ahrensburgian/'long blade' industries than scatter A. However, Gob also includes in his 'epi-Ahrensburgian' British sites traditionally classed as Early Mesolithic such as Star Carr and Thatcham III. This is not supported by scatter C west at Three Ways Wharf, which accords with the broader British evidence that traditionally Early Mesolithic assemblages are morphological and technological adaptations associated with subsistence strategies based on the hunting of woodland fauna. Thus, although there are many traits in common between the 'long blade'/epi-Ahrensburgian and the Early Mesolithic, they are demonstrably distinct technologies produced by different forms of human behaviour and adaptations to different environments and ecosystems.

Technological comparisons

It has already been noted that quality of raw material probably limited the length of blade blank which could be produced. Thus none of the Three Ways Wharf assemblages has an average blade length approaching those of 'long blade' assemblages. Nonetheless, it has been demonstrated that the blade assemblage in scatter C east is significantly longer than that in C west. Differences in degree of nodule decortication and preparation have already been described (Chapter 3). Changes in techniques of platform preparation are also significant (Barton 1989) and the differences in the proportion of faceted to non-faceted blade butts between the Three Ways Wharf assemblages have been described. Fig 213 compares this aspect of the Three Ways Wharf assemblages with 'long blade' sites and Early Mesolithic assemblages of 'Star Carr' and 'Deepcar' type (Jacobi 1978, 308; Reynier in prep). The sites and sources of data in Fig 213 are the following. (The data for the Early Mesolithic sites were kindly supplied by Michael Reynier from his unpublished PhD thesis, and differ subtly from those in the published reports for these sites.)

'Long blade' assemblages: Avington VI, Berkshire (Barton and Froom 1986), Titchwell, Norfolk (Wymer and Robins 1995) and Gatehampton Farm, Oxfordshire (Barton 1995).

Early Mesolithic 'Star Carr' type: Broxbourne 104, Hertfordshire (Reynier in prep), Thatcham III (patinated series), Berkshire (Wymer 1962) and Pointed Stone sites 2 and 3, North Yorkshire (Jacobi 1978).

Early Mesolithic 'Deepcar' type: Thatcham III (unpatinated series), Berkshire (Wymer 1962) and Marsh Benham, Berkshire (Reynier in prep).

Fig 213 shows that the degree of faceting present in both scatters A and C east is comparable with the 'long blade' sites.

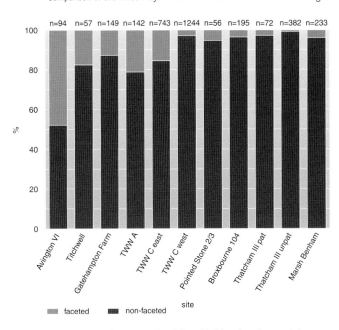

Fig 213 *Blade butt morphology at selected 'long blade' and Early Mesolithic sites*

In contrast, scatter C west clearly falls within the group of Early Mesolithic assemblages.

The Early Mesolithic and scatter C west

In 1932, Clark published *The Mesolithic Age in Britain*, which firmly established the Mesolithic as a period in the prehistoric occupation of Britain. Jacobi (1973; 1976) and Mellars (1974) proposed a formal separation of the Mesolithic into earlier and later phases, based on lithic typology and radiocarbon dates. One of the main identifying features of the earlier Mesolithic was the occurrence of assemblages in which broad (8–11mm wide) obliquely backed points dominated the microlithic component, but which also contained large isosceles triangles and trapezoids and rhomboids (Jacobi 1976, 67). Jacobi also proposed that the earlier Mesolithic forms were replaced around 8500 BP by microlithic forms containing a wide variety of small geometric forms, especially 'micro-triangles' (ibid, 71–5). This scheme is obviously an over-simplification, and some of the associated problems have been pointed out by Jacobi (1987, 163–4) himself, while the same author has highlighted problems associated with the contextual integrity of many of the radiocarbon dates upon which this chronology is based (Jacobi 1994). Nevertheless, the framework remains generally accepted and is the one followed here. The material from Three Ways Wharf scatter C west clearly falls within the Early Mesolithic.

Within the Early Mesolithic, a number of sub-assemblages have been proposed (eg Radley and Mellars 1964; Jacobi 1978, 305–6). These consist of 'Star Carr' type (Clark 1954), 'Deepcar' type (Radley and Mellars 1964) and 'Horsham' type (Clark 1933). Recent research by Reynier (in prep) has attempted a clearer typological and chronological definition of these 'assemblage types'. Although this research is at present incomplete, Reynier has defined these assemblages as follows.

The 'Star Carr' type is dominated by broad, angular,

obliquely truncated points which form 50–60% of the microlith assemblage. The remaining microliths are composed of broad triangles and large trapeziums (10–20% each). Convex backed points and rhomboids are rare.

The microlith component of 'Deepcar' assemblages is dominated by obliquely backed points (60–70%). However, in contrast to 'Star Carr' assemblages, these are less oblique, narrower and often (5–20%) have additional retouch on the leading edge of the tip of the point. Triangles are less common (<5%) but convex backed points are more prevalent (up to 10%). Bi-truncated forms such as rhomboids and lanceolates also increase in frequency (c 5%).

'Horsham' assemblages contain elements of both these technologies. Obliquely backed points again dominate the microlith assemblage (30–40%), but these are small and angular, often with additional retouch on the leading edge. Angular rhomboids and triangles form up to 20% of the microliths. However, the type artefacts of the 'Horsham' assemblages are hollow-based points, typically forming 15–20% of the microlith assemblage on these sites.

Scatter C west

If the British Early Mesolithic really can be subdivided into the 'assemblage types' described above, which does scatter C west most closely match? The absence of hollow-based points would seem to preclude a 'Horsham' type assemblage, while the obliquely backed 'A' type microliths in C west can be paralleled at Star Carr (Clark 1954, 101, fig 35). However, scatter C west also contains a number of narrow obliquely backed points with additional retouch on their leading edge, suggesting a link with 'Deepcar' type assemblages. Three possible interpretations suggest themselves.

1) Scatter C west might be a multiple-phase event. However, the strong spatial patterning together with statistically indistinguishable radiocarbon dates on three deer individuals of two different species suggests that C west is the product of a single event.

2) Scatter C west might represent a transitional stage between 'Star Carr' and 'Deepcar' type assemblages. The radiocarbon dates centring on 9200 BP could support this, since both assemblage types could be current at this time (Reynier in prep).

3) The Early Mesolithic cannot be rigorously divided into chronologically overlapping assemblage types. Since detailed research into these assemblage types is still in progress (M Reynier, pers comm), it would perhaps be unwise to make a judgement on the C west assemblage other than to conclude that it is of Early Mesolithic type.

Conclusions

The date and function of scatters B and D remain uncertain. Scatter C west would appear to date to the Early Mesolithic, which would accord well with the three radiocarbon dates clustering on 9200 BP. Scatter A is best paralleled among the 'long blade' industries of southern Britain and western Continental Europe which date to the end of the Lateglacial and the early Postglacial. Thus the two radiocarbon dates of c 10,000 BP on the horse fauna in scatter A would, if in fact associated with the lithic material, be in agreement with this scheme. The dating of scatter C east is more problematic, since no radiocarbon dates were obtained on the associated reindeer fauna. Typologically and technologically, scatter C east has many similarities with 'long blade' assemblages. However, there are a number of features such as the presence of a hearth, the small size of debitage, and the generally greater range and number of tools, which contrast with 'long blade' assemblages. Nevertheless, on the evidence presented in Chapters 3, 4 and 5 it is possible to suggest that scatters C east and A may be broadly (but not exactly) contemporary, and that both date to the latter part of the period between 10,300 BP and c 9700 BP. It is also argued that scatters A, C east and C west represent subtle differences in functional activity, and that this activity is also chronologically distinguishable. The difference in human behaviour and spatial organisation both on the site and within the wider landscape will be discussed further in Chapter 7, together with the place of the Three Ways Wharf assemblages within the Lateglacial and early Postglacial archaeology of Britain and north-west Europe.

6.6 Integration of lithic use-wear and faunal spatial analysis

Introduction

This section seeks to 'repopulate' the site and reconstruct the human patterns of movement and use of space that produced the lithic and faunal residues. It is acknowledged at the outset that such attempts are difficult, and that the data may be interpreted in many different ways. The difficulties are compounded by the close proximity of scatters C west and C east, since this will inevitably have led to a blurring of the spatial picture. This is particularly true in respect of activities peripheral to each hearth. For instance, it is argued above (6.3) that the antler-working debris adjacent to the eastern hearth was produced by activity associated with C west, not C east. Despite these difficulties, some attempt must be made to visualise the people who created these residues. Otherwise, the study of the lithic and faunal material becomes an end in itself, rather than a study of past human lives and actions, 'the creation of people as subjects' (Barrett 1994, 4).

The preceding sections have dealt with the spatial analysis of lithic and faunal evidence largely in isolation. In this section the three strands of evidence will be integrated, and further interpreted in terms of the 'seating plan' model proposed by Binford (1978a). The work and interpretations of Binford have been used extensively in this analysis. No apology is made for this since his approach can be applied most elegantly to interpreting the Three Ways Wharf data. An integral part of this approach is to understand the space occupied and used by human beings either singly or when congregated.

Freeman suggests that an individual seated on the ground can conveniently reach an area of 2.5m² in front of them, increasing to 3.0m² if the area behind is taken into account (Freeman 1978, 113). This area takes the form of an arc due to the mechanics of the human shoulder and torso (Gamble 1986, 252). In contrast, the physical space occupied by a seated person equates to a circle approximately 1m in diameter. In the following sections the possible seating arrangements of humans on the site are represented by a circle of that size. However, Fig 214 shows the seating space and 'reach area' for comparison.

It was concluded above (6.2) that the main core reduction, tool use and discard areas were centred on the two hearths and corresponded to a drop zone of discarded material. In scatter C west this pattern took the form of two arcs almost encompassing the hearth, while in C east the activity and drop zone was concentrated immediately to the south of the hearth (Fig 180). Surrounding and overlapping with the drop zones were areas interpreted as toss zones, where larger lithic material was discarded (or in the case of some nodules, initially processed). Analysis of the spatial distribution of the faunal material above (6.3) would tend to confirm this interpretation, with drop, toss and even deliberate discard zones being apparent.

Scatter A

In scatter A, it has been suggested that the reindeer upper limb bones representing the main meat-bearing portions of the carcass are clustered, while the other reindeer material is dispersed around the periphery of the site (Fig 181). Due to the relatively low density of lithic and faunal material in scatter A, together with the distortions caused by later features and the continuation of the scatter beyond the confines of the site, the level of spatial analysis was low. Fig 214 shows that the northern concentration of flintwork (SAS 11) and the concentration of meat-bearing upper limb bones lie adjacent to the suggested hearth site, while the southern concentration (SAS 10) lies *c* 4.5m from these zones. In this instance the human 'seating plan' is very tentative, but Fig 214 does suggest that the lithic concentration to the south of the hearth area was not associated with the removal of meat from the upper limb bones. Although use-wear analysis was restricted in scatter A, the results show that scraping hard material, whittling wood and cutting fish were all carried out to the south of the meat-processing area. In contrast, the location of the single *lame mâchurée* within the concentration of upper limb bones could be seen as corroborating the interpretation that this class of artefact is associated with heavy-duty butchery (Barton 1986). However, Fagnart and Plisson (1997, 100–4) suggest that bruised blades were used to hone sandstone hammers. Froom (2005, 38) has likened the artefacts to small cross pein hammers and suggests

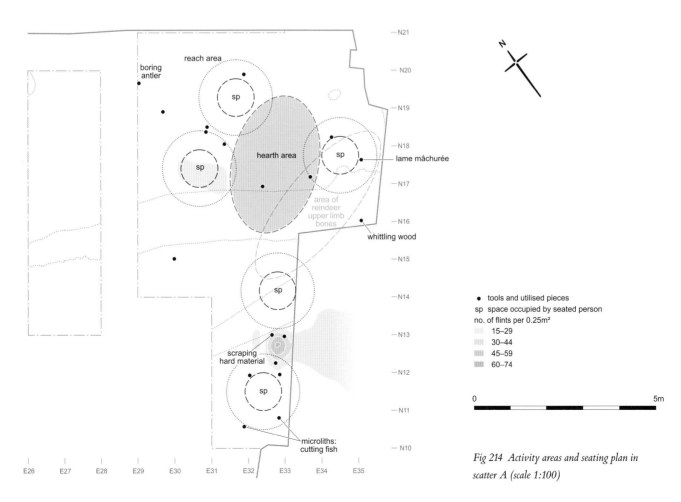

Fig 214 Activity areas and seating plan in scatter A (scale 1:100)

185

that they were used principally for partial faceting of platforms and core front preparation. He also notes that they occur in the densest debitage clusters.

In summary, the meagre evidence from the area available in scatter A suggests the presence of a knapping area and a meat-processing/butchery area on opposite sides of a small hearth. Around the periphery of this area were scattered the low meat-bearing skeletal parts, possibly reflecting toss discard. Four metres to the south was a more concentrated lithic scatter which was possibly associated with non-butchery activities.

Scatter C east

Fig 215 and Fig 182 show the distribution of meat-bearing upper limb bones in scatter C east clustered on the hearth, while the other bones are dispersed around the periphery. It can be seen that the cluster of skeletal material lies across the hearth and along the northern edge of the retouched tool zone. These bones thus form part of the hearth-centred drop zone and illustrate that along with tool production, meat was processed and consumed adjacent to the hearth. This interpretation is

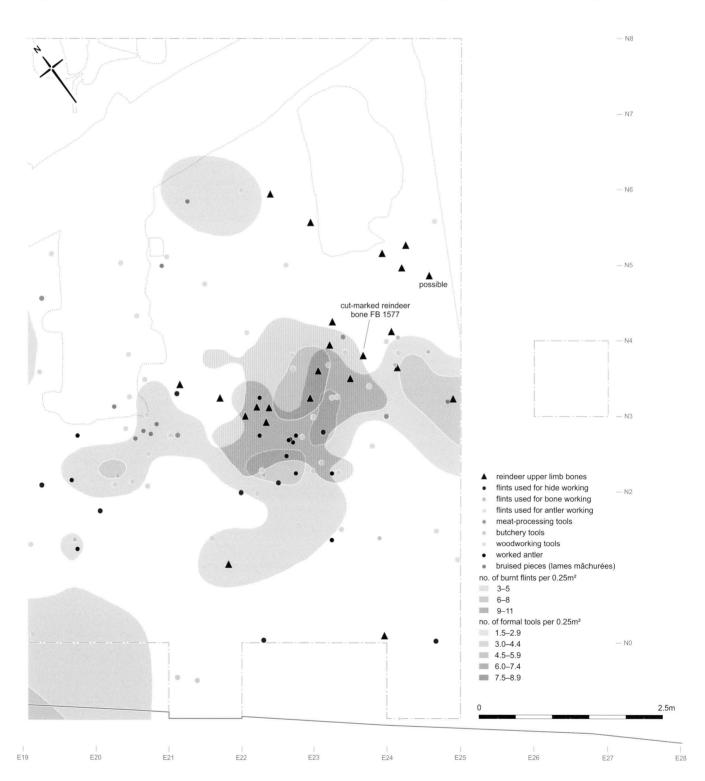

Fig 215 Distribution of used lithics, retouched tools and reindeer upper limb bones in scatter C east (scale 1:50)

reinforced by the presence of a single cut-marked reindeer humerus. Interestingly, the meat-bearing bones lie largely opposite and parallel to the main tool concentrations. As pointed out above (6.3), the use-wear analysis shows that it is difficult to correlate butchery with the hearth-side activity zone. However, Fig 215 shows that three artefacts were used for cutting meat and one for butchery in the central area, suggesting that at least some meat removal took place here. The functional configuration produced by use-wear (Fig 208) would accord with the faunal analysis in suggesting that the three reindeer carcasses which arrived on the site were being completely processed there. However, use-wear also suggests that a fairly wide range of material was being worked in C east, in particular hide, bone and antler. General activity areas have been defined for bone, antler and hide working which extend beyond the central hearth activity zone. The use-wear analysis also provides more detail on the range of activities which took place within the central hearth zone. In Fig 215 it can be seen that bone- and antler-working tools are situated near the hearth. Also present in this area are a small cluster of cortical antler fragments which may be the by-product of antler working, although it has been suggested above (6.3) that these may relate to the Early Mesolithic occupation in scatter C west. However, the main concentration of antler-working tools is to the west of the hearth, surrounding the main concentration of bruised blades and flakes. Hide-working tools are also represented, but their distribution tends to be peripheral to the hearth.

In section 6.3 the distribution of reindeer bones which bear relatively less meat was shown to be more widely dispersed than the upper limb bones, despite some of the former occurring in the central hearth area (Fig 182). This pattern accords with the interpretation of an outer toss-discard zone. In addition, use-wear analysis suggests that it is likely that the outer zone was also the scene of activities, such as hide working and possibly initial carcass dismemberment, which required more open space (Binford 1983, 169–72; Audouze and Enloe 1991, 65–6). The presence of a concentration of flint pebbles and nodules to the south of the hearth (Chapters 1.3 and 3.5) may be a part of this peripheral activity, and could represent either a lithic raw material dump or a setting for smashing bones. However, the proximity of scatters C east and C west will have inevitably produced some blurring and distortion of the spatial patterning around the periphery of the respective scatters, resulting in a palimpsest of activity residues (eg the antler-working debris).

The distributions shown in Fig 215 support the interpretation of the hearth-side area as an activity and drop-discard zone. A 'seating plan' (Fig 216) is shown to illustrate possible human use of space adjacent to the hearth (using the human reach parameters defined above). This proposes that the bulk of the material in C east was created by a small group of people sitting in a semicircle around the southern side of a hearth. A preference for this side of the hearth may reflect prevailing wind direction and therefore the dispersal of smoke from the fire. In that case it would suggest a prevailing wind from OS south-west to north-east.

This interpretation of the spatial patterning in C east seems on balance the most plausible. However, it does not allow for the presence of a shelter within the confines of the excavated area. As mentioned in Chapter 1.3 ('Features and structures'), there are no features which could be associated with such a structure, although any such features would be slight. A shelter need not have existed here, but may have been located a few metres away outside the investigated area, possibly on the higher ground on the crest of the low projecting ridge or valley side (Fig 31). In this scenario, the interpretation of C east as an open-air, hearth-side activity area could still stand. A different interpretation would be to see a shelter located to the north of the hearth, with the hearth near the entrance and the outdoor activity zone around the southern side of the hearth, with a toss zone beyond. Fig 217 shows this interpretation, with a shelter based on those postulated for the Magdalenian levels at Pincevent (Leroi-Gourhan and Brezillon 1966), and the tool and debitage concentrations plotted against the microtopography of the surface of SU40. It can be seen that the shelter is located on higher ground, with the main activity zone on the slope down towards the active stream margin. Of course the relationship of the activity zone to the active stream margin remains the same whichever interpretation is favoured.

On balance, the initial interpretation of C east as consisting of activity and discard zones and the absence of a shelter is favoured here since it is felt that this accords better with the lithic refitting and spatial evidence, such as the dispersed nature of the low meat-bearing reindeer skeletal elements.

Scatter C west

Scatter C west contains an appreciably greater quantity of lithic and faunal material than C east, and its spatial ordering is even better defined.

Fig 218 shows the formal retouched tool contours encircling the central hearth, and these are used to define the central activity zone (above, 6.2). It also shows the distribution of red deer long bones, which serve to define the 'midden' disposal areas described above (6.3), as well as that of worked and cut-marked bone and antler, and of lithic material showing traces of use on these materials.

As has been mentioned elsewhere, the densest bone and lithic concentrations are largely mutually exclusive, and the interpretation of the major bone deposits in C west as discard areas would fit this pattern well. In particular it was suggested above (6.3) that the 'midden' area is the product of long bones being discarded following marrow and grease extraction, while other skeletal elements were disposed of on the periphery of the area.

Fig 218 shows that, although antler-working tools are relatively frequent in C west, they are largely on the eastern side of the central zone and, unlike in C east, are accompanied by very little evidence of worked antler. This could be interpreted in a number of ways. For instance, the majority of antler-working tools may not be associated with C west but with C east. Alternatively, and perhaps more likely, use-wear

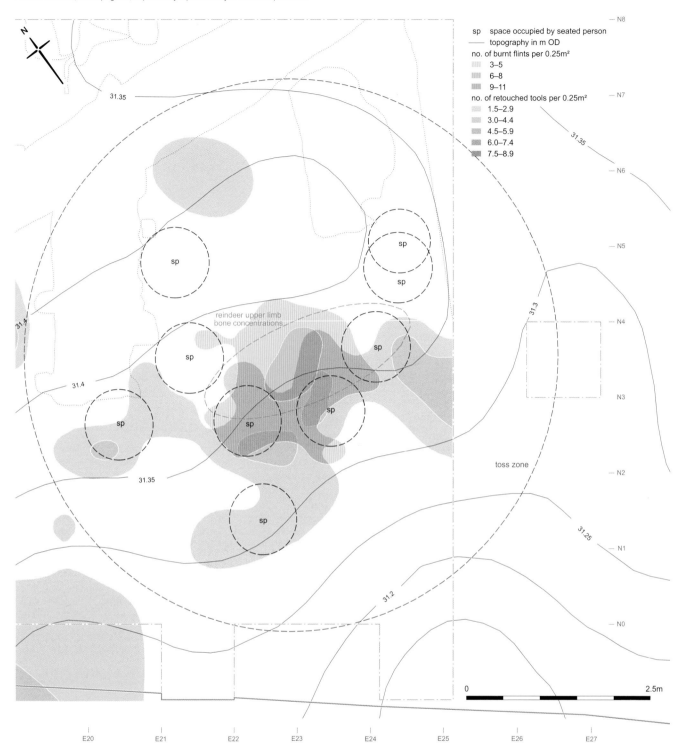

Fig 216 Possible seating plan based on lithic and faunal distributions in scatter C east (scale 1:50)

suggests that antler working was not a primary activity in C west, and the low amount of antler in this area (above, 6.3) suggests that red deer antler was not arriving on the site in any quantity, unlike at Star Carr for example (Clark 1954), although there may be a different activity area comparable to Star Carr adjacent to the stream that was never exposed at Three Ways Wharf. Thus, antler working in C west may have consisted of opportunistic working on a small scale of the little antler material that was present in this hearth area.

Retouched tools used for meat processing and butchery are

also rare in C west, which could support the contention that the bulk of the bone material in this area may have been stripped of meat before arriving on site (above, 6.3). However, it must be remembered that sampling bias in the use-wear analysis towards retouched tools may have contributed to this pattern. The low numbers of cut-marked bones do not add greatly to this discussion, except to suggest that butchery and skinning of swans occurred. The distribution of bone-working tools around the edges of the bone 'midden' has been commented on above (6.4). Fig 218 shows that these patterns are also present to the

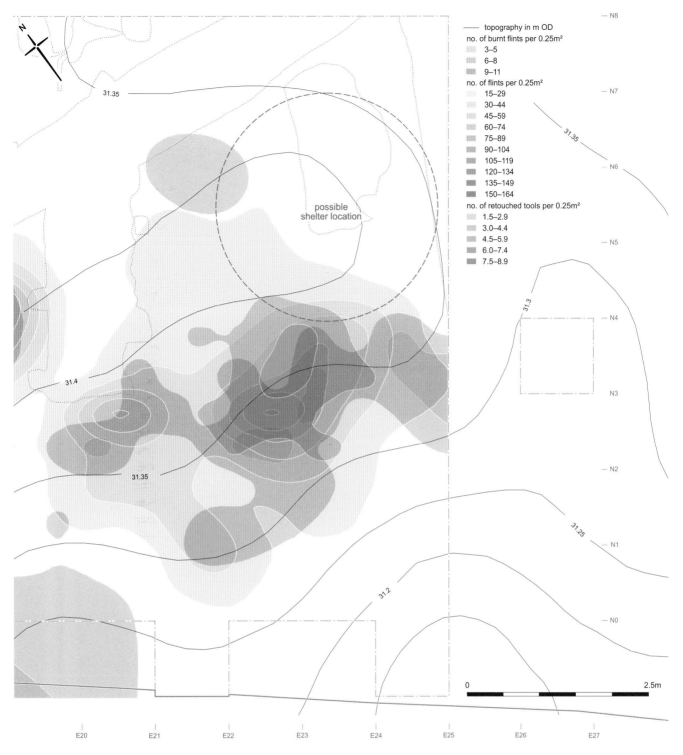

Fig 217 Possible shelter location in scatter C east (scale 1:50)

north-west of the hearth, though with a generally closer match between tool and bone distributions. In the north-west area, it is possible to envisage people seated near the hearth, smashing and working bone before discarding the processed material at the edge of the activity zone. In the south, the patterning of bone-working tools around the larger bone 'midden' suggests either that people may have sat around the midden and picked suitable pieces for working after the bone had been discarded there, or that it simply represents the toss discard of bone-working tools. Interestingly, Fig 218 shows that the antler-

working tools discussed above are distributed on the opposite side of the 'midden' from the bone-working tools.

Use-wear analysis (above, 6.4) suggests that a greater diversity of activities were carried out in C west than in C east, and Fig 218 shows the distribution of wood- and hide-working tools. Woodworking is much in evidence in C west, particularly adzing and chopping wood. The distribution of hide-working tools suffers from the same problems of interpretation as antler-working tools, since the distribution of both types lies centrally to both C west and C east.

189

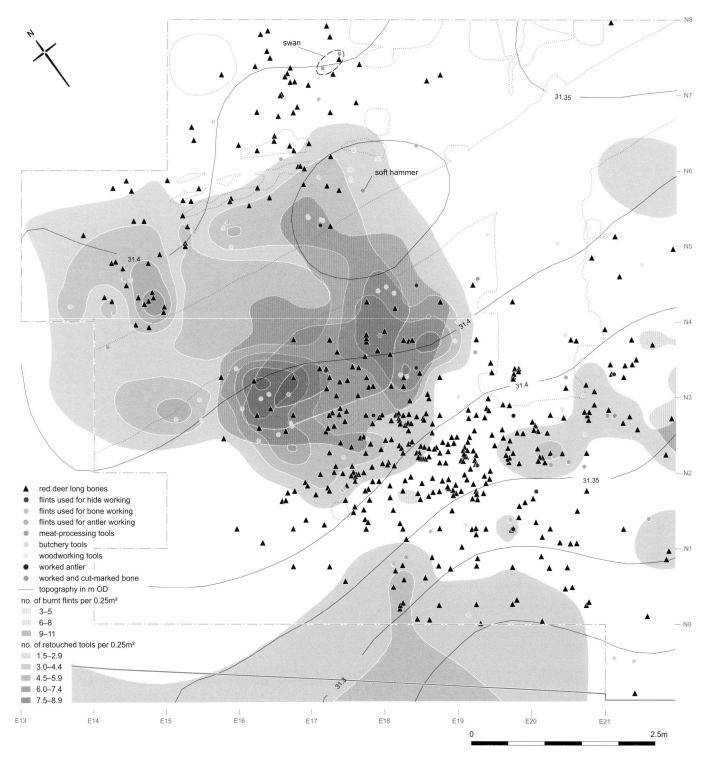

Fig 218 Distribution of used tools and bone debris in scatter C west (scale 1:50)

In scatter C east the activity zone is primarily to the south and either side of the hearth; in C west the zone forms a circle (or two arcs) almost totally encompassing the hearth. In C east the pattern is interpreted as being the result of the prevailing wind direction, with a perhaps less likely alternative seeing a shelter to the north. It has been suggested on faunal grounds that C west represents a longer period of occupation by a larger group of people than C east (above, 6.3), which is a major factor in determining the shape of the activity and drop zones in C west. Fig 219 shows a suggested 'seating plan' for C

west. Binford's studies of the Nunamiut Mask site have shown that where occupation by a number of people occurs over a period of time, the location of the hearth and the arrangement of people around that hearth will vary according to wind direction (Binford 1978a). In scatter C west the main wind direction may have been from site south-east (OS south), taking the smoke from the hearth to site north-west (OS north). Thus the southern area of the hearth, like that in C east, became the main focus of activity, with the retouched tool and debitage contours clearly suggesting that the hearth

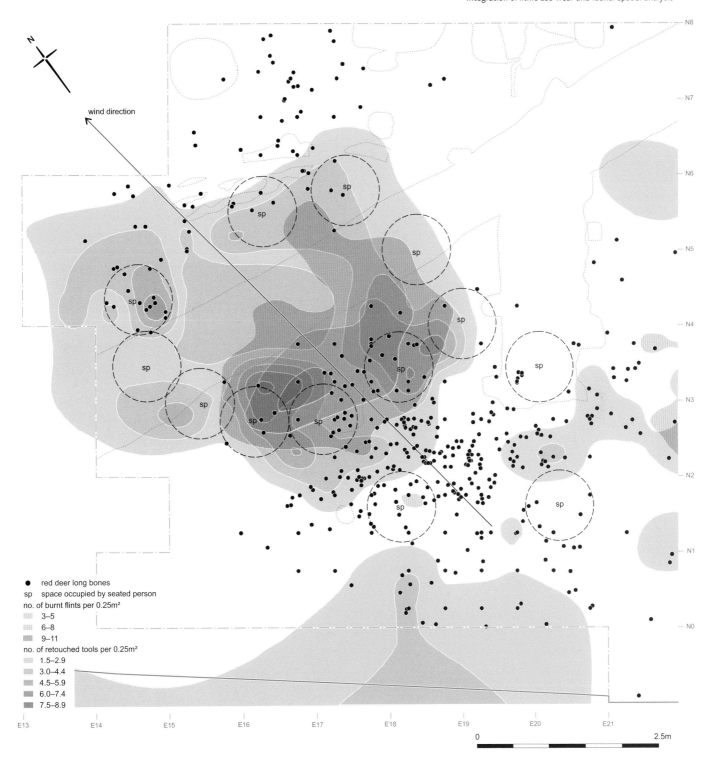

N8

N7

N6

N5

N4

N3

N2

N1

N0

wind direction

sp

sp

sp

sp

sp

sp

sp

sp

sp

sp

sp

sp

• red deer long bones
sp space occupied by seated person
no. of burnt flints per 0.25m²
▦ 3–5
▦ 6–8
▦ 9–11
no. of retouched tools per 0.25m²
▦ 1.5–2.9
▦ 3.0–4.4
▦ 4.5–5.9
▦ 6.0–7.4
▦ 7.5–8.9

E13   E14   E15   E16   E17   E18   E19   E20   E21

0   2.5m

Fig 219 Possible seating plan and interpretation of scatter C west (scale 1:50)

area south of the later ditch was utilised more intensively than the area to the north-west. The bone 'midden' would, therefore, have accumulated as the result of bones being discarded by people sitting on this side of the hearth. Contrary to Binford's model, it would appear that wind direction varied little, since the scatters to the north-west of the later ditch are arranged so that a corridor allowing smoke to disperse to site north-west is still maintained (Fig 219). However, this area would have been smokier than the southern side, which may account for the relatively less dense concentration of material

here. The bones in the north-west would, therefore, have accumulated as a result of people discarding material from the north-west side of the hearth. The location of the hearth also seems to have remained stable within the central area. Thus, the circular shape of the activity zone in C west would be the product of a greater number of people gathered around the hearth compared to C east. Fig 219 shows that it would have been possible to seat up to ten adults around the hearth, with perhaps another two or three picking bone and antler scraps off the midden deposit. In addition to the main hearth in C west, the lithic material near the southern boundary of the site could continue downslope; although bone density in this area is dropping (Fig 159; Fig 160) it is still higher than in the peripheral areas to the north and east. Since this area was unavailable for excavation it is difficult to know whether this material represents part of the toss zone from the C west hearth or the periphery of another lithic and bone scatter.

As with C east, the possible presence of a shelter must also be considered. The very tight spatial clustering of artefacts around the hearth could be interpreted as representing material which built up inside a circular shelter constructed around a central hearth. Topographically, such a shelter would have been located on higher ground (Fig 220) and measured c 4m in diameter. Similar structures have been excavated at Broom Hill, Hampshire (Selkirk 1978), and Mount Sandel, Northern Ireland (Woodman 1985). In the case of Three Ways Wharf,

however, this configuration is considered unlikely, since such a quantity of lithic and faunal material would have made conditions within a structure unpleasant. Moreover, a 'seating plan' consisting of activity and discard areas fits the data well, without having to invoke the presence of shelters. If shelters did exist, then they were probably located away from the excavated area, either immediately to the north-west of scatter C west (Fig 220), or possibly on the higher ground of the alluvial bar (scatters B or D?) or on the crest of the valley side to the east. Evidence of Early Mesolithic activity has since been recovered from Harefield Road, c 300m to the east in just such a location (Barclay et al 1995). If it is accepted that no structures were present at Three Ways Wharf, scatter C west can be interpreted as a task and activity location rather than a habitation site, in other words just one part of a structured occupation site.

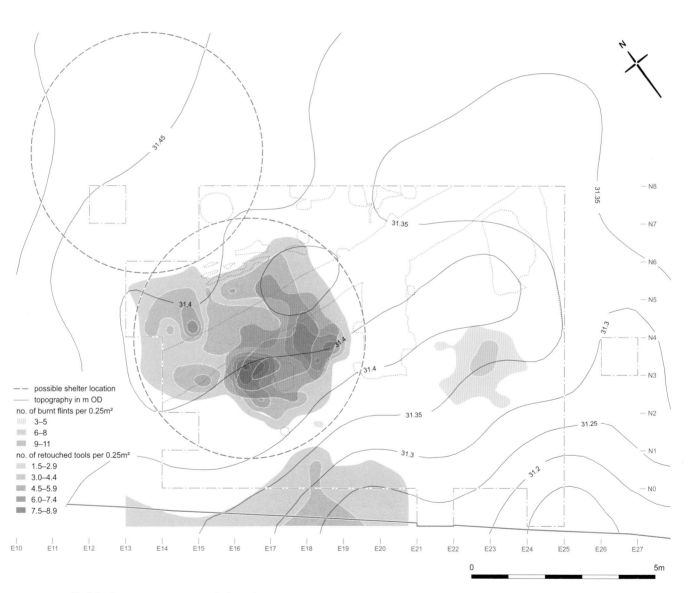

Fig 220 Possible shelter location in scatter C west (scale 1:50)

6.7 Human social structure as reflected in spatial patterning of lithic and faunal material

At the outset of this section, an important point needs elaboration. This concerns the archaeologist's view of hunter-gatherers, which has largely been determined by the nature of the remains available for study. It has been stated that the approach to the study of the Palaeolithic and Mesolithic periods is dominated by a concern with human behaviour in terms of adaptive responses to environmental pressures, whereas in the Neolithic and later periods human beings are more likely to be considered purposive subjects in pursuit of socially defined goals (Thomas 1988, 59). These different approaches are unsurprising, given the differences in the nature of the archaeological evidence available between the earlier and later prehistoric periods. Thus, it is difficult to study 'ritual', religion, social ranking, burial practice and beliefs when the archaeologically detectable expression of these concepts so clearly visible in the Neolithic, as monuments and structured deposition of artefacts, is so conspicuously lacking in the British Mesolithic.

As a result, hunter-gatherers have become dehumanised. We would suggest that beliefs, ritual, religion and social ranking were all present within hunter-gatherer societies, but are archaeologically invisible because they existed as discourse between individuals (Barrett 1994). This discourse will have taken the form of the sung and spoken word, as well as displays of body painting and adornment. Thus, except on rare occasions (eg the pierced antler frontlets from Star Carr), these abstract concepts which are a major part of being human are not observable directly. However, at Three Ways Wharf it is possible to observe the setting where such discourse took place – a group of humans seated around a fire, facing each other and communicating while they carried out their daily tasks. We would suggest that certain people sat in particular places and may have had a leading role in the discourse. In this case the patterning of artefacts can be interpreted in purely functional terms, but it can also be seen as indirectly reflecting the alignment, social makeup and order of the group, and the social discourse which took place between the individuals. Therefore, the spatial patterning of artefacts at sites such as Three Ways Wharf is a product not only of function, but of the need to communicate all the abstract cultural concepts which are usually thought of as being archaeologically undetectable. It is accepted that what was actually communicated around the fire – the beliefs, traditions and fears – can never be known, but we can at least set the scene within which such discourse took place.

The nature of the spatial patterning in scatter A does not allow a higher level of interpretation beyond that suggested by

Fig 214. In scatter C east, the seating plan and other evidence (Fig 215) do not suggest any social differentiation within the group around the hearth. Whether this is a real pattern is a moot point. However, the contrast with scatter C west is interesting. It suggests that C east was the product of a smaller group of humans who had a looser, less rigorous definition of space, although it may also be the result of a shorter occupation.

Spatial ordering in scatter C west is very well defined, and it would appear that certain tasks (such as axe and microlith production, fat extraction and discard) repeatedly took place at prescribed locations around the hearth (Fig 221). To a great extent this formalisation of the use of space would have been determined by factors such as microtopography and the prevailing wind direction (above, 6.6). However, the spatial patterning may also have been influenced by role, age and gender relationships within the human group. For instance, Fig 221 (a) seeks to assign roles to some of the people present around the hearth. This is of course hypothetical and schematic, in that people move around and can undertake many tasks. Nevertheless, when people come together and arrange themselves around a central space for a set activity, certain seating plans often become 'set' and repeated again and again. To use a modern analogy, an extended family sitting down around the table for Sunday lunch will often repeat the same seating plan time and again over many years. The seating plan may be initially directed and ordered depending on age, sex and seniority within the family. This initially formal ordering of space is then perpetuated with little or no further articulation.

From Fig 219 it can be seen that the key positions were on the southern side of the hearth. Possibly four individuals occupied this area, and could have been responsible for the manufacture of axes, microliths and burins, as well as the majority of the extraction of marrow from bones. It is, therefore, possible to suggest that these individuals played a leading role in the activities of the group and the social discourse which took place around the hearth. Although these individuals may also have engaged in other activities, the majority of the bone, antler and hide working appears to have been carried out by the other members of the hearth-side group. Attributing social ranking, age and gender to the individuals is fraught with difficulty, and would exceed the potential of the data presented here. Nonetheless, the composition of the group is interlinked with the functional interpretation of scatter C west, and some suggested scenarios are presented in diagrammatic form in Fig 221 (b–e).

Whichever (if any) of these scenarios approximates most closely to the actual human use of space, they do at least serve as a reminder that artefactual and faunal distributions may reflect the social relationships and interactions between the humans who created them.

a

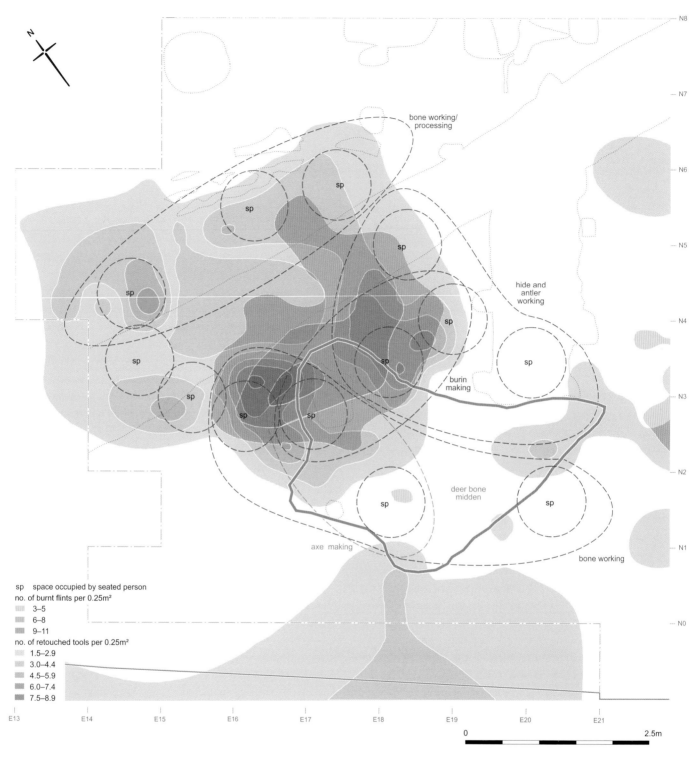

sp   space occupied by seated person
no. of burnt flints per 0.25m²
3–5
6–8
9–11
no. of retouched tools per 0.25m²
1.5–2.9
3.0–4.4
4.5–5.9
6.0–7.4
7.5–8.9

0   2.5m

Fig 221 a – Location of tasks around the hearth in scatter C west (scale 1:50); b–e – different interpretations of the social composition of the human group around the hearth in scatter C west

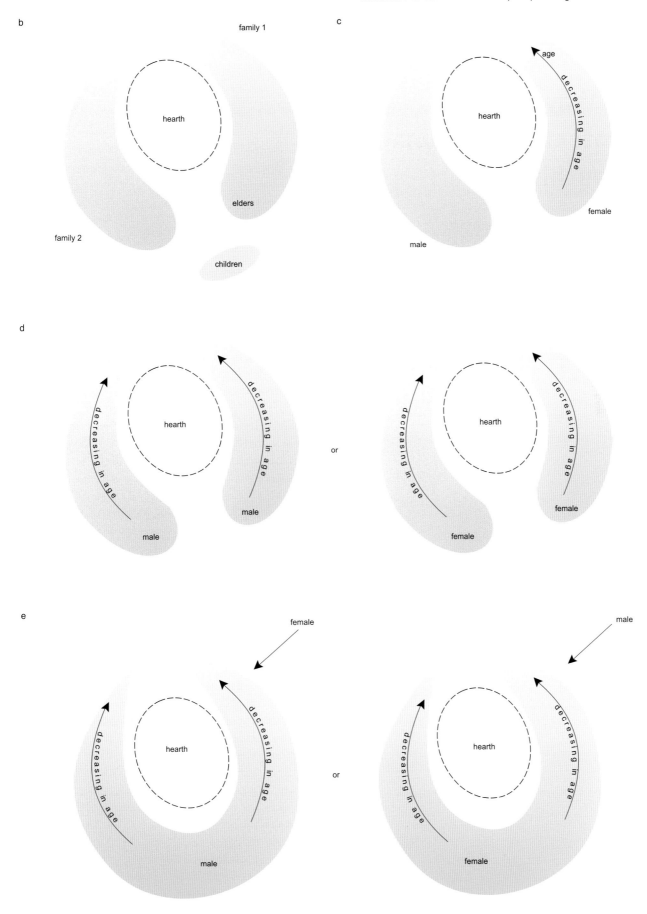

Fig 221 (cont)

Three Ways Wharf: its context and regional relationships

John Lewis and James Rackham

7.1 Environmental reconstruction of the Colne valley in the Lateglacial and early Postglacial

The scatters and deposits at Three Ways Wharf span a period of rapidly changing climatic and ecological conditions in southern England at the end of the last glaciation and the very beginning of the Postglacial, represented by the Younger Dryas or Loch Lomond Stadial, the Pre-Boreal and the Boreal periods (Walker et al 1994; Godwin 1975). The Loch Lomond Stadial has been traditionally assigned to the period 11,000 to 10,000 radiocarbon years BP (Walker et al 1994) and the associated maximum Loch Lomond Glacial Advance to somewhere between 11,000 BP and 10,500 BP (Tipping 1991). The Pre-Boreal, pollen zone IV, lasted from *c* 10,000 BP to 9000 BP, to be followed by the Boreal, zones V and VI (Godwin 1975). The latter period is only represented at Three Ways Wharf by the black humic clay (SU50) sealing the archaeological horizons.

Much further research and recent calibration work on the radiocarbon chronologies of the period (Becker and Kromer 1986; 1991) have indicated great variability in the time sequences for these episodes. In the most recent review, Walker et al (1994) note regional variations for the onset of the Younger Dryas episode, with data from Britain indicating radiocarbon age determinations between 11,300 BP and 10,600 BP for the start of the Loch Lomond Stadial. A similar variability is indicated for the end of the stadial, with the majority of dates falling between 10,200 BP and 9900 BP (Walker and Harkness 1990), although Tipping (1991) has suggested an earlier date close to 10,400 BP. In the London region a radiocarbon date of 11,020–11,160 BP has been obtained for the onset of the stadial from Bramcote Green, Bermondsey (Thomas and Rackham 1996). During the Loch Lomond Stadial the earlier interstadial flora was replaced by tundra and low alpine scrub (Walker et al 1994). The sequence from Bramcote Green shows a drop from a *Betula/Juniperus/Salix*-dominated assemblage in the preceding interstadial to a herb-dominated pollen zone of Cyperaceae, Poaceae, *Artemisia*, *Filipendula*, Caryophyllaceae and *Rumex*. Birch pollen levels continue to fall throughout the stadial sequence. Increasing continentality and aridity is suggested by pollen spectra through deposits of this period (Tipping 1991) with increasing proportions of *Artemisia*, Caryophyllaceae and Cheopodiaceae. Scaife (1982) records shrub, short turf, tall herb, disturbed soil, valley fen and mire, and aquatic communities in pollen diagrams of the period from the Isle of Wight, and a mosaic of these seems likely in the Thames valley. Insect evidence (Atkinson et al 1987) suggests that summer temperatures may have dropped below 10°C at 10,500 BP, with January temperature means of -20°C. Despite the obvious inhospitable character of this period, dated animal bone finds (Table 64) indicate that horse and reindeer were present in Britain throughout this time, although possibly only seasonally for some of it, and the fact that some of these dates derive from humanly modified material suggests a human presence too.

The landscape in the Thames valley can be envisaged as an

Table 64 Radiocarbon dates from Lateglacial and Early Holocene sites in Britain and selected dates from Continental sites

Site	Lab code	Mean	±	Material & species
Inchnadamph	SRR-2105	8300	90	*Rangifer*, antler
Elder Bush Cave	OxA-0812	9000	130	charcoal
Star Carr VP85A	CAR-923	9030	100	
West Heath Common	HAR-7037	9040	90	charcoal
Oakhanger Warren site VII	Q-1493	9040	160	
Badger Hole I	OxA-0679	9060	130	
Gough's New Cave	BM-0525	9080	150	*Homo*
Aveline's Hole	Q-1485	9090	110	*Homo*
Thatcham, Sewage Works	BM-2744	9100	80	hazelnut shell, charred
Oakhanger Warren site VII	Q-1491	9100	160	
Gough's New Cave	OxA-0814	9100	100	*Homo*
Aveline's Hole	OxA-0799	9100	100	*Homo*
Nab Head I	OxA-1496	9110	80	hazelnut, charred
Aveline's Hole	BM-0471	9114	110	*Homo*
Three Ways Wharf	OxA-5559	9200	75	*Cervus*, mandibular teeth
Nab Head I	OxA-1495	9210	80	hazelnut, charred
Oakhanger Warren site VII	Q-1489	9225	170	
Earls Barton	OxA-0500	9240	160	antler
Star Carr VP85A	CAR-926	9240	90	wood, from platform
Seamer Carr sample 2157	CAR-197	9260	90	
Three Ways Wharf	OxA-5558	9265	80	*Capreolus*, mandibular teeth
Three Ways Wharf	OxA-5557	9280	110	*Cervus*, teeth
Marsh Benham	Q-1129	9300	150	
Thatcham	BM-1637R	9320	170	
Gough's Old Cave	OxA-1119	9320	120	*Castor*, mandible
Badger Hole 2	OxA-1459	9360	100	
Star Carr VP85A	CAR-921	9360	110	
Waystone Edge	Q-1300	9396	210	
Thatcham site 5 no. 1	Q-0652a	9480	160	wood, pine
Star Carr	C-353	9488	350	charcoal, assoc with 'brushwood platform'
Thatcham IV	OxA-0894	9490	110	*Alces*, burnt antler
Thatcham V	Q-0652b	9500	160	wood
Star Carr VP85A	OxA-1154	9500	120	*Cervus*, antler frontlet
Thatcham	BM-1636R	9520	120	
Star Carr	Q-0014	9557	210	charcoal, assoc with 'brushwood platform'
Star Carr VP85A	OxA-3345	9580	70	charcoal, 17–17.5cm in sediment column
Star Carr VP85A	CAR-928	9670	120	charcoal underlying platform
Thatcham site 5 no. 2	Q-0650	9670	160	wood
Aveline's Hole	OxA-0802	9670	110	*Rangifer*, shed antler
Marsh Benham	Q-1380	9690	240	
Thatcham	BM-1635R	9700	280	
Star Carr VP85A	OxA-1176	9700	160	worked antler
Star Carr VP85A	OxA-3348	9700	70	charcoal, 31.5–32cm in sediment column
Belloy-sur-Somme (France)	OxA-0462	9720	130	*Equus*, tooth
Seamer Carr	CAR-1020	9720	80	wood/?charcoal
Anston Stones Cave	BM-440B	9750	110	*Rangifer*, bone
Thatcham IV	OxA-0732	9760	120	*Cervus*, worked antler beam
Le Pré des Forges, Marsangy (France)	OxA-0505	9770	180	bone
Thatcham site 5 no. 4	Q-0677	9780	160	wood
Waltham Abbey B-Point	OxA-1427	9790	100	antler
Seamer Carr	BM-2350	9790	180	*Equus ferus*
Thatcham site 5 no. 3	Q-0651	9840	160	wood, birch & pine
Darent Gravels, Kent	BM-1619	9840	120	*Equus*, metapodial
Anston Stones Cave	BM-0439	9850	115	*Rangifer*, bone
Sproughton	HAR-259	9880	120	willow twigs
Belloy-sur-Somme (France)	OxA-0723	9890	150	*Equus*, tooth
Gough's Cave	Q-1581	9920	130	*Rangifer*, antler fragment
Anston Stones Cave	BM-0440a	9940	115	*Rangifer*, bone
Seamer Carr	OxA-1030	9940	100	*Canis*, vertebra
Folkestone	Q-1508	9960	170	mollusc zone a (Kerney 1977)
Kendrick's Cave	OxA-0111	10000	200	*Equus*, mandible
Three Ways Wharf	OxA-1902	10010	120	*Equus*, mandible
Great Doward Cave	OxA-0516	10020	120	*Ochotona* (pika)
Thatcham site 3 no. 1	Q-0658	10030	170	charcoal
Darent gravels, Kent	BM-1674	10080	120	*Rangifer*, bone
Inchnadamph	SRR-1788	10080	70	*Rangifer*, antler

Table 64 (cont)

Site	Lab code	Mean	±	Material & species
Belloy-sur-Somme (France)	OxA-0722	10110	130	*Equus*, tooth
Chelm's Combe	OxA-1782	10140	100	*Rangifer*, mandible
Gough's Old Cave	OxA-1120	10190	120	*Rangifer*, antler
Chelm's Combe	BM-2318	10190	130	*Rangifer*, metapodial
Chelm's Combe	BM-2431	10220	130	*Rangifer*, distal tibia
Chelm's Combe	OxA-1784	10230	110	*Rangifer*, mandible
Roddan's Port (Ireland)	LJ-658	10250	350	*Rangifer*, bone
Belloy-sur-Somme (France)	OxA-0724	10260	160	*Equus*, tooth
Three Ways Wharf	OxA-1778	10270	100	*Equus*, tooth
Messingham	Birm-349	10280	120	
Earls Barton	OxA-0803	10320	150	*Rangifer*, antler; 'Lyngby' axe
Stellmoor (Germany)	Y-152.2	10320	250	
Thatcham site 3 no. 2	Q-0659	10365	170	charcoal, from hearth
Chelm's Combe	OxA-1785	10370	110	*Equus*, metacarpal
Robin Hood's Cave	BM-0603	10390	90	
Flixton site 2	Q-0066	10413	210	
Gough's New Cave	OxA-1461	10450	110	*Rangifer*, maxilla
Robin Hood's Cave	BM-0604	10590	90	
Ossom's Cave	GrN-7400	10590	70	
Elder Bush Cave	OxA-0811	10600	110	*Cervus*, vertebra & cut ribs
Ossom's Cave	OxA-0632	10600	140	*Rangifer*, antler 'spike'
Chelm's Combe	OxA-1781	10600	200	*Rangifer*, metacarpal
Lathum (Netherlands)	OxA-729	10670	160	*Felis leo*, mandible
Kirkhead Cave	HAR-1059	10700	200	
Ossom's Cave	OxA-0631	10780	160	*Rangifer*, mandible
Sproughton	OxA-0518	10700	160	uniserial bone point
Sproughton	OxA-0517	10910	150	uniserial bone point
Chelm's Combe	OxA-1783	10910	110	*Cervus*, mandible
Pin Hole Cave	OxA-1466	10950	120	*Lepus timidus*, partial tibia
Presles (Belgium)	OxA-1344	10950	200	*Cervus*, mandible
Wawcott	BM-2718	10960	100	*Alces* & *Bos* bones
Pin Hole Cave	OxA-1937	10970	110	*Bos*, tibia

open herbaceous tundra landscape, with low scrub and valley bottom mires, occupied at least seasonally by reindeer and horse, and presumably with other animal species such as wolf, bear, pika, fox and various small mammals also present. Little variability can be expected across the area although valleys, such as the Colne, may have been preferentially selected by the large herbivores when moving through the landscape. Some variability over the period can be expected with increasing dryness, and halophyte and steppe elements occurring towards the end of the episode. This may have favoured the horse, which does not like snow-covered ground and can occupy areas of low-quality vegetation and saline steppe (Boyle 1990; Mohr 1971). This species may not have returned to Britain until the latter half of the stadial. The very limited radiocarbon data for the large herbivores during this period show no dates for horse before 10,370 BP (Table 64), although a few dates exist for reindeer earlier in the stadial.

Evidence that the site at Three Ways Wharf was occupied during the Loch Lomond Stadial is suggested by the radiocarbon dating of the horse bone and tooth, which yielded dates of 10,010 BP and 10,270 BP (Table 1), but the association of reindeer with this period cannot be proven, as radiocarbon dates indicate the presence of this species in Britain well into the Pre-Boreal, and no direct dates could be obtained from the

reindeer material from the site.

The latter half of the stadial was marked by fairly rapidly increasing temperatures. The very rapid rise recorded by Atkinson et al (1987), based upon beetle assemblages and the radiocarbon chronology, can no longer be accepted because recent work (Becker and Kromer 1986; 1991) has shown that there is a radiocarbon plateau during the latter part of the stadial, where at least 800 calendar years are concentrated within some 200 radiocarbon years (Fig 222), and it is precisely during this period that increasing temperatures are suggested by the beetle evidence.

The Scottish glaciers appear to have disappeared before 10,000 BP (Walker and Lowe 1980) and by 9800 BP the climate had attained the maximum temperatures of the preceding interstadial (Atkinson et al 1987). During the latter part of the stadial and the early Postglacial birch woodland moved into southern Britain (Huntley and Birks 1983). On the Isle of Wight, Scaife (1982) records increasing juniper at the very end of the stadial followed by the expansion of birch and willow at 9970 BP. This part of the diagram from Bramcote Green is undated, but there is little evidence for either juniper or birch expansion (Thomas and Rackham 1996), which contrasts with work in the Lea valley at Enfield Lock (Chambers et al 1996) where an essentially open landscape dominated by sedges develops some regional birch-pine woodland, with increasing birch, pine and willow. The onset of the birch woodland at this site is dated to 9550 BP. In Kent, Kerney (1977) has defined a sequence of molluscan zones which show a transition from a restricted periglacial fauna typical of open ground to an assemblage in which catholic species have increased and the bare soil species decline. This phase has a radiocarbon date of 9960±170 BP, and is followed by an open woodland assemblage of Boreal age dated to 9305 BP and 8980 BP. The short phase of juniper expansion noted in many pollen diagrams, which may be due to the flowering and expansion of the shrub as threshold temperatures were reached (Iversen 1954), was followed by open birch woodland. Radiocarbon dates suggest that for the first two or three hundred years of the 10th millennium BP reindeer and horse were still present in Britain (Table 64) and, apart from a date of 9760 BP for red deer antler from Thatcham, Berkshire, there is little evidence of woodland mammals. It is, therefore, possible that the two early phases of occupation at Three Ways Wharf could have taken place at any time between the latter half of the stadial and the early part of the Pre-Boreal, perhaps 10,300–9700 BP and including the period during which juniper and open birch woodland was developing. It may be that the seasonal exploitation by these animals of particular areas of Britain changed during this period, with perhaps winter occupation in the latter part, while activity was restricted to reindeer in the summer months during the coldest phases of the stadial.

By the time of the occupation at Star Carr in North Yorkshire (Clark 1954) at c 9700 BP, open birch woodland with an understory of ferns (Day 1995) was present in the Vale of Pickering and much of lowland Britain (Huntley and Birks 1983). In addition, mixed deciduous forest occupied parts of southern England. The Bramcote Green pollen diagram (Thomas and Rackham 1996) shows hazel as the first member of this expanding woodland in east London, followed by oak, elm, lime and alder, a mixed deciduous forest having developed by 8280 BP. The pollen from the deposits sealing the archaeological levels at Three Ways Wharf (Lewis et al 1992; Chapter 2.2) indicates that birch has declined by this time, but the landscape remains fairly open, with pine growing locally and a small deciduous component of oak, elm and hazel. In the contemporary sequence from Enfield Lock in the Lea valley the lowest deposits are characterised by high Cyperaceae values and a low arboreal component (Chambers et al 1996). The low arboreal pollen levels continue into the succeeding local pollen assemblage zone (b), deposits of which have yielded a radiocarbon date of 9545±55 BP. The arboreal component increases in the subsequent pollen zone (c) with more birch, pine and willow pollen, and is also associated with a high charcoal content. A date of 9550±70 BP was obtained for the base of this zone, which records the expansion of birch and pine woodland in the Lea valley at this time. This is significantly later than on the Isle of Wight (Scaife 1982) but establishing its contemporaneity or otherwise with this event at Star Carr is confounded by the radiocarbon plateau. The next zone (d) is characterised by high pine levels and noticeably fewer ruderal

and steppe elements. Increasing hazel levels occur at the top of this zone, and the initial expansion of this species has been dated to 8200±80 BP. This is broadly contemporary with the marked hazel rise in the Bramcote Green sequence (Thomas and Rackham 1996) and suggests that a hiatus exists in this sequence, which may have lost the phase of birch and pine expansion present at Enfield and typical of other pollen diagrams in England.

An undated but broadly contemporary pollen diagram from Church Lammas, Staines, Surrey (Wiltshire 1996), 12.5km downstream from Three Ways Wharf in the Colne valley, shows a high pine count in its basal levels, prior to the expansion of hazel which can probably be correlated with phase (d) at Enfield Lock. Further afield, recent work at both Star Carr and Thatcham can contribute to the picture. At Thatcham, Scaife (1992) suggests a period of pine and hazel dominance, with some deciduous taxa, which is directly dated on hazelnuts to 9100±80 BP. The arrival of hazel in the Vale of Pickering is dated to 9400 BP (Day and Mellars 1994) and the slightly earlier local expansion of the birch woodland at 9500±70 BP (Day 1995). The occurrence of a plateau at this point in the radiocarbon chronology means that no great reliance can be placed on the precision of these dates, although the work of Day and Mellars (1994) perhaps suggests that we can put real calendar dates to the sequence of events at Star Carr if nowhere else. By the time of the Mesolithic occupation at Three Ways Wharf, the plateau effect has ceased and the contemporary environment at Star Carr was still a birch-pine woodland, with hazel just beginning to contribute to the tree cover.

In the London region at this time, c 9200 BP (Table 1), a pine-forested landscape with locally abundant birch and willow appears to be dominant, perhaps with little variation, except in the river valleys. The London Clay lands, chalklands and terrace gravels that surround Three Ways Wharf would all have been forested with pine, with local birch and willow stands perhaps on the valley sides and bottoms. On the evidence of the Enfield (and possibly Church Lammas) sequence few deciduous elements, apart from hazel, appear to have reached the area. Abundant charcoal horizons in levels broadly contemporary with the Mesolithic occupation in the Colne and Lea valleys may testify to human interference, intentional (Mellars 1975; Day and Mellars 1994) or otherwise (Bennet et al 1990; Lewis et al 1992; Huntley 1993; Chambers et al 1996). It is an interesting aspect of the faunal remains from Three Ways Wharf that aurochs, elk and pig are absent. While this may be due to seasonal factors or the hunters' preference, the comparable sites at Star Carr and Thatcham are somewhat earlier, and as we have seen the landscape was open birch forest at Star Carr, while a pine-dominated woodland is indicated at the time of the occupation at Three Ways Wharf. As much as 35 years ago, Mellars (1975) drew attention to the poor prospects that a pure coniferous forest offers animals, and the open birch woodland contemporary with the occupation at Star Carr would have provided a much wider diversity of niches, with local marsh and open water within an open birch woodland being particularly suited to elk and probably aurochs. Bay-Petersen

(1988) notes that all the major species hunted in Denmark – the same as those found at Star Carr – prefer open woodland in a state of succession or regeneration, with open glades and plentiful ground cover. In Canada the highest densities of elk occur during the early stages of forest regeneration, and diminish as mature tree cover increases (Peterson 1955). The pine forests present in the Thames valley a few centuries later would have supported much lower densities of elk, aurochs and wild boar than the Pre-Boreal forests, and red and roe deer may have been the only viable large ungulates available to the occupants of Three Ways Wharf. Even these species would have favoured the woodland edge environment along the river margins and valleys sides. The geographical range of wild boar is likely to have expanded again with the development of a mixed deciduous forest, and similarly with aurochs as human impact opened up this forest. It may be that, in part at least, these environmental changes affected the availability of prey animals, and the elk and aurochs which contributed such an important element in terms of meat to the occupants of Star Carr (Legge and Rowley Conwy 1988) were no longer present in sufficient densities to make their hunting economic. Whether the charcoal horizons noted in many sequences can be seen as the result of intentional firing of the forest to counter a decline in prey density is problematic, since if their origin is similar to the reed charcoal identified at Star Carr (Day and Mellars 1994) they cannot be attributed to forest fires. Until further work is carried out on the identity of the charcoal in these deposits its origin must remain uncertain.

7.2 Comparison with other sites of similar date on a local, regional, national and international scale

The early occupation

Preceding chapters have established that the earliest phases of activity at Three Ways Wharf represented by scatters A and C east were associated with a subsistence strategy based on hunting reindeer and possibly horse. By analogy with other British and Continental sites, and by plotting radiocarbon dates on comparable fauna, it has been demonstrated that both scatters date to somewhere within the period from the amelioration of the Loch Lomond Stadial (Younger Dryas) at *c* 10,300 BP to the replacement of reindeer and horse fauna by woodland species such as red and roe deer *c* 9700 BP in the mid Pre-Boreal. Fig 222 shows that this period equates to over a thousand calendar years, a far from insubstantial length of time. It has also been demonstrated that the early scatters at Three Ways Wharf share affinities with the 'long blade' industry of Britain, which itself is considered part of the north-west European Ahrensburgian technocomplex. Several British and Continental 'long blade' sites have been referred to in previous chapters. However, there are in Britain very few open sites

contemporary with the two Lateglacial or early Pre-Boreal scatters at Three Ways Wharf that have produced faunal material.

While a number of artefacts or humanly modified bones of reindeer and horse are dated to the Younger Dryas (Table 64) and are broadly contemporary with these scatters, most of the contemporary evidence derives from caves or sites where no positive human presence is evident, such as Anston Stones Cave (Rotherham, South Yorkshire), Gough's Cave (Currant 1991) and Chelm's Combe (Cheddar, Somerset), Inchnadamph, Highland, and possibly the site at Flixton 2, North Yorkshire. This latter site contained horse bones (some in articulation) from at least three individuals and including mainly vertebrae (Fraser and King 1954). The faunal assemblage is associated with a 'shouldered point microlith' and was presumed to be a kill site, although no butchery evidence was noted. Although originally associated by Godwin and Walker (in Moore 1954) with pollen zone II, a radiocarbon sample obtained from the deposit containing the horse bones produced a Younger Dryas date of 10,413±250 BP (Table 64). There was some controversy over the dates obtained on reindeer bone from Anston Stones Cave (Clutton-Brock 1986), since they were associated with flint tools believed to be of earlier date, but more recent dates indicate that these results are consistent.

The only contemporary open sites producing faunal remains are at Seamer Carr, North Yorkshire (Rowley-Conwy in prep; Uchiyama et al in prep) and Church Lammas, Staines, Surrey (Rackham 1996), although no radiocarbon dates can yet confirm the date of the Church Lammas sites (below). At Seamer Carr a horse bone is dated to 9790±180 BP, but this find was not associated with any artefactual material (T Schadla-Hall, pers comm) and neither was the dog vertebra dated to 9940±100 BP. Nevertheless, horse bones were found associated with the hearth from which charcoal yielded a date of 9720±80 BP (T Schadla-Hall, pers comm). The presence of roe deer and the complete absence of reindeer from the Seamer Carr bone assemblages (T Schadla-Hall, pers comm) suggest that the human occupation at this complex of sites is later than the early phase of activity at the Colne valley sites, or possibly seasonally different.

Given the paucity of humanly associated faunal evidence, it is extremely difficult to examine human subsistence strategies for this period, other than in general theoretical terms. 'Long blade' industry sites appear to represent a tool kit associated with reindeer and/or horse butchery, probably in close proximity to kill sites (Barton 1989). The lack of hearths or burnt flint at most sites suggests that the activity was very short-lived at any one location (Barton 1995). The restricted tool inventories characteristic of 'long blade' sites can thus be explained in terms of specialised butchery activities of short duration. That many such sites are located in British and Continental river valleys has led to suggestions that reindeer were ambushed at river crossing points (ibid). There is also a suggestion of chronological evolution of the lithic assemblages from the Younger Dryas to the early Pre-Boreal (Barton 1991, 241, table 22.4). Thus the 'long blade' industry has been

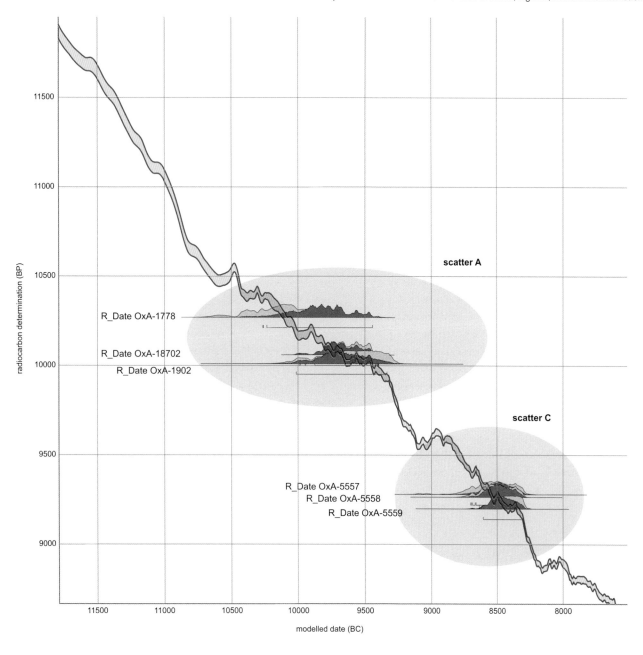

Fig 222 Graph of radiocarbon curve with dated fauna on it, calibrated using OxCal v4.0 (Bronk Ramsey 1994; 2001)

described as a western and probably atypical 'workshop' facies of the classical Ahrensburgian (Gob 1991, 229).

In the light of this general model, how do the data from Three Ways Wharf compare, and can they throw more light on general human subsistence strategies during the period?

Firstly, and most importantly, the faunal evidence from Three Ways Wharf scatters A and C east suggests that in both cases reindeer had been killed elsewhere and partially butchered before the remaining elements were completely processed at the site. This would confirm the general model described above. However, variations in the density and composition of both the Three Ways Wharf lithic assemblages and those of other British and Continental sites need to be explored. In particular, the place of 'long blade' assemblages within a wider settlement system needs to be discussed. Many models of hunter-gatherer settlement patterns have been proposed by researchers in

different regions and periods, for example Binford and Binford (1966), Hole and Flannery (1967) and Price (1978). The different elements of settlement systems are distinguished by variations in density of lithic and faunal material as well as differences in the composition of these assemblages. Such models usually have as their basis ethnographic observations of present-day hunter-gatherer groups. The working model usually accepted for the British Lateglacial and Early Mesolithic has most recently been articulated by Smith (1992, 28–9, fig 3.1). In this model, the home base forms the focus of group activity for most of the group. Hunting and gathering is undertaken by specialist task groups giving rise to kill, butchery and collecting sites. Where these activities take place at a distance from the base camp, hunting (or field) camps serve as temporary camps between hunting grounds and base camp. As mentioned in an earlier chapter, the Early Mesolithic site of Star Carr has recently been reinterpreted in these terms (Legge and Rowley-Conwy 1988).

If the majority of 'long blade' sites are specialist short-duration butchery assemblages, where are the assemblages produced by the other elements of a theoretical settlement pattern, namely kill sites, hunting camps and base camps?

Although very few 'long blade' sites have been adequately excavated, none would at face value appear to fit the other elements of such a settlement pattern. It is therefore reasonable to suggest that either the lithic assemblages forming the other elements of the settlement system remain unrecognised or mis-attributed, or the model does not fit the data for this period. It could be argued that Three Ways Wharf scatter C east, with its hearth and wider range of retouched tools, is a suitable candidate for a base camp. In contrast, the faunal evidence suggests that C east represents a short-stay occupation during which two or three reindeer were processed before the group moved on. It would therefore seem more akin to a hunting camp. However, such models do not accurately reflect the complexity of Lateglacial and Early Mesolithic hunter-gatherer activity. Gamble has pointed out that base camps are few and far between among contemporary northern hunters, and remains sceptical about whether such a class of site has been identified in the Palaeolithic record of Europe (Gamble 1986, 299). The

rarity of suitable data from the British Lateglacial and Early Mesolithic has meant that instead of a model generated by data, the data have been fitted to a theoretical model. The following section is an attempt to reverse this trend.

Assemblage composition

Table 65 and Fig 223 show the retouched tool assemblages (including bruised pieces) from selected 'long blade' sites. It can be seen that there is great variation in the composition of the assemblages, with most consisting of bruised pieces, projectiles (microliths), burins and scrapers. The exceptions are Titchwell, with a high scraper element and no bruised pieces, and Belloy-sur-Somme with a high bruised and low microlith and scraper component. Titchwell, Three Ways Wharf scatter C east and particularly Belloy also stand out in that they contain significantly higher quantities of retouched tools than the other sites (Table 65). It is noticeable that both the Three Ways Wharf scatters contain lower proportions of bruised pieces than the other sites, including the other Colne valley site, Church Lammas. This could indicate a lesser emphasis on heavy-duty chopping/butchery activity at Three Ways Wharf compared with the other sites. Fig 223 shows that variations in the

Table 65 Retouched tool assemblages from selected 'long blade' sites

Tool type	Avington VI	Springhead lower floor	Sproughton	Gatehampton Farm	Titchwell	Belloy	Church Lammas (scat 1)	TWW C east	TWW A
Microliths/points/backed blades	16	1	5	0	5	3	1	31	9
Scrapers & truncated	4	5	6	2	37	29	1	35	1
Serr/dent/notch	0	0	0	0	0	201	1	7	0
Bur/awl/pier/multi	2	7	9	1	16	7	2	15	0
Misc retouched	0	0	0	8	19	65	3	46	9
Bruised pieces	6	4	6	4	0	436	5	8	1
Total	28	17	26	15	77	741	13	142	20

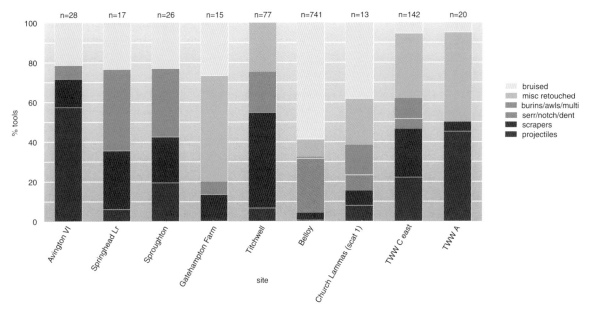

Fig 223 Comparison of the composition of retouched tool assemblages from selected 'long blade' sites

combinations of and emphasis on different tool types within a limited tool repertoire suggest that in addition to reindeer butchery tasks, a range of different site types could be represented by the overall description of 'long blade' industry.

Unfortunately, Fig 223 does not help to define in detail settlement elements within the 'long blade' industry. For instance, although the lithic assemblages in scatters A and C east seem to be the product of short stays and the processing of a small number of reindeer, the lack of similar faunal evidence from other sites restricts comparison. Most of the sites in question have had only relatively small areas excavated (except Belloy-sur-Somme: Fagnart 1991, 213) or have not been fully published. In addition, use-wear analysis at Three Ways Wharf (Chapter 6.4) suggests that tools were used for a multitude of purposes and are not necessarily a guide to site function.

Site size and location

As an adjunct to comparing tool assemblage composition, it is worth considering the size and location of sites. As has been mentioned above, most 'long blade' sites are located in river valleys. The evidence from Three Ways Wharf suggests that they may have been associated with butchery of reindeer and/or horse following a kill. In the case of scatter C east and possibly scatter A, this also involved a stay of short duration, perhaps by four people for up to three weeks. Human use of the landscape appears to consist of small, localised activity areas associated with reindeer processing. Although localised in extent, the concentration of lithic material in scatters A and C east was quite high.

A similar pattern of human activity has recently been uncovered 12.5km to the south of Three Ways Wharf at Church Lammas, Staines (Jones 1995). The site lies on the floodplain of the River Colne just north of its confluence with the Thames. The Geological Survey map for the area suggests that the site is located on an 'island' of gravel draped with alluvium. Excavations have identified three flint scatters typologically similar to the Lateglacial scatters at Three Ways Wharf (Lewis in prep). The major scatter (1) consisted of 260 artefacts including 22 burnt pieces. The tool assemblage comprises a possible broken microlith, one scraper, one notched piece, two burins (on truncations), three miscellaneous retouched pieces, and five bruised blades and flakes (*lames mâchurées*). Preliminary refitting suggests that the scatter is *in situ*. Each of the three scatters is associated with bones of reindeer and in one case also horse (Rackham in prep). Thus both the flint and faunal assemblages at this site are small (fewer than 300 flints and 62 individual bone finds) and suggest a very short period of occupation, although some animal bone has almost certainly been lost as a result of post-depositional processes. The character of these scatters is similar to those at Three Ways Wharf, although the recovered bone assemblages do not allow the same level of analysis. The scatters are several metres apart and appear to indicate separate occupations of the site in the manner already proposed for scatters A and C east. A detailed report on the material from the site is in preparation,

but in the meantime we can speculate on the nature of the Lateglacial occupation in the Colne valley on the evidence of these two sites.

The scatters from Church Lammas and Three Ways Wharf indicate the hunting of reindeer, but in each case there is no evidence for any individual scatter representing more than one episode of occupation or more than three animals being killed. At the Three Ways Wharf scatters the 'camp sites' included hearths and were occupied for between two and 21 days, and most of the carcass of the hunted animals was processed and discarded during the period of occupation. The Church Lammas scatters appear to be of smaller scale and it may be that only part of the butchered carcass was disposed of at the site (Rackham in prep), but collectively this evidence suggests numerous small 'camp sites' of short duration (or, in the case of Church Lammas, possibly initial butchery sites adjacent to kill sites) being located on the floodplain of the Colne near or adjacent to its channels. Fig 223 shows that scatter 1 at Church Lammas and scatter C east at Three Ways Wharf contain the same major tool elements. The variation in the proportions of tools between the two sites can be explained as an artefact of the very small tool assemblage (fewer than 20 pieces) at Church Lammas.

The probable late winter to late spring occupation period, at least at Three Ways Wharf scatter C east, perhaps indicates a nomadic existence by small human groups carrying out opportunistic hunting of reindeer moving through the Colne valley during their spring migration from the North Sea basin. This model has been proposed by Baales (1996) and supported by Johansen and Stapert (1997–8). The reindeer herds may not have been as large as those on the Continent (Smith 1992, 67) and migration need not have involved large-scale movement (Spiess 1979; Boyle 1990; Murray 1994). Nonetheless, individual reindeer herds would have constituted a mobile concentration of food and raw material within the fairly open landscape.

While the evidence that horse was the object of hunting in the Colne valley is circumstantial, the species was definitely present, and it was certainly hunted at Seamer Carr and possibly Flixton in the Vale of Pickering, although the site at Seamer probably post-dates the Colne valley sites (Rowley-Conwy in prep; Uchiyama et al in prep). Horse does not favour snow-covered ground although it can occupy areas with sparse low-quality vegetation (Boyle 1990; Mohr 1971), and it is unlikely to have been occupying the Thames valley during the winter in the Younger Dryas, which as we have seen above was cold continental in climate. Nevertheless, the fact that horse bones have yielded radiocarbon dates throughout the latter part of the Younger Dryas period and contemporary with reindeer (Table 64) suggests that these two species may represent distinctly seasonal occupation with overlapping ranges and occupation of the overlapping parts at different times of the year during the colder phases of the stadial.

A model that might envisage reindeer moving out of winter grazing in the lowlands of the North Sea basin, up the Thames valley and its tributaries, and into central England and perhaps further during the spring, could include small groups or herds of horses moving into the Thames valley during the summer. Thus any horse-dominated assemblages that might be found would indicate summer occupation. Staines may have been a preferential crossing place of the River Thames before the spring melt that would have turned the river into a serious hazard for the reindeer herds if they migrated any later. The later date for horse at Seamer Carr and the absence of reindeer may indicate a period during which reindeer were not present in any density, their range no longer including much of southern England, while horse still survived in the open, lightly wooded landscape prior to the development of the birch and pine forests of the later Pre-Boreal, when woodland species apparently dominate the archaeological assemblages (Grigson 1978; Bay-Petersen 1988).

A second possibility may relate to seasonal differences (above), but by *c* 9700 BP temperatures had risen and vegetational changes had occurred such that occupation by reindeer and horse at different seasons is likely. While we have two radiocarbon dates on horse teeth from Three Ways Wharf (Table 1), no irrefutable association of these horse bones with the reindeer has been demonstrable, despite the juxtaposition of the remains.

What seems clear from the faunal data is that, of the variety of ways in which reindeer can be hunted (Burch 1972; Spiess 1979), the Colne valley sites reflect the opportunistic hunting of single animals or small groups, in other words a foraging (Binford 1980) approach rather than the logistical or planned mass kills during the spring and autumn migrations that are characteristic of sites like Stellmoor (Gronnow 1985) and the Magdalenian of the Paris basin (Audouze and Enloe 1991). It is, therefore, possible that in Britain small groups of humans may have followed the reindeer herds during part of their seasonal movement, removing the need, or desirability, of a 'base camp' that would be occupied for any more than a few days or couple of weeks. This would account for the restricted tool repertoire of the 'long blade' lithic assemblages, the high density of lithics in small scatters and their location in river valleys.

A major problem with this model lies in the extent of the landscape examined at any one 'site' and in establishing contemporaneity between scatters. Due to the relatively small areas excavated on lithic scatter sites (eg 89m² at Three Ways Wharf scatter C), rarely is there an opportunity to study use of the landscape over a large area. Work at Seamer Carr in North Yorkshire has shown numerous overlapping lithic scatters covering very large areas of the Postglacial lake shoreline (Schadla-Hall 1987, fig 3.4; A David, pers comm). The report of 'deer bones' being found 125m to the east of Three Ways Wharf in the 1950s suggests that the low ridge projecting from the valley side at Uxbridge (Chapter 2.2; Fig 31) could be dotted with small lithic and faunal scatters. Some, like scatters A and C west, would not be contemporary. Others, however, like scatters A and C east, could prove contemporary and represent a number of family groups dispersed across the landscape butchering reindeer and horse. If scatters A and C east are contemporary, and if other scatters exist within the vicinity of the excavated site, then the character of the site changes. If this

scenario were true, then we may envisage a model of large numbers of humans engaged in hunting, but dispersing into family-, age- or gender-based groups to butcher the prey. Unfortunately, it is extremely difficult to establish exact contemporaneity between lithic scatters, given the error margins in radiocarbon dating. The only possible way to explore this would be a major refitting programme aimed at investigating links between lithic scatters.

It is, therefore, possible to interpret landscapes such as Three Ways Wharf in two ways. If the flint scatters represent exactly contemporaneous activity, then the sites indicate a large population and a long-stay aggregation site. Alternatively, the scatters are not exactly contemporary but separated in time, in which case the site might represent repeated occupation by smaller groups over many years.

In the absence of evidence for contemporaneity between lithic scatters, it is proposed here that, for Britain at least, the model consisting of small groups of humans following herds of reindeer more closely matches the evidence for the period 10,300–9700 BP. During an earlier period of the Lateglacial, Audouze (1987) notes the absence of base camps in the Magdalenian of the Paris basin and suggests 'multiple short-duration camps used at different seasons and linked with a highly nomadic life' as an alternative to the base camp model.

Artefact refitting at the sites of Oudehaske and Gramsbergen in the Netherlands suggested that prepared cores, blade blanks and tools were carried from site to site (Johansen and Stapert 1997–8, 71). Johansen and Stapert suggest that this pattern may prevail in areas where raw material is scarce. In areas where raw material is more abundant, people would only carry a small selection of tools for use during travel and the first phase of occupation at the next encampment. The data from scatters A and C east are somewhat ambiguous in this respect. For example, many of the cores appear to have been pre-shaped elsewhere, but whether this was tens of miles away, or tens of yards away on the banks of the Colne, is impossible to determine. However, refitting group 10 in scatter C east clearly has many missing blade blanks, and these may well have been carried by the hunters as they moved on to their next encampment.

If this were so, then how does the proposed model compare with the evidence from Ahrensburgian/'long blade' sites of the north-west European mainland? Two of the best-known sites of this period are the blue patinated series at Belloy-sur-Somme in France (Fagnart 1991) and Stellmoor in Schleswig-Holstein, Germany (Rust 1943; Bokelmann 1991). These assemblages clearly represent sites of completely different type.

The Ahrensburgian site of Stellmoor has been reconstructed as a mass reindeer kill and primary butchery location (Bratlund 1991) and dated to around 10,020 BP (Fischer and Tauber 1986, 10). The ploughed-up area of the site covers 30,000m² and is estimated to have produced *c* 2000 tanged points. The radiocarbon dates from Stellmoor suggest that the site was the product of a short time span (ibid), which would accord with its interpretation as a mass slaughter site. However, Stellmoor cannot be regarded as typical of the Ahrensburgian/'long blade' industries. For instance, other excavated sites in the Stellmoor area are much smaller and have produced on average ten tanged points each (ibid).

The site at Belloy-sur-Somme covers an area of at least 1100m² and the lithic assemblage consists of tens of thousands of artefacts (Fagnart 1991, 216). The flint densities and site area are thus several orders of magnitude greater than those at Three Ways Wharf. The faunal remains are poorly preserved and composed mainly of teeth, but are exclusively horse, with no reindeer remains present. Only four individuals are identified, although others may have been present and not survived. Thus the occupation would seem to be of a different nature from that of Three Ways Wharf, and the excavator has suggested that the Belloy assemblage is related to technical activities associated with the working of flint near a rich source of raw material (ibid, 225). As mentioned above, hunting of horse may have taken place during different seasons from that of reindeer. Therefore, sites associated with a subsistence strategy based on horse might be expected to have a different extent and tool assemblage character from those associated with winter reindeer hunting. Nonetheless, published plans of excavated areas at Belloy (Fagnart 1988, fig 87) show a landscape consisting of dense lithic scatters 0.5–1.5m in diameter and 1.5–3.5m apart. If a comparably large area of the low ridge had been available for excavation at Three Ways Wharf, just such a pattern might have emerged, particularly when the distributions of scatters A, C east and D are borne in mind.

The small-scale nomadic exploitation model proposed for the period 10,300–9700 BP should not, therefore, be taken to exclude larger aggregation sites for specific tasks in favourable locations such as Stellmoor, or possibly Belloy-sur-Somme or Swaffham Prior, Suffolk (David 1984). However, these sites may be exceptions rather than the norm, and by and large do not represent 'base camps'. Such a pattern of human activity must be seen against the climatic changes outlined above (7.1), which took place over a period of a thousand calendar years. Put simply, the carrying capacity of the landscape may simply not have been high enough to support a relatively large human population which organised itself into 'base camps' and 'hunting camps'.

While a number of radiocarbon dates suggest a human presence during the 11th millennium BP, they are small in number (eg Barton 1991). This is perhaps not surprising given the climatic deterioration of the Loch Lomond Stadial (Younger Dryas) during the first half of the millennium. Gob (1991, 228–9) has suggested a 'cultural break' between the Tjongerian (or *federmesser*) and the Ahrensburgian of the Netherlands. Cook and Jacobi (1994, 83) have suggested that such a cultural break, if real, may correspond to the coldest part of the Younger Dryas. Therefore, material such as the 'Lyngby' axe from Earls Barton, Northamptonshire, and the 'long blade' assemblages 'would have been left by the earliest travellers and returning settlers as Britain's climate began to improve' (ibid). We may visualise small nomadic 'pioneering' human groups following herds of reindeer and horse further into Britain from a core area in the North Sea basin, as the climate improved from *c* 10,300 BP onwards until the replacement of the cold fauna from *c* 9700 BP.

During this period, it might be expected that changes in climate and vegetation would affect the density, ecology and behaviour of horse and reindeer, which would be reflected in changing exploitation strategies. It has been suggested by several researchers (Taute 1968, 312–13; Gob 1991; Barton 1991; 1998; Johansen and Stapert 1997–8) that these changes may in turn be detected in the subtle differences in both faunal and lithic assemblage composition at 'long blade' sites. For example, we might expect lithic assemblages to evolve and show increasing diversity over time (Chapter 3), perhaps with evidence of stays of longer duration or increasing intensity. It is within this possible context that the subtle differences in the assemblage compositions of scatters A and C east have been interpreted. However, it is stressed that, although we have tended to favour the interpretation of scatter C east as being slightly later than scatter A (though still firmly within the epi-Ahrensburgian 'long blade' industries), this is by no means proven, and the occupations could have been contemporary, if not exactly then perhaps to within a year or two.

While all these aspects are hinted at by other sites in Britain and north-west Europe, the small number of excavated and published sites, let alone the scarcity of sites producing faunal assemblages and radiocarbon dates, does not at present allow these models to be developed further.

Nonetheless, the question has been raised (eg Dumont 1997; Barton and Dumont 2000): do the 'long blade' or epi-Ahrensburgian industries represent an evolutionary stage towards the true Mesolithic, or is there a real break in the pattern of human occupation with the arrival of the full-forest flora and fauna of the late Pre-Boreal after *c* 9700 BP and the associated characteristic Early Mesolithic tool kits?

This author believes that there is a 'rupture' between the people and way of life of the 'long blade' industry and the Early Mesolithic. It is true that many of the techniques and tool types (notably microliths) were pioneered in the Lateglacial and developed further. However, there are so many typological and technological differences between the Lateglacial and Early Mesolithic assemblages that we consider them to be quite distinct. Perhaps more important than lithic typology would have been the changes to the ancient landscape, flora and fauna that occurred in the Early Holocene. Large parts of the North Sea basin would have flooded relatively quickly, leading to rapid disruption of winter grazing grounds and the spring and autumn migration routes of the reindeer herds. This would have had a marked impact on the complex and fragile economic basis of the Ahrensburgian hunting groups. Even more change and adaptation would have been required by the spread of forest, the disappearance of reindeer and the arrival of red deer, with new hunting strategies in new landscapes having to be developed. It is not surprising that stone tool typology and technology underwent a radical transformation, and it is our belief that the complex of Ahrensburgian hunting groups would have fragmented relatively quickly, with only those that were able to adapt surviving. Most importantly, the descendants of the Ahrensburgian groups that did survive and adapt to the Pre-Boreal landscape would no longer be Ahrensburgian. Their ancestors' way of life, technology, and even much of their landscape and the animals they depended upon, would have gone. They might as well be completely different groups of people, apparently separated from their past.

Early Holocene activity

There is likely to have been an interval of several hundred years between the latest of the 'long blade' scatters and the Mesolithic occupation represented by scatter C west at Three Ways Wharf. During this period major changes occurred both in the local vegetation and the fauna available for exploitation (above, 7.1). The woodland-adapted species of red and roe deer replaced the open environment fauna of reindeer and horse which had been the basis of human subsistence strategies for the previous thousand calendar years. Rising sea levels would have led to flooding of the 'core' 'long blade' area of the North Sea basin (Coles 1998), which would have had a major impact on the mobility and territorial range of hunter-gatherer groups. It is unlikely to be mere coincidence that changes in lithic technology and assemblage composition accompanied these changes (Barton 1991).

It has previously been demonstrated that Three Ways Wharf forms part of an extensive early Postglacial landscape in the floodplain of the Colne valley (Lewis et al 1992) (Fig 1). Unfortunately, all the sites documented by Lacaille (1961; 1963) within the Colne valley consisted of collections of artefacts found during gravel extraction rather than by controlled excavation, making it difficult to compare the composition of these assemblages with that from scatter C west. However, all appear to date to the Early Mesolithic. It has also been argued that later Mesolithic sites are more commonly found on the valley sides or further up the valley or its tributaries, and that this may have been in response to the rising water table on the floodplain leading to the transformation of large areas into sedge swamp. Combined with this change in settlement pattern is extensive evidence for burning of vegetation within the Colne valley (Chapter 2.2; Lewis et al 1992), although it is not certain whether this can be attributed to anthropogenic factors. Similar patterns of Early Mesolithic occupation on the floodplains of the Thames and its tributaries, followed by evidence of burning, have been observed elsewhere (ibid) and need not be summarised here. Unfortunately, within the Greater London area very few unmixed Early Mesolithic assemblages have been excavated and even fewer (eg the 'B and Q' site in Southwark (Sidell et al 2002, 11–23) and Creffield Road, Acton (Burleigh 1976)) have been published. This lack of accessible data renders it difficult to make meaningful statements concerning the local earlier Mesolithic other than what has been said above.

At the regional scale, it is worth considering the model proposed by Mellars and Rheindart (1978) to explain the apparent variation in Mesolithic tool kits in terms of underlying geological formation. Briefly, this went as follows.
1) The sand-yielding formations of southern Britain should reflect a higher proportion of hunting equipment than clay or silt formations.
2) On clay and silt formations, there should be a lower proportion of hunting equipment and a greater emphasis on tools associated with other activities such as food processing and general 'home base' maintenance activities.

In the north of the country it had been noted that upland sites displayed high concentrations of microliths, while lower-lying sites produced a greater variety of tool types (Jacobi 1978, 315). In this instance the upland sites were interpreted as upland summer hunting stands associated with seasonal altitudinal movements of red deer (Clark 1972). Fig 224 shows the distribution of Mesolithic sites and finds in western Greater London plotted against the main geological formations. The two main northern tributaries of the Thames, the Colne and the Lea, both bisect the expanse of London Clay, forming a block of clayland landscape 30–40km wide between the two river valleys. A block of landscape of this size could have been exploitable by hunter-gatherer groups based in the valleys of the Lea and the Colne. Fig 224 shows that, in general, Mesolithic activity is confined to the river floodplains and avoids the large expanse of London Clay. Three Ways Wharf scatter C west could be accommodated within the category of lowland or valley bottom 'home base maintenance' sites of the model outlined above.

A notable exception to the lack of activity on the London Clay is the site at West Heath, Hampstead (Collins and Lorimer 1989), which is situated on the junction of the Bagshot sands with the surrounding Claygate Beds and London Clay at an altitude of 100m (Fig 224). It is therefore a site located on sandy deposits surrounded by clay and is the closest approximation to an 'upland site' in Greater London. The sand 'island' acted as a favoured location, since the site evidently saw repeated occupation throughout the Mesolithic (ibid). However, the major part of the assemblage dates to the early phase of the period, and makes an interesting comparison with Three Ways Wharf. From Fig 225 it can be seen that, compared with Three Ways Wharf scatter C west, West Heath has a greater emphasis on 'hunting' equipment (eg microliths and backed bladelets). Conversely, 'maintenance' tools such as burins, awls or piercers, core tools and miscellaneous retouched pieces form a higher proportion of the assemblage at Three Ways Wharf than at West Heath.

It should be remembered that these functional interpretations of sites are based on typological classifications. A growing body of use-wear data (Chapter 6.4) suggests that tools could be used for a variety of purposes. In particular, at Three Ways Wharf microliths seem to have been used for cutting, whittling and boring wood, and cutting hide and meat, as well as being used as projectile points. While it is likely that the majority of microliths were used as projectiles, particularly at upland sites, the diversity of usage should not be overlooked. Nonetheless, and even though the West Heath tool assemblage includes far fewer microliths than, for example, the Pennine sites (Jacobi 1978), the contrasts between it and Three Ways Wharf would tend to support the model outlined above. Analysis of assemblage composition suggests that West Heath represents an

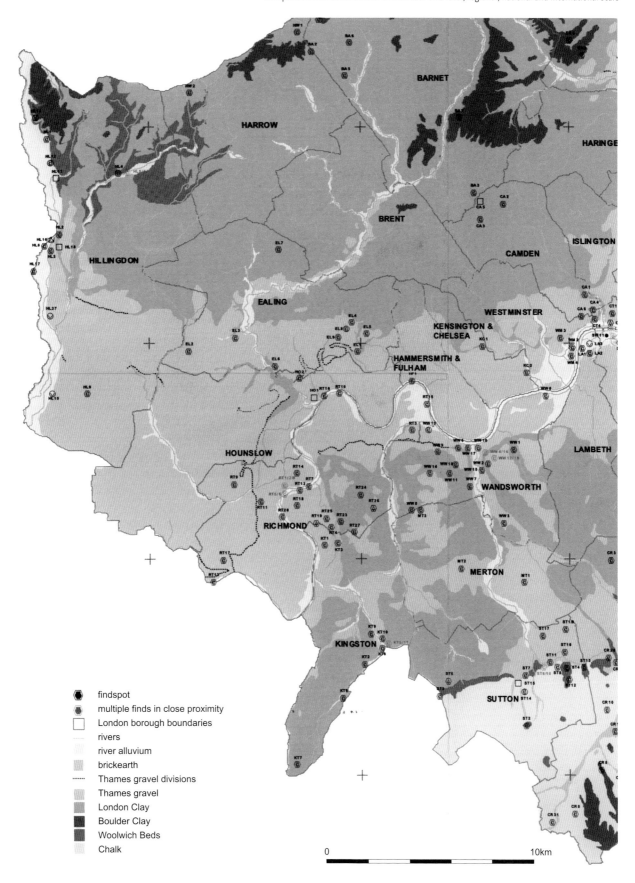

Fig 224 Mesolithic finds in the western part of Greater London plotted against simplified geology and topography (scale 1:175,000)

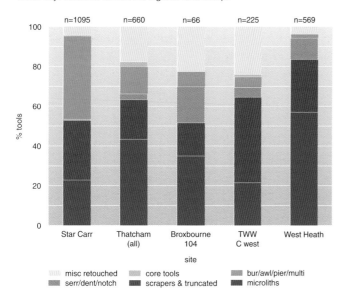

Fig 225 Comparison of the composition of retouched tool assemblages from selected Mesolithic sites

Table 66 Faunal spectrum of large mammals from Star Carr, Thatcham, Barry's Island and Three Ways Wharf

Species	Thatcham	Star Carr	Barry's Island*	TWW C west
Horse	1		1	
Red deer	8	26	37	15
Roe deer	6	17	5	2
Elk	1	12	2	
Aurochs	2	16	6	
Pig	7	4		

* Data based upon total MAUs as opposed to MNIs; figures therefore somewhat higher than those from the other sites (calculated from data supplied by P Rowley-Conwy)

'upland' hunting base, while Three Ways Wharf scatter C west would fall within the 'base camp' element of the traditional settlement system described above for the early Pre-Boreal. We are fortunate in that the quality of the faunal and lithic data at Three Ways Wharf allows a more detailed analysis of the function of the site within the broader Mesolithic landscape.

The Early Mesolithic period in Britain is scarcely better served by archaeological sites with faunal remains than the preceding period. The site at Seamer Carr, North Yorkshire, has been mentioned but the faunal assemblages from this site are unpublished, although woodland elements such as roe deer are present. The classic sites of Star Carr, North Yorkshire, and Thatcham, Berkshire, appear on the basis of the radiocarbon dates to be a little earlier than Three Ways Wharf (Table 64; Day and Mellars 1994), and another site in the Vale of Pickering, Barry's Island (P Rowley-Conwy, pers comm), as yet undated, may be broadly contemporary with Seamer Carr and Star Carr, although there is some evidence for reworking of material in a stream channel (T Schadla-Hall, pers comm) which may have 'mixed' the assemblages. Some cave sites certainly contain contemporary material, but relating any but the directly dated bones from these caves with the lithic assemblages is problematic.

The faunal assemblages from Star Carr (Fraser and King 1954; Legge and Rowley-Conwy 1988), Thatcham (King 1962) and Barry's Island (P Rowley-Conwy, pers comm) offer the only comparative data for the scatter C west fauna (Table 66), and of these only the Star Carr material has been studied in depth (Legge and Rowley-Conwy 1988). The most startling difference between Three Ways Wharf and all three of these sites is the species spectrum. Among those larger mammals most likely to have been hunted for food, the Three Ways Wharf fauna is lacking in diversity and contrasts with the other sites where most species are represented. There are a number of factors which might be responsible for this lack of diversity.
1) Day and Mellars (1994) have postulated extended periods of occupation at Star Carr or in its immediate vicinity, and such repeated occupation – even if confined largely to the summer months (Legge and Rowley-Conwy 1988) – may be expected to have resulted over a period of years in a diverse 'catch'. It is difficult to argue a similar case for Thatcham and Barry's Island simply because the data are not available, but the distributional analysis of the faunal remains from Three Ways Wharf has suggested that the Early Mesolithic site may represent a single period of occupation. In that case the site might reflect a seasonal camp specifically concerned with the hunting of red deer.
2) We have suggested that the hearth area and midden reflect the final stages of processing of the carcass and bones and may, therefore, represent only a part of the actual settlement site. This would allow for the possibility that debris from other species was discarded at another location.
3) We might postulate that the availability of these different game species varied with the season, such that a site of short-duration, single-period occupation, or specifically seasonal occupation, would not have been exploiting the whole spectrum of species available over a longer time span.
4) These differences may reflect faunal changes associated with the chronology of the sites and the environmental conditions previously described.

In principle none of these arguments alone appears able to account for the full variability, and it is likely that all will be contributing to the picture. We have seen that horse is present through at least the latter half of the Younger Dryas and the early Pre-Boreal, but that little evidence for this species occurs after 9500 BP. The occurrences at Thatcham and Barry's Island may either reflect an early episode of occupation or, as the finding of horse in both scatters A and C at Three Ways Wharf suggests, represent the residual occurrence of bones (whether naturally occurring or the result of human activity) within a later occupation deposit. This latter possibility does not, apparently, hold true for the Seamer Carr material (T Schadla-Hall, pers comm), and if we accept this it follows that the absence of horse from Star Carr might indicate that the Seamer Carr sites with horse should be considered as earlier in this sequence.

It is possible, as suggested above, that the absence of elk at Three Ways Wharf could also be attributed to chronological differences. A radiocarbon date of 9490±110 BP (OxA-0894) was obtained on burnt elk antler from Thatcham site IV (Table 64) and a similar or slightly earlier date can probably be assigned to the Star Carr specimens, to judge by the dates from the site altogether (Mellars and Dark 1998; Dark et al 2006). Population densities of elk are significantly lower than for red deer (Bay-Petersen 1988) and, during a relatively short period of occupation at Three Ways Wharf, there may have been no opportunity to hunt elk.

The absence of pig is less easily explained. Only at Thatcham does this species occur with any frequency, while it is completely absent from Barry's Island, only 3km from Star Carr. It seems likely that the absence of pig and aurochs from the assemblage at Three Ways Wharf may be due to the suggested single period of occupation of relatively short duration and a probable lesser density of these species in the pinewoods of the Boreal as discussed above (7.1). Although scatter C west is interpreted as a location where bones were smashed for marrow extraction, there is little reason to suppose that the marrow bones of pig and aurochs were less 'desirable' than those of red or roe deer, and they might, therefore, have been disposed of elsewhere. Only a cultural or social control could account for such selection.

Season of occupation may well have influenced these figures. Jochim (1976) and Price (1978) predicted the annual resource utilisation of various foods for inland Mesolithic sites, and Price (1982) suggested that the wide diversity of species and artefacts at Star Carr supported an interpretation of the site as a base camp. Price's model allows for some variability in the utilisation of different species at different times of the year, with red deer being predicted as the largest contributor during the late winter months (Price 1978). He later noted that such models do not provide reliable estimates of past diet (Price 1989), but game availability could readily account for variation in species composition between sites. The preliminary interpretation of Barry's Island as a winter site (P Rowley-Conwy, pers comm), and the tentative conclusion that Three Ways Wharf is a late winter to late spring or early summer site, may account for the dominance of red deer in these assemblages. This suggestion is reinforced by the consideration of the site types (below).

In this discussion we have only considered the large mammals, although smaller species also occur at the site and swans were definitely hunted, with at least one of the bones classed as comparable with whooper swan. There is no evidence of swan at other Early Mesolithic sites in Britain, although whooper and mute swan are common on Mesolithic sites of the Boreal and Atlantic periods in Denmark (Clark 1948; Grigson 1989; Rowley-Conwy in prep). The presence of the likely whooper swan is suggestive of winter occupation (Grigson 1989) since this species nests on swampy and marshy tundra and taiga in northern Scandinavia and Russia today. However, climatic conditions in Pre-Boreal Britain were somewhat different from those of today, and given that the species has nested in Scotland

in recent times (Peterson 1993) the possibility cannot be ruled out that it was nesting in Britain during the Pre-Boreal and need not indicate a winter occupation.

Having considered species availability, we should now turn to the site type as indicated by the lithic and faunal assemblages. As discussed above for the earlier occupation, the base camp/hunting camp model is strongly ingrained in the archaeology of the Early Mesolithic. If the anatomical composition of the scatter C west faunal assemblage at Three Ways Wharf suggests specialised marrow/grease extraction from a restricted range of species, the lithic assemblage composition and use-wear profiles imply that a wider range of activities took place, leading Grace to interpret the assemblage as a 'home base' (Chapter 6.4). The spatial analysis and 'seating plan' model discussed in Chapter 6.7 suggests that extracted marrow was the primary support of the occupation, but that other members of the group or groups also carried out a variety of tasks within the social sphere of a central hearth. One of the most important aspects of the faunal assemblage is that it represents the very last phase of the processing cycle, indicating that the kill, initial butchery, and possibly even further butchery and processing took place elsewhere within the landscape. In trying to identify these other elements of the settlement system, we must compare Three Ways Wharf with the few other sites producing faunal and lithic assemblages.

There are considerable difficulties in comparing aspects of the Three Ways Wharf lithic and faunal assemblage with the results from Star Carr and Thatcham. Most importantly, both the Thatcham (Wymer 1962) and Star Carr (Day and Mellars 1994) assemblages are the products of more than one occupation, whereas it has been argued previously that Three Ways Wharf scatter C west is the product of a single occupation. Much of the interpretation of the activities being carried out at Three Ways Wharf relies on the recording of the large quantities of unidentifiable or barely identifiable bone fragments. It was precisely these fragments which tended to be discarded or not collected during the study and excavation of the other two sites in the 1950s. Whether this occurred at Star Carr and Thatcham is not known for certain, but P Rowley-Conwy (pers comm) has alluded to 'winnowing' of the faunal collection at Star Carr after retrieval, whereas Gale Sieveking (pers comm), who actually excavated at the site, has assured us that all the material that could be recovered from the deposits was collected, and T Schadla-Hall (pers comm) recalls meeting the man who backfilled the Star Carr excavations and who himself recalled commenting on the small pieces of bone that were present in the spoil being returned to the trench. This hearsay evidence is both contradictory and insufficient to allow any assessment of what may have been discarded or not collected, and we have no choice but to work with the reported material only.

Two features of the Star Carr faunal remains are significant in these comparisons. Firstly, the largest component of the assemblage is antler. Legge and Rowley-Conwy (1988) recorded 259 fragments of red deer antler, of which 163 were worked in some way, and 63 unshed antlers of roe deer derived from at least 39 heads. The high frequency of these remains and their inconsistency with the apparent sex ratio in the postcranial material led these authors to conclude that much of the antler was imported independently of the postcranial material. This would represent specialised large-scale antler processing activity (Clark 1954) in complete contrast to scatter C west at Three Ways Wharf. The second significant aspect of the Star Carr faunal material is the large number of bone and antler artefacts such as barbed points, worked tines and antler mattocks, most of which appear to have been completed functional objects; evidence of antler working in the form of 'groove and splinter' technique was also well represented. No such objects were found at Three Ways Wharf. Given that the majority of the Three Ways Wharf faunal assemblage represents the very last stage of animal processing, interpreting some of the Star Carr remains as the discard of points used in hunting for the butchery and defleshing of carcasses could account for their absence in scatter C west. The large number of scapulae, radii, ulnae and lower fore- and hindlimb bones at Star Carr may reflect the discard of bones that were of little further use after butchery and defleshing (Fig 226). Marrow and grease extraction appear

to have been of less importance or absent at Star Carr since femora, proximal humeri and proximal tibiae are largely missing (Fig 226), and these constitute some of the most desirable bones for grease extraction (Binford 1978b).

Barry's Island, on the basis of preliminary results (P Rowley-Conwy, pers comm), includes elements of both Star Carr and Three Ways Wharf within its small collection (Fig 226). Mandibles are the most common bone (cf Star Carr) while innominate bones are next in frequency (in contrast to Star Carr and Three Ways Wharf) and long bone splinters are very common (cf Three Ways Wharf), and red deer is the most common species (cf Three Ways Wharf). The collection is small, and these finds could derive from a smaller-scale or shorter-duration occupation that combines parts at least of both the Star Carr and Three Ways Wharf elements of a potential site complex. Thus, some of the more obvious contrasts with Star Carr could be attributed to seasonal factors, although, as we have seen above, these differences could just as well be due to the loss of a spatially distinct element of the Star Carr assemblage. One thing that is clear from all these assemblages is the relative absence of vertebrae; this is consistent with these bones having been left at the kill site, although the atlas and axis appear to occur with consistently greater frequency than the other vertebrae, and were presumably removed with the skull when this was also taken.

If the faunal assemblages suggest a difference in site function and seasonality between Star Carr and Three Ways Wharf, are these differences reflected in the tool assemblages? From Table 67 and Fig 225 it is clear that there are major differences.

The Star Carr assemblage contains large quantities of microliths and scrapers, burins, awls and piercers, but particularly burins. The dominance of burins appears more pronounced in Table 67 due to the rejection of 120 'core scrapers' (Clark 1954, fig 33, F4, 6, 8, 9) as retouched tools. Rather, these seem to be cores with platform edge and arête abrasion and modification similar to that observed at Three Ways Wharf, and linked to blade production. Microwear studies of a small sample of the burins (Dumont 1987, 85) show that they were principally used for antler working, with bone working also prominent. This accords perfectly with the abundant evidence of antler working at Star Carr (above).

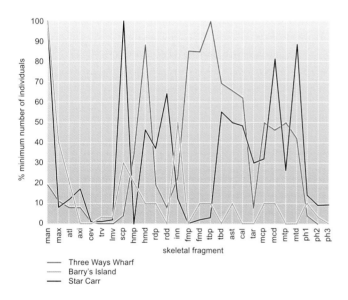

Fig 226 Plot of red deer bone frequency at Barry's Island, Star Carr and Three Ways Wharf

Table 67 Retouched tool assemblages from selected Early Mesolithic sites

Tool type	Star Carr	Thatcham III (pat)	Broxbourne 104	Marsh Benham	West Heath	TWW C west	TWW C east
Microliths/points	248	24	23	24	324	48	31
Scrapers & truncated	330	13	11	46	151	97	35
Serr/dent/notch	5	4	12	28	61	11	7
Burins	336	1	5	12	7	6	15
Core tools	7	0	0	1	3	4	0
Awl/pier/multi	123	2	4	0	5	2	5
Misc retouched	46	3	15	20	54	69	46
Total	1095	47	70	131	605	237	139

However Star Carr is interpreted, it is clear that one of the major activities there was the manufacture of antler and bone points.

Burins, awls or piercers also form a substantial component at Thatcham, though not as great as that at Star Carr. Despite poorer preservation conditions at Thatcham, worked bone and antler points and bodkins were present. It should be remembered that at Thatcham all the excavated scatters were combined to produce total tool counts (Wymer 1962, 338). It is possible that specialised bone- and antler-working areas existed, but have been masked by the homogenisation of the assemblage in the published report. Both Star Carr and Thatcham contrast with Three Ways Wharf, where bone and antler working was on a much smaller scale, and where burins form a much smaller component of the assemblage.

In scatter C west scrapers form the major tool component. Use-wear analysis shows that woodworking was the main function of these tools, followed by bone and antler working and hide working. In contrast, at Star Carr hide working was the major function, followed by bone and antler working and woodworking. It is, therefore, possible to suggest that tool assemblage composition coupled with use-wear analysis does reflect at least the major activities carried out at particular sites. In this respect Fig 225 suggests that Broxbourne 104, situated on the floodplain of the River Lea in Hertfordshire, is closest in assemblage profile to scatter C west at Three Ways Wharf.

In conclusion, Star Carr and Three Ways Wharf represent different elements within Early Mesolithic settlement systems. Having demonstrated that certain sites are associated with specialised tasks such as fat or marrow extraction and antler working, we must examine the spatial patterning of these sites in the landscape. From the foregoing discussions it is clear that a number of different models can be postulated to explain lithic and faunal variation between sites. Some of the main factors affecting this variation are human group size, seasonality, site function, procurement strategies and storage of resources. Differences in emphasis of any one or more of these elements result in models which differ in scale of human activity and patterning while still fitting the data. Some of these models will be discussed below.

Model 1: the traditional base camp/hunting camp model

According to the traditional model (Smith 1992, fig 3.1), if Three Ways Wharf is interpreted as a 'base camp' and Star Carr as a 'hunting camp' (Legge and Rowley-Conwy 1988), then it should be expected that there would be considerable spatial separation between the two elements in each case. The absence of certain skeletal parts at Star Carr and their presence at Three Ways Wharf could be neatly explained by the removal of meat-bearing limb bones to the base camp. The emphasis on antler working at Star Carr could be accounted for by the need to 'retool' and refurbish hunting equipment at a temporary camp, and the presence there of many complete antler points could be attributed to their having been discarded, possibly following butchery of the carcasses. At Three Ways Wharf there are also

hints of a curation strategy in the lithic assemblage, for instance among the axes. However, there are equally plausible alternative models which may more accurately reflect the complexity of site type and hunting strategy.

Model 2: multiple repeat occupations

Binford's models (Binford 1978a; 1978b) based on Inuit data are unlikely to be directly applicable to an environment where food and other resources were more readily available, evenly distributed and less seasonally determined. A model that defines a hunting camp as distinct from a base camp seems likely to reflect merely length of occupation rather than distinctly different activities. A seasonally nomadic existence, with sites being occupied for several weeks, and preferred locations being returned to repeatedly and possibly at the same season, might account for most of the variability between sites in terms of scale and species diversity. Each of these camps could include spatially distinct activity areas which might be several to tens of metres apart, depending upon the local topography, and with density and definition dependent upon group size, season of occupation, length of occupation and number of repeat occupations. Day and Mellars (1994) have proposed extended periods of occupation at Star Carr which, if the seasonal data is to be believed, must represent a series of seasonally consistent repeat occupations, in contrast to the interpretation of Three Ways Wharf scatter C west as representing a single phase of activity. The extent of the Star Carr site is apparently very much larger than the area excavated by Clark (T Schadla-Hall and N Milner, pers comm; Milner 2007) and consistency of the faunal data throughout this potential area cannot be assumed. Repeat occupations at the site may not have been seasonally consistent, and if they were located on a stretch of the lake shore rather than precisely over previous occupations, the unexcavated deposits might include faunal assemblages that are seasonally different in character. The resultant spatial patterning would be similar to that recovered from Seamer Carr (Schadla-Hall 1987). Three Ways Wharf scatter C west is important precisely because it appears to reflect just a single phase of activity lasting several weeks and is not a palimpsest of Mesolithic activity, although an earlier Lateglacial occupation did occur at the site.

Model 3: task groups and contemporary settlement elements

As discussed above (Chapter 6.3), the Three Ways Wharf assemblage would fit quite well as the hearth-side waste of the Star Carr site. It is now clear that the excavated portion of this latter site is merely a part of the original occupation area and, as Price (1982) noted, reflects the toss zone for the larger pieces away from the settlement. An increasing density of flints upslope towards the edge of the excavated area and the decline in bone preservation (Clark 1954) indicates that all the bone and fragments that may have existed on the upslope part of the site and areas beyond the limits of excavation have been lost as a result of post-depositional corrosion in acid soil. The practical location of the settlement hearths upslope on dry land and all the activities which would have taken place around these are, therefore, not reflected in the bone assemblage recovered. Legge and Rowley-Conwy (1988) failed to consider this in their analyses, although they acknowledged that the sample derived from a 'toss zone'. The absence of many small bone fragments and long bones such as the femur could, therefore, be explained by their removal to the fireside where cooking, fine bone and antler working, and marrow and grease extraction may have been taking place.

The relative absence of antler, skull and vertebrae at Three Ways Wharf, and the occurrence of smashed long bones and small-scale antler working, perhaps reflects exactly those activities missing at Star Carr and, leaving aside for the moment the potential impact of seasonal differences and species diversity, these two sites could represent spatially distinct areas of a single type of site complex.

It is relatively easy to suggest that the 'scatter C west element' of the Star Carr site would have lain upslope from Clark's excavations, but it is more difficult to say where the 'Star Carr element' of the Three Ways Wharf site was. In Chapter 2 it was demonstrated that scatter C west lay on the side of a low ridge extending across the valley bottom, adjacent to an active stream. It is, therefore, possible that the 'Star Carr' activity element lay some metres south of C west, on the edge of the stream. Local newspaper reports in the 1950s of bones and antlers being recovered during building works some 125m east of the site could fit the bill, but it remains a possibility that these two elements need not always be located within the same site complex.

In this model it is possible to envisage different task groups, perhaps composed of members of multiple family groups selected on a gender or age basis, carrying out different specialist activities in separate but adjacent segments of the landscape (Fig 227). This scenario has implications for assessing the total size and social structure of human groups at this period. For example, it would imply a large population composed of multiple family groups cooperating in the hunting, butchering and processing of prey. In addition specialist tasks such as bone, antler, hide and wood working, and lithic tool production, would have been divided among the members of the group. As we have seen in Chapter 6.6, there are hints of this task division visible in the seating plan around the C west hearth (Fig 219). If this model were applicable, then one could envisage a division of labour not only around a hearth at a specialist task location but between the different elements of a landscape composed of roughly contemporary activity locations (Fig 227). This suggests the ordered division of labour and sharing of resources for the good of the group. From this it follows that the population size of the group would be quite large and composed of many family units. This model differs from the others in terms of scale and contemporaneity of activity.

The faunal data from Three Ways Wharf could certainly be interpreted in this way. For instance, in addition to the 'Star Carr element' being close by, other task sites such as the location where the main limb bones were defleshed, and the meat consumed or dried, could also be tens of metres away (Fig 227). If all the red and roe deer were killed during a relatively short space of time, it would imply the cooperation of a number of hunters or hunting parties. Similarly, the total meat yield of 15 red and three roe deer present at Three Ways Wharf would suggest a population much larger than that suggested by

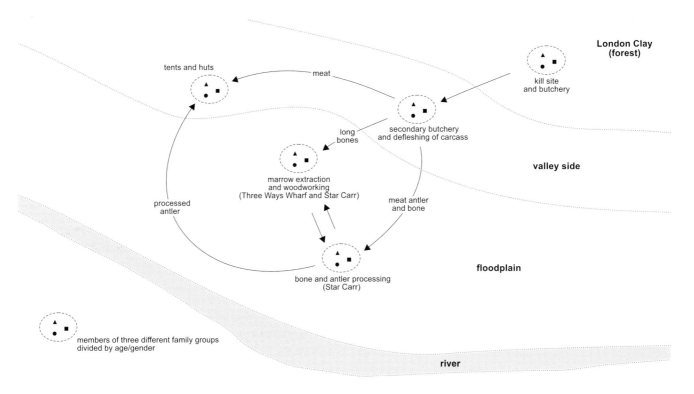

Fig 227 Diagrammatic representation of the task group model

the seating plan in Chapter 6.6 (Fig 219; Fig 221, a). The suggestion that much of this meat may never have reached the hearth side at Three Ways Wharf implies that it was processed and consumed elsewhere, with scatter C west concerned with marrow and grease extraction. However, the possibility that the marrow- and grease-rich bones were cached and stored would account for their high frequency, and this could have been achieved by a much smaller group of people (model 4).

Model 4: small-scale, seasonally determined activity

This model also acknowledges that Star Carr and Three Ways Wharf represent different elements in a settlement system. However, unlike model 3 (Fig 227), the size of the human group concerned is much smaller and seasonality of occupation is far more important in determining the activity and the subsistence strategies employed. As has been described above, Star Carr has been interpreted as a summer hunting camp (Legge and Rowley-Conwy 1988) which also involved specialised antler and bone working activities. Elsewhere in this report it has been argued that Three Ways Wharf represents a late winter or early spring occupation in part sustained by marrow and fat extraction from bones which may already have been largely defleshed when they arrived on site. Bone and antler working was very small-scale, although other tasks (notably woodworking) were undertaken. These differences may be explained by the subsistence strategies employed by respective groups at different times of the year.

The Star Carr and Barry's Island assemblages are the only ones which can be compared on any level with Three Ways Wharf. Rowley-Conwy has noted the presence of numerous shaft fragments in the small collection of bone from Barry's Island, most of which are likely to have derived from the red deer, and has used their presence to suggest marrow processing (P Rowley-Conwy, pers comm). This is the only comparable assemblage to scatter C west, and Rowley-Conwy's tentative interpretation of this site as a winter occupation perhaps accords with the Three Ways Wharf evidence. Marrow extraction is a relatively high-cost exercise (Binford 1978b, 44) in terms of fat/calorific return for effort and is likely to have been much more of a priority during the winter (and particularly late winter) and early spring months, when human fat reserves were low, the hunted animals were lean, and few other fat sources were available (Speth 1991). In contrast, during the summer months hunted ungulates would have carried greater fat stores within the meat and alternative sources were available. The need for marrow fat processing and grease extraction during the summer would be reduced, and summer occupation sites might show significantly less long bone destruction. Certainly it would be more difficult to store unprocessed long bones for any length of time during the summer months and Binford notes that the Nunamiut tended not to store marrow bones in the summer because they spoiled (Binford 1978b, 100). Whether the apparent absence of large numbers of small long bone splinters from the Star Carr assemblage should be put down to its proposed summer occupation (Legge and Rowley-Conwy

1988), or the 'winnowing' of the original sample (above), is a dilemma. However, if the faunal assemblages do reflect seasonal variation, what does this say about Three Ways Wharf and activity patterns?

The concept of caching material to be used elsewhere or at a later date has been employed by Gamble in his model of northern hunters (Gamble 1986). Collection and caching has also been used by Legge and Rowley-Conwy (1988) to overturn Clark's original interpretation of Star Carr as a winter site. Interestingly, at the winter site of Three Ways Wharf, which would have had access to shed antler, this commodity is scarce. If the seasons of occupation at Star Carr and Three Ways Wharf are judged correctly, we have a situation where antler is collected in the winter for working in the summer. However, it is in respect of the meat-bearing bones that caching as a strategy has its greatest effect on modelling human group size and behaviour. It has been noted above that the potential meat content of the skeletal material at Three Ways Wharf suggests a length of occupation or size of group far in excess of that suggested by the seating plan. However, if the majority of the faunal assemblage was not the product of a large hunt, but represents the processed remains of cached marrow bones, then the picture is changed. We would then have a sequence of events as follows (Fig 228).

1) A small group of one or two families move around the landscape in the late summer/early winter, hunting red and roe deer; this results in upland 'hunting stand' type sites, or sites such as West Heath. Initial butchery is carried out close to the kill site and the main meat-bearing carcass portions are brought back to the campsite and shared out.

2) The group consume enough meat to satisfy their immediate needs, and dry and store the remainder. During this period they may work antler stored from the winter to retool hunting equipment, thus producing 'Star Carr type' sites.

3) During the winter the group's activities become centred more on valley bottoms, following altitudinal movements of red deer. Meat is consumed and stored as before. In addition, the defleshed long bones and other high marrow- and grease-bearing bones are carefully preserved and cached to provide a store of lipids for the period of the year (late winter/early spring) when this vital dietary component is at its most scarce. The total number of animals predated may be high, but this total will have been accumulated over several weeks in ones and twos, rather than through mass slaughter or large-scale collaborative hunting. Since the period of predation may be long and the number of prey killed at any one time is small, the cache will accumulate slowly, but by late winter will have reached an impressive size with (as at Three Ways Wharf) a large number of individual animals represented, though of restricted species range and anatomical content. During winter such a cache could be stored in snow drifts or perhaps high enough up trees to be above the level of fly activity, out of the way of scavengers and cooled by the wind.

4) During late winter/early spring, at the time of greatest stress on lipid availability, the small group make camp near the site of the long bone cache, which is at last utilised to sustain the

late summer to mid winter

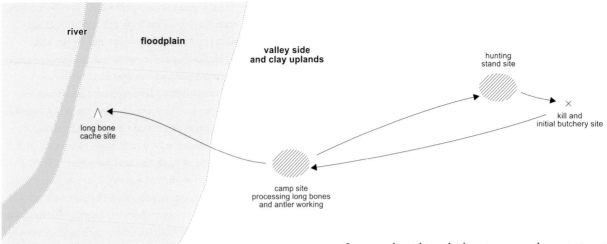

late winter to early spring

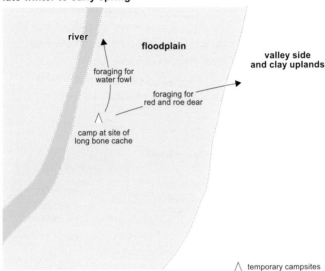

⋀ temporary campsites

Fig 228 Diagrammatic representation of small-scale, seasonally determined activity

group over this difficult period. Further raw materials for survival as well as dietary supplements are provided by hunting other species such as swan, the occasional roe deer and perhaps beaver. During this period antler is collected for storage, perhaps with some initial processing such as cutting off the tines and reducing the length of the beams. In addition, the usual maintenance activities such as hide and wood working are carried out. All this activity would produce a lithic and faunal assemblage very similar to that at Three Ways Wharf scatter C west, and one which could be interpreted as a specialised late winter/early spring 'camp'.

Summary and conclusions

From the models described above it can be seen that the data from Three Ways Wharf, like those from Star Carr, can be interpreted in a number of ways. Model 1 may be too simplistic

a framework within which to interpret the variations in site type and lithic and faunal assemblage. Model 2 may be inherently untestable, since the present crudity of radiocarbon dating makes establishing sequential occupation on such a fine scale impossible. Our own personal preference is for models 3 and 4, which are more socially and seasonally complex variations of model 1. The implications for human group size and social structure of each model are quite different. Model 3 envisages a large band made up of many family groups. Labour and effort are coordinated between the family groups, with task groups being formed to carry out the various procurement and processing activities required for survival. These activities take place at locations which are adjacent or separated by tens of metres. This would produce a landscape containing 'favoured locations' consisting of numerous, partially overlapping lithic and faunal scatters. Both the population size and degree of social interaction in this model are high. In model 4 the band size is relatively small, consisting of one or two family groups. The band moves seasonally around the landscape, which together with a caching strategy produces lithic and faunal scatters of varying character in different locations. Repetition of this pattern over a number of years would also lead to a landscape of 'favoured locations'. The Colne valley contains just such a Mesolithic landscape of favoured locations, a pattern repeated in the valleys of other Thames tributaries such as the Lea and the Kennet.

It is felt that model 4 most closely matches the Three Ways Wharf data and, unlike model 3, does not depend on the unproven presence of different task areas close to the site. Also, the overall band size and degree of social organisation required by model 4 are much lower than those required by model 3. While not ruling out these aspects of model 3, it is again felt that they remain to be corroborated by data from other sites.

It is clear that the resolution of many of these problems depends primarily on the excavation and publication of more sites with *in situ* faunal and lithic assemblages. However, a factor often overlooked is the need to excavate very large areas of Lateglacial/Early Holocene landscape in order fully to recover the spatial distribution of lithic and faunal material. Even the excavations at Three Ways Wharf only provided a 'window' on this landscape. It should be remembered that the landscape contains 'sites' ranging in size and type from Star Carr and Three Ways Wharf to a scatter of flakes, representing a single knapped pebble, such as that at Cowley Mill, 1km south of Three Ways Wharf (Stewart 1989). The excavations at Seamer Carr have, as previously stated, revealed a complex series of lithic scatters over a very large excavated area (Schadla-Hall 1987), and the final publication of this site will undoubtedly clarify the data recovered at Three Ways Wharf and at Star Carr, and the models outlined above.

7.3 Changing patterns of human activity, 10,000–8200 cal BC

The preceding section suggested subtle changes in patterns of human behaviour during the end of the Lateglacial and the Early Holocene. These may be summarised as follows.

In Britain the return of severe climatic conditions during the Loch Lomond Stadial (Younger Dryas) led to a curtailment of the human activity which typified the Lateglacial Interstadial.

Following the amelioration of the Loch Lomond Stadial

(Younger Dryas), human 'recolonisation' of Britain (or at least activity on an increasing scale) spread from the North Sea basin and north-west Europe. This took the form of small human groups following herds of reindeer and horse, and possibly seasonally exploiting these resources. Humans adapted to exploitation of a resource (the reindeer herd) which was individually concentrated but widely separated in space from the next such concentration, and which moved across a largely open landscape (Fig 229, a). The mode of subsistence was thus highly mobile, producing a settlement pattern consisting of kill sites with temporary camps for butchery and other tasks in close proximity. Repetition of this activity over many years may have led to a landscape consisting of small, dense scatters of lithic material dispersed at 'favoured locations'. Alternatively, several groups may have acted together and carried out processing adjacent to each other, producing a similar archaeological pattern. Almost all the carcass was processed at the temporary butchery camp, with perhaps enough meat retained to last until the herd moved on and the next kill and camp could be made at a new location. Three Ways Wharf scatters A and C east could both have been produced by humans subsisting in this way. Some Continental sites, such as Belloy-sur-Somme and Stellmoor, suggest larger congregations of human groups and/or functional differences in site-specific activity.

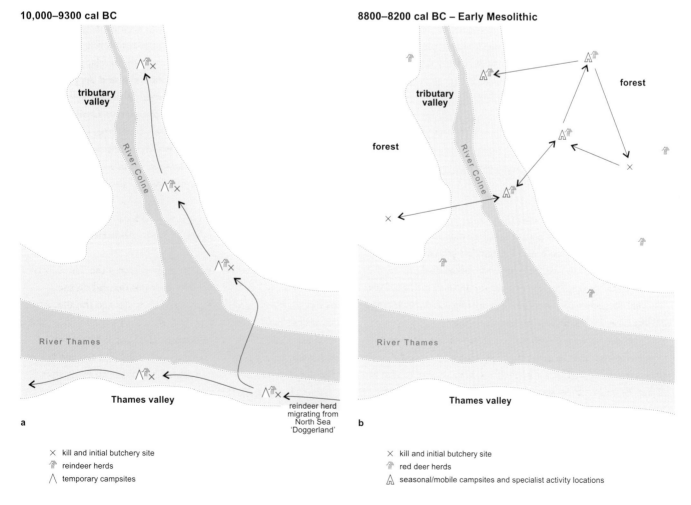

10,000–9300 cal BC

8800–8200 cal BC – Early Mesolithic

× kill and initial butchery site
⚔ reindeer herds
∧ temporary campsites

× kill and initial butchery site
⚔ red deer herds
⩔ seasonal/mobile campsites and specialist activity locations

Fig 229 a and b Diagrammatic comparison of subsistence strategies 10,000–9300 cal BC and 8800–8200 cal BC

This subsistence pattern was followed for perhaps a thousand calendar years, during which time changes in the composition of the flora and fauna may be reflected in a subtle evolution of lithic typology and technology.

The earliest true Mesolithic assemblages occur after *c* 9300 cal BC and seem to be synchronous with the replacement of reindeer and horse by species adapted to the increasingly wooded environment of the Pre-Boreal such as red and roe deer. It is surely no coincidence that these events occur virtually simultaneously. It is argued in this report that changes in environment and fauna are reflected not only in lithic tool technology but in patterns of human behaviour and subsistence. Red and roe deer represent a less concentrated and less mobile resource than reindeer. They do not form large herds which travel long distances through a mainly open landscape but form small herds which are more evenly distributed through the woodland (Fig 229, b). Instead of the small, highly mobile bands following a mobile resource of the previous thousand years, it is argued that human groups became relatively larger in size and comparatively less mobile with longer-duration occupation of points in the landscape. Increasing variation in site type and activity location emerged as a consequence, together with the development and growth in importance of increasingly sophisticated curatorial strategies, such as caching of food and raw material resources. This interpretation of Three Ways Wharf and other British evidence is in direct opposition to a model proposed for the Continent by Fischer and Tauber (1986). In this model the replacement of reindeer by more territorial big game is seen as favouring a lower human population and possibly shorter periods of habitation at different settlements (ibid, 12). Whether there was a genuine difference in subsistence strategies either side of the North Sea lowland plain is a moot point, and the difference in interpretation may simply reflect the different emphasis on evidence derived from different patterns of fieldwork.

7.4 Further potential of the archive

The majority of the aims of the excavation and post-excavation analysis (Chapter 1.3 and 1.4) have been met. The data from Three Ways Wharf have shed new light on human behavioural adaptations at the end of the Lateglacial period. Most importantly, during the Early Mesolithic occupation of scatter C west, it is possible to suggest that the space occupied by different individuals around a campfire, and the different tasks they performed, can be recognised. However, there are many other questions which have arisen and many alternative models which could be tested using the data in the site archive. For example, a more extensive refitting programme might be aimed at identifying links between scatters A and C east. Further use-wear analysis might concentrate on an extensive sample of the unretouched debitage. As mentioned previously, any future faunal analysis could focus on patterns of skeletal breakage.

On a broader scale, Three Ways Wharf has demonstrated the archaeological potential of fine-grained alluvial deposits present on the floodplains of the Thames and its tributaries. Any future fieldwork in advance of development must take into consideration the nature of the archaeology of this period, and employ adequate evaluation and excavation strategies to assess and maximise this potential. Furthermore, any opportunity to excavate large areas of the palaeo-landscape should be seized upon. In the absence of such opportunities, the information from many smaller-scale evaluations and excavations can be used to paint a picture of the relict landscape, provided that consistent research aims and recording methods are adopted.

In national terms, Three Ways Wharf joins a very small group of sites which have provided *in situ* lithic and (most importantly) faunal assemblages. Although these assemblages are not as spectacular or well-preserved as those at Star Carr, Three Ways Wharf is currently the only site which can provide data on the mode of human activity at the transition between the Lateglacial and Holocene periods.

FRENCH AND GERMAN SUMMARIES

Résumé

Elisabeth Lorans

Uxbridge, dans le Middlesex, est situé à la périphérie nord-ouest du Grand Londres, près de la rivière Colne, affluent majeur de la Tamise. Le site de Three Ways Wharf occupe un terrain bas dans la plaine alluviale à la limite nord-ouest de la ville actuelle. Entre 1986 et 1990, des fouilles ont révélé cinq zones de dispersion de matériaux lithiques et fauniques en place.

La zone A consistait en un assemblage de « longues lames » tardiglaciaires associées à des restes de chevaux et de rennes. Deux datations radiocarbones effectuées sur les ossements de chevaux suggèrent une présence humaine autour de 10 000 BP. Une troisième, plus récemment obtenue, a confirmé les datations précédentes.

Les zones B et D étaient de petite taille et difficiles à dater mais la zone D est probablement à attribuer aussi au Tardiglaciaire.

La zone C était composée de deux occupations chronologiquement distinctes, C est et C ouest. La première associait une industrie de « longues lames » à des restes fauniques de chevaux et de rennes. Aucune datation par radiocarbone n'a pu être obtenue à partir des restes osseux mais cette phase est probablement incluse entre 10 300 BP et 9600 BP environ et est donc globalement contemporaine de la zone de dispersion A. La seconde consistait en une concentration dense de matériel lithique du début du Mésolithique et en un assemblage faunique dominé par le cerf. L'attribution chronologique fut confirmée par trois datations par radiocarbone indiquant une activité humaine au début de l'ère postglaciaire vers 9200 BP. L'analyse de la faune suggère une occupation de fin d'hiver ou de printemps, marquée par l'extraction de graisse et de moelle des os longs de cerfs accumulés.

Le principal apport de ce programme de recherche a été de dater et de caractériser l'activité humaine et les stratégies d'approvisionnement à la transition Glaciaire/ Postglaciaire, une période mal connue en Grande-Bretagne. Cet objectif fut atteint par l'analyse technique et typologique du matériel lithique, par l'étude de la faune et par l'analyse spatiale des artefacts et des restes osseux. Au cours du travail, de nombreuses pistes de recherche ont émergé, tandis que d'autres se sont révélées infructueuses. La possibilité de changements des structures sociales en cette période de la Préhistoire a été prise en compte.

Zusammenfassung

Manuela Struck

Uxbridge, Middlesex, liegt an der nordwestlichen Peripherie von Groß-London und nahe dem Fluss Colne, ein Hauptnebenfluss der Themse. Die Fundstätte Three Ways Wharf befindet sich an einer tief liegenden Stelle im Überflutungsgebiet des Colne am Nordwestrand der heutigen

Stadt Uxbridge. Ausgrabungen von 1986 bis 1990 legten hier insgesamt fünf ungestörte Stein- und Tierknochenstreuungen frei.

Streuung A bestand aus einer „Langklingen"-Industrie des Spätglazials vermischt mit Pferde- und Rentierresten. Zwei C14-Daten von Pferdeknochen lassen die Anwesenheit von Menschen hier um 10 000 v.H. vermuten. Eine dritte vor kurzem vorgenommene C14-Bestimmung bestätigte die zuvor gewonnenen Daten.

Streuungen B und D waren klein und schwer zu datieren, wobei Streuung D wahrscheinlich ebenfalls in das Spätglazial gehört.

Streuung C repräsentiert zwei chronologisch unterschiedliche Nutzungen, und zwar C-Ost und C-West. Streuung C-Ost steht in Verbindung mit einer „Langklingen"-Industrie und enthielt auch Pferde- und Rentierknochen. C14-Daten wurden anhand der Knochen nicht gewonnen; diese Phase fällt aber wahrscheinlich in die Periode 10 300 bis ca. 9600 v.H. und ist dadurch ungefähr zeitgleich mit Streuung A.

Streuung C-West bestand aus einer besonderen Konzentration frühmesolithischer Steinartefakte und Tierreste, unter denen Rothirschknochen vorherrschten. Diese Zeitstellung wurde durch drei C14-Daten bestätigt, die menschliche Aktivitäten für eine frühe postglaziale Periode um 9200 v.H. belegen. Die Tierknochenanalyse legt eine Nutzung während des späten Winters und Frühjahrs nahe, während der vornehmlich Fett und Knochenmark aus den gehorteten Langknochen des Rotwilds gewonnen wurde.

Der hauptsächliche Vorstoß des Three Ways Wharf-Projekts war die Datierung und Charakterisierung menschlicher Aktivitäten und Strategien zur Existenzsicherung während des Übergangs von der Eiszeit zur postglazialen Ära, einer wenig verstandenen Periode in Großbritannien. Dies wurde erreicht durch die Auswertung der Steinbearbeitungstechnologie und -typologie, der Tierreste sowie der Verteilungsmuster von Artefakten und Skelettresten. Im Verlaufe der Untersuchungen ergaben sich viele ungeplante neue Forschungsansätze, während andere sich als unproduktiv erwiesen. Möglichen Hinweise auf soziale Veränderungen in dieser prähistorischen Periode wurden ebenfalls erwogen.

BIBLIOGRAPHY

Ahlen, I, 1965 Studies on the red deer, *Cervus elaphus* L, in Scandinavia, *Swedish Wildlife Res* 3, 177–376

Allen, T G, 1995 *Lithics and landscape: archaeological discoveries on the Thames Water pipeline at Gatehampton Farm, Goring, Oxfordshire, 1985–92*, Thames Valley Landscapes Monogr 7, Oxford

Andrews, P, 1995 Experiments in taphonomy, *J Archaeol Sci* 22, 147–54

Arnold, H R, 1993 *Atlas of mammals in Britain*, Inst Terrestrial Ecol Res Pub 6, London

Atkinson, T C, Briffa, K R, and Coope, G R, 1987 Seasonal temperatures in Britain during the past 20,000 years reconstructed using beetle remains, *Nature* 325, 587–92

Audouze, F, 1987 The Paris basin in Magdalenian times, in *The Pleistocene old world: regional perspectives* (ed O Soffer), 183–200, New York

Audouze, F, and Enloe, J, 1991 Subsistence strategies and economy in the Magdalenian of the Paris basin, France, in Barton et al 1991, 63–71

Avery, B W, 1980 *Soil classification for England and Wales*, Soil Survey Monogr 14, Harpenden

Avery, B W, and Bascomb, C L (eds), 1974 *Soil survey laboratory methods*, Soil Survey Monogr 6, Harpenden

Baales, M, 1996 *Umwelt und Jagdökonomie der Ahrensburger Rentierjäger im Mittelgebirge*, RGZM Monographien 38, Mainz

Bal, L, 1982 *Zoological ripening of soils*, Wageningen

Ballin, T B, and Jensen, O L, 1995 Farsundprosjektet – stenalderbopladser på, in *Lista, Varia* 29, 268–323, Oslo

Barclay, A, Boyle, A, Bradley, P, and Roberts, M R, 1995 Excavations at the former Jewsons Yard, Harefield Road, Uxbridge, Middlesex, *Trans London Middlesex Archaeol Soc* 46, 1–25

Barrett, J C, 1994 *Fragments from antiquity: an archaeology of social life in Britain, 2900–1200 BC*, Oxford

Barton, R N E, 1986 Experiments with long blades from Sproughton, near Ipswich, Suffolk, in *Studies in the Upper Palaeolithic of Britain and north-west Europe* (ed D A Roe), BAR Int Ser 296, 129–41, Oxford

Barton, R N E, 1989 Long blade technology in southern Britain, in Bonsall 1989, 264–71

Barton, R N E, 1991 Technological innovation and continuity at the end of the Pleistocene in Britain, in Barton et al 1991, 234–45

Barton, R N E, 1992 *Hengistbury Head, Dorset: Vol 2, The Late Upper Palaeolithic and Early Mesolithic sites*, Oxford Univ Comm Archaeol Monogr 34, Oxford

Barton, R N E, 1995 The long blade assemblage, in Allen 1995, 54–64

Barton, R N E, 1997 *English Heritage book of Stone Age Britain*, London

Barton, R N E, 1998 Long blade technology and the question of British Late Pleistocene/Early Holocene lithic assemblages, in *Stone Age archaeology: essays in honour of John Wymer* (eds N Ashton, F Healey and P Pettitt), Oxbow Monogr 102 (Lithics Stud Soc Occas Pap 6), 158–64, Oxford

Barton, R N E, 2005 *Ice Age Britain*, rev edn, London

Barton, R N E, and Dumont, S, 2000 Recolonisation and settlement of Britain at the end of the last glaciation, in *Tardiglaciaire* 2000, 151–62

Barton, R N E, and Froom, F R, 1986 The long blade assemblage from Avington VI, Berkshire, in *The Palaeolithic of Britain and its nearest neighbours: recent trends* (ed S N Collcutt), 80–4, Sheffield

Barton, R N E, Roberts, A J, and Roe, D A (eds), 1991 *The Late Glacial in north-west Europe: human adaptation and environmental change at the end of the Pleistocene*, CBA Res Rep 77, London

Bay-Petersen, J L, 1978 Animal exploitation in Mesolithic Denmark, in Mellars 1978, 115–45

Becker, B, and Kromer, B, 1986 Extension of the Holocene dendrochronology by the Preboreal pine series, 8800 to 10,100 BP, *Radiocarbon* 28(2B), 961–7

Becker, B, and Kromer, B, 1991 Dendrochronology and radiocarbon calibration of the Early Holocene, in Barton et al 1991, 22–4

Bennett, K D, Simonson, W D, and Peglar, S M, 1990 Fire and man in Postglacial woodlands of eastern England, *J Archaeol Sci* 17, 1–8

Bennett, K D, Whittington, G, and Edwards, K J, 1994 Recent plant nomenclatural changes and pollen morphology in the British Isles, *Quat Newsl* 73, 1–6

Bergman, C A, Barton, R N E, Collcutt, S N, and Morris, G, 1987 Intentional breakage in a Late Upper Palaeolithic assemblage from southern England, in *The human uses of flint and chert: proceedings of the Fourth International Flint Symposium, Brighton, 1983* (eds G de G Sieveking and M H Newcomer), 21–32, Cambridge

Biard, M, and Hinguant, S, 2004 Paléolithique supérieur final ou Mésolithique ancien?: le site du Buhot à Calleville (Eure), *Bulletin de la Société Préhistorique Française* 101, 597–600

Binford, L R, 1978a Dimensional analysis of behaviour and site structure: learning from an Eskimo hunting stand, *Amer Antiq* 43, 330–61

Binford, L R, 1978b *Nunamiut ethnoarchaeology*, New York

Binford, L R, 1980 Willow smoke and dogs' tails: hunter-gatherer settlement systems and archaeological site formation, *Amer Antiq* 45, 4–20

Binford, L R, 1983 *In pursuit of the past*, London

Binford, L R, 1984 *Faunal remains from Klasies River mouth*, Orlando

Binford, L R, and Bertram, J B, 1977 Bone frequencies and attritional processes, in *For theory building in archaeology: essays on faunal remains, aquatic resources, spatial analysis and systemic modelling* (ed L R Binford), 77–153, New York

Binford, L R, and Binford, S R, 1966 A preliminary analysis of functional variability in the Mousterian of Levallois facies, *Amer Anthropologist* 68, 238–95

Blankholm, H P, 1991 *Intrasite spatial analysis in theory and practice*, Aarhus

Blankholm, H P, and Price, T D, 1991 *Arcospace: a package for spatial analysis of archaeological data, Version 3.0*, Aarhus

Boas, F, 1888 *The central Eskimo*, repr 1964 with an introduction by Henry B Collins, Lincoln, Nebr

Bokelmann, K, 1991 Some new thoughts on old data on humans and reindeer in the Ahrensburgian tunnel valley in Schleswig-Holstein, Germany, in Barton et al 1991, 72–81

Bonsall, C (ed), 1989 *The Mesolithic in Europe: papers presented at the Third International Symposium, Edinburgh, 1985*, Edinburgh

Bordes, F, 1967 Considérations sur la typologie et les techniques dans la Paléolithique, *Quartär, Jahrbuch für Erforschung des Eiszeitalters und der Steinzeit* 18, 251–62

Bordes, F, 1970a Observations typologiques et techniques sur le Périgordien supérieur de Corbiac (Dordogne), *Bulletin de la Société Préhistorique Française* 67, 105–13

Bordes, F, 1970b Réflexions sur l'outil au Paléolithique, *Bulletin de la Société Préhistorique Française* 67, 199–202

Bouchud, J, 1966 *Essai sur le renne et la climatologie du Paléolithique moyen et supérieur*, Périgueux

Bouma, J, Fox, C A, and Mdema, R, 1990 Micromorphology of hydromorphic soils: application for soil genesis and land evaluation, in Douglas 1990, 257–78

Boyle, K V, 1990 *Upper Palaeolithic faunas from south-west France*, BAR Int Ser 557, Oxford

Brain, C K, 1981 *The hunters or the hunted?: an introduction to African cave taphonomy*, Chicago

Bratlund, B, 1991 A study of hunting lesions containing flint fragments on reindeer bones at Stellmoor, Schleswig-Holstein, Germany, in Barton et al 1991, 193–207

Bronk Ramsey, C, 1994 Analysis of chronological information and radiocarbon calibration: the program OxCal, *Archaeol Comput Newsl* 41, 11–16

Bronk Ramsey, C, 2001 Development of the radiocarbon calibration program OxCal, *Radiocarbon* 43(2A), 355–63

Brooks, J, Grant, P R, Muir, M, van Gijzel, P, and Shaw, G (eds), 1971 *Sporopollenin: proceedings of a symposium held at the Geology Department, Imperial College, London, 23–25 September 1970*, London

Bullock, P, Fedoroff, N, Jongerius, A, Stoops, G, and Tursina, T, 1985 *Handbook for soil thin-section description*, Wolverhampton

Bunn, H T, 1983 Comparative analysis of modern bone assemblages from a San hunter-gatherer camp in the Kalahari Desert, Botswana, and from a spotted hyena den near Nairobi, Kenya, in *Animals and archaeology: 1, Hunters and their prey* (eds J Clutton-Brock and C Grigson), BAR Int Ser 163, 143–8, Oxford

Burch, E S, 1972 The caribou/wild reindeer as a human resource, *Amer Antiq* 37, 339–68

Burchell, J P T, 1938 Two Mesolithic 'floors' in the Ebbsfleet valley of the lower Thames, *Antiq J* 18, 397–401

Burleigh, R, 1976 Excavations at Creffield Road, Acton, in 1974 and 1975, *London Archaeol* 2(15), 379–83

Catt, J A, 1979 Soils and Quaternary geology in Britain, *J Soil Sci* 30, 607–47

Chambers, F M (ed), 1993 *Climate change and human impact on the landscape: studies in palaeoecology and environmental archaeology*, London

Chambers, F M, and Mighall, T M, 1991 Palaeoecological investigations at Enfield Lock: pollen, pH, magnetic susceptibility and charcoal analyses of sediments, unpub

Environ Res Unit, Univ Keele, rep

Chambers, F M, Mighall, T M, and Keen, D H, 1996 Early Holocene pollen and molluscan records from Enfield Lock, Middlesex, UK, *Proc Geologists' Assoc* 107, 1–14

Clark, J G D, 1932 *The Mesolithic age in Britain*, Cambridge

Clark, J G D, 1933 The classification of a microlithic culture: the Tardenoisian of Horsham, *Archaeol J* 90, 52–77

Clark, J G D, 1948 Fowling in prehistoric Europe, *Antiquity* 22, 116–30

Clark, J G D, 1954 *Excavations at Star Carr: an Early Mesolithic site at Seamer near Scarborough, Yorkshire*, Cambridge

Clark, J G D, 1972 *Star Carr: a case study in bioarchaeology*, Addison-Wesley Modular Pub 10, Reading, Mass

Clark, R L, 1982 Point count estimation of charcoal in pollen preparations and thin sections of sediments, *Pollen et Spores* 24, 523–35

Clutton-Brock, J, 1986 New dates for old animals: the reindeer, the aurochs and the wild horse in prehistoric Britain, *Archaeozoologia* 1, 111–17

Coles, B J, 1998 Doggerland: a speculative survey, *Proc Prehist Soc* 64, 45–81

Coles, B J, 2006 *Beavers in Britain's past*, WARP Occas Pap 19, Oxford

Collcutt, S N, and Macphail, R, 1995 Soil micromorphology and magnetic susceptibility, in Allen 1995, 12–13

Collins, D, and Lorimer, D, 1989 *Excavations at the Mesolithic site on West Heath, Hampstead, 1976–81*, BAR Brit Ser 217, Oxford

Conneller, C, and Schadla-Hall, T, 2003 Beyond Star Carr: the Vale of Pickering in the 10th millennium BP, *Proc Prehist Soc* 69, 85–105

Cook, J, and Jacobi, R, 1994 A reindeer antler or 'Lyngby' axe from Northamptonshire and its context in the British Late Glacial, *Proc Prehist Soc* 60, 75–84

Cooper, L P, 2006 Launde, a terminal Palaeolithic camp-site in the English midlands and its north European context, *Proc Prehist Soc* 72, 53–93

Corbet, G, and Ovenden, D, 1980 *The mammals of Britain and Europe*, London

Cornwall, I W, 1968 *Prehistoric animals and their hunters*, New York

Correia, M, 1971 Diagenesis of sporopollenin and other comparable organic substances: application to hydrocarbon research, in Brooks et al 1971, 569–620

Courty, M A, Goldberg, P, and Macphail, R I, 1989 *Soils, micromorphology and archaeology*, Cambridge

Currant, A P, 1989 The Quaternary origins of the modern British mammal fauna, *Biol J Linnean Soc London* 38, 22–30

Currant, A P, 1991 A Late Glacial Interstadial mammal fauna from Gough's Cave, Somerset, England, in Barton et al 1991, 48–50

Dark, P, Higham T F G, Jacobi, R, and Lord, T C, 2006 New radiocarbon accelerator dates on artefacts from the Early Mesolithic site of Star Carr, North Yorkshire, *Archaeometry* 48, 185–200

David, A, 1984 Swaffham Prior: results of fieldwork, unpub notes

Davis, L B, and Reeves, B O K, 1990 *Hunters of the recent past*, London

Day, S P, 1995 Devensian Lateglacial and Early Flandrian environmental history of the Vale of Pickering, Yorkshire, England, *J Quat Sci* 11, 9–24

Day, S P, and Mellars, P A, 1994 'Absolute' dating of Mesolithic human activity at Star Carr, Yorkshire: new palaeoecological studies and identification of the 9600 BP radiocarbon 'plateau', *Proc Prehist Soc* 60, 417–22

Deeben, J, Dijkstra, P, and van Gisbergen, P, 2000 Some new ^{14}C dates from sites of the Ahrensburg culture in the southern Netherlands, *Notae Praehistoricae* 20, 95–109

Delpech, F, and Rigaud, J-P, 1974 Étude de la fragmentation et de la répartition des restes osseux dans un niveau d'habitat paléolithique, in *Premier Colloque international sur l'industrie de l'os dans la préhistoire: abbaye de Sénanque, Gordes, avril 1974* (ed H Camps-Fabrer), 47–55, Aix-en-Provence

Devoy, R J N, 1979 Flandrian sea level changes and vegetational history of the lower Thames estuary, *Phil Trans Roy Soc London* B ser 285, 355–407

Dimbleby, G W, 1985 *The palynology of archaeological sites*, London

Douglas, L A (ed), 1990 *Soil micromorphology: a basic and applied science*, Developments in Soil Science 19, Amsterdam

Dumont, J V, 1987 Mesolithic microwear research in north-west Europe, in Rowley-Conwy et al 1987, 82–9

Dumont, J V, 1997 Nouvelles recherches sur la transition tardiglaciaire-préboréal dans le Sud et l'Est de l'Angleterre, in Fagnart and Thévenin 1997, 517–27

Egorov, O V, 1967 *Wild ungulates of Yakutia*, Jerusalem

Ellis, C J, Allen, M J, Gardiner, J, Harding, P, Ingrem, C, Powell, A, and Scaife, R G, 2003 An Early Mesolithic seasonal hunting site in the Kennet valley, southern England, *Proc Prehist Soc* 69, 107–35

Elsik, W C, 1971 Microbiological degradation of sporopollenin, in Brooks et al 1971, 480–511

English Heritage, 1989 *Management of archaeological projects*, London

English Heritage, 1991 *Management of archaeological projects*, 2 edn, London

Evans, J G, Davies, P, Mount, R, and Williams, D, 1992 Molluscan taxocenes from Holocene overbank alluvium in central southern England, in Needham and Macklin 1992, 65–74

Faegri, K, 1971 The preservation of sporopollenin membranes under natural conditions, in Brooks et al 1971, 256–72

Fagnart, J-P, 1988 *Les Industries lithiques du Paléolithique supérieur dans le Nord de la France*, Revue Archéologique de Picardie, spec no. (1–2), Amiens

Fagnart, J-P, 1991 New observations on the Late Upper Palaeolithic site of Belloy-sur-Somme (Somme, France), in Barton et al 1991, 213–26

Fagnart, J-P, and Plisson, H, 1997 Fonction des pièces mâchurées du Paléolithique final du bassin de la Somme: caractères tracéologiques et données contextuelles, in Fagnart and Thévenin 1997, 95–106

Fagnart, J-P, and Thévenin, A (eds), 1997 *Le Tardiglaciaire en*

Europe du Nord-Ouest: actes du 119e congrès national des sociétés historiques et scientifiques, section de pré- et protohistoire, Amiens, 26–30 octobre 1994, Paris

Fischer, A, and Tauber, H, 1986 New C-14 datings of Late Palaeolithic cultures from north-western Europe, *J Danish Archaeol* 5, 7–13

Fletcher, M, and Lock, G R, 1991 *Digging numbers: elementary statistics for archaeologists*, Oxford Univ Comm Archaeol Monogr 33, Oxford

Fraser, F C, and King, J E, 1954 Faunal remains, in Clark 1954, 70–95

Freeman, L G, 1978 The analysis of some occupation floor distributions from earlier and middle Palaeolithic sites in Spain, in *Views of the past: essays in old world prehistory and paleoanthropology* (ed L G Freeman), 57–116, The Hague

Froom, R, 2005 *Late Glacial long blade sites in the Kennet valley: excavations and fieldwork at Avington VI, Wawcott XII and Crown Acres*, Brit Mus Res Pub 153, London

Gamble, C, 1986 *The Palaeolithic settlement of Europe*, Cambridge

Gardiner, J, Allen, M J, Lewis, J S C, Wright, J, and Macphail, R I, in prep A long blade site at Underdown Lane, Herne Bay, Kent, *Proc Prehist Soc*

Gibbard, P L, 1985 *The Pleistocene history of the middle Thames valley*, Cambridge

Gibbard, P L, Wintle, A G, and Catt, J A, 1987 Age and origin of clayey silt 'brickearth' in west London, England, *J Quat Sci* 2, 3–9

Gob, A, 1991 The early Postglacial occupation of the southern part of the North Sea basin, in Barton et al 1991, 227–33

Godwin, H, 1940 Pollen analysis and forest history of England and Wales, *New Phytologist* 39, 370–400

Godwin, H, 1975 *History of the British flora*, Cambridge

Goldberg, P, and Macphail, R I, 1990 Micromorphological evidence of Middle Pleistocene landscape and climatic changes from southern England: Westbury-sub-Mendip, Somerset, and Boxgrove, West Sussex, in Douglas 1990, 441–8

Gordon, B, 1988 *Of men and reindeer herds in French Magdalenian prehistory*, BAR Int Ser 390, Oxford

Goudie, A S, Viles, H A, and Pentecost, A, 1993 The Late Holocene tufa decline in Europe, *Holocene* 3, 181–6

Grace, R, 1989 *Interpreting the function of stone tools: the quantification and computerisation of microwear analysis*, BAR Int Ser 474, Oxford

Grace, R, 1990 The limitations and applications of functional analysis, in *The interpretative possibilities of microwear studies: proceedings of the International Conference on Lithic Use-wear Analysis, 15–17 February 1989 in Uppsala, Sweden* (eds B Gräslund, H Knutsson, K Knutsson and J Taffinder), 9–14, Uppsala

Grace, R, 1993 The use of expert systems in lithic analysis, in *Traces et fonction: les gestes retrouvés: actes du colloque international de Liège, 8–10 décembre 1990* (ed P C Anderson), ERAUL 50, 389–400, Liège

Grace, R, in prep Use-wear analysis: the state of the art, *Archaeometry*

Grace, R, Ataman, K, Fabregas, R, and Haggren, C M B, 1988 A multivariate approach to the functional analysis of stone tools, in *Industries lithiques: tracéologie et technologie* (ed S Beyries), BAR Int Ser 411, 217–30, Oxford

Grigson, C, 1978 The Late Glacial and Early Flandrian ungulates of England and Wales: an interim review, in *The effect of man on the landscape: the lowland zone* (eds S Limbrey and J G Evans), CBA Res Rep 21, 46–56, London

Grigson, C, 1989 Bird-foraging patterns in the Mesolithic, in Bonsall 1989, 60–72

Grimm, E, 1991 *TILIA and TILIA*GRAPH*, Springfield, Ill

Grøn, O, 1995 *The Maglemose culture: the reconstruction of the social organisation of a Mesolithic culture in northern Europe*, BAR Int Ser 616, Oxford

Gronnow, B, 1985 Meiendorf and Stellmoor revisited: an analysis of Late Palaeolithic reindeer exploitation, *Acta Archaeologica* 56, 131–66

Guilloré, P, 1985 *Méthode de fabrication méchanique et en série des lames minces*, Paris

Habermehl, K H, 1961 *Altersbestimmung bei Haustieren, Pelztieren und beim jagdbaren Wild*, Berlin

Halsey, C, 2006 The former Sanderson site, Oxford Road, Denham UB9: an archaeological post-excavation assessment and updated project design, unpub MOL rep

Havinga, A J, 1964 Investigation into the differential corrosion susceptibility of pollen and spores, *Pollen et Spores* 6, 621–35

Havinga, A J, 1967 Palynology and pollen preservation, *Rev Palaeobot and Palynol* 2, 81–98

Havinga, A J, 1971 An experimental investigation into the decay of pollen and spores in various soil types, in Brooks et al 1971, 446–79

Healey, F, Heaton, M, Lobb, S J, Allen, M J, Fenwick, I M, Grace, R, and Scaife, R G, 1992 Excavations of a Mesolithic site at Thatcham, Berkshire, *Proc Prehist Soc* 58, 41–76

Higham, T F G, Jacobi, R M, and Bronk Ramsey, C, 2006 AMS radiocarbon dating of ancient bone using ultrafiltration, *Radiocarbon* 48(2), 179–95

Hinton, P, and Thomas, R, 1997 The Greater London publication programme, *Archaeol J* 154, 196–213

Hole, F, and Flannery, K V, 1967 The prehistory of south-western Iran: a preliminary report, *Proc Prehist Soc* 33, 147–206

Housley, R A, 1991 AMS dates from the Late Glacial and early Postglacial in north-west Europe: a review, in Barton et al 1991, 25–39

Huntley, B, 1993 Rapid Early Holocene migration and high abundance of hazel (*Corylus avellana* L): alternative hypothesis, in Chambers 1993, 208–15

Huntley, B, and Birks, H J B, 1983 *An atlas of past and present pollen maps for Europe: 0–13,000 years ago*, Cambridge

Iversen, J, 1954 The Late Glacial flora of Denmark and its relationship to climate and soil, *Danmarks Geologiske Undersogelse*, 2 ser 80, 87–119

Jacobi, R M, 1973 Aspects of the 'Mesolithic Age' in Great Britain, in *The Mesolithic in Europe* (ed S K Kozlowski), 237–65, Warsaw

Jacobi, R M, 1976 Britain inside and outside Mesolithic Europe, *Proc Prehist Soc* 42, 67–84

Jacobi, R M, 1978 Northern England in the 8th millennium BC: an essay, in Mellars 1978, 295–332

Jacobi, R M, 1987 Misanthropic miscellany: musings on British Early Flandrian archaeology and other flights of fancy, in Rowley-Conwy et al 1987, 163–8

Jacobi, R M, 1994 Mesolithic radiocarbon dates: a first review of some recent dates, in *Stories in stone: proceedings of anniversary conference at St Hilda's College, Oxford, April 1993* (eds N Ashton and A David), Lithic Stud Soc Occas Pap 4, 192–8, London

Jochim, M A (ed), 1976 *Hunter-gatherer subsistence and settlement: a predictive model*, New York

Johansen, L, and Stapert, D, 1997–8 Two 'Epi-Ahrensburgian' sites in the northern Netherlands: Oudehaske (Friesland) and Gramsbergen (Overijssel), *Palaeohistoria* 39/40, 1–87

Jones, P, 1995 An interim report on the excavations of an Upper Palaeolithic site in Staines, Surrey, unpub Surrey Archaeol Unit rep

Kelsall, J P, 1957 *Continued barren-ground caribou studies*, Can Wildlife Service, Wildlife Management Bull 1 ser 12, Ottawa

Kelsall, J P, 1968 *The migratory barren-ground caribou in Canada*, Can Wildlife Service Monogr 3, Ottawa

Kemp, R A, 1985 The decalcified Lower Loam at Swanscombe, Kent: a buried Quaternary soil, *Proc Geologists' Assoc* 96, 343–54

Kerney, M P, 1977 A proposed zonation scheme for Late Glacial and Postglacial deposits using land mollusca, *J Archaeol Sci* 4, 387–90

King, J E, 1962 Report on animal bones, in Wymer 1962, 355–61

Lacaille, A D, 1961 Mesolithic facies in Middlesex and London, *Trans London Middlesex Archaeol Soc* 20, 101–49

Lacaille, A D, 1963 Mesolithic industries beside Colne waters in Iver and Denham, Buckinghamshire, *Rec Buckinghamshire* 17, 143–81

Lacaille, A D, 1966 Mesolithic facies in the transpontine fringes, *Surrey Archaeol Collect* 63, 1–43

Lack, P, 1993 *The atlas of wintering birds in Britain and Ireland*, Calton

Lane, P J, and Schadla-Hall, R T, in prep *Hunter-gatherers in the landscape: archaeological and palaeoenvironmental investigations in the Vale of Pickering, North Yorkshire, 1976–97*

Lawrence, M J, and Brown, R W, 1973 (1967) *Mammals of Britain: their tracks, trails and signs*, rev edn, London

Legge, A J, and Rowley-Conwy, P A, 1988 *Star Carr revisited: a re-analysis of the large mammals*, London

Leroi-Gourhan, A, and Brezillon, M, 1966 L'Habitation magdalénienne no. 1 de Pincevent près Montereau (Seine-et-Marne), *Gallia Préhistoire* 9, 263–385

Lewall, E F, and Cowan, I McT, 1963 Age determination in black-tailed deer by degree of ossification of the epiphyseal plate in the long bones, *Can J Zool* 41, 629–36

Lewis, J S C, 1991 Excavation of a Late Glacial and early Postglacial site at Three Ways Wharf, Uxbridge, England: interim report, in Barton et al 1991, 246–55

Lewis, J S C, 2000 The Upper Palaeolithic and Mesolithic periods, in *The archaeology of Greater London: an assessment of archaeological evidence for human presence in the area now covered by Greater London* (ed MoLAS), 45–62, London

Lewis, J S C, in prep *The Lateglacial lithic assemblage from Church Lammas, Staines, Surrey*

Lewis, J S C, Wiltshire, P E J, and Macphail, R, 1992 A Late Devensian/Early Flandrian site at Three Ways Wharf, Uxbridge: environmental implications, in Needham and Macklin 1992, 235–46

Lyman, R L, 2008 *Quantitative paleozoology*, Cambridge

MacDonald, G M, Larsen, C P S, Szeicz, J M, and Moser, K A, 1991 The reconstruction of Boreal forest fire history from lake sediments: a comparison of charcoal, pollen, sedimentological and geochemical indices, *Quat Sci Rev* 10, 53–71

Macphail, R I, 1990 Soil report on Three Ways Wharf, Oxford Road, Uxbridge, Middlesex, unpub AML rep 27/91

Macphail, R I, 1994 Soil micromorphological investigations in archaeology, with special reference to drowned coastal sites in Essex, *SEESOIL, J SE Engl Soils Discussion Grp* 10, 13–28

Macphail, R I, in prep The soil micromorphology from the Lateglacial site at Church Lammas, Staines, Surrey, in Lewis in prep

Mellars, P, 1974 The Palaeolithic and Mesolithic, in *British prehistory: a new outline* (ed C Renfrew), 41–99, London

Mellars, P, 1975 Ungulate populations, economic patterns and the Mesolithic landscape, in *The effect of man on the landscape: the highland zone* (eds J G Evans, S Limbrey and H Cleere), CBA Res Rep 11, 49–56, London

Mellars, P (ed), 1978 *The early Postglacial settlement of northern Europe*, London

Mellars, P, 1987 *Excavations on Oronsay: prehistoric human ecology on a small island*, Edinburgh

Mellars, P, and Dark, P, 1998 *Star Carr in context: new archaeological and palaeoecological investigations at the Early Mesolithic site of Star Carr, North Yorkshire*, McDonald Inst Monogr, Cambridge

Mellars, P, and Rheindart, S C, 1978 Patterns of Mesolithic land-use in southern England: a geological perspective, in Mellars 1978, 371–96

Mills, J, 1984 Excavations in Uxbridge, 1983–4, *London Archaeol* 5(1), 3–11

Milner, N, 2007 Fading star: Star Carr, *Brit Archaeol* 96, 10–14

Mohr, E, 1971 *The Asiatic wild horse: equus prezvalskii Polialoff, 1881*, London

Moore, J W, 1954 Excavations at Flixton, site 2, in Clark 1954, 192–4

Moore, P D, Webb, J A, and Collinson, M D, 1991 *Pollen analysis*, Oxford

Munsell, 1992 *Munsell soil colour charts*, rev edn, New York

Murphy, C P, 1986 *Thin-section preparation of soils and sediments*, Berkhamsted

Murray, N, 1994 A study of settlement pattern, mobility and subsistence in Britain and north-west Europe during the last glaciation, unpub PhD thesis, Univ Edinburgh

Needham, S P, and Macklin, M G (eds), 1992 *Alluvial archaeology* in Britain: proceedings of a conference sponsored by the RMC Group plc, 3–5 January 1991, British Museum, Oxbow Monogr 27, Oxford

Newcomer, M H, 1976 Spontaneous retouch, in Second International Symposium on Flint, 8–11 May 1975, Maastricht (ed F H G Engelen), Nederlandse Geologische Vereniging, Staringia 3, 62–4, Maastricht

Newcomer, M H, Grace, R, and Unger-Hamilton, R, 1986 Investigating microwear polishes with blind tests, J Archaeol Sci 13, 203–17

Newcomer, M H, Grace, R, and Unger-Hamilton, R, 1988 Microwear methodology: a reply to Moss, Hurcombe and Bamforth, J Archaeol Sci 15, 25–33

Noddle, B A, 1973 Determination of the body weight of cattle from bone measurements, in Domestikationsforschung und Geschichte der Haustiere: internationales Symposion in Budapest, 1971 (ed J Matolcsi), 377–89, Budapest

Ohnuma, K, and Bergman, C A, 1982 Experimental studies in the determination of flaking mode, Bull Inst Archaeol 19, 161–70

Olausson, D, 1985–6 Intrasite spatial analysis in Scandinavian Stone Age research, Meddelanden från Lunds Universitets Historiska Museum ns 6, 5–25

Ordóñez, S, and Garcia del Cura, M A, 1983 Recent and Tertiary carbonates in central Spain, in Modern and ancient fluvial systems (eds J D Collinson and J Lewin), Int Assoc Sedimentol Spec Pub 6, 485–97, Oxford

Pedley, H M, 1990 Classification and environmental models of cool freshwater tufas, Sediment Geol 68, 143–54

Pelegrin, J, 2000 Les Techniques de débitage laminaire au Tardiglaciaire: critères de diagnose et quelques réflexions, in Tardiglaciaire 2000, 73–86

Peterson, R, 1993 Collins field guide: birds of Britain and Europe, 5 edn, London

Peterson, R L, 1955 The North American moose, Toronto

Preece, R C, and Robinson, J E, 1982 Mollusc, ostracod and plant remains from early Postglacial deposits near Staines, London Naturalist 61, 6–15

Price, T D, 1978 Mesolithic subsistence – settlement systems in the Netherlands, in Mellars 1978, 81–113

Price, T D, 1982 Willow tales and dog smoke, Quarterly Rev Archaeol 3, 4–7

Price, T D, 1989 The reconstruction of Mesolithic diets, in Bonsall 1989, 48–59

Rackham, D J, 1979 Rattus rattus: the introduction of the black rat into Britain, Antiquity 53, 112–22

Rackham, D J, 1982 Mid-Devensian mammals in Britain, unpub MSc thesis, Univ Birmingham (Isleworth)

Rackham, D J, 1996 Church Lammas, Staines, Surrey: animal bone assessment report, unpub Surrey Archaeol Unit rep

Rackham, D J, in prep The animal bones from excavations at Church Lammas, Staines, Surrey, in Lewis in prep

Rackham, O, 1986 The history of the countryside, London

Radley, J, and Mellars, P, 1964 A Mesolithic structure at Deepcar, Yorkshire, England, and the affinities of its associated flint industries, Proc Prehist Soc 30, 1–24

Ratcliffe, P R, and Staines, B W, 1982 Red deer in woodlands: research findings, in Roe and red deer in British forestry (ed Brit Deer Soc), 42–53, Warminster

Reimer, P J, Baillie, M G L, Bard, E, Bayliss, A, Beck, J W, Bertrand, C J H, Blackwell, P G, Buck, C E, Burr, G S, Cutler, K B, Damon, P E, Edwards, R L, Fairbanks, R G, Friedrich, M, Guilderson, T P, Hogg, A G, Hughen, K A, Kromer, B, McCormac, G, Manning, S, Bronk Ramsey, C, Reimer, R W, Remmele, S, Southon, J R, Stuiver, M, Talamo, S, Taylor, F W, van der Plicht, J, and Weyhenmeyer, C E, 2004 IntCal04 terrestrial radiocarbon age calibration, 0–26 cal kyr BP, Radiocarbon 46(3), 1029–58

Reynier, M, in prep Site report for Broxbourne 104

Rigaud, J-P, 1978 The significance of variability among lithic artefacts: a specific case from south-western France, J Anthropol Res 34, 299–310

Roberts, M B, 1986 Excavation of the Lower Palaeolithic site at Amey's Eartham Pit, Boxgrove, West Sussex: a preliminary report, Proc Prehist Soc 52, 215–45

Rowley-Conwy, P, in prep Animal bones from the Vale of Pickering Research Trust excavations 1985–98, in Lane and Schadla-Hall in prep

Rowley-Conwy, P, Zvelebil, M, and Blankholm, H P (eds), 1987 Mesolithic north-west Europe: recent trends, Sheffield

Rozoy, J-G, 1978 Les derniers chasseurs: l'Épipaléolithiqe en France et en Belgique, essaie de synthèse, Bulletin de la Société Archéologique Champenoise, spec no. (June), Charleville

Rust, A, 1943 Die alt-und mittelsteinzeitlichen Funde von Stellmoor, Neumünster

Scaife, R G, 1982 Late Devensian and Early Flandrian vegetation changes in southern England, in Archaeological aspects of woodland ecology (eds M Bell and S Limbrey), BAR Int Ser 146, 57–74, Oxford

Scaife, R G, 1992 Pollen analysis, in Healey et al 1992, 66–70

Schadla-Hall, R T, 1987 Recent investigations of the Early Mesolithic landscape and settlement in the Vale of Pickering, North Yorkshire, in Rowley-Conwy et al 1987, 46–54

Schadla-Hall, R T, 1989 The Vale of Pickering in the Early Mesolithic in context, in Bonsall 1989, 218–24

Selkirk, A, 1978 Broom Hill, Braishfield: Mesolithic dwelling, Current Archaeol 63, 117–20

Sharrock, J T R, 1987 The atlas of breeding birds in Britain and Ireland, London

Sidell, J, Cotton, J, Rayner, L, and Wheeler, L, 2002 The prehistory and topography of Southwark and Lambeth, MoLAS Monogr 14, London

Smith, C, 1992 Late Stone Age hunters of the British Isles, London

Sonneville-Bordes, D de, and Perrot, J, 1956 Lexique typologique du Paléolithique supérieur, Bulletin de la Société Préhistorique Française 52, 408–12

Sparks, B W, 1961 The ecological interpretation of Quaternary non-marine Mollusca, Proc Linnean Soc London 172, 71–80

Speth, J D, 1983 Bison kills and bone counts: decision-making by ancient hunters, Chicago

Speth, J D, 1991 Nutritional constraints and Late Glacial adaptive transformations: the importance of non-protein energy sources, in Barton et al 1991, 169–78

Spiess, A E, 1979 *Reindeer and caribou hunters: an archaeological study*, New York

Stace, C A, 1991 *New flora of the British Isles*, Cambridge

Stapert, D, 1989 The ring and sector method: intrasite spatial analysis of Stone Age sites, with special reference to Pincevent, *Palaeohistoria* 31, 1–57

Stewart, I, 1989 Assessment report of excavations at Cowley Mill Road, Middlesex, unpub MOL rep

Street, M, 1991 Bedburg-Königshoven: a Pre-Boreal Mesolithic site in the lower Rhineland, Germany, in Barton et al 1991, 256–70

Sturdy, D A, 1972 Reindeer economies in late Ice Age Europe, unpub PhD thesis, Univ Cambridge

Sturdy, D A, 1975 Some reindeer economies in prehistoric Europe, in *Palaeoeconomy: being the second volume of papers in economic prehistory by members and associates of the British Academy Major Research Project in the Early History of Agriculture* (ed E S Higgs), 55–95, Cambridge

Tardiglaciaire, 2000 *Le Tardiglaciaire en Europe centrale et septentrionale: actes de la table-ronde international de Nemours 1997*, Mémoires du Musée de Préhistoire d'Ile-de-France 7, Nemours

Taute, W, 1968 *Die Stielspitzen-Gruppen im nördlichen Mitteleuropa: ein Beitrag zur Kenntnis der späten Altsteinzeit*, Fundamenta A5, Cologne

Taylor-Page, F J, 1971 *Field guide to British deer*, Oxford

Tegner, H, 1951 *The roe deer: their history, habitats and pursuit*, London

Thomas, C, and Rackham, D J, 1996 Bramcote Green, Bermondsey: a Bronze Age trackway and palaeoenvironmental sequence, *Proc Prehist Soc* 62, 221–53

Thomas, J, 1988 Neolithic explanations revisited: the Mesolithic–Neolithic transition in Britain and southern Scandinavia, *Proc Prehist Soc* 54, 59–66

Tipping, R, 1991 Climatic change in Scotland during the Devensian Late Glacial: the palynological record, in Barton et al 1991, 7–21

Tooley, M J, Rackham, D J, and Simmons, I G, 1982 A red deer (*Cervus elaphus* L) skeleton from Seamer Carr, Cleveland, England: provenance of the skeleton and palaeoecology of the site, *J Archaeol Sci* 6, 365–76

Uchiyama, J, Clutton-Brock, J, and Rowley-Conwy, P, in prep Animal bones from the excavations at Seamer Carr, Yorkshire, 1977–86, in Lane and Schadla-Hall in prep

Walker, M J C, and Harkness, D D, 1990 Radiocarbon dating the Devensian Lateglacial in Britain: new evidence from Llanilid, south Wales, *J Quat Sci* 5, 135–44

Walker, M J C, and Lowe, J J, 1980 Pollen analyses, radiocarbon dates and the deglaciation of Rannoch Moor, Scotland, following the Loch Lomond Advance, in *Timescales in geomorphology* (eds R A Cullingford, D A Davidson and J Lewin), 247–59, Chichester

Walker, M J C, Bohncke, S J P, Coope, G R, O'Connell, M, Usinger, H, and Verbruggen, C, 1994 The Devensian/Weichselian Lateglacial in north-west Europe (Ireland, Britain, north Belgium, the Netherlands, north-west Germany), *J Quat Sci* 9, 109–18

Ward, G K, and Wilson, S R, 1978 Procedures for comparing and combining radiocarbon age determinations: a critique, *Archaeometry* 20, 19–31

Whallon, R, 1973 Spatial analysis of Palaeolithic occupation areas, in *The explanation of cultural change: models in prehistory: proceedings of a meeting of the Research Seminar in Archaeology and Related Subjects held at the University of Sheffield* (ed C Renfrew), 115–30, London

Whallon, R, 1978 Spatial analysis of Mesolithic occupation floors: a reappraisal, in Mellars 1978, 27–35

Wiltshire, P E J, 1996 Church Lammas, Staines, Surrey: assessment of palynological potential of subsurface sediments, unpub Surrey Archaeol Unit rep

Wiltshire, P E J, and Edwards, K J, 1993 Mesolithic, Early Neolithic and later prehistoric impacts on vegetation at a riverine site in Derbyshire, England, in Chambers 1993, 157–68

Woodman, P C, 1985 *Excavations at Mount Sandel, County Londonderry, 1973–7*, N Ireland Archaeol Monogr 1, Belfast

Wymer, J J, 1962 Excavations at the Maglemosian sites at Thatcham, Berkshire, England, *Proc Prehist Soc* 28, 329–61

Wymer, J J, and Robins, P A, 1994 A long blade flint industry beneath Boreal peat at Titchwell, Norfolk, *Norfolk Archaeol* 42, 13–37

Wymer, J J, and Rose, J, 1976 A long blade industry from Sproughton, Suffolk, *E Anglian Archaeol Rep* 3, 1–15

Yalden, D W, 1991 History of the fauna, in *The handbook of British mammals* (eds G B Corbet and S Harris), 3 edn, 7–18, Oxford

INDEX

Compiled by Margaret Binns

Page numbers in **bold** indicate illustrations and maps
All street names and locations are in London unless specified otherwise
County names within parentheses refer to modern counties